THE MODERN LIBRARY
of the World's Best Books

RENAISSANCE PHILOSOPHY

VOL. I

THE ITALIAN PHILOSOPHERS

Selected Readings from Petrarch to Bruno

RENAISSANCE PHILOSOPHY

VOLUME I

THE ITALIAN PHILOSOPHERS

Selected Readings from Petrarch to Bruno

EDITED, TRANSLATED, AND INTRODUCED BY

Arturo B. Fallico and Herman Shapiro

DEPARTMENT OF PHILOSOPHY

SAN JOSE STATE COLLEGE

THE MODERN LIBRARY

NEW YORK

FIRST MODERN LIBRARY EDITION, FEBRUARY 1967

 Published in New York by Random House, Inc., and simultaneously in Toronto, Canada, by Random House of Canada Limited.

Library of Congress Catalog Card Number: 67-11590

Manufactured in the United States of America

THE MODERN LIBRARY
is published by
Random House, Inc.

questo libro é dedicato agli studenti di Calabria e ai loro bravi maestri

PREFACE

THIS VOLUME is the first in a projected series designed to make the writings of selected Renaissance philosophers available in English translation. The present volume contains selections drawn from the writings of the Italian thinkers of the period; the next will treat of the philosophers in other European countries. Although this division is admittedly artificial in the sense that the general intellectual climate in which they worked was roughly the same for all the Renaissance thinkers, it is yet not wholly arbitrary; for it seems to us that there are differences between the thought of the Italians and that of other Europeans significant enough to merit separate treatment. But this will become evident in the second volume of *Renaissance Philosophy*.

Excepting only the continuing pioneer work contributed by a few specialists whose findings, unhappily, have not yet trickled down for inclusion within our standard college texts in the history of philosophy, Renaissance thought has been almost totally neglected. The principal reason for this is more readily understood than condoned. In the philosophical literature of the period we simply do not find thinkers of the magnitude of a Plato or an Aristotle, of a Scotus or an Ockham, of a Descartes or a Hume: that is, no single figure or cluster of figures pre-eminent enough to call forth all the available might of scholarly investigation. For the historian of philosophy, however, the neglect of an entire chapter of intellectual history on this ground is indefensible. Who today reads Christian Wolff? Yet, Kant did; and if we wish to understand Kant, we should, too. In an entirely similar manner, the philosophical thought of the Renaissance provides important clues for understanding the modern thinkers. Thus, if we really hope to understand the wide difference in outlook which obtains between, say, Ockham and Bacon, a thorough grasp of the intellectual currents of the Renaissance is indispensable.

Broadly, four basic currents are discernible in the thought of the Renaissance: Humanism, Platonism, Aristotelianism, and that of the independent Philosophers of Nature. Accordingly, this volume is divided into four sections, each containing writings representing one of these four major traditions. Each selection has been chosen to exhibit a significant philosophical tendency or position characteristic of the school of thought with which its author's name has become identified. In order to accomplish this we found it necessary, in many instances, to make available writings that had never before been rendered into English. We shall have more to say later concerning these translations.

Humanism, originating in Italy and spreading gradually throughout the rest of Europe, was the broadest and most pervasive of the intellectual movements of the period. No matter what accretions of meaning may have since become attached, to the men of the Renaissance who first coined and employed the term, a "Humanist" was one whose intellectual pursuits centered around a program of what we would now call classical studies. Despite the fact that such pursuits can scarcely be regarded as philosophical in themselves, the Humanists have come to be recognized as occupying an important place in the history of Western philosophy. It was, in the first place, their researches into the literature of classical antiquity that made the writings of the ancient philosophers generally accessible for first-hand study and restatement; again, the Humanists' use of classical literary genres as a vehicle for philosophy, undertaken in conscious revolt against the strictures of Scholastic terminology and method, brought about a complete metamorphosis in the style of philosophical literature—a contribution which is far from unimportant; further, it was the Humanists who formulated, for centuries to come, the classic pattern of formal education. In this latter connection, their selection of the name *studia humanitatis* ("the humanities") for their subjects, is significant: for it reveals that characteristic emphasis upon the centrality and worth of man which defines the entire scope of their philosophical concern. Accordingly, when we turn to the Humanist philosophical literature, we find it to be exclusively taken up with subjects and problems of a moral nature. Although these Humanist writings on moral philosophy lack neither originality of treatment nor matter, they tend, for the most part, to display the influence of ancient precedent. Thus we find among the favorite topics of discussion, such classic themes, for example, as fate and fortune, the relative merits of the active and contemplative life, the felicity and afflictions of human life, man's freedom, and, of course, his dignity.

Section I of the present volume is devoted to the writings of the Humanists. The selections from Petrarch's *De remediis utriusque fortunae* and Alberti's *Intercoenales* deal with various aspects of fate, fortune, and the vicissitudes of human life; Valla's brilliant dialogue, *De libero arbitrio,* attempts to bring new insight to the age-old debate on human freedom; the section closes with Manetti's celebrated statement on the dignity of man: *De dignitate et excellentia hominis*. In this latter selection there emerges a particularly clear picture of the profound difference between medieval and Renaissance conceptions of man's place in the universe.

The whole tradition of Humanism lies at the core of the movement which has come to be known as Renaissance Platonism. The Platonist thinkers of the period, indeed, were so thoroughly steeped in Humanist learning that many historians still regard them as constituting a wing of Humanism rather than a distinct and unique group. But there appear to be good grounds for challenging this view: first, the Platonist thinkers significantly enriched and modified their Humanist background by combining it with sources never tapped by the Humanists; and second, the range of their philosophical interests extended quite beyond the limited orbit of problems that typically moved the Humanists.

With respect to the first point, the writings of Marsilio Ficino prove most instructive. Under the patronage of

Cosimo de' Medici, Ficino, in 1462, founded the famous Platonic Academy at Florence. It was the express purpose of this celebrated circle to revive the Platonic philosophy in Italy. First and foremost, this required that the basic writings of Platonism be made available. By 1468, Ficino himself had completed the immense task of translating the entire Platonic *corpus* from the Greek. But aside from Plato, who remained always his richest mine of inspiration, Ficino's sources included Plotinus; writings attributed to Orpheus, Pythagoras, Hermes Trismegistus, and Zoroaster; and an impressive variety of works composed by Latin, Arabic, and assorted Neoplatonist authors. Yet other members of the Platonist circle—notable among these being the brilliant Pico della Mirandola—quickly added the writings of the Jewish Cabalists and the Greek Aristotle along with Aristotle's Greek, Arabic, and Latin commentators.

With reference to the second point, it is important to note that Christianity had always lent itself most readily to expression in Platonist, or rather Neoplatonist, terms; for it was in the attempt to give meaning to this curious pagan-Christian cordiality that Ficino and the Platonists were led to wander into metaphysical and cosmological realms well outside the Humanist pale. In brief, as the Platonists saw it, the thought of pagan antiquity was to be understood as constituting a continuous series of progressively developed attempts to articulate the full Truth embodied, finally, in divine revelation. Hence, the congeniality remarked above. Seen thus, no ancient or exotic philosophical or religious tradition was to be despised, as each warranted searching study for the purpose of discovering and assessing its proper role in the unfolding of the one Truth. On the one hand, then, the Platonist vision both legitimatized and broadened the devoted study of classical antiquity begun by the Humanists; and on the other, it set the stage for that major program of intellectual synthesis which is so characteristic a feature of Renaissance Platonist thought.

Section II of this volume is devoted to the writings of the Renaissance Platonists. Our first selection, Pico's *Epis-*

tola to the Venetian Humanist Ermolao Barbaro, with its sober defense of Scholastic literary "barbarism," seemed to us worthy of inclusion for two principal reasons: first, it reveals the significant difference in attitude toward Scholasticism that divides the Humanists—who were generally hostile toward the Aristotelians—from the Platonists, who tended to feel that the views of the Aristotelian thinkers also embodied some share of the truth; second, Pico's closing remarks show quite clearly that the Platonists regarded themselves as dissociated from Humanism—at least in its narrowest and most pedantic form.

Our second selection is Ficino's revealing little work, *De sole*. In this fine example of the solar literature of the period we see the founder of the Florentine Academy attempting to synthesize age-old and multiphased doctrines concerning the sun with his own Neoplatonized version of Christianity.

The third selection is another work by Pico: a writing in which, once again, there is exhibited this syncretism which is so typical of the Platonist program. At the age of twenty-four, Pico announced himself prepared to dispute nine hundred theses in public, at Rome, against any and all challengers. Among other things, the theses set forth purported to show that Hellenism and Jewish Cabalism were readily reducible to a Platonized system of Christianity; and that the philosophies of Plato and Aristotle were really in basic agreement. This third selection is the *Oratio*, or Introduction, to the main body of Pico's nine hundred theses.

This famous piece of writing has often been singled out by historians as a prime and exquisite example of the typical Humanist emphasis on the dignity of man. Without question, it is that. But this should not be accounted surprising since, as we indicated earlier, Renaissance Platonism presupposes the whole tradition of Humanism before pressing beyond. In this connection, it is significant to note that only the opening portion of Pico's *Oratio* sounds the Humanist theme, while in the latter parts he proceeds to do what the more philosophically naïve Humanists never seemed interested in doing: to set the conception of man's exalted and unique position in the universe within a metaphysical framework. Here it would be instructive for the student to compare Pico's statement with that of Manetti.

The Platonist movement of the Renaissance was famous for its doctrine of love. Ficino himself, in his commentary on Plato's *Phaedrus,* held that the love of which Plato speaks and the love of which St. Paul speaks are one and the same: the love, that is, of Absolute Beauty, which is God. This theme was developed and embroidered by the Platonists in many ways; none, however, dealt with it more brilliantly, or with greater sensitivity and insight, than Leone Ebreo. We have chosen to close the section on Renaissance Platonism by presenting one—the first—of Ebreo's celebrated *Dialoghi di amore.*

Intellectual historians are still divided in their estimates of the philosophical value of Renaissance Aristotelianism. One tradition of scholarship, presumably taking its cue from the polemics directed against the Aristotelians by the Humanists, tends to dismiss the Aristotelianism of the period as philosophically stunted and atavistic. At the other extreme, there are those historians who regard the work of the Humanists and Platonists as the outpourings of literary amateurs, and champion the Aristotelians as the only true representatives of philosophical thought in the Renaissance. Both views require modification: Aristotelianism appears to have been quite as vital and productive as the Humanism and Platonism of the time; and it is only by adopting an extremely narrow conception of philosophy that one can summarily dismiss the writings of the Humanists and Platonists as philosophically barren.

Italian Renaissance Aristotelianism exhibits only a marginal interest in Scholastic theology. The roots of Aristotelianism were deeply set in the Italian universities, and in these centers the study of theology had always been subordinate to the study of medicine and law. Although not averse to dealing with metaphysics, the Italian Aristotelians, characteristically, were drawn to the natural sciences and logic. Recent research has done much to show that these thinkers—particularly those connected with the University of Padua—made important contributions to the methodology and terminology of the natural sciences. Thus it is possible to read the traditional hostility between the Humanists—with their professional emphasis upon the *studia humanitatis*—and the Aristotelians—with their primarily scientific interests and academic associations—as roughly analogous to the present-day rivalry between the sciences and the humanities.

Characteristically, the Renaissance Aristotelians conducted their philosophical inquiries along purely rational and Aristotelian lines. Fully aware that reason and a proper rendering of Aristotle might lead to conclusions diametrically opposed to orthodox belief, the Aristotelians, refusing to compromise either their philosophical principles or their religious convictions, held stanchly to the view that the tenets of faith and the findings of philosophy may very well be at variance. This is not to say, however, as some historians have maintained, that the Aristotelians subscribed to a crude theory of "double-truth"; nor is there any convincing evidence to support the charge that their stand was a hypocritical device employed to mask secret disbelief or even atheism. Until more facts are made available, it is perhaps not injudicious to regard the Aristotelians as standing, in this matter, at a crossroad: viewed retrospectively, their position may be understood as a widening and deepening of the breach between faith and reason already effected in the late medieval period; and seen projectively, it may appear a step in the direction of free thought.

Section III of this volume is made up of selections drawn from the writings of Renaissance Aristotelians. For centuries, the question of how God's foreknowledge could be reconciled with human freedom had exercised the best minds in Christendom. The first selection in this section, an extract from Pomponazzi's *De fato, de libero arbitrio, et de praedestinatione*, shows the famous Paduan submitting this problem to a careful critical analysis. Conducting his inquiry throughout under the aegis of natural reason,

Pomponazzi is led, finally, to conclude that no one has ever succeeded in effecting a philosophically acceptable reconciliation; and, indeed, that the two—God's foreknowledge and human free will—cannot obtain simultaneously. Here, it would be most instructive for the student to compare Pomponazzi's handling of the problem with that of Valla.

Although Aristotle's *Poetics* was not unknown to the Middle Ages, it was not until the Renaissance thinkers focused on this work that it began to receive the serious attention which its contents merit. So successful, indeed, was the exploitation it received at this time, that long after the rejection of his physical theories, Aristotle's philosophy of art continued to exert its influence on aestheticians. Among the first of those thinkers who surrendered to the spell of Aristotle's *Poetics* was the famous philosopher-poet, Torquato Tasso. The section on the Renaissance Aristotelians closes with the first of Tasso's influential and hotly debated *Discorsi dell'arte poetica*.

The Renaissance Philosophers of Nature, as the label suggests, were chiefly concerned with natural philosophy and cosmology. Still, this shared concern does not adequately mark them off from the Humanists, Platonists, and Aristotelians of the period; it was, rather, an attitude held in common toward their subject matter which sets them apart as a unique and significant group.

As we have seen, Humanist, Platonist, and Aristotelian alike took pride in relating their views with some one or other of "the ancients." Not so with the Philosophers of Nature. It was, indeed, their proudest boast—one found repeated time and time again in their writings—that their investigations into nature were to be carried out in an independent and original manner: one wholly freed from the weight of any established tradition. It is precisely this deliberate and sweeping repudiation of all accepted philosophical authority in the province of their special concern which characterizes the Renaissance Philosophers of Nature.

But the intellectual fund of centuries is not thus easily

dismissed. A thoughtful reading of the selections excerpted from their writings will prove that ancient authority, although explicitly and emphatically denied ingress at the front gate by the Philosophers of Nature, was inadvertently carried through the gate concealed in the basic presuppositions of the Nature Philosophers themselves. Still, the attitude of these thinkers is highly significant: for their bold seeking after originality reflects a conviction the truth of which was to be confirmed in a spectacular fashion by their immediate successors—the conviction that it was possible for "the moderns" to acquire, on their own, knowledge from which "the ancients" had been effectively barred.

Section IV contains selections drawn from the works of the Philosophers of Nature. The opening selection, a portion of Telesio's *De rerum natura iuxta propria principia*, is to be approached with some caution. Telesio's writing is not easy to understand until the whole direction of his thought is grasped. It would be well, therefore, for the reader to go through the Telesio selection twice, not attempting at the first reading to grasp every detail of his ingenious and novel theory, but attempting rather to comprehend the sweep of his thought. Once it has become clear where he is headed, a second reading will unravel most of the intricacies and clarify most of the details. Such tangles as are then found to remain may well be attributed to Telesio himself, whose writings are not wholly free of inconsistencies.

A deep fascination with magic and things magical runs through much of Renaissance thought. The question of just how this occult current can be thought of as functioning within the context of a philosophical inquiry into nature is best answered with reference to the work of Campanella, a segment of whose engrossing *Del senso delle cose e della magia* is presented as the second selection.

It seems most appropriate to close this section, and this volume, with a sampling taken from Bruno's *De l'infinito, universo e mondi*. Bruno's is without question a Renaissance genius; yet, many features of his unfolded vision prove modern enough to undergo adoption and development at the hands of subsequent thinkers. The resemblance between certain key passages in the writings of Bruno and Galileo has long been noted; the similarities of thought between Bruno and Spinoza do not appear to be entirely coincidental; and Bruno's monads, upon analysis, seem quite faithfully to shadow forth those of Leibniz.

To be sure, it is not yet possible to establish the precise nature of the debt owed the Renaissance thinkers by those of subsequent times. Nonetheless, it seems clear that each of the major movements of the period foreshadows certain important developments of later thought. To the following centuries, the Humanists bequeathed the heritage of classical education and the scholarly methods of research. Platonist thought may be seen as pointing directly to the idealist metaphysics of the modern period; there, too, its stress upon the share of truth to be found in all philosophical and religious doctrines would find enlightened expression in the doctrines of natural religion and universal tolerance. In many ways, the thought of the Aristotelians, despite the fact that these thinkers did not themselves expressly embrace these views, relates to later developments in naturalism and free thought. Finally, the Philosophers of Nature appear to have paved the way for the more freely speculative philosophies of modern times.

With one exception, the present editors are responsible for the translation of each selection in this book. The selections from Pomponazzi's *De fato* was rendered into English by the precise scholarship of our friend and colleague, Professor Frederick Scott of the Department of Philosophy at San Jose State College. As with the great majority of selections presented in this volume, that contributed by Dr. Scott has never before appeared in English translation. It would serve no clear purpose here to enumerate the problems encountered in translating these selections: any scholar who has himself attempted to translate the Renaissance thinkers is aware of the frustrations, difficulties, and dangers involved. All of our final decisions touching on the matter of language were conditioned by one concern: to mirror the meaning of the original document as faithfully as possible.

Principally, this volume has been designed for use in connection with college courses in the history of philosophy or humanities. Our own introductions to each thinker provide brief biographical data. At the end of each section there appears a selected list of Suggested Readings citing readily available works in which the thought and times of the men represented in the section are authoritatively set forth and examined.

We wish here gratefully to acknowledge the interest expressed in this volume by so many of our friends and colleagues. We are particularly grateful to Professor P. O. Kristeller of Columbia University, and to Professor N. W. Gilbert of the University of California at Davis, both of whom took time out of their busy schedules to suggest the names of those Renaissance figures whose writings would be most appropriate to an anthology of this sort. Needless to say, the present editors are fully responsible for the final selection. Finally, we wish to express a similar debt of gratitude to Dott. Aldo di Perna of Naples, and Goffredo Iusi of Cosenza, for their efforts in our behalf in connection with certain bibliographical problems.

A. B. Fallico
H. Shapiro

Saratoga, California
1966

CONTENTS

I

RENAISSANCE HUMANISM

FRANCESCO PETRARCA

FRANCESCO PETRARCA, *the first great representative of Renaissance Humanism, was born in Arezzo in 1304. He studied law at Montpellier and Bologna. He spent the period 1326–1353 at Avignon, which was then the seat of the papal Curia. In 1353, Petrarch returned to his native Italy, never to leave it again. He died in Arquà, near Padua, in 1374. He was an avid collector of manuscripts, a tireless classical scholar, and a great poet. His Latin prose writings include formal orations, historical works, invectives, dialogues, numerous tracts and carefully polished letters. Among these prose writings, four are of special philosophical interest:* De secreto conflictu curarum mearum; De vita solitaria; De sui ipsius and multorum ignorantia; *and* De remediis utriusque fortunae.

On the Remedies of Good and Bad Fortune

DIALOGUE 1

On the Prime of Life, and the Hope of Long Life

Joy and Hope. I am in the prime of life: I shall yet live a long time.

Reason. Lo! The first vain hope of mortal men: a hope which has already deluded many thousands, and will continue to do so.

Joy and Hope. I am in the prime of life.

Reason. A vain and short-lived joy. Even as we speak, the flower withers!

Joy and Hope. I am quite sound.

Reason. Who will call that sound which lacks much, while that which it has is uncertain?

Joy and Hope. But there is a certain law and a fixed term of living.

Reason. Who made the law? What is the fixed term of life? Surely it is a most unjust law that is not equally applied to all men; and, indeed, this one is so variable that nothing is more uncertain in the life of man than the term of his life.

Joy and Hope. Nonetheless, there is a certain term and measure of life which has been set forth by the wise.

Reason. It is not in the power of him who receives it to set the term of life. This, rather, is in the power of Him who gives it: God. But I understand: You are thinking of a term of some seventy or—if the individual be somewhat more robust—eighty years. He, however, who attains to such an age finds life to be all pain and travail. Indeed, it is possible that your hopes have been extended even further than this by him who said, *the days of a man's life are many times a hundred years.* Now this, as we know, is an age which but few attain; but granting that that which happens to few were to happen to all, what would it then profit?

Joy and Hope. A great deal, in truth; for the life of young men is the more secure the further it is from old age and death.

Reason. You deceive yourself. Nothing is safe to a man: but that which is most dangerous for him has its source in heedlessness. Nothing is closer to life than death; when they seem to be at the greatest remove, they are closest together. The one always passes, the other draws inexorably nigh. Try as you may to escape, death is ever at hand and hangs over your head.

Joy and Hope. Well, at least for now, youth is present and old age is absent.

Reason. Nothing is more fleeting than youth; nothing more treacherous than old age. Youth tarries not, but slips away in its delights; old age, following immediately after, softly, in darkness and silence, strikes men unawares; just when she is thought to be far off, she stands at the door.

Joy and Hope. My youth is in the ascendant.

Reason. You put your trust in a most treacherous thing. This "ascendancy" of which you speak is, in reality, a decline. This brief life is furtively, silently, between play and dreams, soon dissolved by unstable time. Would that God would permit us to realize in the beginning, as we do at the end, the rapidity with which time unfolds and the brevity of life! To one just commencing, it seems endless; to one who is leaving, it seems as nothing; and that which first seemed a century, is seen at the last as hardly an instant. We discover the fraud, therefore, when it is no longer possible to foil it. This is why, frequently, the counsel given to youth, which is at once incredulous and untried, is in vain; lacking in wisdom of its own, youth has contempt for the wisdom of others. And so the follies of youth, while innumerable and colossal, remain nonetheless covert and unknown to their very authors. Nothing serves better to unveil them than old age, which sets them clearly before the eyes of those who have perpetrated them and are their accomplices. Youth does not realize what it should have been, before it becomes what it has become—and then it can become nothing else. Were one able to foresee it on his own, or were one capable of believing those who instruct him, he should be one in a thousand, and would wax a happy youth. He would not drag his life along so many tortuous ways, for virtue alone provides the straight and narrow path.

Joy and Hope. My age is without fault.

Reason. How can it be faultless if from its very inception it is steadily chipped away; if it is broken up in minute fragments from the very instant in which it is given us? The sky turns with a continuous motion, the moments steal away the hours, the hours steal away the days; this day destroyed another, as that other has destroyed yet another; and so on, relentlessly. So, as Cicero affirms, pass the months; so pass the years; so time passes and hurries. It flies, as Virgil says, "without agitating its swift wings."

Thus, as in sea voyages, the end arrives suddenly, without the traveler anticipating it or even thinking about it.

Joy and Hope. These are my early years, still far from the end.

Reason. Within the cramped limits of life, nothing is far off.

Joy and Hope. In every regard the beginning is farthest from the end.

Reason. Yes, in every respect: but this would be an exact observation only if everyone's life were of equal duration. Little children frequently, and in many ways, incur death. More often than not the end is close even when it seems far away.

Joy and Hope. Without doubt, these are my greenest years.

Reason. Despite the fact that few are aware of it, from the very moment that we began to speak some change has occurred; and during the very instants of syllabification some little life has passed away—something has been subtracted from the fading flower of the years. What then has the tender youth more than the old and wrinkled man, except this brief and transitory prime that we are talking about? A flower which fades a little at each instant; an age in which I find nothing sweet and joyous, since youth is aware that it will become, more swiftly than it takes to tell, what age now is and has already become. And he who closes his mind to this is demented. The only difference I would concede between youth and old age is that if both were dragged to their death, one might be considered more happy than the other: the one, that is, who is first to offer his neck to the ax. It seems to me that the one who had to wait would in some way be the more unfortunate of the two; for while their situations are thus different, the one who remains until last can hope for something which might permit him to escape the agony of his companion, and live on. Death alone can save a young man from old age. In brief: in a small space of time there can be no great felicity; and for a truly great soul, nothing that is so brief can seem desirable. Awaken, all you who sleep! The hour has come!

Open your sleepy eyes! Learn, once and for all, to think of eternal things—to love them, to desire them; and yield up to time itself that which is transitory. Learn to detach yourself willingly from those things which cannot remain with us for very long, and to leave them, in spirit, before they leave us.

Joy and Hope. Mine is a green and fixed age.

Reason. Anyone who calls any age "fixed," lies. Nothing is more wanton than time. Time is the wheel of all ages. Can you conceive of it as fixed? O vanity! Nothing is fixed—in this very instant they take you away!

DIALOGUE 2

Physical Beauty

Joy. My physical beauty is of a rare order.

Reason. This is no more fixed than time; with him it comes, and with him it goes. Stop time, if you can, and you may, perhaps, also hold beauty.

Joy. My physical beauty is of the first quality.

Reason. You lean on a most inconstant base. Even the body passes as a shadow; and yet you feel that an accidental quality—one that is only momentarily with the body—will remain? Even if the substance remains, accidental qualities can depart; but if the substance goes, they cannot but leave. I have not here even remarked that of all the qualities which desert the mortal frame, none flees more swiftly than beauty. Its delicate flower no sooner shows itself, then it vanishes from under the very gaze of him who gives it admiration and praise. Frost burns it, a puff of wind shakes it; it is struck by enemy hands, or trodden underfoot by passers-by. Glorify yourself, and take your pleasure; here, with great leaping bounds comes she who will strip you of your thin-veiled covering. It is death that makes us see the vanity of human beauty—and not only death: old age, the course of just a few years, or even the sudden fever of a few hours is enough. Even discounting this, beauty must consume itself in the very course of its existence, and end in nothing. In the final analysis, the joy that beauty brings in its train when it arrives upon the scene is not equal to the sorrow that it evokes when it departs. If I am not mistaken, that beautiful Roman emperor was thinking this when he wrote to a friend: "Remember—nothing is more acceptable than beauty, and nothing can be more brief." But even if it were a natural gift that was constant and lasting, I would still fail to see what was so desirable about this shimmering loveliness which lacks all substance: it covers over much ugliness and many revolting things with a skin-thin veil which deceives and beguiles the senses. We must take pleasure in goods that are real and of substance, not in those that are empty and transitory.

Joy. My physical beauty is a thing of exquisite grace.

Reason. You are blindfolded; your feet are chained; your wings are entangled. It is not easy for you to see truth, to follow virtue, or to elevate your soul. Beauty has distracted many who sought honesty, and led them to its opposite.

Joy. O, my wondrous physical beauty!

Reason. True: wondrous. But what is there to remark in such vanity? From how many truly delectable things does beautiful youth abstain! How many travails does it rush to meet! How many sacrifices do the young impose upon themselves, not in order to become really beautiful, but simply to appear to be so. From mere infatuation with beauty alone, they become forgetful of health and pleasure! How many hours it wastes in making itself beautiful, to the neglect of so many honest, useful, and necessary things! Keep it. I do not envy you this brief and passing good, this vain joy. Your enemy dwells within your own house; and what is worse, it is an enemy both tender and pleasing. You are in the company of that which steals your tranquility and your time; you possess what continually tortures you and gives you grief. You are a very producer of dissensions;

a tinder of passions; a door wide open to hatred as well as love. You may be liked by women, but you are detested by men—or at least suspected by them. For nothing ignites the jealousy of husbands as much as physical beauty—a thing yet most ardently desired. Nothing is more powerful in disturbing hearts, and for this reason nothing is viewed with greater suspicion.

Joy. I possess extraordinary beauty.

Reason. Usually it drives young men of little judgment where it is not meet for them to be: they, judging it to be as legitimate as it is desired, come to the point where they believe they can derive gain from this, their good, without ever reflecting upon what is right. This has already provoked many ugly, premature deaths.

Joy. Mine is a rare beauty.

Reason. But in a short time that youthful bloom in your beautiful cheeks will pass. The blonde hair will fall out, and those that remain will whiten. Those smooth cheeks, that serene brow, will become lined with deep furrows; those flashing and smiling eyes, like two luminous stars, will be dulled by the veil of sadness. Those teeth, white and smooth as ivory, will be covered with a corrosive film, and will no longer display their old luster: indeed, they will not appear to be the same. That proud head, those smooth shoulders, will bend; the delicate throat will sag; you will begin to suspect that those weathered hands and those deformed feet are not your own. No sense in continuing: the day will come when you will no longer recognize yourself in the mirror. And all this ugliness, which you consider so far removed, will come upon you, if you continue to live, in less time than it takes to tell. I speak of this because, when you stand agape in the presence of this novel condition, you will not say that I did not predict it. If you believe me now, these transformations will one day not shock you so much.

Joy. At least for now my beauty is resplendent!

Reason. In this connection, no expression could be more apt than that of Apuleius: "Wait a moment, and it will be no more!"

Joy. Up to this instant, my physical beauty is perfect.

Reason. How much more I would prefer perfect spiritual beauty! There is, in truth, a beauty of the soul, which is so much more exquisite and more secure than that of the body; and it, too, obeys the laws of good order arising from the harmonious disposition of parts. It would have been much better to prefer this, and to dedicate oneself to it, since time does not consume it, nor do sickness and death destroy it. You admire perishable things.

Joy. Without a doubt, at least for the moment, mine is an uncommon beauty.

Reason. As in many other things, so also in this, the middle road is to be preferred. If on account of this physical beauty you do not become enraptured with yourself and do not devote yourself to pleasing others beyond what is meet, and if you come out of it with chastity, sobriety, and modesty, there will accrue to you no small credit.

Joy. Good looks make the spirit serene.

Reason. Quite the contrary! Physical beauty torments the spirit and too often drags it into danger. What sense is there in taking pride in that which is not of your own doing, and in possessing that which cannot obtain for any length of time? To own it has never given glory to anyone; indeed, many have acquired glory in ridding themselves of it. Not to mention other traits, what constitutes Spurina's glory is not the beauty she received from nature, but the ugliness which she brought upon herself.

Joy. I try to combine virtue with beauty.

Reason. Should you succeed, then I will truly consider you fortunate and will, with everyone else, think of your beauty as even more resplendent and your virtue as the more gentle. Although Seneca writes that "those are in error who say that virtue is more welcome in a beautiful body," I think, nevertheless, that his rebuke would be just only if they had said "greater," or "more perfect," or "more profound." But since the "more welcome" refers here not to virtue as such, but to the judgment of those who make this statement, it seems to me that Virgil did not err in speaking as he did. In sum: the fascination of beauty has in itself nothing solid and nothing desirable, although, if it presents itself in accompaniment with virtue and combines, thus, the regard that we hold for both, I will admit that we can say that beauty may serve virtue as an ornament, not unpleasing to see but fragile and of brief duration. By itself, however, I would call beauty a burden for the spirit, and regard it as a useless decoration.

DIALOGUE 49

Dear Love

Joy. I enjoy a dear love.

Reason. You are destined to be overwhelmed by its sweet betrayals!

Joy. I burn with my sweet love!

Reason. Well said: you burn! Truly, love is a hidden fire, a wound that gives pleasure, a delicious poison, a sweet bitterness, a delectable ailment, a joyous torment, an attractive death.

Joy. I love, and I am loved in return.

Reason. That you love, you may well know; but that you are loved in return is not certain—unless you can prove it by the words which your beloved utters in sleep!

Joy. There can be no doubt that I am loved!

Reason. It seems to me that she has convinced you; but it is not difficult to convince those who wish to be convinced. Every lover is blind and credulous. If you wish me to believe her protestations of love, show me a document written by your beloved—a document written on soft snow and witnessed by the south winds! But you are mad to believe any woman: especially if she be flighty. Sex, the senses, superficiality, the habit of lying, deceit—these things, each and all together, render suspect whatever comes from her lips!

Joy. The object of my love surely delights my soul, and I burn sweetly.

Reason. Do you believe the words of the famous teacher of love who said: "So that you may enjoy the happiness of your ardor and sail by propitious winds"? Yours are words dictated by desire, not by wisdom. So far as I am concerned, the more sweetly you burn, the more I would enjoin you to employ caution and remove yourself from the fire. This malady is most dangerous when it gives most pleasure: too often a most unhappy outcome destroys all the sweetness.

Joy. I love and I am loved.

Reason. Let us grant that such is the case: is this not a double bind? The tighter the knot, the more difficult it is to undo. I would cast a better prognosis for you if you loved and were not loved in return! It is true that some people declare both the fortunate and the unfortunate loves to be equally harmful since, if the soul becomes used to favors, it rebels at difficulties. But I believe that nothing is more conducive to loving than being loved; and, conversely, I think that nothing is more efficacious in halting our love than knowing that we are not loved and that we will never be. Such a thing, of course, could never be believed by blind and smitten minds such as are possessed by those who love, since it applies to the class of those about whom it has been written: "Lovers seek one another in their dreams."

Joy. I love with happiness.

Reason. He who will not see what woes are forthcoming is obviously stunned; but he who takes pleasure in his pain must be mad!

Joy. I confess it: to love gives me happiness!

Reason. I would prefer that it was detestable and tiresome to you. You would then be relieved of this ailment the sooner, and there would be hope of a full recovery. As it is, the delight feeds your infirmity, for one who takes pleasure in being ill refuses to become healthy.

Joy. That may be; but, according to my view, love is a noble thing.

Reason. Each person speaks what he knows. I, instead,

consider love a vile thing and a weakness capable of unnerving and debilitating even the strongest of men. Let me retail something which, although known to all, is nonetheless never recalled without the shock of surprise: for the remembrance of great events evokes surprise even in those who know them. Now I shall not go into all the cases: indeed, I hardly think this to be necessary, or even possible: but let me speak of the two most eminent generals of the two most famous peoples in the whole world. Julius Caesar, conqueror of Gaul, Germany, England, Spain, Italy, Thessaly, Tessaglia, Egypt; later to be victorious in Armenia, in Pontus, in Africa, and again in Spain: he, while in the midst of so many victories, was defeated because of the love of a queen. Hannibal, victor at Ticinus, at Trebia, at Transimenus, at Cannae, later destined to be defeated in his own country, was first conquered by love at Salapia in Apulia and—what is even more unpardonable—love for a prostitute! How powerful do you think an evil must be which can smash with one light blow souls so steadfast, hearts so firm? How powerful is that which is capable of binding with such thin thongs, such swift feet and strong arms? Now I shall not even refer to the fables which, nonetheless, contain their own truth: Jove, transformed into different animals; Mars, ridiculously imprisoned in a net; Hercules, spinning with his strong hands; Leander, who died in the waves; Biblida, who perished in tears; Procri, struck by the sword of his servant; Pyramus, dying by his own hand; Hyphin, dying at the end of a rope. I put aside that which is more credible and, indeed, quite well known: the generals of the Greeks fighting for love, and Troy in flames. Leaving aside all these examples, and a thousand others similar to them, the two which I first mentioned are sufficient to prove, by the eminence of their names and by historical documentation, what I have been telling you.

Joy. I love. What would you say if I hated, since you thus condemn love?

Reason. In the way in which you conceive them, I condemn them both; and I will not call something "good" simply because it is different from or the opposite of another called "bad." Two contraries equidistant from the middle, that is, from virtue, are two extremes: they are equally evil.

Joy. So you think that it is evil to love? I confess that I know of nothing better than this "evil"!

Reason. I believe you, by Hercules, knowing your temperament! Still, your opinion cannot change the facts.

Joy. Let him who so chooses hate it; I shall continue to love!

Reason. In themselves, love and hate are indifferent things. In reality, just as we can eulogize hatred of vice and love of virtue, so we can condemn hatred of virtue and love of vice. In brief, it would be difficult for you to find anything which is, in itself or as such, so worthy of detestation or of praise that with but a slight change it could not merit either condemnation or praise. As for you, consider what you love.

Joy. What is it that I love which differs from what others love?

Reason. Not everyone loves the same things. There were those who loved God with such fervor as to think themselves fortunate to be able to sacrifice themselves, their very lives, everything, for this love. Others, without aiming so high, felt the same for pure and simple virtue or for their country. If all the objects of love were numerable, I should here name them for you, but they are as the sands of the beach.

Joy. I've never been in heaven; what is more, I have never seen virtue: I love what can be seen!

Reason. If you love nothing but what is visible, you can love nothing that is great. Why do you not see the truth of the well-known precept: "Do not love that which is seen, for that which is not visible is eternal"? You, whose spirit is blind and who trusts his eyes, are not capable—I won't say "of loving"—but of thinking or understanding eternal things! You seek what is destined to perish with you, covering your shameful feelings with the thin pretense of sincerity; what you call "love" is truly lust; and this you cultivate, making of it—if I may so—a god, who you then think can exculpate you of your immeasurable guilt. What could be more unjust than that, the example for which is set by a god? Go then: raise an altar to your god and burn incense; let him pull you up to heaven. But the true God of heaven will surely thrust you and your god into the pit!

Joy. You interpret the lightheartedness of youth in the worst possible way. Forgive me, but I love!

Reason. If you must seek forgiveness of those you have offended, forgive yourself! The only harm you do is to yourself. To what reefs, O you unfortunate one, you are leading your small boat!

Joy. I like to live this way, and I don't understand what prohibits my doing so.

Reason. To sin is a misfortune; it is worse to take pleasure in it. It is a very great misfortune to love sin and to justify it; but misfortune reaches its height when the quest after pleasure joins with the conviction that one is doing good thereby!

Joy. I love and I cannot do differently—nor do I wish to!

Reason. But you could, if you wished to! Perhaps, with the passing of the years, you may wish to do so. It often happens this way in other things, but it happens this way most especially with your malady. May time naturally bring, at last, the remedy for your illness.

Joy. There will never come a day when I shall not love!

Reason. More power to you! Enjoy yourself, go mad, delight in your dreams—when you awaken you will weep!

Joy. I shall never weep! I shall sing and console myself with poetry, as all lovers do.

Reason. Here is a profession about which it would be possible to say many things. Indeed, I insist upon doing so, since you have brought me to it. Among the many kinds of madness, that of people in love is the most extraordinary; and not only among the common people, where habits are suggested by instinct and every excess is understandable, but as well among the cultured men of Rome and Greece. You know that the Greek poets, as your own, have written on the loves of others as well as their own. Many have, as a consequence, derived fame from this source—a source from which they should rather have deserved contempt! Among the Greeks, the most tolerable is Sappho: her age, her sex, her lightheartedness—everything serves to excuse a young girl. But how can we excuse Anacreon? or Alcaeus? both of whom were not only great poets, but strong men, famous for what they did for their country. And among your poets, how shall we judge Ovid, Catullus, Propertius and Tibullus, whose every lyric is about love? But why talk about poets—men to whom, for some unknown reason, the greatest license is granted? Why not rather rebuke the philosophers, who are supposed to provide us with guides for living? And here, by Bacchus, you can be proud that your own have been much more serious than the Greeks! It is difficult to find one, among yours, who is so degenerate that he has not at least openly condemned this vanity—even if he has himself fallen prey to it. Among the Greek philosophers, on the other hand, not only the common breed but those most astute, like the Stoics, and even Plato himself (which is a surprising thing), we know to have been involved in this error. The Stoics want the wise man to love; and certainly, if we agree on the kind of love, they are not wrong. The wise man will love God, as I have said; he will love his neighbor, he will love virtue, his country, his parents, his children, his brothers, his friends and, if he is really wise, he will also love his enemies—not for themselves, you understand, but for the sake of Him who wishes us to do so. In all of these loves, what, I ask, is the place of beauty? In Cicero's *Tusculanarum*, we read this definition: "Love is the attempt to actualize friendship under the species of beauty." Who is so blind as not to see what beauty pretends for itself? Consequently, Cicero rightly asks: "What is it, in truth, this love of friendship? Why don't we love an ugly young woman, or a beautiful old one?" Age and beauty, with their charms, are no doubt at the base of that "friendship"—so called, euphemistically, rather than that "lasciviousness" which it really is, as anybody with good and open eyes can readily see! Thus, everything returns to the same point: if in nature there is a kind of love without anxiety, without coarse desires, without sighs, without burning thoughts, then let the sage enjoy it, "for he is free from every passion," as Cicero goes on to say—free, that is, from every agitation and from every anxiety, for these are states of soul that the wise man must, above all, eschew. At all events, we cannot change the truth of things as we can, by talking, change their appearance. But our discourse is at this moment concerned with lustful love only, which, no doubt, has many more serious defects than those that I have pointed out. So much for the Stoics. I turn now to Plato, prince of philosophers, in fact—as we say—the God of Philosophers. (Even if this be disputed by many, in this controversy one must align himself not with the judgment of the many, but with that of the greatest and best.) Plato, I say, doubtless an exceptional man, wrote much about his loves—even the base ones. (I maintain, with all respect to Plato, that for the philosopher all passions are questionable, and none are permitted him.) He wrote, indeed, more licentiously than one might expect from a person who bears such a name. However, he did write, and the writings remain; and he felt no shame for this blot on his immense fame, any more than he feared the judgment of posterity; for such fears were quite won over by the impetus of the passion which pressed on his soul, and by the sweetness of the style which moved the pen. This sweetness, even in shameful subjects and filthy material, is so great in him that you can see the light of his genius, as rays of sun on mud, reflected in the Epicurean writings. And I can see that just this sort of following after Plato caused many others to leave behind writings which they would have done better to destroy, or not to have written at all. I think that this can yet induce many others to do the same; but I speak only of the most famous. I have said much to deplore this madness, and much more could be said; and as concerns the remedy, not a few things yet remain to be said. Regarding what you call the "consolation" of this evil, which you imagine can come to you from poetry, let your answer be the question that Horace raises in a few verses: "Do you think that by poetry you can remove from your heart the pains, the regrets, the heavy thoughts?" By talking, by singing, love is fed, love is inflamed, and not extinguished; for this reason the songs that you remember, and the lyrics you recite, can effect no cure, but can only irritate the wounds.

Joy. Your admonitions, and the experiences you relate begin, finally, to make me believe! Let the rest alone, therefore, and turn to the remedies.

Reason. Many in the past have sought them; among those, Naso, a strange doctor, more interested in sickness than in health. He gives us advice which is sometimes frivolous, sometimes base, but never without some value. Others, too, have written of the remedies: Cicero, for example, did so with powerful directness. All in all, I can approve only a few remedies selected from the many advanced: change your residence—this is becoming to the body and is also an aid for the sick soul; avoid and run away from every minute thing that recalls the beloved face; occupy yourself, and dedicate yourself to other projects, thoughts, which help to destroy the traces of the old malady; think continually and intensely how shameful, how sad, how unfortunate and, in the end, how brief, impermanent, and really empty is that which one seeks to obtain in the face of so many obstacles; think, too, of how easily and how much better one can satisfy oneself in other ways and by different means; one can also develop complete contempt for it, and stay away from it by viewing it as being one among the most vile things. Quiet reserve has served as a cure for many; and this is particularly the case with sensitive hearts; for they dislike scandal and ridicule, and they experience pain on being pointed out, and being on everyone's tongue; and when the ugliness of the thing comes into view, fruitless, shameful, dangerous, sorrowful, they have reason for regret. Finally, putting aside all excuses and false opinions, it will help to accept what is the truth: and in this, neither nature nor destiny nor the stars can help, but only a lightness of soul and an open judgment. The cure depends on the patient; it commences when he begins to will with firm faith and has broken with the sweet ties of habit; this is a laborious undertaking, doubtless, but it is possible for him who wishes it. "One must demonstrate, in this, as in any other kind of disturbance," says Cicero with great profundity, "that one is dealing with something that is voluntary, chosen, self-created. As a matter of fact, if love were natural, all would love, and would always love, and love in the same way; and neither shame nor reflection nor satiety would suffice to end it." Satiety itself is placed by some among the remedies; others think that a new love can chase away an old one, as a nail can drive a nail. Some such method was suggested by friends to Artaxerxes, king of the Persians, and it was followed by good results, as Josephus wordily attests; I will say nothing of these results, but I really must protest the choice of the remedy. These two latter methods are sometimes useful, I admit, but I consider them always dangerous. If you are not cured by one of these that I have previously mentioned, or by some combination of them, then you must go back to the causes of the sickness. If I am not mistaken, the principal and most important ones are health, beauty, wealth, idleness, and youth. As with physical maladies, the spiritual ones are cured magnificently by their contraries: bad health, ugliness, poverty, intense preoccupation, and old age—which is an excellent cure for all the errors of youth. These are extreme remedies; hard, of course, but quite proportionate to the nature of the illness.

DIALOGUE 92

Fame

Joy. I have achieved an immense fame.

Reason. I do not understand how great things can squeeze themselves into what is little! If you gauge the limits of time and of place, you must admit that they can contain no great fame. Nor will I object to the idea that the whole earth is but a point; and that nature has made it in large part uninhabitable, even as chance has made it in large measure inaccessible. Nor will I object to the idea that the present instant is even less than a point; and that, in addition, it is unstable, and runs out so rapidly that the mind can scarcely conceive it. The parts of time are two, and these are never present: they are such that one taxes us with the cares of memory, which is so untrustworthy, and the other with the anxiety of waiting. I accede also to the idea that all of time, taken together, is so broken and confused by torrential rains, excessive heats, epidemics, the inclemency of the seasons and, finally, by its own ruinous flowing, that frequently one epoch has nothing to relate it with another. And as with time, so also with space. You can see how that which is very well known in one place, cannot even be recognized in another. Examples of this kind are by the hundreds and I shall not bother to enumerate: everyone knows them, and they serve to make us see clearly just how great can be the fame that mortals can possibly attain on earth!

Joy. I have attained all the fame that my condition allows.

Reason. If unmerited, though short, go in peace; if merited, enjoy it; not because you possess it, but rather because you have deserved it.

Joy. I sought for fame.

Reason. True fame can be sought only with good works. Take care to look into that from which your renown derives, in this way you will see if you have acquired genuine fame; for if it was only chance that gave you fame, chance can also rob you of it.

Joy. Many are the varieties of fame.

Reason. Take care that what you hold to be true fame is not but a false image. In human matters, self-deception is not uncommon!

Joy. There is a superabundance of fame.

Reason. As no poor man tries to pass for a rich man

except to impress his neighbor, so too, no fool tries to pass himself off as a person of great value. Still, both know very well, no matter what the judgment of others, how much money they have in their purse, and how much virtue in their soul.

Joy. I am resplendent in my fame!

Reason. If it corresponds to merit, use it with moderation so that you may not dirty it with the blot of pride; otherwise take care not to deceive others.

Joy. My fame is splendid.

Reason. Try to deserve it, or else cast off a garment that is too heavy for you. It is better not to be famous than to be mendaciously famous. If true fame requires so much effort to conserve, what can you hope from false fame? To take the spotlight is always difficult. It is difficult because there is an infinity of persons observing you from everywhere. Truly famous persons are rare; and the anonymous, mediocre, and envious public, by the law of contrast, hates them. It is a serious matter to attempt to hide oneself in the midst of so many insidious enemies: you are not allowed to close your eyes to all who stare at you so fixedly and with such rapt attention.

Joy. I show myself in all my fame!

Reason. You probably would do better to hide yourself! For certainly you would be safer. A poet who has said many superficial things said this, which is profound: "He who knew how to hide himself, lived well."

Joy. I am famous. Everyone knows me. My position makes me quite conspicuous.

Reason. Envy insinuates and penetrates even into hidden places. Do you think you can avoid that which confronts your fame? It means little that some few have gained in stature by being in the public eye; for very rare are those who do not receive a bad name, and harm, from being known to all. The saying of Claudius, "Presence diminishes fame," is well known. How much more must knowledge diminish it? Rarely are men what they appear to be!

Joy. Everyone says that I am famous.

Reason. You take light from the cloud which covers you. If you came out of your cloud for a single instant, as great as is your vainglory, so great should your true lack of fame appear!

Joy. But my fame is genuine!

Reason. No one can know this better than you. Fame, as certain wise men have said, is almost a shadow of virtue; it accompanies it and follows it. Often, too, fame even precedes virtue, as we see in the cases of those adolescents of good disposition whom the hopes of men elevate to fame even before their virtue has come to fruition. This sort of fame acts often as a stimulant, which excites the generous and modest soul, elevating it and helping it to fulfill the hopes of the elders; but it acts as well to cast down foolish and presumptuous souls. Hence the disappointing transformation of famous youths into unknown old men. The truth of the matter is that eulogy helps the wise and harms the foolish. A shadow cannot exist by itself, it is always the shadow of something. Do you want your fame to be genuine? Make sure that your virtue is real and steadfast.

DIALOGUE 108

Happiness

Joy. I am happy.

Reason. Do you think that even being pope, emperor, or the possession of absolute power and riches would serve to make you happy? You are fooling yourself! These conditions make one neither happy nor unhappy. All they do is exhibit the individual naked, just as he is; and even if they were efficacious, they would render him unhappy rather than happy, just as do all those dangers in which the very roots of human miseries are sunk.

Joy. I am happy.

Reason. Unhappy you! You, who in the midst of so many evils have the hope of being happy!

Joy. I am happy.

Reason. Probably you do believe it, but you are in error; for this reason, nothing can add to your happiness, but a great deal can add to your unhappiness. Not to know one's own misery is the greatest misery of all!

Joy. I am happy.

Reason. This is what Pompeius Magnus said under the very daggers of his executioners! Yet (if you look deeply into the truth), he was never happy; even when it seemed to him that he was supremely happy and at the very height of prosperity.

Joy. I am happy.

Reason. You are happy? Then you are an exceptional journeyman! If, on this rough and difficult road, you are able to be happy while being dragged into a thousand dangers, without knowing where they will eventuate, you are a marvelous traveler! If under these conditions you are really happy, you are as no one has ever been before, or—as can easily be predicted—ever will be. Who, pray tell, can be happy in the midst of misfortunes? No one can have happiness until he departs this vale of miseries. Among mortals, only two examples of happy persons are to be found: one of these, Quintus Metellus, was proclaimed to be happy both by public opinion and by history. Nonetheless, I know from more dependable sources that he was not so happy as is commonly believed: at times he suffered atrocious injuries (and to double his unhappiness) at the hands of vile and inferior men. The happiness of all others is just as false, as appears quite clear. Silius was said to be happy; but his cruel life and cruel death proclaim otherwise. If Alexander of Macedon and Julius Caesar were always very fortunate, they nevertheless lived constantly in disquiet: they were constantly involved in turbulence, and therefore never happy. Besides, death came to them prematurely: the death of the first came in the midst of war; and it came for the other, unexpectedly, after victory. One died by poison, the other by the blade. The happiness which the Scipios had gained in war ended with the unjust exile of the first, and the unworthy and unjustified death of the second. It would lead us too far afield to discuss the vicissitudes of each so-called "happy" man, so I turn to the most significant example: Emperor Augustus. He, above all others, seems to be regarded by everyone as having been happy. His throne was the highest; his peace the most lasting; the course of his life, and its termination, was tranquil; and, what is more, he enjoyed a constant serenity of soul and of habit. Who would presume to question his happiness? Yet, those who have studied his life in greater detail do not think he was happy. His external appearance, in fact, is quite in conflict with his intimate and private life: he lacked male sons of his own; his adopted children and his nephews died, and some of them suffered a fate even worse than death—exile. Then too, he suffered treachery at the hands of the most vile among men; frequent plots against his life; the repeated adulteries of his only and beloved daughter, and of his niece; and, finally, he was succeeded by an unwelcome heir, selected more out of necessity than will—a man absolutely unworthy of him and the empire. If, then, none of these was happy, either find me someone who is like you, or try to be happy without company; failing this, listen to an opinion which is more like the truth. I repeat it to you: before death, no man is happy!

Joy. I feel myself to be happy.

Reason. I think I know the happiness of which you speak. You are happy either by your own error, as a poet has said—and this is a miserable happiness, as I have already said—or else you are happy because of your soul's own virtue—and this is not complete happiness, although it represents the right road toward happiness. And another observation: when I examine all the details, I confess that I am surprised about the dreams of happiness that some men entertain, and of the promise of happiness which they make to others. They may be acute with regard to many things, but in this matter they are blind. There are two views of happiness: some say there is required the accumulation of all possible goods and their continued possession —in which case anyone can see for himself how many things a man would be lacking who directed his life to attaining happiness in this way; for he would learn that all the goods that are lacking are transient and uncertain —or else, as others say, virtue alone is capable of everything. Those, indeed, who live according to virtue and are thought to be happy may truly be close to it. Yet they must live a life which is continually concerned with the struggle against temptation; they must be forever exposed to a crowd of grave dangers; and they can never be sure of themselves until the end. Whether they know it or not, these dangers are vitally important to the whole quest, because there can be no happiness without error and lack of security!

Joy. It seems to me that I am happy.

Reason. You have given the answer: if error made us happy, few would be unhappy! Vain, therefore, is happiness: in addition, it is very brief, for no man when in error can maintain happiness. Truth alone is steadfast. Error, instead, is something vain and fleeting: it dissolves in one's arms like smoke or a shadow, if one seeks to embrace it. She will come at last, who will, with great vigor, eject fantasies, expose false pleasures, fix the true price for human felicity, and put an end to dreams! Meanwhile, ask any of those of whom we have previously spoken—ask all who were reputed to be happy and who thought themselves so —ask them in what state they find themselves; and where; and what opinion they now have of that brief happiness. They will be silent. But Truth will speak for them and bear witness that although thought happy, they were all, in reality, most unhappy!

DIALOGUE 121

The Quest for Peace

Hope. I hope to have my soul in peace.

Reason. Why hope for peace? Wouldn't it be better to procure it? You will find it as soon as you begin to pursue it in the right spirit.

Hope. I hope to have my soul in peace.

Reason. Only those who are at war hope for peace. Who brings war into your soul if not you, yourself? It is shameless to hope and to expect from others what you deny yourself.

Hope. I hope to have my soul in peace.

Reason. May I ask when, and from whom, do you hope for that which you, yourself, can give yourself, now? that indeed, which none but you can take from yourself? Put down the weapons of desire and resentment and you will have complete peace of spirit!

Hope. I hope to have my soul in peace and in quiet.

Reason. How? What you are doing is directly opposed to peace; you are fighting against your own hope! All that is requisite is that men devote as much energy to saving themselves as they devote to sending themselves to hell. Perennial agitation and trouble of spirit costs much more than peace and tranquillity. Between hopes, the desires of humans, and their attempts to realize these, there is such a contrast that each individual seems to have not one heart but many—and all in discord!

Hope. I hope for tranquillity.

Reason. I marvel at where you derive this eternal hunger for hope! Poor mortals! As soon as you get what you hope for, again you direct your hopes toward distant things, and then, beyond these to yet others. Is tomorrow more luminous than today? Why are the things of the future the most desirable to those who desire them? For some, nothing more than hope is yearned after; and these would never accept any other more sure result in place of their hope. To these, I can wish nothing more than that they become old among their vain hopes; always postponing until tomorrow while divesting themselves of all goods today. Finally, they comprehend that they have hoped in vain: looking back, they see that they have sought vainly in other places for that which was always at hand!

Hope. I hope to have peace and tranquillity of spirit.

Reason. A great part of being human consists in shadows. So many mortals feed on wind and take delight in fantasies. How many, by these hopes, fall into conflict and despair!

LEON BATTISTA ALBERTI

LEON BATTISTA ALBERTI *was born in Genoa in 1404, the illegitimate son of a famous Florentine. Artist, sculptor, architect, musician, and scholar, Alberti personifies the Renaissance ideal man. His Latin was good enough to enable him, while still a student, to write a comedy that was mistaken for a work of Terence. He studied law and natural philosophy at Bologna. In 1428 he went to France and Germany as secretary to Cardinal Albergati; in 1431 he was invited to Rome as Cardinal Moulin's secretary. He accompanied Eugene IV on a diplomatic mission to Florence in 1434, and was with Pius II on a similar mission to Mantua in 1459. The first of these trips brought him into contact with Brunelleschi, Donatello, and other great Florentines; the second resulted in his being commissioned to draw plans for Sant'Andrea at Mantua. He died, admired and beloved by all, in 1472. Al-*

berti, in addition to his other accomplishments, was a prolific writer. From his pen we have poems, plays, dialogues, and tracts on diverse subjects. Most notable among his longer works are De re aedificatoria *and* Momus, *or* De principe. *A similarly notable smaller work,* Intercoenales, *reflects the ideas that pervade* De principe.

Three Dialogues

FIRST DIALOGUE: RELIGION

Libripeta. This place seems quite religious and pious to me, for in it, as in the widely celebrated house of Simon, many have come to retreat from the cares of life. But here comes Leopide, for whom I was waiting.

Leopide. Greetings, Libripeta. Have the sacrifices detained me in the temple longer than you expected?

Lib. You were much too long. What business had you with the gods that required such lengthy devotions?

Leop. Is it perhaps wrong to honor the gods fully, and to pray that they be favorable to our entreaties?

Lib. Of course, the celestial beings are sure to listen to you there—under those sacred domes which hide the mob of priests!

Leop. But don't you know that everything is full of gods?

Lib. Then you could have performed here, under this fig tree, those same rites which a superstitious habit of the ignorant induced you to perform in the temple! But tell me, did you plead your own cause before the painted gods, or did you plead the cause of others?

Leop. Why do you ask?

Lib. Because I would think it presumptuous of you if, thinking that you were dearer to the gods than others, you felt that your words would be more efficacious than the words of those who are in need of aid. Anyway, I believe that those who go near the gods ought, principally, to ask for present and future goods, and the ability to hold on to them, and that evils be dissipated. What do you say?

Leop. Yes, I think you are right.

Lib. But do you wish the gods to be foolish, and to become your accomplices and lackeys? Do you realize that any goods which they granted you would have to be taken from others? What servant could be more vile than one who could be commanded to commit such a misdeed? And who would be so vicious as to order his cutthroats to enrich him by robbing others?

Leop. I understand what you wish to convey; but I have not asked them to be thieves—if anything, I regard them as good workers who can help me to grow my own cabbages.

Lib. How the gods, if they only knew, would despise your shamelessness!

Leop. But you, Libripeta, don't you admit that the help of the gods is of great value to men in their adversities?

Lib. And you, Leopide, don't you admit that men are themselves the cause of their afflictions? Come, climb this fig tree and hang yourself on this branch—then pray to the gods for help! If you had not weakened yourself by poring so long over your books you would be neither pale nor sick to your stomach. The evils of men are provoked by men themselves. Believe me, sailors would never have conceived of gods capable of calming tempests if they had not risked their lives on the sea. Ever since men, by their own foolishness and ineptitude, have brought grave ills upon themselves, they have developed the habit of turning to the gods; and even when acting thus, while yet pretending that the divinities can halt that which they themselves have provoked, they can be seen, not praying, but engaging in contests or quarrels. Now if men avoided the causes of evil, they would never need the gods to rescue them; and if you believe that it is men who hurt other men, what is required is not the intercession of a god but, rather, the rule of men over themselves. But if, finally, it were the gods themselves who caused the evil, believe me they would not cease their practice because of your prayers. To be oppressed by misfortune is man's heritage; but even if the source of our sorrows lay with some other—fate, say, or destiny, or time—without doubt they would still occur, as they do, in accord with the divine will and in utter disregard—O you who call yourself religious—of your pleas and your fasts. Furthermore, do you really think that the gods are like us poor homunculi? Do you conceive of them as beings who, like men, imprudent and impulsive, make sudden decisions only suddenly to reverse them? I hear, instead, from those who cultivate letters, that in the complex administration of the universe the gods are extremely industrious, and that they conduct the world with an order which is almost invariant. Things being what they are, you are a raving madman if you believe that the gods would deviate from the basic and primeval course of things to institute new patterns and works because of your fables and pleas. Again, it would be an extremely vile form of slavery for the gods to surrender their plans to suit your will and needs. Finally, it is well to remember that according to religious people, the gods move the sun, the moon, and all the other stars through the ether; that they agitate the seas; that they send the winds and lightning, and regulate an infinite number of other such awful things—they are just too busy and certainly do not have the time to listen to the foolish and empty supplications of men. It is said that they are attentive to even the smallest things; in that case, they must listen much more willingly to the pure sounds of crickets and cicadas than to the foolish requests of men. In any event, the gods are badgered only by the prayers of scoundrels; for good men remain content with what they have, and suffer their misfortunes in silence. Bad men know no limit or measure when it comes to asking for special favors or for aid in their misfortunes.

Leop. All that you have said, Libripeta, I consider to have been said only for the purpose of talking. In my opinion that the prayers and pledges of good men are not unwelcome to the celestial beings, I remain unshaken. I will remain always convinced that piety helps us to avoid many deserved woes, and that the gods are supremely helpful toward those who deserve help. Goodbye.

SECOND DIALOGUE: VIRTUE

Mercury. Virtue, the god has asked me by letter to come here to meet you. I have come to find out what you wish from me; after that, I shall return to Jove.

Virtue. Greetings, Mercury. I thank you, because your pity and benevolence have made it possible for me to avoid being despised by the whole circle of gods.

Mer. I await what you have to tell me. Be very brief, because Jove has ordered me to return to him with all possible speed.

Vir. Can I not speak even with you about my plight? How can I ever receive satisfaction for the offenses done me if not only supreme Jove, but you as well, whom I have considered a dear brother, will not hear my complaints? O woe! Where can I take refuge? From whom can I seek help? Thus despised, I prefer being a piece of wood to being a goddess!

Mer. Once and for all, go ahead and talk—I am here now at your disposal.

Vir. All right—but see how naked and ugly I am! Now my condition was brought about by the cruelty and maliciousness of the goddess Fortune. There I was, garlanded, in the Elysian Fields among my friends Plato, Socrates, Demosthenes, Cicero, Archimedes, Polyclitus, Praxiteles, and other such sages and artists who had, in their lives, piously revered me as a saint. While we were talking together, the goddess Fortune, insolent, proud, domineering, and surrounded by a host of armed followers, turned to me and asked in a bellicose manner: "How does it come about, you common thing, that you do not make obeisance when your superiors arrive upon the scene?" Grieving, because of this unlooked-for insult, and also somewhat irritated, I replied: "Supreme goddess, you cannot thus mark me a commoner, nor, if it is necessary for me to make obeisance to superior gods, do I believe that I have to defer, in shame, to you!" Immediately upon hearing this, she lunged at me to do me an injury; nor shall I repeat the insults she heaped upon my head while this was going on. Plato, the philosopher, then began to make a speech directed against her, touching on the subject of the duties pertaining to gods. But she, feigning shock, shrieked: "Away, blabberer! Lackeys should not come to the defense of the gods!" The orator Cicero also prepared to speak against her, when suddenly, out of the mob of armed men surrounding her, Mark Antony, showing his gladiator's flanks, leaped forth and struck Cicero a devastating blow in the face. It was then that my other friends, taken by fear, ran for their lives. Neither Polyclitus with his brush, nor Phidias with his chisel, nor Archimedes with his lens, nor the others who were similarly armed, could defend themselves against these truculent warriors trained to sack, kill, and wage war. So, abandoned by the men, and as well by all the gods that were present, unhappy me was kicked and pummeled; they tore off my robe, left me prostrate in the mud, and went their way singing! Even in this condition, as soon as I was able, I came here to inform Jove, the All Highest. I have been waiting here for a month now, to be presented to him; I inquire about this audience of all the gods who come and go, and every time I hear a new excuse. The gods tell me that "pumpkins have to flower at their own time," and that they have to busy themselves with the various colors of butterfly wings! How is it that they always find some way to put me off and to ignore me? The pumpkins have flowered! The butterflies soar in splendor! The farmer takes care that the pumpkins do not die for want of water, but I am favored neither by the gods nor by men! For this reason, O Mercury, I pray and invoke you, who have always been the bearer of men's wishes to the gods, that you plead my sacred and just cause; and I seek haven with you, for I have put all my hope in you. Act, I pray you, so that I may not be rejected, and made, moreover, a laughing-stock. It would be a disgrace affecting the whole order of divinities if even stupid little men were to come to despise me.

Mer. I have listened; I am very sorry. I must tell you, in the name of old friendship, that you have undertaken to plead a most unpopular cause. Indeed, Jove himself, not to speak of the other gods, claims that he owes to Fortune the benefits which he has received, and he holds a profound respect for her power and strength. For it is Fortune who sends the gods to heaven, and who uses her lackeys, whenever she wishes, to depose them. Therefore, if you are wise, you will melt silently into the host of lesser deities and remain there unnoticed until such time as Fortune will have forgotten her hatred of you.

Vir. In that case, I shall remain hidden for all eternity! And so I shall go my way, naked and despised.

THIRD DIALOGUE: FATE AND FORTUNE

Philosopher's Friend. O philosopher, I approve of your theory according to which the minds of men are completely free and separated from their bodies during sleep; and I would, above all else, like to hear from you about your very beautiful dream having to do with Fate and Fortune. Recount it, therefore, now that we have leisure, so that I may be pleased with you because you have seen more in sleeping than we see while awake.

Philosopher. My dear friend, I shall do as you wish; and you will hear something worth committing to memory.

Here it is. I had been awake long into the night reading the ancient doctrines on Fate, and while I admired many of the theses of the authors, very few, nonetheless, seemed to me wholly satisfactory. Thus, within myself, I sought for something more. Tired by my long vigil, I fell into deep slumber. It seemed to me that I was located at the summit of a very high mountain amid a numberless host of shades of men—or so they seemed to me. From the height, I looked out upon the whole landscape; the mountain was rendered inaccessible by rocks and steep precipices, and only the narrowest of paths led to the top. Around the mountain, turning tortuously upon itself, there streamed a very rapid and whirling river, and the innumerable host of shades descended in an endless progression toward the river by way of the narrow path. Wholly absorbed by the prospect and by the innumerable multitudes of shades, I was so overcome at this point that I did not even look to see what lay beyond the river, nor did I seek to learn whence the shades came to the mountain top. What fascinated me particularly, were the extraordinary things that transpired in the river; and these were truly wondrous. No sooner did a shade become immersed in the river than it took on the visage and body of a child, and then, as the river carried it farther and farther, I saw the body begin to age. It was then that I began to speak: "If there is, O shades, in you any trace of humanity, if ever you have fellow feeling for humanity, tell me, I pray you, the name of this river, for it belongs to humanity to instruct men."

Then the shades responded: "You are mistaken, man, if by your corporeal vision you take us to be shades of men. We are in fact, even as you, celestial sparks destined to live like men."

I then replied: "Happy am I indeed if I have merited from the gods the privilege of knowing more about you; for it somehow seems to me a divine privilege to know where you come from, from what parents, and from what place."

The shades answered me: "Cease, man, cease to seek beyond that which it is granted man to know; cease to inquire into the mysteries of the god of gods. Know that to you, and to all souls encased in flesh, only so much can be revealed. To satisfy your curiosity, so far as it is allowed, I shall tell you the name of this river: it is *Bios*."

I was profoundly struck by these words. Pulling myself together, I said: "I pray you, celestial gods, speak this name in Latin so that I may better understand; now I am prepared to give the Greeks all the honors they deserve, but it doesn't seem to me a mean thing that I love my own language."

Then spoke the shades: "In Latin, the name of the river is 'Life,' or 'Mortal Existence'; its further banks are Death, for whoever reaches them becomes dissolved once again into a shade."

"Marvelous thing!" I replied, "but how is it that I see some shades, I know not which, who float about on inflated skins with their foreheads raised high above water, while others are being tossed about, helter-skelter, in the river, buried by the waves, struck by the rocks, and barely able to lift their faces out of the water? Why, pray tell me, good god, such a difference?"

And the shades: "Those whom you perhaps consider more secure on account of the inflated skins are actually, instead, in the gravest danger; for the river is full of sharp reefs. See how those skins, blown and pompous, tossed onto the reefs by the waves are broken and fail? Unfortunate are those who trust themselves to the skins. See how, here and there, in the middle of an eddy, abandoned and without support, they are flung against the rocks? These are most deserving of compassion, for their course is hard indeed. If the shades maintain their skins intact, these yet provide no guarantee; if they abandon them, the currents drag them until they no longer appear anywhere in the river. Much better is the fate of those others who, trusting to their own strength from the start, swim the whole course of Life. In fact, those run the best course who, having trust in their ability to swim, learn to rest for a moment by holding to the rear of a boat, or by leaning on one of the boards which you see carried along in the river; avoiding the reefs with great effort, they direct themselves gloriously to the beach, almost as if they were winged. So that you may properly grasp all this, know that we, impelled by nature, are all greatly drawn to them and greatly desire to help them, which we do to the degree that it is in us to help them to their safety and their glory. And you mortals usually ascribe to these the names 'honorable,' 'industrious,' 'serious,' 'zealous,' 'thoughtful,' 'active,' and 'frugal.' Those who prefer the skins, instead, are not considered by us as worthy of any particular favor because of their riches or their greatness; rather, we hold them in contempt and consider them deserving only of what you call 'hatred,' 'perfidiousness,' 'shamelessness,' 'cruelty,' and similar vices, out of which the skins are woven."

Then I: "I am truly pleased that some lean on the little boats, and that still others sit at the boat's prow, while yet others, as I see, work to repair the boats when they become disabled. They who do good to others by offering a helping hand to those who are in difficulty, and who succor the good, are most worthy of the praise and gratitude of men and the favor of the gods."

And then the shades: "Your sentiments are correct, O man; and we wish you not to ignore that all who go on the little boats, so long as they want things in moderation, so long as they are just, wise, honest, and never cease thinking worthy thoughts, enjoy the favor of all the gods. None among men who are struggling in the river is more welcomed by the immortal gods than those who, in the little boats, look to faith, to simplicity, and to virtue. This is the only concern of the gods: to support the voyages of those little boats which are deserving because of their bearing and virtue. And this, among other reasons, because they safeguard the peace and tranquillity of many. The little boats that you see mortals call 'empires'; but despite the fact that they are very useful in successfully running the course of the river, you still will not find in them a constant and stable defense against the roughest reefs of the river. In fact, when the waters race most swiftly, then the bigger the ship the greater the danger; they are smashed against the reefs by the power of the waves. It happens quite often that they overturn in such a way that even the most capable and expert do not succeed in staying afloat amidst the great wreckage and the crowd of survivors. While the smaller boats, under the control of those who guide them, easily become submerged, they are yet superior in this: that they, more easily than the large boats, can pass between the reefs. But the maximum capacity to avoid shipwreck in any type of boat belongs to those whose crews are ready and able to meet any eventuality with attention, with faith, with diligence and every concern, including a willingness to expose themselves to the work and the dangers for the common safety of all involved. Take note, however, that among mortals, none can be considered more secure than those few who are seen running here and there in the river with absolute confidence, looking attentively in all directions, and holding on to secure boards; and these boards mortals call 'good arts.' " Thus spoke the shades.

I then asked: "Why is it not better, with the aid of virtue and justice, to stay on the boats and face the dangers than to run the course of Life on a single bit of flotsam?"

The shades answered: "A great soul will seek even a very small boat, rather than an isolated board; but one possessed of a free and placid disposition will rightly avoid the great travails and continuous dangers of large ships. Add to this, that those who content themselves with private goods consider public tumults and the follies of the multitude as burdensome; besides, it is very difficult to maintain just equilibrium, decorum, tranquillity, and a sweet idleness among the ignorant mob. These are all things which, if they be lacking, will rapidly cause the destruction of king, helmsman, and crew in every boat. Thus, those who sit at the helm must see to it, above all, that the boat does not end on the reefs or the banks because of their, or their gods', lack of attention. They must be certain that it is not overburdened with useless cargo. It is the duty of a wise prince to jettison, if necessary, not only his own possessions but even himself, if need dictates that the ship be lightened. Those things which are considered by some as difficult to do without, because they make for a secure and placid life, are disdained by the truly moderate and simple souls. Note further that it is well to see to it that the great number of persons seated at the prow do not lead the boat into danger or capsize it. I trust I need not even mention that it must be the navigator's constant concern to avoid those reefs, not less dangerous than hard, that tear at the rudder, break into the benches, or disrupt the beat of the oars; again, you cannot subdue, except with force, the insolent and belligerent; and it is not without great risk or loss that there is always on board the inept, the useless, and the lazy who, when danger arises, do not offer a hand, abandoned as they are to sloth, and slow as they are to action, so that the ship which holds them easily perishes on this account."

Thus, the shades had spoken; and I remained in silence, struck no less by what I had heard than by what I had witnessed. Turning my eyes to the river, I asked again: "But who are those that I see struggling in the waves in the midst of straw, with their heads barely above water? Tell me, I pray you, about all that I see."

And then said the shades: "They are among the worst of mortals: 'suspicious,' 'jealous,' 'calculating,' as you call them; with their perverse nature and depraved habits they do not want to swim, but amuse themselves by impeding the strokes of others. They are very similar to those that you see contriving, by fraud, to steal with one of their hands now a skin, and now a board, while the other hand clings tenaciously on to the rushes that grow in the mud under the water. These rushes are the most irksome thing in the river; and this kind of activity is such that those who engage in it muddy their hands, and their hands remain muddy forever; these you usually call 'avaricious' and 'opportunistic.' Those that you see immediately behind them, leaning on jellyfish, are called 'sycophants,' 'evil,' and 'shameless.' The remaining ones, finally, of whom you can see only the feet, those who are being tossed hither and thither by the waves like useless tree trunks, show what they are: they are those whom the philosophers descry as subhuman because of their way of life—they are the libidinous, the gluttonous, submerged in desire and lost in sloth. But now, offer supreme honor to those that you see there, set apart from the crowd."

And I, looking in all directions, said: "In truth, I see no one who is separated from the multitude."

And the shades: "How can you miss those who, with wings on their feet, fly with such agility and rapidity over the waves?"

Then I: "I seem to see one; but why should I do homage to him? What have these done?"

Answered the shades: "Does it seem to you that those have little merit, who—simple and uncorrupted—are considered by men as divine? The wings that they bear represent truth and simplicity, and their winged sandals signify contempt for transitory things. Justly, therefore, are they considered divine, not only because of these divine endowments, but also because they were the first to construct the boards that you see floating in the river; these boards, upon which they carved the titles of the good arts, are a great help to those who are swimming. Those others, similar to the gods, but who nevertheless do not entirely emerge from the waters because, although they have their wings whole, they lack the winged sandals, are demigods; and they are most deserving of being honored, and are to be venerated as being immediately below the gods. It is their merit to have enlarged the boards by adding pieces of flotsam to them; further, they engage in the admirable enterprise of collecting the boards from the reefs and the beaches, in order to construct new ones and to proffer these works to those who still swim in midstream. Render, O man, honor to these; render then the thanks that are their due for having offered excellent help with these boards to those who run the difficult course of Life."

This is what I saw and heard in my sleep; and I seemed, in a marvelous way, to have been somehow admitted to the presence of the winged gods. Then, suddenly, it appeared to me that I had fallen into the river; and that there were neither boards, nor skins, nor any other supports to aid me in staying afloat. And so I awakened; and thinking over my vision, I thanked sleep for having brought so clearly to my understanding the meaning of Fate and Fortune. If I interpret my vision correctly, I learned that Fate, which runs according to its own proper order, is nothing more than the course of events in the life of men. I learned that Fortune favors those who, at the moment of their fall into the river, find near them either whole boards or a sound boat. I learned that Fortune is hard for those of us who fall into the current where it is necessary for us to overcome the impetus of the waves by respiteless swimming. In any event, we should never ignore the fact that in human affairs, prudence and industry are worth a very great deal.

LORENZO VALLA

LORENZO VALLA *was born in Rome in 1406/7. After completing his studies in the city of his birth, he taught at the University of Pavia from 1430–1433. In 1435* Valla *entered the service of King Alfonso of Aragon; and in 1448 he returned to Rome to become papal secretary and professor at the university. He died in 1457. Aside from his numerous translations, among which were works written by Xenophon, Homer, Herodotus, and Thucydides, he penned a number of original treatises, letters, invectives, monographs, dialogues, and assorted historical writings. His tract exposing the apocryphal character of the Donation of Constantine, which led to charges against his orthodoxy, is still a model of philological-historical research. Among the most important of his philosophical writings are* Dialecticae disputationes, *and the two dialogues:* Devoluptate, *and* De libero arbitrio.

On Free Will

TO GARZIA, BISHOP OF LERIDA

It is my most particular wish and heart's desire, most excellent and learned bishop, that all Christians, and especially the theologians, stop paying court to philosophy and wasting their energies on it. They should stop giving it the status of equal, of sister—even patroness—of theology. I believe, indeed, that these people have a false conception of our religion when they suppose that it has need of being supported by philosophy. This mistake was not made by the ancients whose works defy the centuries; and these men were followers of the apostles: true columns in the Lord's temple. In fact, if we view the matter rightly, all the heresies of those times, which were not a few, derived almost entirely from philosophical origins. Thus philosophy did not assist but, rather, seriously injured sacred theology.

Those of whom I speak, claim that philosophy was born to extirpate heresies, whereas it is really that seedbed in which they are born. They do not realize that those very saintly fathers of antiquity were not equipped with the arms of philosophy with which to unmask error. Indeed, these ancients fought bitterly against philosophy itself, sending it into exile like Tarquin the Proud, forbidding its return. Were they so unarmed and helpless? How then were they able to conquer so great a part of the world? You who do possess such armament are not even able to defend that which they have left you as a patrimony! This is most lamentable and undignified! Why then do you not follow in the track of your fathers? If not their reason, at least the authority and success of these men should have led you to emulate them rather than embark on new paths. It seems to me that the doctor who experiments with new and still untried medication, instead of curing his patient with medicines already proved by experience, is odious and execrable. I should judge in the same way the helmsman who favors an uncharted course to that long used by others to save their ships and merchandise.

You have arrived at such a point of insolence that you think no one capable of becoming a theologian who does not employ the precepts of philosophy after having learned these most assiduously. You regard as fools all those who previously ignored, or wanted to ignore, these precepts. O times! O customs! There was a time, in the Roman Senate, when neither citizens nor strangers were permitted to speak in a foreign tongue, but only in that of the city. You, however, who may be regarded as senators of the Republic of Christ, are better pleased to employ pagan than ecclesiastical language.

But I shall have many opportunities, in other situations and upon other occasions, to speak of these matters. At present, I wish to show that Boethius, only because he loved philosophy to excess, did not deal correctly with the subject of free will in the fifth book of his *Consolation of Philosophy*. I have previously replied to his first four books in my work on *True Good*. Now I shall attempt to discuss and resolve this problem with the greatest diligence possible; and, so that it might not seem purposeless after so many writers have dealt with this topic, I shall have something original to add.

Although spurred by my own desire to do this work, I was excited further by a recent discussion with Antonio Glarea, a very learned and very acute man; one who is dear to me not only because of his ways, but also because he is a fellow citizen of San Lorenzo. I have set forth, in the sequel, the nature of our discussion, recounting it as if the discussion were proceeding and not narrated, avoiding in this manner the too frequent interpolation of "I said" and "he said." I cannot understand why Marcus Tullius, a man of immortal genius, claimed that he used this method in his book called *Laelius*. For when an author relates things that are said, not by him, but by others, in what way can he insert "I said"? This usage is found in Cicero's *Laelius*, which contains a debate between Laelius and his two sons-in-law, Gaius Fannius and Quintus Scaevola. The story is told by Scaevola, while Cicero, together with some of his coterie, is listening without presuming to enter into conversation with him out of respect for his age and dignity.

But let us return to the subject. Having come to see me around noon, and finding me unoccupied, seated with some members of my family, Antonio made a few introductory remarks appropriate to the subject and the occasion, and then continued as follows:

Antonio. The problem of free will appears to me to be most difficult and, indeed, arduous: one from which depends every human action, every right, every wrong, every reward, and every punishment, not only in this earthly life but in the future one, as well. This question is of such magnitude that it is hard to say whether there is another more compelling or less clear. Often, with myself and with others, I have puzzled over this problem, but I have not yet succeeded in finding a solution, and remain, therefore, disturbed and confused within myself. Nevertheless, I will never stop seeking, nor will I ever despair of finding the solution, even while I know that so many have been deluded in their hope of discovering the answer. Now I would like to have your opinion on this matter—not only because I may achieve my end by survey and examination of everyone's opinion, but also because I know well your subtle and penetrating judgment.

Lorenzo. As you say, the question is arduous and difficult. Indeed, I am not sure that anyone has ever properly grasped it. Yet there is no reason for you to be disturbed and confused, even if you never resolve it. Is it right to irritate oneself if one cannot solve a problem that no man has ever solved? Furthermore, you know many who possess things that we do not and this need not be disturbing, but rather should be borne with a calm and serene mind. One may be noble, another masterful; one may possess riches, another genius and eloquence; yet others may possess several of these endowments together; and still others, possess them all; but he who is a just evaluator of these human conditions, and is aware of his own industry, will not complain because he lacks these goods. Besides, he will not say that one must be grieved for not being endowed with bird wings, which no human bears.

If we were to be sorrowed by all that we do not know, our lives would be rendered bitter and hard. Do you wish me to enumerate all of the things that remain unknown to us? Not only divine and supernatural things, such as the question under discussion, but also the human ones which can enter the ambit of our understanding? In brief, the things of which we are ignorant far outnumber those that we know. It is for this reason that the Academics, although incorrectly, affirmed that we know nothing completely.

Ant. I fully agree with what you say. But I am impatient and intellectually hungry, incapable of restraining my appetite. What you say about the wings of birds—that one must not mourn their lack since no one has them—is something I can appreciate. However, must I forswear wings if, like Daedalus, I could obtain them? How much more marvelous are the wings I desire! With them, I might fly not merely from the prison of walls, but from the prison of errors to that fatherland where our souls, and not merely our bodies, are born. Let us leave the Academics to their convictions: they who, while universal in their doubt, nevertheless did not doubt their own doubting; they who, while affirming that we know nothing, nevertheless did not abandon searching. Well we know that more recent thinkers have added many new ideas to what was previously known. Their example and their teaching must encourage us to discover still others. Cease, therefore, I beg you, to take from me this desire to search; for if you rob me of this, you would rob me also of every commitment to inquiry unless, of course, you succeed in satisfying my quest, as I hope and profoundly desire.

Lor. How can I satisfy what no one else has been able

to? What can I say about books? If they convince you, nothing else remains for you to seek; and if they do not, then I can do no better. This is the best that I can say to you. Yet you will see how pious and just it is for you to declare war on all books, even the most respected ones, and not be satisfied with any.

Ant. I well know it might seem intolerable and almost a sacrilege to remain unsatisfied with books that have been regarded as authoritative for so long; but you are careful to note how these books are in disagreement on a great many matters, defending, as they do, opposing opinions, and there are very few whose authority places them above question. Indeed, on other questions I do not reject the authors; for it seems to me that now one and now another says things that are quite probable. But on this matter—the one on which I wish to converse with you—I will, with your consent and that of others, not agree with anyone. What can I say when Boethius himself, who is acclaimed by all for having dealt with this argument, does not succeed in completing his own undertaking but takes refuge at certain points in the fictional and imaginary? He says, for instance, that God, by means of intelligence that transcends reason, eternally knows all things, having them all present. But I cannot aspire to the knowledge of intelligence and eternity, being as I am only a rational being who knows nothing outside of time. I suspect that Boethius himself did not understand what he said, even if what he said was true—which I do not believe. As a matter of fact, we cannot suppose one to be saying the truth when his discourse remains incomprehensible to him and to everyone else. And so, although rightly having initiated the discussion, he did not properly conclude it. If you agree with me on this, I shall be well satisfied with myself; if not, please be kind enough to expound more clearly what Boethius said so obscurely. In either case, reveal to me your opinion.

Lor. What a request you make of me: to offend Boethius by either condemning him or correcting him!

Ant. Are you calling it an offense to tell the truth about someone or to clarify his obscurities?

Lor. Still, it is despicable to do this to great men.

Ant. Certainly it is more despicable not to show the right way to one who errs and asks for help.

Lor. But what if I myself am ignorant of the way?

Ant. Just this way of putting it, "I am ignorant of the way," is characteristic of him who has no desire to show the right way! Please, therefore, do not refuse to bare your soul.

Lor. What if I should tell you that I share your opinion about Boethius, and that I, as you, do not understand him and cannot explain this question?

Ant. If you are speaking the truth, I will not be so mad as to insist on asking you for more than you can give; but take care not to fail me in your office as a friend by being impatient or by lying!

Lor. What do you wish me to explain to you?

Ant. Whether the precognition of God is opposed to the freedom of the will; and whether this problem has been justly treated by Boethius.

Lor. We shall see later about Boethius; but if I do what you ask you must make me a promise.

Ant. What promise?

Lor. That if I have treated you generously at lunch, you will not also want to stay for dinner.

Ant. What lunch? What dinner? I don't understand what you mean.

Lor. I mean that you will be satisfied with this discussion alone and will not then add a second.

Ant. Second, did you say? This one alone is more than sufficient! Therefore, willingly do I promise that I shall not "ask for dinner."

Lor. Come, then: put the question.

Ant. Very well: If God foresees the future, the future cannot happen differently from the way that He foresaw. Thus He foresees Judas betraying, and it is impossible for Judas not to betray—it is necessary that he betray—for if it were otherwise, God forbid, we could not admit God's providence. This being the case, it is necessary to believe that mankind lacks freedom of the will. Nor am I speaking solely of evil men: in fact, just as these necessarily have to do evil, so good men have to do good—if we can at all name "good" or "evil" those who have no freedom of will, or call their actions "just" or "unjust" when these are necessary and forced. You yourself can see the consequences of this: that God can praise the justice of the one and deplore the injustice of the other; rewarding the one and punishing the other would seem, to put it frankly, the very opposite of justice, since the actions of men necessarily follow the foreknowledge of God. Let us, therefore, put aside religion, piety, sanctity, ceremonies, and sacrifices; let us expect nothing from Him, let us cease praying to Him, or invoking His forgiveness; let us no longer try to direct our souls toward the good; let us rather do what we please, since God foreknows our injustice and our justice. Thus, if we are free, He does not know our future before it happens; and if we are not free, He is not just. This is what makes me doubt.

Lor. You have not limited yourself to simply proposing the question, but have eviscerated it! You say that God foreknew the betrayal of Judas: did He also induce him to betray? This doesn't seem right to me. Because God foreknows an action of man does not mean that his action is necessitated, because he may perform it quite willingly—and what is voluntary cannot be necessitated.

Ant. You must not think that I shall give up so easily or that I shall run away without blood and sweat.

Lor. Courage, my friend! Come close and fight at close quarters—not with spear but with sword!

Ant. You say that Judas acted voluntarily and not, therefore, out of necessity. Indeed, to deny that he acted voluntarily would be supreme impudence. What do I say to that? I say that this act of will was certainly necessitated since God foreknew it. That which He foreknew was what Judas necessarily had to will, and do, so that divine foreknowledge would not be false.

Lor. I do not understand why it should seem to you that God's foreknowledge necessitates our will and our actions. In fact, if *fore*knowledge determined the actual being of the thing *fore*known, *knowledge* should similarly determine the actual being of the thing *known*. However, if I judge you correctly, you will never say to me that a thing *is* because you *know* it is. You know, for example, that it is now day; but is it day because you know it? Or do you know it because it is day?

Ant. Go on.

Lor. This same argument goes for the past. I know that eight hours ago it was night, but it is not my knowledge that determines it to have been night; it is, rather, the fact that it was night by which I know that it was night. And, to go beyond this, I anticipate that in eight hours it will be night again. Is it for this reason that it will become night? Now, if man's foreknowledge is not the cause of something occurring, neither is God's.

Ant. Your comparison is deceiving: to know the present and the past is one thing, but it is an entirely different thing to know the future. When I know that something is, this does not vary; the day which this is, cannot not be. Also the past does not differ from the present; for we did not notice the day after it had past, but we knew it while it was occurring and was present. I learned that it was night when night was present, and not when it had passed. In cases like this, I will concede that something has been or is, not because I know it, but that I know it because it is or has been. But the question is different as regards the future, for the future is contingent; and what is contingent cannot be known with certainty. Thus, if we do not wish to deprive God of foreknowledge, we must confess that the future is certain and, consequently, necessary—and it is this which deprives us of freedom. Do not say, therefore, as you did a moment ago, that future events are not determined merely because God foreknows them, but that He foreknows them because they will be; for you thus do offense to God by insinuating that it is necessary for Him to foreknow future events.

Lor. You have come to the fray very well armed and equipped—but let us see which of us is fooling himself, you or me. First of all, I will respond briefly to this last difficulty: you say that if God foreknows the future because it is to be, then He is necessitated in His knowledge, being forced to foreknow the things to come. Now this is not to be attributed to necessity, but to His nature, His will, His power—unless the fact that God cannot sin, die, or abandon His own knowledge be construed as a weakness rather than as divinity and power. Thus, when we say that He cannot but foreknow the future, which is a kind of wisdom, we do not offend Him, but do Him honor. I will not hesitate, therefore, to say that God cannot but foreknow the things that will be. I pass now to your first point: that the present and the past are unalterable, and hence knowable, while the future is contingent and therefore cannot be foreknown. I ask you if it could be changed that in eight hours night will fall; that after summer, there will be autumn; after autumn, winter; and after winter, springtime; and after springtime, summer?

Ant. These are natural events and they follow always the same pattern. I am talking about voluntary matters.

Lor. And how about fortuitous ones? Can God foreknow them without rendering them necessary? That it is raining today, that I find a treasure tomorrow—will you concede that these things can be foreknown without predetermining them?

Ant. Why should I not so concede? Do you think that I have such an erroneous conception of God?

Lor. Take care not to err when you affirm that you are saying the truth! If, in fact, you concede this to me, why then do you doubt voluntary acts? The one and the other events can be interpreted in the same way.

Ant. This is not true. Those, in fact, which are fortuitous, follow their own nature, and therefore doctors, sailors, and farmers usually anticipate many things which they predict for the future from knowledge of the past, which is something that cannot be done with voluntary acts. Anticipate which foot I shall move first, and I will disprove your prediction by moving the other.

Lor. Who has ever been so keen as our Glarea? He thinks that he can impose on God as did that character in Aesop who went to ask Apollo, just for the sake of deceiving him, if the sparrow which he had hidden under his cloak was dead or alive. You are asking not me but God to predict! I cannot prophesy even if the grapes will be good, and you ascribe this prophetic power to ordinary farm folk. But by affirming that God does not know which foot you will move first, and really thinking this way, you involve yourself in a grave sin.

Ant. Do you seriously believe that I am affirming this? Or am I, rather, just asking it for the sake of discussion? In any event, it seems to me that you are dodging the issue, and that with this speech of yours, you are trying to avoid a real fight.

Lor. You talk as if I fight for love of victory rather than love of truth. Look at the ground that I have lost! Do you concede that God now knows your will even better than you know it?

Ant. I concede it.

Lor. It is also necessary that you concede to me that you will do nothing other than what your will decides.

Ant. Without a doubt.

Lor. How then can He be ignorant of the action if He knows the will which is the source of action?

Ant. You are wrong! Not even I know what I will do, let alone know what I will want. I, in fact, do not want to move absolutely this or that foot, but only the foot that is other than what He has predicted. Hence, if you compare me to God, just as I do not know what I will do, so He does not know.

Lor. What could possibly be the fruit of such caviling? He knows that you will act in a way different from what He will say, or that you will move the left foot first if He said you would move the right. Hence, whatever He should say, He knows with certainty what will happen.

Ant. But which of the two will He say?

Lor. Are you talking about God? Let me know your will and I'll tell you what will happen.

Ant. Come now: try and know my will!

Lor. You will move first the right foot.

Ant. Here's my left!

Lor. And will you say that my prediction was false? Even when I knew all along that you would move the left foot?

Ant. Then why did you say other than you thought?

Lor. To deceive you by your own deception, and to surprise you when you wanted to surprise me!

Ant. But in His answer, God would not lie. And you are wrong in answering for that other when He would never say what you say.

Lor. But you told *me* to predict. Hence, I had to answer not for God but for myself.

Ant. You are certainly changeable! A moment ago you were saying that I told not you, but God, to predict. Now you say the contrary. Let God tell me which foot I am going to put forth first!

Lor. This is ridiculous! You talk as though He could respond.

Ant. But if He so willed, couldn't He respond?

Lor. Do you think that the truth can lie?

Ant. What then would He reply?

Lor. Without doubt He would tell what you are about to do, but while you would not be listening, He might tell me or someone else. And after He did this, do you think He would have predicted truly?

Ant. Without a doubt. But what do you think would happen if He predicted it to me?

Lor. Believe me, you who hope so much to deceive God, if you listened to Him, or if you knew with certainty what He has predicted, moved by love or by terror you would hasten to do His will! But let us put aside all this which has nothing to do with foreknowledge. It is one thing to foresee and another thing to predict the future. Speak, therefore, about foreseeing, but forget about prediction.

Ant. Agreed. For the things that I have said were not intended so much to defend my thesis as to confute you. I return, therefore, to the point where I maintained that it was necessary for Judas to betray since this is what God foresaw—unless we wish to eliminate providence altogether.

If it were possible for things to go differently from what is foreseen, providence would be out of the picture; if instead, we admit that it was impossible, out goes freedom of the will, and this would be a thing no less unworthy to God than if we should deny His providence. So far as I am concerned, I would prefer that He be rather less wise than less good. The latter would hurt the human race, but the former would not.

Lor. I laud your moderation and probity. For where you cannot win you do not persist in fighting, but concede the point and pass on. This new defense, however, seems to me to be at the base of the argument which you set forth a while back. Therefore, in replying to you, I deny that the possibility of an event occurring, which is different from the one foreknown, carries with it as a consequence the idea that foreknowledge can be deceived. What is in the way of admitting both things? What militates against its being true that something can turn out differently than it will immediately happen? The possibility of an event is an entirely different thing from its future occurrence. I could be married, a soldier, or a priest; but does this make me any one of these? Not at all. Though I can equally well act in a way different from what will happen, yet I shall not. Judas possessed the possibility of not sinning, even though it was foreseen that he would; but he preferred to sin, and this preference of his was foreseen. In this way, foreknowledge is valid, even as free will. This latter will choose one of the possibilities, since it is impossible to act in two different ways at the same time. Yet, whatever one chooses, the Lord foreknows it by His light.

Ant. Here I have you! Do you ignore, perhaps, the philosophical principle according to which everything that is possible must be admitted to be? Is it possible that anything can occur different from what has been foreseen? One may admit that it can; and from this it becomes clear that foreknowledge is deceived, since it is possible for things to happen different from the foreseen.

Lor. You have the courage to use the formulae of the philosophers on me, as if I had not the courage to contradict them! The principle which you offer—whoever asseverated it—seems to me to be quite absurd. I can, in fact, move my right foot first, and let us assume that this is what happens. I can equally well move first the left before the right, and the right before the left. Thus, on the basis of your position regarding possibilities, I shall arrive at the impossible; and in this way you might understand that it cannot be conceded that all that can happen must happen of necessity. Therefore, it is possible that you can act differently from what God foreknows, and nevertheless not act differently; nor can you therefore deceive Him.

Ant. I will not object further, and having broken all my arms I will not pretend to fight, as they say, with nails and teeth. But if you can explain this thing to me at greater length, and clearly convince me, I will listen to you.

Lor. You yearn for some new praise of your probity and reserve, being, as you are, always equal to yourself. I will do then what you ask, which I would have done anyway. The things that I have said up to this point were not the things that I had planned to say but, rather, those required by the necessity of having to defend myself. Listen now to what I have to say—and perhaps it will convince you, too—about foreknowledge not impeding freedom. But first, if you please, tell me whether you wish me to be brief or, for love of clarity, to extend myself a bit.

Ant. To tell the truth, those who talk clearly seem to me to talk briefly; and the more prolix are, by far, the most obscure, even when they speak in a few words. Further, the abundance of talk carries with it something proper to persuasion; hence, having asked you from the start to speak in the clearest possible manner on the argument, there is no reason why you should doubt my wish in this. But do as you think best; in any case, I shall not oppose my opinions to yours.

Lor. It pleases me to do as you wish; and what you desire, I too think best. Now then: Apollo, that god who was so much celebrated by the Greeks, knew by his own nature and by the concession of all the other gods, all future things. Not only knowing those things which concerned men, but those as well which concerned the gods, he gave oracles, true and indubitable, to all pleaders—that is, if we can believe what has been said. Let us concede that this was the truth, without objection. Sextus Tarquinius consulted him to find out what would happen to him. Let us imagine that the god responded with a verse, as was his custom:

> A miserable exile you will become,
> Destroyed by the irate city.

To which Sextus replied: "What do you say, Apollo? What have I done to you for you to announce such a cruel fate? Why assign to me such a sad death? Take back, I pray you, your forecast, give me a happier future. Be good to me, for I bring regal gifts." To which Apollo answered: "Your gifts, young man, are certainly gratefully accepted, and, in return, I have given you your oracle; no doubt this is unhappy and sad, and one which I myself would wish were happier, but it is not in my power to make it so. I know fate: I don't fix it. I can prophesy fortune, not change it. I happen to be an announcer, not an arbiter. I would announce happier things to you if happier things were to befall you; in all this, I am blameless. Nor could I oppose my own misfortunes, if I predicted them. If you wish, accuse Jove; accuse the fates; accuse the fortune upon which depends the causes of events. In them is power and will; in me, only foreknowledge and prediction. You asked me for the truth, and I could not lie; you came to my temple from a distant land, and I could not send you hence without answering. Two things be far removed from me: lying and keeping silent." Could Sextus not have retorted in this way: "It is your fault, Apollo. That by your wisdom you predict my fate; if you had not predicted it, none of it would then happen to me"?

Ant. Not only would it be unjust for Sextus to speak thus, but it is incredible that anyone would respond in this manner.

Lor. How then should he answer?

Ant. You tell me.

Lor. Why not, perhaps, in this manner: "I, O holy Apollo, thank you for not having deceived me by lying, and for not having answered my request with silence. But tell me, I beg you, why Jove is so unjust with me and so cruel as to assign me, an innocent adorer of the gods, so tragic a fate without my being a miscreant or sinner"?

Ant. If I were Sextus, I would certainly respond to Apollo in this way; but what would Apollo say?

Lor. "And you, Sextus, call yourself innocent and without blame? Do not deceive yourself! The sins that you will commit, you may be sure, will be yours: the adulteries, treasons, perjuries, and the pride which is your heritage, are to blame." To this, Sextus would probably respond: "To you instead must be attributed the guilt of my crimes; for having foreseen my sins, it was necessary for me to commit them."

Ant. Sextus would be not merely unjust if he answered in this way, but mad!

Lor. And what would you have answered in his place?

Ant. Nothing, really.

Lor. If then Sextus has no valid claim to make against Apollo's foreknowledge, certainly Judas has no reason to blame God's foreknowledge. And if this is the way things are, I think that I have answered the question about which you were disturbed and confused.

Ant. I am truly satisfied and wholly illumined, which I hardly anticipated; and for this reason I hold for you a gratitude which I might call immortal. What Boethius was not able to give me, you have given me!

Lor. And now I wish to tell you something concerning Boethius, because I know you expect me to and because I promised to do so.

Ant. What can you tell me of Boethius? I welcome anything that you might say.

Lor. Let us take up again with our fable. You think that Sextus has no answer for Apollo? I ask you, what would you say to a king who refused you an office, or a magistracy, on the excuse that in this office or magistracy you would commit capital crimes?

Ant. "I swear to you, O king, by this strong and faithful right hand of mine, that I shall never commit crimes in such an office."

Lor. Imagine that Sextus says the same thing to Apollo: "I swear, O Apollo, that I will never do as you say."

Ant. And Apollo?

Lor. Certainly he would not respond as a king, for a king does not know what will happen in the way that God knows it. Apollo, therefore, might say: "Must I then be a liar, O Sextus? Am I ignorant of what will happen? Do you think that I spoke as I did in order to warn you? Or to pronounce an oracle? I repeat to you: You will be an adulterer, a traitor, a perjurer, proud and evil."

Ant. That is a speech worthy of Apollo. What could Sextus possibly say now?

Lor. You mean you can't think of what he might say in his defense? Would he allow himself to be condemned so easily?

Ant. But what if he is guilty?

Lor. He is *not* guilty! It is only being announced that he *will* be. If Apollo announced such a thing to you, I think you would run to pray, and you would supplicate not Apollo but Jove, to have your heart and your fate changed.

Ant. This I would do; and at the same time make Apollo out a liar!

Lor. You speak well, But if Sextus cannot make him out a liar, if his prayers are vain, what will he do then? Will he not become indignant? Will he not become irritated? Will he not come out with laments? "And so Apollo, am I not able to abstain from my crimes? Can I not pursue virtue? Can I not change my evil soul? Am I not free?"

Ant. This would be a very powerful answer by Sextus, and also, in truth, a just one. But what will the god say?

Lor. "This is the way things stand, Sextus. Just as Jove has created the wolf rapacious, the hare timid, the lion courageous, the ass stupid, the dog angry, the sheep gentle, so also has he made some men sweet and some hard; in some he has generated the propensity to crime and in still others the propensity to virtue; to one he has given a corrigible disposition and to another an incorrigible one; to you he has assigned an evil soul, incapable of correction. For this reason you will act viciously—out of the qualities of your character; and Jove will punish you according to your actions and your works. And that this must happen he has sworn by the Stygian marshes."

Ant. Apollo has excused himself very well, but at the cost of accusing Jove. I would, in fact, be much milder with Sextus than with Jove. For he would have reason to ask: "Why is the crime mine, and not that of Jove? If I cannot but do evil, why does Jove condemn me for this guilt? Why does he punish me without cause? Anything that I do, I do not freely but necessarily. Am I able to oppose myself to his will and to his power?"

Lor. This is precisely what I wished to elicit with my fable. This is the whole point of the story: that, while we cannot separate the knowledge of God from His will and His power, by employing the device of Apollo and Jove, we could achieve with two different gods—each god being endowed with his own proper nature—what cannot be achieved with one. The one was employed for creating the character of men, the other for knowing. This was done so that it might become manifest that providence is not the cause of necessity, but that all which occurs, whatever it is, must be referred to God's will.

Ant. Now you throw me back into the same abyss whence you had delivered me! There now grows in me a doubt similar to the one respecting Judas. In the case of Judas, necessity was attributed to God's foreknowledge; it seems here, instead, to be referred to His will. But does it matter in what way our liberty is taken away? You deny that it is foreknowledge which annuls freedom, and say instead that it is God's will. We're right back where we started from!

Lor. Did I say that freedom is annulled by God's will?

Ant. But doesn't it follow? Can you resolve this doubt?

Lor. Who will resolve it for you?

Ant. I will not go until you do!

Lor. But this violates our agreement! You are not content with the lunch, but want also the dinner!

Ant. So you tricked me into making a promise? But promises which are exacted by deceit are not valid. Nor do I consider myself to have been given a lunch if you force me to vomit what I have eaten—or, to put it differently, if you send me away just as hungry as when I came.

Lor. Believe me, I did not wish you to promise in order to deceive you. What advantage would this have been to me when I could have refused you lunch to begin with? But having eaten so generously that you felt obligated to thank me, you are now ungrateful because, as you say, I have forced you to vomit, or am sending you away hungry. You requested lunch, not dinner; and you expect ambrosia and nectar, which are divine and not human foods. I have offered you fish and birds from my own preserves, and wine from the suburban hills—the ambrosia and nectar you can seek from Apollo and Jove!

Ant. What are these poetic figures "nectar" and "ambrosia"? Let us leave these vain things to fictitious divinities—to Jove and to Apollo. I would wish that you serve the dinner from those inns and taverns where they give a complete meal.

Lor. Do you think perhaps that I am so base as to send away a friend who comes to dine with me? I did, of course, see where the discussion was leading, and so I provided quickly for myself, eliciting from you a promise that you would not ask for more after the first question. Thus, I act with you not only in accordance with right, but with justice. You may very well, if you can believe a friend, find with others the dinner that you did not find with me.

Ant. I shall no longer annoy you; nor shall I be ungrateful to a benefactor and a friend. But to whom are you directing me for enlightenment?

Lor. If I knew to whom to send you, not only would I send you to dine, but I would myself join you at the dinner!

Ant. Is it your belief, then, that no one is in possession of these divine foods?

Lor. Can I think otherwise? Have you perhaps not read

the words of Paul about the two sons of Rebecca and Isaac? He said:

For the children being not yet born, neither having done any good or evil, that the purpose of God according to election might stand, not of works, but of him that calleth; it was said unto her, The elder shall serve the younger. As it is written, Jacob have I loved, but Esau have I hated. What shall we say then? Is there unrighteousness with God? God forbid. For he saith to Moses, I will have mercy on whom I will have mercy, and I will have compassion on whom I will have compassion. So then it is not of him that willeth, nor of him that runneth, but of God that sheweth mercy. For the scripture saith unto Pharaoh, Even for this same purpose have I raised thee up, that I might shew my power in thee, and that my name might be declared throughout all the earth. Therefore hath he mercy on whom he will have mercy, and whom he will he hardeneth. Thou wilt say then unto me, Why doth he yet find fault? For who hath resisted his will? Nay but, O man, who art thou that repliest against God? Shall the thing formed say to him that formed it, Why has thou made me thus? Hath not the potter power over the clay, of the same lump to make one vessel unto honour, and another unto dishonour? [*Romans* 9:11-21.]*

And further on, as if blinded by the great light of God's wisdom, he exclaims:

O the depth of the riches both of the wisdom and knowledge of God! how unsearchable are his judgments, and his ways past finding out! [*Romans* 11:33.]

Now if that vessel, thus elected, which, lifted to the third heaven, hearing the mysteries which man is not permitted to utter, was nonetheless incapable of saying or even perceiving them, how could anyone else investigate or hope to understand such things? And take note that freedom of the will is not said to be impeded by the divine will in the same way as by foreknowledge. The will has, in fact, as cause, an antecedent cause in God's wisdom. Hence, the fact that He

* This and the subsequent Biblical quotations follow the King James version.

blinds some and has pity on others stems from very good cause, namely, that He is both wise and good. For it is impious to say otherwise, as if the supreme good were not performing supreme good. In foreknowledge, however, there is no antecedent, nor any cause whatever of justice and goodness. We do not ask: "Why does He foreknow this?" We ask, rather: "Why does He will this?" What we really want to know is this: How is God good if He takes away free will? For He would have taken it away if it were impossible for things to occur differently from what He foreknows. But in no way does He necessitate; nor does He deprive us of our freedom by blinding some, as He does, and having pity on others. For this He does out of His supreme wisdom and sanctity, even if His reasons appear hidden in mystery as in a secret vault. I know very well that many have had the presumption to seek out these reasons, saying that all who are either blinded or condemned are justly made so, for we all belong to that race which was corrupted and fell through the sin of the first parent. But, just to use one argument, forgetting all the rest, why did even Adam, who was made of uncorrupted matter, become hardened in sin and throw the whole race into the mud?

Something similar happened to the angels, some of whom fell into sin while others stayed on the straight path, although all were of the same substance, of the same uncorrupted root, maintaining even now—if I may be permitted to say so—the very same substance and quality of that golden root. Nor did these latter angels convert themselves into a better substance, nor the former into a baser, by choice. Some had the honor of being chosen, almost as if vessels for the Lord's table, while the others can be considered as vessels hidden from His sight because, more despicable than if they became mud, they gathered every mite of ugly filth, making their plight more pitiable even than that of men. For more grievous is the harm to the gold of which angels are made when it is polluted with filth than to the silver of which men are fashioned. Therefore, in Adam the original silver—or, if you prefer, the clay—was never transformed, but remained the same as it was before. As it was with Adam, so it is with us.

Does not Paul say that a vessel of noble use is made of the same clay as one of mean use? And that a noble vessel is not made of corrupt matter? We are, then, vessels of silver and not of mud; and we have for too long a time been considered ignominious vessels of death and damnation, but not necessarily given to evil. God has, indeed, infused death into our being because of the first sin of the parent in whom all of us are guilty; but He has not charged us with the guilt which comes with being hardened in sin. Paul says:

> Nevertheless death reigned from Adam to Moses, even over them that had not sinned after the similitude of Adam's transgression, . . . [*Romans* 5:14.]

Now if by the sin of Adam we had become sinners in our very being, certainly the grace of Christ would have freed us so that we would no longer be hardened in sin. But this is not the case. Many of us are, in fact, hardened in sin. It is for this reason that all who are baptized are, by the death of Christ, freed from original sin and death. But only some pursue that piety which goes beyond baptism, while others remain blinded like Adam and some of the angels. Let anyone explain, then, why God blinds some and shows mercy to others, and I will call him an angel rather than a man, although I do not believe that such things are known even to the angels. Indeed, these things were not even known by Paul—from which you can gather in what respect I hold him! Now if these matters are unknown to the angels who look constantly upon the face of God, how can we be so presumptuous as to wish to know them? But before I finish, I must speak of Boethius.

Ant. You remembered Boethius just in time. I was just thinking of him. He sought to know just such things and to be able to teach them to others; not, it is true, in the same way as Paul, but nonetheless with the same end in view.

Lor. Not only did he trust too much in his own powers,

attempting what was beyond them, but he did not have the same end in view as Paul—nor did he complete what he had begun.

Ant. Why do you say that?

Lor. I shall tell you. What I wanted to say is this: Paul begins by telling us that the grace of God does not depend on man who wills and acts, but on His mercy. Boethius, however, concludes, in intent if not in words, that it depends not on God's grace but on man, who acts and wills. Nor is it sufficient to speak of God's providence without touching on His will, just as you, to take the case at hand, have shown: not content with the explanation of the first question, you sought also to ask about the second.

Ant. If I understand you, I would say that you have rendered a most just verdict on Boethius. I don't think even he would object.

Lor. What then do you suppose was the cause that led Christians to move away from Paul and to forget him, even while they treated the same subject that the apostle was concerned with? What is more, in his whole writing of *Consolation,* nothing at all is found about our religion: nothing of all the precepts which lead to the blessed life—and not so much as a hint of Christ!

Ant. I think this was because he loved philosophy too much.

Lor. You understand very well. I hold that no one who loves philosophy so ardently can possibly please God. Therefore, Boethius, following a kite instead of the south wind, brought his wine-laden fleet to strange shores and exotic places instead of to a port of his own country.

Ant. You have proved all of this.

Lor. Let us come, then, to the end and conclude once and for all that I have satisfied you, as at least I believe, on the question of the foreknowledge and will of God, and also on Boethius. What I shall add is not to instruct you, but rather for the sake of exhortation, although you, who have an honest mind, have no need of exhortations.

Ant. Go ahead, then. Exhortation is never useless or inappropriate, and I am accustomed to accept it gladly both from acquaintances and from the most intimate friends—among whom I have always numbered you.

Lor. And I shall exhort not only you but all the others present, and especially myself. I was saying, then, that neither men nor the angels know the reasons why the divine will condemns some and saves others. Now if, on account of ignorance of this and many other things, the angels do not come to love God any less, nor do they fail in their ministry, nor regard their beatitude as diminished, shall we by reason of a similar ignorance lose faith, hope and love? Shall we rebel, as against a tyrant? And while we give our faith to the wise even without good reason, but only on their authority, should we not have faith in Christ who is the wisdom and the virtue of God? He wishes everyone to be saved from the death of sinners: to be converted and to live. And while we trust our money to good men without any receipt, from Christ—who never deceived anyone—must we request a guarantee? And while we entrust our life to friends, should we not entrust it to Christ who, for our salvation, took on the life of the body and the death of the cross? We do not know the reasons—and what does it matter? We remain firm in our faith, and not in the probabilities of reason. Would knowing, perhaps, strengthen our faith? Of greater worth is humility. The apostle says: "Mind not high things, but condescend to men of low estate." * Is the knowledge of divine things useful? Much more useful is love. The apostle says again: "Knowledge puffeth up, but charity edifieth." † And so that you may not be misled into believing that this is said only with respect to the knowledge of human things, he states further: "And lest I should be exalted above measure through the abundance of the revelations, there was given to me a thorn in the flesh, . . ." ‡ Let us not seek any profound science. Let us guard ourselves against being like the philosophers who, calling themselves wise, became frauds; and who, not wishing to appear ignorant of anything what-

* Romans 12:16.
† I Corinthians 8:1.
‡ II Corinthians 12:7.

soever, while disputing about everything under the sun, looked to the heavens, attempting to scale its heights as if—if I may say so—they wished to invade it. But they, like proud and rash giants, were hurled back to earth and buried in hell like Typhoeus of Sicily. Among the chief of these was Aristotle, in whom God first revealed and then condemned the pride and the temerity not only of Aristotle himself, but of the other philosophers as well. As a matter of fact, when Aristotle could not discover the nature of Euripus, throwing himself into its depths he was swallowed up, speaking as follows: "Since Aristotle did not grasp Euripus, Euripus won over Aristotle"! What could be more proud and more foolish? And how could God by a more clear verdict condemn his genius and that of others like him than by letting him be driven mad by his excessive desire to know, and kill himself thus?—a death, as I see it, even more miserable than that of Judas. Let us, then, run away from the desire to know the absolute truth. Let us join, rather, the ranks of the humble. Nothing is more becoming to the Christian than humility. In this way, we may know God more truly. It was written: "God resisteth the proud, and giveth grace to the humble." * In order to obtain such grace, I shall no longer indulge in curiosity about such a question, so that in seeking the divine majesty I may not be blinded by the light. And I hope you will wish to do the same. I had to say this, not so much for your sake or for that of your friends, but to show you my most personal belief.

Ant. Your exhortation has bared your very soul in its most profound conviction, and has also excited ours greatly—if I may speak thus for the others. But tell me, do you intend to record this conversation of ours so that others may know of it?

Lor. Well said. Let us permit all others to judge this, our discussion, if it be worthy; and let us send it first of all to the Bishop of Lerida, whose judgment, I am sure, will be favorable, and whose approval would most certainly help me to face the disapproval of anyone else. I respect his

* I Peter 5:5.

opinion more than Antimachus respected that of Plato, or Tullius that of Cato.

Ant. You cannot do or say anything more correctly; I beg you to act as quickly as possible in this matter.

Lor. I shall.

GIANOZZO MANETTI

GIANOZZO MANETTI, *whose works characteristically combine profound faith with great erudition, was born in Florence in 1396 and died in Naples in 1459. He was the honored friend of several powerful political figures, and secretary to Pope Nicholas V. He was the familiar, as well, of some of the most celebrated men of letters of his day. Among other scholarly contributions, he is famous for his translation of Aristotle's moral writings. He also composed a number of original works, among which the following are particularly noteworthy: an apologetic work in twenty books,* Adversos Judaeos et gentes pro catholica fide; *a historical work,* De illustribus longaevis; *and the dialogues* Dialogus consolatorius de morte filii *and* Dialogus in domestico et familiari quorundam amicorum symposio. *Unquestionably his most famous work, written in four books, was* De dignitate et excellentia hominis.

On the Dignity and Excellence of Man

Dedicated to Alfonso of Aragon

PREFACE

O SERENE PRINCE, it was a custom among the ancient sages who recorded their thoughts, to dedicate the fruits of their work to princes. This they did, I think, for two reasons: first, to make known to their good princes their love and their good wishes; and second, because their work, thus dedicated, took on greater authority. I, myself, desire to follow this laudable custom of the learned and to walk in their shadow. To their reasons for dedication, I have added two others. These are particularly apt for the affixing of your name to this new work which I have composed—a work titled *On the Dignity and Excellence of Man*. The first of these reasons is that I wished to suggest by this dedication how all the endowments of man's soul and body, and all of the privileges of man as a whole, such as are put forth by me in the first three books, unite and are exemplified in your most worthy and admirable person. In truth, I should now like to be specific about this, and I would do so, if I did not fear the charge of being a sycophant. At any rate, this thing has already been expressed with meticulous attention to detail in writings other than my own. One point, however, I cannot leave unmarked: everything of good that I have treated extensively and in depth in this work seems to me indisputably true when referred to the singular, admirable, and almost divine endowments of your person. Here is my second reason: when recently I was with you in Naples, as Florentine ambassador, I had the opportunity to read a monograph on the same subject as my own. Written by Bartholomeo Fazio, a man of great learning and elegance, the work was deserving of great renown and celebration. This work of Fazio was dedicated to the great pope, Nicholas V. Not long afterward, finding myself with you, close by that very famous and most honored Greek Tower, and talking at length with you —you who are so learned and gentle—about wise men, somehow we recalled in particular the monograph in question. Afterward, you kindly and cordially invited me to write a work on the same topic. I, who desired above all to please your Majesty, did not hesitate to reply that nothing could be more dear to me than to serve and please you. Thus, as you know, I promised most willingly and joyfully to compose this work, and to dedicate it to you. I began the writing a little after; but owing to pressing obligations I did not immediately succeed in completing it. I turned to it again a bit later, and would, no doubt, have then finished it, if the unexpected visit of Emperor Frederick III to Italy had not taken me away from the work. In fact, I had to go to Rome as Florentine ambassador in order to attend his coronation, and I remained there until he left. After returning from this mission, I finally put the last touches to my work. In order, then, to fulfill my promise and to satisfy my obligation toward so magnanimous a creditor, as well as for the other reasons mentioned above, I dedicate it to you.

I have divided the work into four books, not accidentally or by chance, but after careful and considerable reflection. In fact, having carefully and diligently considered each endowment of the human body, and then those of the soul, and finally those of the human person entire, it seemed to me not inappropriate, but most proper—for the greater dignity of the argument as well as the clearer and easier comprehension of it by all—to treat the material separately, in single books, so that I might handle it with more ease and power. It is on this account that I have treated—with as much care and diligence as was possible to me—in Book I, the great endowments of the human body; in Book II, the particular privileges of the rational soul; and in Book III, the admirable properties of the whole man. Having accomplished this in the three first books, I thought of adding a fourth, in which to confute what had been written of man by many untried authors. These men lauded death, and wrote of the misery of human existence; and I felt it necessary to treat their views, because my own are so violently in opposition. I have thus put this volume together with care, and with supreme devotion. It is being sent to you at Naples, from Florence. I petition and beg you most humbly not to disdain this small gift, but to accept it with a warm soul. It is sent to you in profound devotion.

BOOK IV

On the praises and on the good of death: on the misery of human existence

UP TO this point, in the three preceding books, I have expounded broadly and at great length, with clear and open language, so far as my limited capacities have allowed, all that seems particularly to refer to the singular and outstanding dignity and excellence of man. And I thought that the moment had arrived when I should conclude my work. This is something that I would doubtless have done if I had not thought it germane to my task to confute those statements made by many ancient and modern writers who have written on the advantages of death and in its praise, as well as on the misery of human existence: statements, that is, which seem utterly to contradict the substance of this treatise. Moreover, in this, my refutation of the aforementioned frivolous and false views, I have decided to pursue a certain order so that my discussion will be more pointed and strict. I will answer, therefore, briefly, and in direct accord with the nature of the position under scrutiny and the arguments given in its support: first, with regard to what is said about the fragility of the human body; second, the ignobility of the human soul; and last, with regard to what has been said about the human person taken as a whole.

Let us begin, then, with the body of man. Many serious and learned men thought that the body of man, exposed and defenseless in its very nature, is so fragile, so weak, and so utterly unstable, that it cannot sustain cold, heat, hunger, thirst, and other such corporeal impositions without injury. When man surrenders himself to repose and to sleep, they say, it is again a sign of his weakness and corruptibility. They affirm, moreover, that even the things which are most pleasing to man—things without which he could not survive—are generally harmful and destructive. Loud and sudden noises, too much light, bad odors, bitter tastes, and hard knocks also, according to this thesis, bring about great debilitation in the human organism. Staying awake or sleeping, food and drink, can also be harmful at times. Again, even a change of water, a variation in the quality of wine, the blowing of the wind and, generally, the most feeble causes, the smallest impositions, appear to affect the human body for ill. The body, supposedly, is constituted in such a way that it is affected adversely by the slightest variation of its unstable elements. All of this, it is claimed, can be clearly and simply shown to be true by numerous experiences, manifest evidences, and abundant examples; or by referring to the authority of Aristotle, Seneca, Cicero, and Pliny as well as any number of other Greek and Latin authors, sacred and profane. But I shall not pause to cite all of those who, in many places in their writings, try to establish and demonstrate this thesis. Aristotle, for example, in a passage in the Ethics, writes: "Sight and hearing, as the books of the Physicists maintain, are tiring." Cicero, further, in his *Tusculanarum quaestionum libri quinque*, states: "Nature has given us weak bodies, and given them over to pains which are intolerable and to diseases which are incurable; she gave us as well infirmities of the soul to correspond."

Now it would be difficult to enumerate the many species of ailment with which our bodies are afflicted from head to toe. Being weak by nature, and rendered even weaker by disease, these ailments make for a quick death; or, so to say, the body flies daily, in the manner of a very swift bird, toward ultimate doom. It is clear that human life is brief—almost instantaneous. Seneca, in many places in his works, and especially in his *Consolatione ad Helviam matrem*, greatly laments the body's weakness. Pliny, in his *Naturalis historia*, having first expressed himself with regret on the frailty of the human body, writes that nature has been not so much a mother to us as a stepmother. Job, moreover, calls this house of ours terrestrial: he sees it as a lowly shack—a thing which we inhabit made of earth, of clay, and of mud. It is this view, indeed, that the Holy Father, Innocent III, in the book titled *On the Misery of Human Existence*, wished to explicate and enlarge. He added many other things, touching on the vileness of the matter with which Adam's body was formed; the vileness of that matter of which the bodies of other men are formed; and holds that God made the human body out of the mud of the earth. He insists, further, that the planets and the stars were made by omnipotent God out of fire; that the winds and the currents were made out of air; that the fish and the birds were made out of water; and that man and the other beasts were made out of earth. He maintains that the bodies of men are conceived of seed and sperm; and he concludes that the matter of the first man was much more vile and ignoble, comparatively speaking, than that of any other animate being, since the earthly element is the most vile and ignoble. He declares that the bodies of men other than Adam are born like those of the dumb beasts, with the single difference being, perhaps, that the embryos which are conceived—that is, the yet imperfect fetuses of men—are drawn upward and nurtured in the maternal uterus by menstrual blood. Pope Innocent seems to have accepted this theory, as applying only to the human body after its conception, and not to those of other animals. But to these other animals he attributes many characteristics which we ordinarily think of as belonging to men alone—as viciousness, shame, and ignominy. I shall not, however, in the interest of brevity, mention all of these; let it suffice for me to note that such views as these are typical of the statements which many worthy authors habitually present in order to demonstrate the weakness and fragility of man.

Now let us look at what is said concerning the vileness of the human soul. In Book II of this work, where I referred to various opinions of different authors regarding the condition and quality of the soul, I said, among other things, that there have been some philosophers who thought that the soul was something corporeal; so, for example, said Thales, Anaximander, Anaximenes, Anaxagoras, Diogenes, Leucippus, Democritus, Heraclitus, Empedocles, Hippias, Arcesilaus, Zeno, Aristoxenus, and Varro. Nor are there lacking some who deny its existence altogether. Dicaearchus, for example, who, imagining that the soul is nothing, affirms that it is nothing but a vain and empty name, and that we speak improperly when we speak of "besouled" or "animated" beings. Then there were many others who, while denying that it was something corporeal in itself, held nevertheless that it derived from the potency of matter and that it is—to use an expression of the theologians—*extraduce*. And all of these men believed that human souls perish with their bodies; not only those who taught that the soul was something corporeal, but also those who contended that souls were spirits destined to die with their bodies, as we know was the case with the Epicureans. They said, in fact, that the soul is disturbed by illnesses of its own no less than the body, and that it suffers from a variety of diseases. Just as they saw many illnesses in bodies, such as migraine, ophthalmia, polyps, splenetic ailments, swelling of the hands, gout, pains in the sides, pains of the bladder, worms, fevers, and other such afflictions which often torment bitterly and bring men, in the end, to certain death; so also they argued that there were various species of malady affecting the soul. These, they held, came to torment it by dividing it in two before leading it to its destruction. They placed in the category of such disturbances emulation, resentment, pity, anguish, grief, pain, lamentation, anxiety, modesty, and desperation; under fear they classified idleness, prudery, terror, timidity, fright, fainting, and disturbance; in the category of self-pleasing the listed ill-will, pleasure, and boastfulness; finally, in the category of lust they placed excitement, ire, hatred, unfriendliness, discord, need, desire, and so on. These, and many other perturbations of the soul, Cicero has cited in an outstanding and elegant manner in some of his own writings. Those who thought the souls of men to be immortal believed that they were altered and shaken by various disturbances only so long as the body was alive. Now when the connection between the two contrasting natures is dissolved, according to some, the souls, depending upon the particular case, enter an appropriate animal body and dwell therein. Later, with the inevitable corruption of this corporeal instrument, they are forced to take yet other bodies. In this way, according to this opinion, because of the almost infinite variety of animal bodies, there is a perpetual, even an eternal, life of the soul. Pythagoras of Samos is considered as the initiator of this theory. He learned about the immortality of the soul from his teacher, Pherecydes of Syros, who was the first of the naturalists to maintain it; and Pythagoras, not being able to understand how there could be a soul without a body, developed this theory of, as we might call it, eternal recurrence. It was for this reason that, in his statutes, Pythagoras prohibits men from eating animal flesh; because the souls of friends and family members long deceased should not be driven out of these animals and forced to transmigrate.

According to still others, souls fly about aimlessly for "hundreds of years," as the poet says—for a very long time, that is—either in this hot and turgid air or in the pure ether. Either they arrive at last in the heavens or they fall into Tartarus, depending upon the condition of their previous life. Thus, be souls mortal or immortal, it would seem, according to these diverse philosophies, that we can conclude that human souls whether embodied or disembodied, whether they endure of themselves or inhabit bodies which are not their own, whether they fly upward through the ether or descend into hell are never free of affliction. For the moment, it is enough to have noted these views regarding the complete lack of dignity of the human soul.

Let us now go on to consider briefly what certain worthy authors have said to show the ignominy and the conditions worthy of vituperation and contempt that relate to the whole person and the life of man. Now if the two elements of which man is composed were truly as we saw them to be in the theories sketched above, who could doubt that the resulting composite would not contain, in full, the nature and character of its components? Therefore, to whoever considers the nature and condition of man with care and intelligence, man must appear, quite clearly, as fragile, impermanent, and ignoble; as subject to affliction by an almost infinite variety and number of illnesses and perturbations. Thus, many ancient wise men, full of learning, considering these and many other similar defects of the soul and body no less than the evils of human life, after examining and analyzing them, have lamented the human condition at length in many places in their writings. The philosopher Hegesias of Cyrene expounded with sumptuous elegance on the many evils of human life. Ptolemy, King of Egypt, is said to have prohibited him from "entering the schools, because many, having heard him, committed suicide." Having been prohibited by his sovereign to discuss the matter aloud, he could not be stopped from recording his doctrines; and so he composed a beautiful dialogue in which he introduces a character who, while permitting himself to die of neglect, was saved by friends to whom he then enumerated the evils of life. Even Crantor, in one of his *Consolations*, openly endorses this doctrine, introducing, according to Cicero, a certain Terinaeus Helysius who, with great sadness, laments the death of his son. This man, having journeyed to the oracle of Apollo in order to ask the reason for such misfortune, was enlightened by three verses inscribed on a tablet:

> The ignorant minds of men are throughout life steeped
> in error;

Euthynous is dead by the will of fate.
Therefore his death was a good for you, and for him.

Alcidamas, a famous ancient rhetorician, according to Cicero, is said to have written a eulogy on death, which seems to have consisted particularly in an enumeration of the woes of man. Marcus Tullius, in that beautiful and famous book *De consolatione*, dealt with this theme of human misfortunes so touchingly, and he so bemoaned and lamented the lot of man, that his readers desired nothing more, as some have said, than to depart this world.

Pliny, finally, in a passage of his *Naturalis historia*, states that nothing exists which is at the same time more miserable and more proud than man. He declares, in fact, and demonstrates that other animals have only a concern for food, without other cares, while man, in addition to the care that he shares with the brutes, is daily tormented by an infinite number of other concerns. Herodotus' tale concerning Cleobis and Bliton, children of a certain priestess, Argia, makes a similar point. While she was going to the city in a carriage in order to perform a solemn sacrifice according to the custom, it happened that her horses foundered. Her sons, being present, stripped off their clothes and having anointed their bodies with oil, placed themselves in the harness in place of the horses. And so the priestess was drawn to the temple by her sons. It is said that she then prayed to the goddess for the greatest gift that can reward filial love. The young men then dined with their mother, and went to sleep. Both were found dead in the morning. A similar prayer is remembered in connection with Trophonius and Agamedes. These two had erected a temple to Apollo at Delphi; and praying to the god, they requested for their work and all their labors no small reward. Without specifying, they asked simply that they be granted "the supreme good of man." Apollo promised it. These men, having been found dead after three days, pay testimony to the fact that man's supreme good was judged to be death. It was later that other gods added to this the gift of prophecy. There is also the story of Silenus, whom the poets claim had been made a prisoner by King Midas. He was released, it seems, because he taught the king that the best thing was for no man to have been born or, if born, to die as quickly as possible. And this, they write, was the reason for the king's having granted him his freedom. We know that Euripides, as well as many other poets, employed this adage to his advantage. Indeed, this view lies at the heart of certain customs pursued in Asia. In certain places there, neighbors and friends are invited to the homes of those families who have lost a member due to serious ailment, in order to join in weeping over the evils of life. These friends then all follow the deceased to the burial ground in a festive mood and celebrate his departure. On grounds such as these, Cleombrotus, even though nothing evil had befallen him, nevertheless thought it better to die; accordingly, he threw himself from a rock into the sea. So also, Socrates, though he could easily have got out of jail, preferred to die. Cato Uticensis killed himself; and is said to have been happy at departing from this life. He found, it would seem, a good reason for dying in the victory of Caesar. So, to conclude, many other pagans, supremely wise and strong, were induced to take their own lives for such reasons. They bore, indeed, with serenity and even joy, their own deaths as well as the deaths of friends and loved ones.

But why cite any more examples from the pagans, when Solomon clearly displays the same opinion in Ecclesiastes? Where, commencing with the vanity of all things, and pursuing this note, he is led to say, at a certain point:

> So I hated life; because the work that is wrought under the sun was grievous unto me; for all is vanity and a striving after wind. [*Ecclesiastes* 2:17.]

A little further on he writes:

> For that which befalleth the sons of men befalleth beasts; even one thing befalleth them; as the one dieth, so dieth the other; yea, they have all one breath; so that man hath no pre-eminence above a beast; for all is vanity. All go unto one place; all are here of the dust, and all re-

turn to the dust. Who knoweth the spirit of man whether it goeth upward, and the spirit of the beast whether it goeth downward to the earth? [*Ecclesiastes* 3:14.]

And a bit further on he says:

Wherefore I praised the dead that are already dead more than the living that are yet alive; but better than they both is he that hath not yet been, who hath not seen the evil work that is done under the sun. [*Ecclesiastes* 4:2.]

Elsewhere he says:

A good name is better than precious oil; And the day of death than the day of one's birth. [*Ecclesiastes* 7:1.]

Statements of this kind are frequent. Even Job, in that famous and sacred dialogue, says:

Man that is born of a woman
Is of few days, and full of trouble.
He cometh forth like a flower, and withereth;
He fleeth also as a shadow, and continueth not. [*Job* 14:1.]

And elsewhere:

Is there not a time of service to man upon earth?
And are not his days like the days of a hireling? [*Job* 7:1.]

And again:

Now my days are swifter than a runner;
They flee away, they see no good.
They are passed away as the swift ships;
As the vulture that swoopeth on the prey. [*Job* 9:25.]

And a little further on:

Wherefore then hast Thou brought me forth out of the womb?
Would that I had perished, and no eye had seen me!
I should have been as though I had not been;
I should have been carried from the womb to the grave. [*Job* 10:18.]

Six hundred passages, similar in nature, too lengthy to cite particularly, can be found scattered throughout this

Book. Even Ambrose, Bishop of Milan, a very saintly and learned man, did not hesitate to deal particularly with the good of death. He wrote, indeed, a special work in which he set forth the many evils of human life. In support of his conclusions, he refers not only to the passages just quoted, but to many others as well. From here, he then moves on to respond against certain objections which he had raised himself, concerning the despicability of death. He classified these objections into three varieties, and then confuted them. Finally, at the conclusion of the book, he attempts to demonstrate and verify what he had set forth at the outset. But let us turn away from Ambrose and direct ourselves to the already mentioned treatise dealing with the misery of human life, composed by Innocent. In this work, starting from the first origins of man, and going through to the ultimate end, Innocent sets forth many arguments designed to prove his thesis. From these, we have gathered those which seem to us to be most worthy of attention as pertinent to our own purpose in this work. I cite them, that is, in order to provide a full confutation.

Innocent, then, after having spoken of the vile putrescence which obtains once the embryo is conceived, remarks that everyone, male and female alike, when born—and even before sinning because of age—wails and laments as a sign of the true misery of man's nature. He states, in fact, that when born, all males wail and cry in *ha*, while females, instead, lament in *heu*. To support this observation, he refers to the commonly recited verse: "All sons of Eve say *ha* or *heu*." He then explains this name, *Eve*, as being nothing but *heu* and *ha*, which are the exclamations of grief. He says, finally, that before the sin she deserved to be called *Viraginem*, and afterward, *Eve*. Taking, in one way or another, these and similar arguments which seemed to him to provide the best and most solid basis for his future edifice, Innocent then goes on, at great length, to speak of nudity, lice, spit, urine, foul stools, the brevity of life, old age, the many travails and pains of mortals, the many anxieties, imminent death, the many kinds of torment, and all the rest of the afflictions of the human body.

Now if we, with the help of God and according to our capacities, can succeed in confuting, as we wish, all these statements, we can then conveniently terminate our discourse. There will but remain to us, at the end of this work, the task of admonishing ourselves and our readers to recognize as gifts of the omnipotent Lord those highest and most felicitous conditions of our human nature which were discussed in detail in the three preceding books. These conditions, as we saw, are such that we can live in this world always happy and well-functioning; while afterward we may hope to dwell eternally in the Divine Trinity, from which we have received all these gifts. Desiring, therefore, very much to confute all the above arguments from their very foundation, we shall, in our response, follow the same order in which we have initially set these arguments forth. We shall begin with the body. We feel no hesitancy in responding as we do to the arguments touching on its weaknesses and discomforts.

The doctors of our Faith attest to the fact that the human body, which, as we said above, was made of slime of the earth by omnipotent God, was constructed in such a way that it is in part mortal, because of the first parents' sin; and in part capable of becoming immortal, should it refrain from sin. The first man, in fact, is said to have had a mortal body which was in a certain sense immortal. Now we are accustomed to ask whether he had both qualities by reason of the nature of his body, or if, instead, the immortality came to him through the beneficence and privilege of Grace. In any case, they say that in that first stage, man was made in such a way that, had he chosen it to be so, he would never have died. In the second stage—since by sinning he left his pristine condition—they affirm that he degenerated and became corrupted, thus becoming liable to the certain penalty of death. But in the third stage—that of the glorious resurrection—they say that he will become immortal with the aid of Grace; but we shall show this in greater detail at the end of this work, with God's assistance. Therefore, every bodily weakness, every disease, and all other discomforts mentioned above, are not to be thought of as contracted because of man's nature, but because of the blot of sin. Hence, the evils that man is thought now to possess must not be attributed to nature but to original sin, as was said above. We must, therefore, stop all the lamenting and weeping of writers, sacred and profane, which speak in praise of death and its advantages. We must stop all this talk, as well, about all other ailments, seeing that these derive neither from God nor from nature but from sin. "But," some may object, "even if this is conceded, could one not, nonetheless, conclude that human bodies, by nature or—as you are trying to show—by sin, received and transmitted this subjection to fragility, to sickness, to death, and to all other evils? Couldn't it be argued that the subjection to which they were condemned, whatever it may be and whatever its cause, appears natural, and goes back to the beginning of creation? There is no doubt, you see, that the law of death, and the afflictions of all other human evils, applies from birth to all humans in every epoch." Now then, even if we conceded this, and much more, yet, if we were not so skeptical and so ungrateful, obstinate and delicate, we should yet recognize that in this, our daily life, we possess many more pleasures than pains. There is not, in fact, a human act—and this is a marvelous thing—which, if we consider its nature with care and attention, does not show itself to be one from which man can derive some pleasure. Thus, through our various external senses—such as sight, hearing, smell, taste, and touch—man enjoys pleasures so great and potent that many of them appear to be superfluous, excessive, and overabundant. It would, in fact, be difficult if not impossible to express the pleasures that man derives from the open and clear view of beautiful bodies; from the hearing of various sounds, symphonies, and harmonies; from the perfumes of flowers and similar things; from tasting sweet and pleasing foods; and, finally, from touching extremely pleasing things.

And what shall we say of the internal senses? Words are wholly inadequate to express the delights that come from the sense which the philosophers have called "common" in determining the differences between sensible things; or the pleasures derived from the various imaginings of different substances and accidents; or in judging, in remembering and, finally, in understanding. If men, in life, tasted those pleasures, and those delights, rather than tormenting themselves on account of the annoyances and despairs, they should be happy rather than weep; and they should console themselves rather than lament—and all the more as Nature has provided numerous remedies against cold, heat, pain, fatigue, and illness. All these remedies are sure antidotes against these ailments; and what is more, they are not irritating, annoying, or bitter, as is the case with medicines, but they are, rather, soft, sweet, delectable, and pleasurable. In the same way that we enjoy satisfying hunger and thirst when we eat and drink, so also we enjoy becoming warm, or becoming cool, or resting. Moreover, in a certain way our perceptions of taste appear much more delectable than all our tactile perceptions with the exception of the sexual ones. These latter pleasures are the supreme guide, the only one, no doubt, that did not come about by chance, but—as the philosophers say—"for clear reasons and evident causes." It seems quite planned that from coitus there would be derived an enjoyment greater than is derived from eating and drinking; for in this, Nature intended, above all, to conserve the species rather than the individual; and the species, as we know, is conserved through the union of the male and female, whereas individuals are conserved by the absorption of food which, so to speak, renews what is destroyed. Understood in this way, all the pernicious opinions concerning fragility, heat, cold, fatigue, hunger, thirst, bad odors, bad tastes, unpleasing sights, tactile contacts, wants, sleeplessness, dreams, foods, drinks, and similar human ailments will appear frivolous, vain, and inconsistent. Thus they must appear to all who consider, with a little diligence and accuracy, the nature of things. As a matter of fact, the references cited above from Aristotle, Cicero, Seneca, and Pliny are confuted and refuted by what we have said: for sight and hearing are laborious and annoying functions only when they are overdone and abused. When, however, we use these and the other senses in a measured and moderate manner, not only do we not become jaded and tired, but we become restored. And if it is impossible to deny what Cicero said—i.e., that nature has given us weak and fragile bodies—she nonetheless, let it be noted, has also furnished us abundantly with many remedies for their weaknesses and fragilities. Further, if we look on this, our corporeal domicile, as made of clay and mud, as that most patient man says, and view it as matter's *infima species,* we must remember that this, doubtless, could not be otherwise; for such a marvelously delicate constitution is most appropriate to serve as receptacle for the human soul. Having thus responded to and stilled the arguments of the ancient authorities, it remains for us to confute, briefly, the arguments of Pope Innocent III. To these we now apply ourselves, ready and armed.

Now if, as Innocent thinks and says, the body of the first man was made of mud, while the bodies of other beings, both animate and inanimate, were made from the other elements—which we concede without argument, appear by their nature to be more noble than the earth—then it is curious that this human structure, composed of terrestrial matter, should appear so much the more noble and excellent in comparison with all other beings. For the winds and the planets and the stars, even though made of air and of fire, remain nevertheless insensible and inanimate. Yet one would think that they should by far excel the nature of fish, birds, and those of brute animals, which came, like man, to possess life from the earth. But this rational animal, provident and sagacious, has, in fact, a body which is a great deal more noble than that of the beasts, because it is more capable of operating—it is capable of speaking and of understanding—and these are functions of which the beasts are deprived. Similarly, it can be considered greater than the wind and the stars—things that are lacking in sense—as also superior to the fish, birds, and other things that are animated. Indeed, the human body, even though it does not share a common matter with any of these beasts, nonetheless appears to be superior. The human body, in a word, was, in its own proper nature, made in such a way that without original sin it would never have perished, as I recall having remarked and demonstrated above. This is a characteristic that no other body possesses. It is for this reason that the terrestrial element must be considered so much the more admirable and noble than all the others. Failing this, we must take the view that although composed of an element which is by nature more ignoble and vile than the others, it was nonetheless, in the body of man, sublimated and exalted over the others. But let these brief considerations regarding the body of the first man suffice. As regards all other bodies, and the observations made on their conception and the formation of their embryos, we, wishing to give a very brief answer, will say only that our bodies were given in the beginning the same condition as that of other perfect animals. Indeed, even a better condition: for our bodies take their origin from seed which is better and more delicate; they are nourished and grow by a blood which is richer and more pure. For sperm derives from excess of food, and—according to the opinion of all doctors—blood is generated from the same substance. Hence, the more delicate and noble the food of an animal, the more excellent will be the sperm and blood derived from its residues. Thus the sperm and blood of man must be much superior to that of other animals, since human food is considered more noble than the food of all other animals. I shall ignore the other remarks of Innocent, on nudity, weakness, and such, since I feel that I have touched on these sufficiently, to the extent that I was capable of doing so, in my general remarks above. Let us go on now to combat, briefly, the opinions referred to above concerning the baseness of the human soul.

We'll forget about Dicaearchus and those who have held that the soul does not exist, that it is an empty name, and that it is vain to speak of animals as "besouled" beings. These people professed such doctrines concerning the human mind only to prove themselves completely lacking in both mind and sense. They never seem to have considered that they were themselves possessed of these things. In this error, they were joined by Thales, Anaximander, Anaximenes,

Diogenes, Leucippus, Democritus, Heraclitus, Empedocles, Hippias, Arcesilaus, Zeno, Aristoxenus, Varro, and all others who maintained that the soul was something corporeal, derived *extraduce* from the potency of matter, and that it was destined to die with the body. To these fools, and—so to speak—fat and lazy philosophers, I will repeat some of the same things that I said in Book II of this work. There, among other things, I cited the words of our Cicero who, in everything, agreed with Catholic truth and faith: "The soul has no terrestrial origin, because there is nothing mixed or composite in the soul; nor is there anything which appears to have been born or formed of earth. Further, there is nothing humid or airy or fiery about it; for none of these can have the power of memory, of mind, of thought, the capacity to retain the past, to predict the future, to embrace the present—these are all divine endowments, and can come only from God. The power and the nature of the soul is, therefore, unique and apart from all known common natures. Hence, whatever it may be, that which feels, that which knows, that which has vigor and lives is celestial and divine and, therefore, necessarily eternal." Aristotle himself, the prince of philosophers, sees thought as transcending all mixed and simple bodies. He posits a certain fifth nature from which mind emerges. He held, in fact, that thinking, seeing, and other such faculties could not possibly derive from the above-mentioned bodies. According to what Cicero once said about him: "Aristotle, who is by far the greatest intellect—with the exception, naturally, of Plato—having considered those four well-known kinds of principles from which all is born, believes that there is a fifth nature from which the soul is born. To think, to anticipate, to teach, to learn, to remember, to love, to hate, to desire, to fear, to suffer, to enjoy, and such like, are not features, as he sees it, of any of the four kinds; and so he adds another kind, without name, and calls the entelechy of the soul by a new name—a name which almost suggests continuous motion without rest."

But let us turn to the Epicureans now, and to other pedestrian philosophers of their ilk. To these, who maintained that souls perish together with their bodies, let us refer all that we have already said in Book II of this work. Let us, however, not be so tedious as to repeat all these things here. As for those who believe—since they are incapable of understanding a soul without a body—that souls can retain their immortality only by transmigrating, I shall only refer briefly to a text of Cicero. In the work which he wrote at Tusculum, Cicero says: "Many however are opposed, and think that souls are as if condemned to capital punishment. But they can give no other reason for regarding the immortality of the soul as incredible, except that they are unable to conceive of the condition of a soul without a body. It is as if they already knew all about the condition of the soul when in the body: how it got there; what its dimensions were; and where it was therein located. But even if it were possible to see all that is hidden within an individual man, would the soul be visible? Let those reflect on this who declare that they cannot understand a soul without a body—let them consider further what they can understand of the body itself. I, when I consider the nature of the soul, find it much more difficult and more obscure to understand the condition of the soul in the body, where it finds itself as in a strange house, than when it is free of the body and gains the free sky, its proper home. No doubt, we find it difficult to comprehend that which we have never seen; still, we can certainly grasp God himself in thought —and the divine soul freed from the body, as well."

We come now to the arguments directed against the whole person of man. First of all, let us consider the authorities, and then the arguments themselves. As regards the authority of Hegesias, of Crantor, Alcidamus, of Cicero, of Pliny, Herodotus, Euripides, Cleombrotus, Socrates, Cato—some of whom merely wrote in praise of death, while others destroyed themselves altogether because death freed them of the woes and misfortunes of life—we must note that the opinions of these ancient Gentiles must be considered as especially suspect. No one in his right mind doubts that the things created by God are all good. Sacred Scripture attests to this fact. Things being so, man, for whom all these goods were created, must be seen not only as good himself, but, so to speak, as more than good. Human life, therefore, cannot be as universally miserable as these men held. Indeed, were it so, it would then follow that that which is essentially good would find itself in perennial misery; and since this, patently, is not the case, without doubt the authorities referred to above—poets, orators, and philosophers who have written at length on the misery of human existence—appear to have provided arguments that are false, frivolous, and empty. And this, shown by argument to be false, finds further confirmation in the celebrated testimony of St. Augustine who, in Book XXII of the *City of God*, wrote: "Just as that nature which is capable of feeling is, even suffering, superior to the stone, which cannot suffer; so also the rational nature is more noble, even if unhappy, than that nature which lacks reason and sense. For this reason there is no misery in it. This being the case, such a nature—created with such excellence that even though transitory it may attain beatitude and unite with the immutable and supreme good—will never be satisfied unless it is blessed, and only God can assuage this thirst; this nature, I say, is vicious if it does not adhere to this good." Lactantius confirms this as well in various parts of his *Institutions*, when he refutes the opinions of Cicero and others who, in some of their writings, praised death. Lactantius writes: "At the beginning of his *Consolations*, Cicero maintains that men are born to suffer for wrongdoing. He repeats the same thing later, almost attacking anyone who does not recognize that life is full of misfortune. Quite rightly, then, he declared himself to be involved in error and in miserable ignorance of the truth." Immediately afterward, Lactantius says: "Those who talk of the good of death, argue thusly in their ignorance: 'if there is nothing after death, death is not an evil because it releases us from consciousness of pain; if the soul survives, then death is a good because immortality follows.'" With his admirable eloquence, Lactantius completely destroys all such opinions and refutes them, showing them to be totally false. As for the famous cases of Socrates, Cleombrotus, and Cato, we hold that these were led to kill themselves not by the thought of human misfortune and a contempt of life but, rather, in the hope of immortality. If this were not the case, they would never have been praised so highly for their greatness of soul by so many writers. To flee the trials of life is not the mark of the strong and magnanimous but, rather, as Aristotle says, of the weak and irresolute. Even Pythagoras forbids turning away from life without the order of a chief, who is God. The same point is exhibited also in that speech which Socrates made before his judges when he received the death sentence: "A great hope, O judges, takes possession of me that your sentence of death is a good for me; it is, in fact, necessary that one of two things occur: either that death takes away every capacity to feel, or that we go to another place far from here," and so on. The fact that Cleombrotus read a book of Plato's on the immortality of the soul proves that he killed himself for no other reason than that he believed what Plato wrote on the subject. Augustine, in Book I of the *City of God* also attests to the fact that Cleombrotus read that work before killing himself. We must think the same of that great and vigorous Cato who—if he had killed himself merely to avoid the ill-fortune expected as a result of Caesar's victory—would have sinned more than all of the other ancient suicides; nor, if this were the case, would he have merited the extravagant praises heaped upon him by even the profane writers. This opinion seems also to have been that of Augustine, especially in the same work, the *City of God*. Furthermore, Plutarch, in his treatment of Cato's life, states that before Cato killed himself, he too read Plato's book.

To the sacred authorities, Solomon, Job, and Ambrose, I think we must reply differently. Now Solomon, in *Ecclesiastes,* spoke deliberately in such a way that all inhabitants of the earth would understand him—as a very clear and simple orator, that is. This is quite obvious from the use of the Hebrew name *Koheleth,* and the Greek name *Ecclesiastes.* For this reason he speaks in such a manner that in many places he seems openly to contradict and confute himself. Thus, the statement cited above, in which he regards man's death as equal in value to that of the animals, is strongly contradicted by what he says at the end of the work when, speaking of man, he says, among other things:

> Before the silver cord is snapped asunder,
> And the golden bowl is shattered,
> And the pitcher is broken at the fountain,
> And the wheel falleth shattered into the pit;
> And the dust returneth to the earth as it was,
> And the spirit returneth unto God who gave it.
> [*Ecclesiastes* 12:6.]

He contradicts himself also as regards those two other cited passages, the first being when he states:

> Wherefore I praised the dead that are already dead more than the living that are yet alive; [*Ecclesiastes* 4:4.]

and the other being the statement:

> A good name is better than precious oil;
> And the day of death than the day of one's birth.
> [*Ecclesiastes* 7:1.]

These statements are in direct contradiction to many passages in the same work, but especially to these two:

A living dog is better than a dead lion; [*Ecclesiastes* 9:4.]

and:

Go thy way, eat thy bread with joy,
And drink thy wine with a merry heart;
For God hath already accepted thy works. [*Ecclesiastes* 9:7.]

It was because of these internal contradictions that there arose such a variety of contrasting opinions regarding the sanity, and even the evil, of the doctrines contained in Ecclesiastes. Hence, those first doctors and teachers of the ancient Hebrew church, who soon after the death of our Redeemer established the order of the Hebraic books which they now use—teachers who, in Hebrew, are called *Rabbis* —discussed at length the question of whether Ecclesiastes should be included among the authentic works of sacred Scripture together with the prophetic works, or whether they should not condemn and burn it. Doubtless, it would have been decided that this work should be given to the flames by these teachers, and destroyed forever, if it did not contain, at the last, these words:

> Fear God and keep His commandments; for this is the whole man, [*Ecclesiastes* 12:15.]

and so on.

Now as regards the numerous contrasting utterances of the most patient Job, we hold that that Book was composed by the great saint and legislator, Moses, as a dialogue on divine providence. It was thus necessary that there be stated the various opinions which represent the different protagonists. We do not hesitate to declare these passages false and fallacious, because Job himself, and his three friends—precisely with respect to the above-cited passages—appear to have been refuted by the high and wise Elihu. He was, indeed, admonished and advised by the Omnipotent to change them into other passages that are true and certain. With regard to Ambrose and similar doctors, if there be men who insist upon citing the authority of their meditations on the good of death, we respond that they wrote most clearly and openly in their works on the beatitude and happiness of the future life awaiting souls; on the goods to be realized when souls are separated from bodies; and on that marvelous, almost incredible, resurrection of bodies after the Last Judgment. But we shall speak more of this at the end of this book. Since, then, we have, according to our capacities, confuted all the other passages drawn from the works of the sacred and pofane writers referred to above, we must now pause to consider the arguments of Pope Innocent.

The first and principal foundation of our Innocent—that upon which it pleased him to erect the entire edifice called *On Misery*—is the death of all men. This he stated correctly at the beginning of his work, where, discussing human misfortunes, he writes these words: "All are born weeping; and in this, they express the misery of our nature. The male, newly born, says *ha*, and the female, *heu*. It is as a certain wise man who says: 'and so will say all who are born of Eve.' What then is *Eve* if not *heu ha*? The same exclamation with which we express the extremity of sorrow. Indeed, after the great female sin, she deserved to be called *Eve*," and so on. Innocent believes he has here established an excellent foundation for his edifice; but in truth, his base is such that, as our poet says,

> Were it not for the fact
> that reverence for the Highest Keys
> forbids me this, . . .

I would not hesitate to declare what he has said to be banal, puerile, and greatly out of keeping with the dignity of the pontifical estate. We shall content ourselves, however, with but a moderate discussion of these words, because of the high veneration which his sanctity merits. We shall limit ourselves, then, to satisfying in a measured way the requirements of our own present project. First, it is proper briefly to consider this so-called "solid and adamantine foundation." For if we examine this with proper diligence and care, we can then more easily understand and grasp the inadequacy of the rest, based as it is on a weak and shifting ground, rather than rocks and diamonds. Indeed, the venerated words of sacred Scripture clearly show how false, how far from the truth, is what he says concerning the two natural exclamations which, as he supposes, are the clear and manifest expression of human misery and misfortune. At the beginning of Genesis, Moses, inspired by the Divine Spirit, says:

> And the man called his wife's name Eve; because she was the mother of all living. [*Genesis* 4:20.]

She was called, then, by this name "Eve" because she was the mother, the origin, and the principle of all men who had to be born and propagate themselves from her as from a primal root. Clearly, this is what the sacred words of the Latin text disclose. This appears with even greater clarity in the Hebraic version; in fact, the supreme prophet, describing in the aforementioned Book the origin and the development of all things, says:

And he named his woman Aia;

and wishing to give the reason for this name, Moses quickly adds:

For she had to be the mother of all who live.

Of all men, that is, who, by the excellence of their human nature—or as the Greeks say, with even greater clarity, because of *antonomasia*—had rightly to be called "living"; and the living, in the Hebrew, are regarded as such. Our own Jerome, the most accurate of all the sacred translators of the Greek and Latin, always rendered the Hebraic term as *Eve*, for euphony. The same holds with what Innocent writes in connection with *viragine*; when he affirms, that is, that before the sin she deserved to be called *viragine*, while after the sin *Eve* was most appropriate. For this statement turns out to be as false as the previous one examined; especially if you consider carefully and diligently the following precise words of the same prophet:

And Adam said: "This is now bone of my bones and flesh of my flesh; she should be called *virago*, because she was taken out of man." [*Genesis* 2:23.]

While the matter is clear enough in the Latin tongue, it appears even more clear and manifest in the Hebraic. In the Hebrew, he says:

And she shall be called *Hisca* because she was taken from out of *Hisc*;

now *Hisc*, in the Hebrew, is a word which derives from "man." St. Jerome, in order to keep his translation most faithful, and fully aware of the etymology of the word in question, rendered the Hebraic *Hisca* by *viragine*—a word which is derived from *vir* which means, in the Latin, "man." Flavius Josephus, in Book I of his *Antiquitates Judaicae* confirms the truth of all this with these words: "In Hebrew, the female is called *Hisca*. So the name of the woman for them was evidently *Eve*, which means the mother of all the living." Having thus shown in the clearest light the initial error of our Innocent, an error which occurs at the very foundation of his work, what must we think concerning that which was erected upon it? Is it, in fact, likely that he stated the truth in the balance of his work when we see the grave error with which he begins? This is an egregious error; an error into which he would never have fallen had he not been completely ignorant of the Hebrew tongue.

Now let us consider briefly some of his individual arguments, first recalling, in order to refute them, the various headings, all of which relate to the misery of man: his nudity; the fruits of men and the fruits of trees; the evils of old age; the brevity of life; the travails of mortals; the various occupations of men; and the different anxieties and miseries, which he expounds in great number, but which we will not list in the interest of brevity. In order to proceed with some order in this our confutation, we shall speak at the outset concerning the nudity of man. In regard to this, Innocent says as follows: "Man is born naked, and naked he returns. He comes poor, and he departs poor." To this we make answer that it was necessary for man to be born in this way, precisely because of his grace and beauty. If, indeed, man was born draped with various coverings and pelts, it would be difficult to describe how horrible would be the appearance of little babies. Precisely because of the excellence of our nature, it could not happen otherwise; and even if it had been otherwise, Nature would never have left the human body, the most beautiful, and without doubt the most marvelously accomplished of all her works, hidden under some other covering. She would never conceal its beauties with deforming and inappropriate veils. Now we could, had we wished, have answered differently with respect to the natural vestments, the skin, of the newly born; we did it this way, however, because in the same passage we read that this writer has used vicious words against even this natural covering with which we are all born. He, in fact, says: "And if anyone protests that he does come dressed into this world, let him but attend to the kind of dress he wears: it is an ugly thing to say, ugly to hear, and ugly to see—it is a bloody little skin." Now to be just, we should remark that what he probably referred to was the *secundina*, which is the name which doctors have given to that membrane with which children are born. All children, by necessity, have this with them at birth and cast it off immediately thereafter.

But what shall we say concerning the fruits of men and of trees which Innocent employs by way of analogy? He uses it in this way right after his discussion of nudity: "Go, investigate the herbs and the trees: they produce their own flowers, leaves, and fruits, while you produce only lice, nits, and fleas. The former, of themselves, produce oil, wine, and balsam; and you, man, produce spit, urine, and feces. They, of themselves, diffuse sweet odors; but you produce abominable and foul smells." Going on in this way, he makes abundant similar comparisons which we will not here mention for the sake of measure and decorum. One could answer to these objections of the aforementioned supreme pope that his comparison of men to plants is absurd and irrelevant. The proper "fruits" of man are not those of turpitude, superfluity, dirt, and wastes; rather we must consider human fruits to consist in such things as acts of the intellect and the will; for it is these which man, by his nature, is born to produce. Nature does not specifically aim to produce in man the products mentioned above: they come, rather, as a result of a certain necessity which arises with regard to food and drink; and yet, it is marvelous and almost incredible that these things which I have called "superfluous" in respect of man's nature still appear to be quite utilitarian—at least according to what doctors tell us about such things as spit, urine, stools, and hair. The spit of a man who is hungry, for example, is a cure for the bite of venomous serpents; it is of efficacy, as well, in curing certain ailments of the eyes. Urine admirably relieves and even cures constipation, and preserves sight. Dried phlegm, placed on the nostrils, promotes sleep in those who suffer from insomnia; and human feces and hair—which latter, according to the Scriptures, "not one of which should disappear"—help in fertilizing the fields in a way far superior to any other fertilizer.

What shall we say concerning the inconveniences of old age and the brevity of life? As before, we do not lack in appropriate responses. If, indeed, we know that at the beginning of human history, our forefathers lived for some nine hundred years—which fact leads Innocent, by comparison, to despise our actual life which he regards as most brief—we must remind ourselves that this happened because God, without doubt, was providing wisely and justly for humans. For if humans at the outset enjoyed but a brief duration of life, human nature could not have propagated itself; humans could not have erected cities; and discovered the sciences and the arts. But after all these things, necessary to men, were established and made known, the longevity of man, it is true, began to diminish little by little. Proceeding thus, it arrived, finally, at this, its present span. Flavius Josephus, in the already cited *Antiquitates Judaicae*, appears to confirm this; he remarks that God conceded a lengthy life to the ancient fathers of our religion as an initial gift. Not long afterward, beginning with the death of Terah, father of Abraham, after pointing out that he had lived two hundred and fifty years, Josephus adds these words: "Now it has come about that after Moses' generation, the life of men has become continuously more brief; for after Moses, human longevity was set at one hundred and twenty years." Men who live now, however, no longer have need of such longevity: for the health of the human race has been conserved; many cities have been erected; the many useful arts are available to us; and the human race has been propagated. As a matter of fact, to accomplish all of our human projects, and to live fully, well, and happily, the life that we now live is more than sufficient. That this is the actual case today is clearly and openly demonstrated by Seneca, in his work *On the Brevity of Life*, where he confutes the well-known adage concerning the longevity of art and the brevity of existence. In order to deal competently with the arguments touching on the inconvenience of old age, we have merely to compare these not only with the pleasures and the delights of the life previously lived, but as well to those which old age may itself enjoy. Whoever troubles to make such a comparison will be led to the reasoned position that the pleasures of life, in general, far outweigh the evils that have occurred and continue to occur to men. Concerning the toil and labor of mortals, we respond just as we did with regard to the evils of old age. We think, indeed, that the pleasures which accrue to man for his labors far outweigh the pains. Indeed, if we consider with accuracy and diligence the various activities of man, we will discover that while it may be true that we always suffer some discomfort in activity, it is also true that every activity yields more pleasure than the pain involved in the effort of performing it. It is a famous dictum of Aristotle that men necessarily enjoy life; indeed, that same philosopher, in Book X of his *Ethics,* where he speaks of pleasure, affirms and demonstrates that pleasure is absolutely inseparable from man's activities. Even more noteworthy, he declares at this point that pleasure is bound to human life itself in such a way that it can in no way be divorced from it. His words are these: "That pleasure becomes complete through the various senses is manifest; for, indeed, we say that seeing and hearing give us pleasure." A bit later, having shown that all such activity yields pleasure, he adds: "But let us not now discuss the question as to whether we choose life for the sake of pleasure, or pleasure for the sake of life; for these things are so closely tied together that they cannot be separated, since without activity there is no pleasure, and every activity is completed by the attendant pleasure." Man, therefore, seeks pleasure throughout his whole life, from the time of his birth to the time of his death. This being the case, doubtless, as we have stipulated above, the pleasures of life far outweigh the pains.

As regards the various cares and anxieties of men, I believe that one must respond in the same way. It is best not to be too wordy about things so clear and manifest; and consequently, so that we may not ourselves be led to say more than is required by the character and conditions of the matter at issue, this is all we shall say. Moreover, the arguments to the contrary set forth above, and everything that may be said to make the case for human misery, can easily be destroyed and abundantly refuted with reference to the final resurrection of the flesh. When we are born again, certainly we will again take on our dead bodies: but then without blot, without corruption, without weakness, without deformity. We shall all be renovated in supreme glory; and all shall be completely free of infirmity and blemish, the discomforts which now plague us, and those difficulties which afflict us daily from every quarter. Not only this, but our bodies will also be furnished with ornaments of singular splendor, as we shall now try to explain in brief by indicating the different and admirable conditions accruing to the bodies of the blessed.

The first condition is perpetual and eternal health, lacking all infirmity, and completely immune to all disease. Concerning this condition, the psalmist speaks in many places, and particularly in the psalm where he says:

Praise, O my soul, the Lord
who heals your infirmities.

The second condition is eternal youth. Eternal immunity of the body, that is, would not help man if it were not accompanied by the blessing of continuous youth; neither would immortality be of any value—even though one were fully healthy—if he were so oppressed and burdened by the years that he had to support himself with a cane. All shall be reborn in the fullness and vigor of age thirty. As the apostle said:

Until we all arrive at the unity of faith, at human perfection, the measure of age and the fullness of Christ.

Christ suffered the cross at thirty years of age, after having ended His retreat; and so, having shown himself to the world at thirty years, we too will be reborn at that age. Not only shall we have the same age as Christ but, marvelous to say, we shall have as well His same stature; it will be as the apostle says:

And He said that they shall conform with the image of His Son.

The third condition will be the freedom of bodies. Our bodies, which are now oppressed by so many necessities, so many burdens, and so many corruptions deriving from sin, will become light, subtle, free, and unblemished. The fourth condition will be beauty without blight. If, indeed, corporeal beauty without blight consists in a harmony of parts yielding a certain sweetness of appearance, then certainly there will be perfectly complete beauty when there is no longer any incongruity of parts; and at that time, a certain marvelous and divine effulgence will appear, diffuse itself necessarily, and bring perfect harmony and grace to the whole. Thus it is written in the sacred books:

The just will shine like the sun in the realm of their Father.

The fifth condition will be the elimination of passivity and the addition of immortality. The dwellers in that realm, indeed, will be tormented by neither cold nor heat; by neither hunger nor thirst; neither will they be tormented by old age, nor by any other affliction. The sixth condition will be uninterrupted peace; for there man will have peace wholly, completely, and eternally. The seventh condition will be everlasting joy without grief; for God will wipe every tear from the eyes of His saints. Never again will tears be shed; never again will there be anguish; nor will laments and wailing ever be heard; for all this ends with our mortal and temporal life. Having thus abundantly, with what we have said, confuted all possible objections to this, our worthy attempt to proclaim the dignity and excellence of man, it remains for us to touch on certain things, similarly worthy of remark, concerning the rewards and joys of the blessed, and the punishments and pains of the damned.

Anyone who knows even a little of the sacred books knows that the praises of the blessed have been great and numerous. Above all, they enjoy the glorious and sweet vision of the divine Majesty; as the apostle Paul says:

> Now we see as through a glass darkly and by enigmas, but then we shall see face to face. [*I Corinthians* 13:12.]

Again, there is John the evangelist, who says:

> We shall be like Him because we shall see Him as He is.

Matthew, too, openly and clearly confirms this in that famous and well-known sermon delivered by our Lord on the mountain:

> Blessed are the pure in heart, for they shall see God. [*Matthew* 5:8.]

We could thus recall and cite by the hundreds other such testimony from divine Scripture; testimony confirming that the just of the earth will see God. But fearing that we might be too prolix, we shall deliberately eschew such an enumeration, especially since the whole question at issue is so clear and obvious that there can be, really, no doubt or uncertainty about it. Some ask whether in the heaven of the saints God shows himself to corporeal eyes, to the eye of the mind, or to both; as concerns this, there have been various opinions offered by men of supreme doctrine and sanctity; however the case may be in regard to it, it seems clear that the blessed somehow do contemplate that marvelous mirror of all things human and divine, and it is utterly impossible to say or to comprehend sufficiently the great joy involved in this beatific vision. If even the sight of gems is so delightful to us, or the sight of the stars, or the sight of the beautiful and harmonious human figure, what must it be like to be in the presence of almighty God? Without question, that delight will be so great as to render us immensely, uninterruptedly and infinitely happy forever. That such a remarkable and incredible joy will come to us through the vision of God can surprise no one; one has but to consider that all things are reflected in God by a light which is more radiantly clear than our daily light. It is as Gregory puts it in his holy writings: "What will he not see who sees Him who is everything?" What more can one say of this immense and infinite joy? The Catholic doctors and their dogmas have stated it in the most manifest way when they tell us that this divine vision is the grace of the blessed light, and that its privation, conversely, constitutes the principal pain and misery of those who are damned. When you consider the splendor, subtlety, agility, impassivity, beauty, immortality, which are the most outstanding and admirable conditions of these glorified bodies, the nature of their endowments and singular privileges will become manifest and shine forth in an incredible way. Indeed, the bodies of the blessed will be so resplendent that nothing human can be compared to them, or even approach them, in their immense and great splendor. Wishing to express the radiance of these glorified bodies through some analogy with corporeal things, the prophet Isaiah and the evangelist Matthew, unable to find anything more splendid than the sun, chose to compare the blessed condition to the splendor of this orb. One wrote:

> The just will shine like the sun in the presence of God;

and the other, regarding the transfiguration of Christ on Mount Tabor, said:

> His face shone as the sun.

The souls of the blessed will appear so fine that neither doors, nor walls, nor any other corporeal barrier could offer them resistance. It shall be just as Christ indicated when, having entered through closed doors after the resurrection, He appeared to His disciples. Moreover, they will be so agile that no weight will hinder their going wheresoever they wish. This too is in accord with the plain example of Christ, who, in order to succor His disciples when they were in danger, walked on the Sea of Galilee with dry feet. They will appear as impassive, beautiful and immortal; for no element will drag them down, no turpitude will deform them, and no illness will weaken them at that time when they enjoy seeing the infinite congregation of the blessed, joined with the host of saints, intoning hymns together. If, indeed, friendship is so sweet in this human world where suspicions are so many, where deceptions abound, and where dangers daily threaten, can you imagine what sweetness attaches to that divine and reciprocal charity in the realm without deception and without change? When we see the full glory and splendor of this heavenly Jerusalem with our own eyes, we shall exult supremely; for its foundations and the walls around the twelve circles are all of different gems, and the twelve doors are equally each made of pearls, and each is a pearl, as John the evangelist states at the end of the Apocalypse. When the blessed in their eternal happiness will see all this, while the damned are forced to remain in eternal torment, without question they will be filled with supreme and infinite joy.

Now to these joys of the blessed there will correspond an equal number—nay, more—of torments for the miserable damned. Indeed, first of all they will be deprived of the vision of God, the lack of which modern theologians call "the punishment of the damned." This torment is considered so great, according to the famous opinions of Chrysostom and Augustine, that any exile from the heavenly realm would prefer being placed in hell to being denied the vision of God. To this great punishment there is added the torment of an infinite and insufferable, sulphurous fire; the damned are subjected as well to horrible odors, cold, and other such infernal torments. These latter the theologians usually refer to as the "damnations of sense." To all this horror one should add the moans, cries, and loud shrieks of the damned who continuously lament. What can we say of this terrible sight, involving an infinite number of men damned to such intolerable tortures? It is a thing so horrible, so fearful, that we can neither think about it nor speak of it. Consider, further, how desolate they will be when they understand that their damnation is for eternity; that they are to be kept in eternal torment with no hope of future redemption, while the blessed, filled with eternal and infinite joy, are to be forever gratified, happy, and exultant.

But let us now conclude this work of ours with a final touch. We have shown abundantly, in order, in the first three books of this work, how marvelous and how great is the dignity of the human body, how great and sublime is the soul, and how great and outstanding is the excellence of the fully constituted man. Then, in this fourth book, we resolved and confuted the arguments that seemed to oppose us and to contrast with our views. It but remains for us to exhort, briefly, our contemporaries and posterity to observe the divine commandments with care and diligence, so that they may ascend to the eternal celestial realm. Therefore, we humbly pray and supplicate, O very serene prince—to return to your Majesty, at last, as after a long voyage—not only to you, but as many others as well who may read this work, that they observe and execute the divine commandments. If everyone, according to his capacity, tries to conduct himself in this way, he will obtain temporal privileges as well as eternal rewards. Furthermore, without question, all careful observers of these divine precepts have been fated, from birth onward, to be fortunate in this life as well as eternally happy and blessed. We earnestly pray all eventual readers of our work to observe diligently this brief and affectionate exhortation, even at the cost of forgetting all the rest that we have written. Accomplish what we shall briefly try to say: O men, O king, princes and sovereigns, since you have been set in places of such great dignity and excellence that all that is on the earth, in the waters, and in the sky is under your sovereign control, take to heart virtue. Shunning all vices, love virtue with all the power of your soul and your body. Love it, I pray you, observe it, follow it, embrace it in such a way that, continually practicing it, you will be not only happy but blessed, and become thus similar even unto immortal God. Your duties, as regards understanding and acting, you have in common with omnipotent God; consequently, by acquiring and cultivating virtue, you may attain the beatitude of a tranquil immortality. You may emulate that Eternal Prince: He is always understanding, acting, and contemplating. These, indeed, are the proper projects of God himself; and in your own perpetual and eternal beatitude you will enjoy one and simple joy like Him, and dwell in eternal exaltation to the sound of everlasting hymns. This, then, I had to write for you, O most serene prince, concerning the dignity and excellence of man; and all the things which I have so abundantly explained above, I feel to be supremely true every time I turn my eyes and my mind to the singular and admirable endowments of your person and its precious privileges. Wherever, indeed, we have shown with diligence and care every single good quality of human nature, we knew you to possess them in your body and soul. The many excellent and outstanding human endowments and parts, admirably united and converging into a unity, we see illuminated in the single person of King Alfonso; he seems not to have been born according to the common law of nature but, rather, to have been formed and elected by the omnipotent Lord himself.

Suggested Readings

FRANCESCO PETRARCA

BARON, H. *The Crisis of the Early Italian Renaissance*, 2 vols. Princeton, 1955.

KRISTELLER, P. O. *Eight Philosophers of the Italian Renaissance.* Stanford, 1964.

MOMMSEN, T. E. *Medieval and Renaissance Studies*, ed. E. F. Rice. Ithaca, 1959.

PETRARCA. *Secret*, trans. W. H. Draper. London, 1911.

———. *On His Own Ignorance and That of Many Others*, trans. H. Nachod, in E. Cassirer *et al.*, eds., *The Renaissance Philosophy of Man.* Chicago, 1948.

RUEGG, W. *Cicero und der Humanismus.* Zurich, 1946.

TRINKAUS, C. *Adversity's Noblemen.* New York, 1940.

ULLMAN, B. L. *Studies in the Italian Renaissance.* Rome, 1955.

WHITFIELD, J. H. *Petrarch and the Renaissance.* Oxford, 1943.

WILKINS, E. H. *Studies in the Life and Works of Petrarch.* Cambridge, Mass., 1955.

LEON BATTISTA ALBERTI

COATES, W. H., *et al. The Emergence of Liberal Humanism*, vol. 1. New York, 1966.

MANCINI, G. *Vita di L. B. Alberti.* Florence, 1911.

MICHEL, P. H. *Un idéal humain au XVe siècle, La pensée de L. B. Alberti.* Paris, 1930.

SAITTA, G. *Il pensiero italiano nell'umanesimo e nel Rinascimento.* Bologna, 1949.

LORENZO VALLA

BAROZZI, L. and SABBADINI, R. *Studi sul Panormita e sul Valla.* Florence, 1891.

GAETA, F. *Lorenzo Valla.* Naples, 1955.

KRISTELLER, P. O. *Eight Philosophers of the Italian Renaissance.* Stanford, 1964.

MANCINI, G. *Vita di Lorenzo Valla.* Florence, 1891.

VALLA, LORENZO. *The Treatise of Lorenzo Valla on the Donation of Constantine*, trans. C. B. Coleman. New Haven, 1922.

———. *On the Freedom of the Will*, trans. C. Trinkaus, in E. Cassirer *et al.*, eds., *The Renaissance Philosophy of Man.* Chicago, 1948.

GIANOZZO MANETTI

KRISTELLER, P. O. *Renaissance Thought.* New York (Harper Torchbooks), 1961.

———. *Renaissance Thought*, vol. 2. New York (Harper Torchbooks), 1965.

II

RENAISSANCE PLATONISM

GIOVANNI PICO DELLA MIRANDOLA

Giovanni Pico *was born into a noble family in Mirandola in 1463. He studied law and philosophy at Bologna, Ferrara and, from 1480–1482, Padua. Expert in Greek and Latin, he learned Hebrew and Arabic at Perugia, where he also became interested in the Jewish cabala. By 1486 he had composed the nine hundred theses which led to charges against his orthodoxy. Pico fled to France to evade capture, but was nevertheless arrested in 1488. He was released owing to the intervention of several Italian princes and he then returned to Florence, where he enjoyed the protection of the Medici. There, until his death in 1494, he made a brilliant addition to the learned circle that had gathered around Ficino. Considering the brevity of his life, Pico was quite prolific. He composed poems, letters, commentaries, and a number of original philosophical tracts. Aside from his nine hundred theses and the famous* Oratio, *he is well known for* Heptaplus *and* De ente et uno.

Letter to Ermolao Barbaro

Dear Ermolao: I cannot hold back what it is that I feel for you; nor can I help but feel all that it is proper to feel toward one who possesses every grace to so eminent a degree. Would that God had made the power of my intellect equal to the task of extolling your merits, and the force of my style capable of expressing, at least this once, what it is that I feel always! Well do I know that my poor attempts to do you honor fall infinitely far below the sublime height of your worth. Know that between my words and what I feel lies the same distance as between my feeling and reality. Do you really think me so presumptuous as to aspire to your greatness? All can admire you, very few can emulate you, none can equal you.

I should consider myself fortunate, indeed, if what I wrote could, in some small measure, approach you, my Ermolao. Your very style—to speak of nothing else—which you consider to be of such little worth, strikes and delights me in a truly wondrous way. It is wise, serious, poised, erudite, powerful, and ingenious; it contains nothing of the common or trivial, in either language or structure. Together with Poliziano, I read and read again all the letters which you have sent to us; and—when we can get them—those which you have sent to others as well. The latest ones invariably outdo the preceding ones; and new graces seem to flower with each letter, causing us to catch our breath by reason of the excess of delight which they engender.

It is quite extraordinary how you can persuade, and how you can direct the reader's very soul wherever you wish. I marked this always in your letters, but particularly in your most recent one: the one in which you ridicule the "barbarian philosophers," who, you say, are commonly regarded as "uncouth, uneducated dolts." Desirous of living beyond death, these men, as you say, never truly lived even when alive; while if they were yet alive, they would live in desperation and shame.

By Hercules! When I read this I was thunderstruck! Overwhelmed by bitterness, how I regretted all the effort I had expended in study—six whole years of work! I was inconsolably desolate over having spent my time and energies on so worthless an enterprise. Fruitless, the hours spent in studying Thomas, Scotus, Albert, and Averroës! Misspent, the best years of my life! Utterly wasted, those many sleepless nights! Gone forever, the time in which I could have won for myself a reputation in letters!

In my musings, I could not help but imagine what any of these men, were he alive today and still in possession of his keen wit, might have said in his own defense. It occurred to me, finally, that some one of them, a bit more eloquent, perhaps, than his fellows, might have responded as follows in defense of his "barbarism."

"We lived, O Ermolao, in fame; and so we shall continue to live in the future. Not, of a certainty, in the schools of the grammarians—not there where they instruct little boys—but among the philosophers, in the circle of the wise, where they do not spend their time quibbling about the mother of Andromache, the children of Niobe, or other such inanities, but where, instead, the principles of things, human and divine, are investigated. In our ruminations, our researches, and in our attempts to cast light on the nature of things, we were sometimes so subtle, so acute, and so painstaking that we may, perhaps, appear to have been overscrupulous and cautious: but is it ever possible to be overscrupulous and too careful where the search for truth is involved?

"He who would rebuke us for intellectual weakness or pettiness—let him come forth! He will soon discover that the "barbarians" had Mercury not merely, as some, on the tongue, but in their hearts. He will discover, too, that while they may have lacked eloquence, they yet did not lack wisdom; and further, that to divorce these is as much a violence as to marry them is illegitimate. For who would not condemn the use of such blandishments as hair ornaments and cosmetics in a maiden? Who would not condemn these in a Vestal Virgin?

"There is such a contrast between the task of an orator and that of a philosopher that none greater can be imagined. For what does the rhetorician do but seek to lie, to deceive, to be circuitous, and to insinuate? You take pride in maintaining that it is your business to influence the will, to make black appear white, and white, black; and that you can, with words, elevate, destroy, support, or annul anything that you wish; finally, it is your claim that with the near magical lure of eloquence, you can transform, at will, things themselves in appearance and character. Not, of course, that they become by your magic what you say; yet, while not becoming so, they can be made to appear to the listener as you wish them to appear. But what else is this than pure deception, pure imposture, pure deceit? The orator, in fact, always either exaggerates the nature of what is real by magnifying it or, by reducing the force of his words, degrades it. All the while, that is, he gives false impressions by his words, and coolly deceives, in the way in which a phantasm or a simulacrum deceives.

"Can such a one have any affinity with the philosopher, whose sole purpose is to know, and to demonstrate the truth to others? No philosopher could serve the truth who sought merely to create impressions and to seduce with language. It would be as if, not having faith in our ability to capture reality, we were to seek by deception to have men accept our views. Thus, sacred Scripture was written in spare language and not with eloquence. For in every argument concerned with truth, nothing is more foreign and vicious than the stress upon style. This passionate searching after words is more suitable to legal disputes than to inquiries directed toward knowledge of natural and divine things. Thus it is not worthy of those who sit in our Academy; it is proper only for those who occupy themselves with political intrigue, and who seek the adulation of the mob which values, rather, the flower than the fruit.

"Have you not heard the saying: 'Robes of the same cloth are not fitting for all men'? We yield that the flow of language can be graceful, attractive, and pleasurable; but in the philosopher it is neither appropriate nor welcome. Who is not tolerant of the extravagant poses, gestures, and expressive glances employed by actors and dancers? But who, while not condemning these in the actor and dancer, would fail to condemn these affectations in the ordinary man and in the philosopher? When we behold a young girl of ready wit and graceful manner, we appreciate her and would embrace her; yet we would condemn these same features in a mature woman. It is not we, therefore, but the others who are reprehensible: those who celebrate the Bacchanals at the feet of the Vesta: those who sully the high purpose and purity of the philosopher with the cheap tricks of the actor.

What Synesius says of youth, we can verily say of speech: 'Adorned oration is a shameful thing.' It is for this reason that we prefer our kind of speech—straightforward, weighty, and precise—to any eloquently ordered oration; for these latter carry with them always the suspicion of corruption. All profanation must be kept from the robe of Athena and other sacred things.

"But all else aside, nothing is more foreign to philosophy than that which smacks of ostentatiousness or vulgar display. Socrates used to say that shoes from Sicyon, while certainly comfortable and stylish, were just not for him. The tastes of the man-of-the-world, whether in food or in discourse, differ from those of the philosopher who indulges in such things only as necessity demands. If the former neglected such things, he would soon lose his status, while if the latter sought such things, he would no longer be a philosopher. If Pythagoras could have lived without eating, he would have abstained even from cabbages; if he could have expressed his thoughts by means of facial expressions or with less effort than it takes to employ language, he would not have spoken at all, so far removed was he from addiction to the *bon mot* and the finely turned phrase. And we must be wary of all such pretty show: for the listener, charmed by the attractive exterior, might dig no further: he might not pierce to the marrow and blood which, as we know, oft runs infected under an attractively made-up face. Indeed, it is just this way with those who, having learned to turn a pretty phrase, attempt to mask the fact that there is nothing in them save what is vain and empty. They can only entertain and amuse their listeners or readers with displays, catchy modulations, and euphony. If the philosopher did this, Musonio would say that it is not a philosopher who speaks, but a flautist piping. Let it not be considered a defect in us that we do not that which it would be truly defective for us to do. We are not concerned with the manner in which we write, but the matter which we set down. Actually, we consciously strive to avoid the ceremonial and the niceties of discourse; we are not concerned that our language may or may not be pleasing or gracious, but only that it be informative, serious, and severe enough to guarantee its precision. We neither seek nor expect the applause of theater goers for having stimulated them with euphonious and sonorous strains such as are employed in the theaters to show what is false and what sweet; we hope for and desire, rather, the silent admiration of the few who can recognize and ponder these truths, dug from the inner recesses of nature and brought to men from the abode of Jove. We seek to present some matter so thoroughly researched that there remains no room for doubt, and so solidly presented that there remains no need for further discussion.

"Let all admire in us not our elegance but our care and concern in research; the subtlety of our observations; the severity of our judgment; our ability to synthesize; our capacity to disentangle or unravel what is snarled. Let us be admired for a concise style, strong enough to bear arguments of great weight; for our handling of a wealth of problems, judgments, and solutions. Let them, if they will, admire our expertness in the elimination of ambiguities, and in the destruction of inanities. Let them admire the way in which we seek to explore the unknown; to destroy what is falsely asserted; and to demonstrate the truth by means of unassailable arguments.

"It is on these grounds, O Ermolao, that we hope to avoid that oblivion to which you would consign us. I can assure you, we shall continue to defend ourselves thus to future detractors as well. And if, as you say, the vulgar regard us as uncouth and uneducated, we feel honored on this account, and not shamed. It was never our intention to write for the vulgar: we wrote for you and your kind. The ancients discouraged the attentions of the ignorant by employing enigmas; we, similarly, try to bar the ignorant from our feasts, for they would surely make them inedible with the bitter rind of their words. Those who are forced to release their treasures when they know that they cannot carry them very far are accustomed to cover them over with debris and refuse so that no unworthy and casual passers-by will take them up. So, too, the philosopher must be concerned to hide his teachings away from the unworthy public; for the mob can neither understand nor appreciate them. What the crowd wants is cheap theatrics: something equal to their capacities and meriting, thus, their plaudits.

"Do you wish me to present you our way of speech in an image? It is precisely as the Silenus of Alcibiades. This was a statue of crude, unappealing, even despicable appearance: but filled with a rare and precious content of gems. Thus, if you see but the outside, you see a monster; but if you seek within, you discover a god.

" 'But,' you may say, 'it is our ears that are offended; they simply cannot abide the harsh, raucous cacophony; and these barbarous terms fill us with fear by their very sound.' O man of refined tastes, be all ears when you go to the players of flutes and pipes, but when you go to the philosophers, be receptive in your very self: in the depths of your being! Here, have the ears of Tyanaeus: the ears with which he, having freed himself from the body, was able to hear not earthly Marsyas, but heavenly Apollo who played on his divine lyre the ineffable harmonies of a hymn to the universe. Listen to the words of the philosophers in this way and they will seem to you as sweet as honey. Thus will you become the envy of Nestor.

"But let us dispense with this pompous discourse. To criticize a philosopher, who is concerned to speak carefully and with precision, for his lack of stylistic elegance is not a sign of refined taste but of insolence. It is as if one were to become irritated and indignant with Socrates because, while discoursing on virtue, his sandals were untied, or his toga was disarranged, or his fingernails were improperly pared. Cicero demands of the philosopher not eloquence but doctrine and reason. He knew very well that it is the use of the mind, and not the speech, that characterizes the wise and educated man. He insisted that the arguments be valid, not the speech correct; and that the internal rather than the external word be counted. With us philosophers it is meet that the Muse be in our souls rather than on our lips; for then we shall be rendered impotent neither by corrosive anger nor by debilitating weakness. Finally, let harmony regulate our soul: a harmony which is often destroyed by the theatrics of the poet. Plato, indeed, suspecting this, was led to expel the poets from his Republic, leaving it to be governed by the philosophers. He implied, moreover, that the philosophers too were to be expelled if they began to imitate the poets and Sophists.

" 'But,' Lucretius will say, 'even if the writings of philosophers require in themselves none of the adornments of speech, it is yet necessary to soften the austerity of their doctrines, so that in order to beguile improvident youth it is better to mix that bitterness which cures illnesses with honey.' Perhaps, Lucretius, this would be most proper if you were writing for children or for the vulgar; but in any case you would have done so—for you prepared not only wormwood, but also the most virulent of venoms! At all events, we must have very different standards; for it is not our wish to lure the vulgar but, rather, to rid ourselves of them. We do not wish to prepare vile wormwood, but nectar. 'But,' Lactantius will object, 'the truth implanted in the soul of the listener may be given even greater inpetus if, in addition to appealing to its power, it is made more attractive by a proper speech.' If you, O Firmian, had been as assiduous in your study of the Scriptures as you were in your study of false controversies, you would not have said this! Indeed, you might have been moved to confirm what I am saying no less brilliantly than you confuted the sayings of others. Tell me, I pray you, what can more powerfully move and persuade than the sacred Writings? They do not merely move, they do not merely persuade, rather they compel and agitate; they carry with them the weight of the Law, rugged and simple, vitally alive, flaming, cutting, penetrating to the very depth of the soul, transfiguring the whole man with marvelous power. Alcibiades says that while he remained unmoved by the elaborate and ringing orations of Pericles, he was far from unmoved by the naked and simple words of Socrates. He goes on to say that these words, even though unadorned, so exalted him, and so took him out of himself, that he did whatever Socrates ordered. But why dwell on these well-known examples? If he who listens is not a fool, what else does he expect from pompous discourses but treachery?

"Three things, above all else, convince: the life of him who speaks, the truth that he declares, and the reverence with which he speaks. These, O Lacan'tius, are the qualities which lend credibility to the philosopher: that he be just, that he be truthful, and that he be honestly searching—not after that oratorical pomp which comes from the gentle groves of the Muses, but after that which emerges from that terrible cavern where, as Heraclitus says, 'the truth hides.'

" 'But,' someone might observe, 'let us examine the question, O friend, putting aside all contention. Wisdom is, in itself, something venerable and divine; granted, it has no need for extrinsic adornment; but what harm is there in adding this to it? Who can deny that that which is beautiful in itself becomes even more resplendent when it is adorned?' It is I, my friend, who will deny it: if you add decoration, you despoil the splendor of many things. Nor should radiance be added to these things; for by their very nature they are in such perfect condition that any change can only diminish their perfection. Would you place plaster over a marble palace, and cover it with white? You would destroy its dignity and beauty. In the same way, wise and philosophical discussions are not enhanced, but disfigured, by whitewash. What more? Is it not well known that cosmetics ruin beautiful features? In general, no matter the ornamentation you choose, it hides whatever it is put on, and carries ostentation in its train. Thus if what was there first was superior to the ornament, this latter, whatever it may be, will do harm rather than good. Therefore, philosophy offers itself naked and in full view: it wishes to be seen entire, it wishes to be exposed to all judgments, because it knows that it possesses in its entirety the grounds for universal admiration. When you veil it, it is beauty that you hide. It wants only to be accepted pure and whole; anything you mix with it corrupts it, adulterates it, and transforms it. It must maintain its pristine and simple individuality. For this reason, we must not toy with rhetorical figures, we must not be pleased at prolixity, we must not abandon ourselves to euphemisms or to the audacity of neologisms—not in a thing so serious, not in a thing of such magnitude; for in such matters it would be wrong to add, subtract, or transform anything.

"Here you may very well respond: 'We will concede that it is not your task to speak with rhetorical flourishes; still, though you are not pretentious on this point, you do discourse in Latin; so that while you do not employ flowery language you do, at any rate, explain yourself in the Latin tongue. Now I do not demand that your speeches be polished, but neither do I wish them unkempt; let your words be neither too casually nor too carefully chosen. We do not require that your speeches entertain, but let them at least not offend.'

"Very good: now you are beginning to agree with us. But I should now like to examine this Latin of yours which, as you maintain, the philosophers ought to respect even as they fail to do so. For example: instead of saying *a sole hominem produci*, as you do, we say *causari hominem*. You then immediately begin to hoot, quite justly, that 'This is not Latin!' In this you are as I say, quite correct. You are even more correct when you say: 'This is not said in the Roman fashion'; but if you conclude, therefore, that 'This is not correct,' then you will be in error. An Arab and an Egyptian will say the same thing; they may not say it in Latin, but they will be nonetheless correct in saying it. For the names of things are either imposed upon them by convention or by nature. It could very well be the case that a human society agrees upon the meaning of a word; if so, then that word is the correct one to attach to the things which it has been agreed upon to represent. This being so, what is there to halt those philosophers, whom you call 'barbarians,' from themselves getting together to agree upon common language norms which are just as sacrosanct to them as the Roman tongue is to you? If the assignment of names is purely arbitrary there is no reason to view ours as wrong and yours as right. If you do not wish to dignify our tongue by calling it 'Roman,' call it instead 'French,' or

'Spanish,' or even, if it pleases you, what the vulgar call 'Parisian.' When these men speak to you they will be derided for many things and, to a great extent, they will not be understood. But the same thing will happen to you when you speak to them. Remember the Greek saying: 'Among the Athenians, Anacharsis speaks incorrectly; but the Athenians do the same among the Scythians.'

"But if the rightness of names is dependent upon the nature of things, should we consult the rhetorician about this rightness, or should we repair to the philosopher, who alone examines and clarifies the nature of all things? Perhaps what the ear rejects because of its harshness, reason may yet prefer as consonant with reality. 'But why do they introduce these innovations and employ a non-Latin tongue, if they were born among Latins?' The fact is, O Ermolao, that they could not waste the time—for they were occupied with reading in the sky the laws of fate, the character of events, and the order of the universe; they were busy reading in the elements the vicissitudes of life and death, the powers of simple elements, and the composition of mixed elements—they could not, I say, at the same time take note of the peculiarities, laws, and properties of Cicero's, Pliny's, and Apuleius' Latin. They sought what is accepted in nature and what is not accepted in nature; they were not concerned, while doing this, for how their findings would affect the Romans.

"But to yield your point for the sake of discussion, let me concede that eloquence and wisdom join in mutual ties. Philosophers have effected the separation between wisdom and eloquence; while historians, rhetoricians, and poets have, as Philostratus complains, separated eloquence from wisdom. You must not doubt that these latter will continue to enjoy great fame, while the former will go down in infamy. But think about what you are saying: Cicero prefers wisdom less eloquent to empty loquacity; we do not prize money for the way it is coined, but for the kind of metal of which it is made. No one prefers false Roman money to German coins of pure gold. Those who separate between the heart and the tongue are mistaken; but how many are all tongue without heart? Do they not themselves, as Cato says, reduce themselves to glossary deaths? Without a tongue one can live, even if not comfortably; but one cannot live at all lacking a heart. A man is not refined who does not concern himself with literary eloquence; but a man is not a man who lacks philosophical concern. Wisdom, though lacking eloquence, can serve; but unwise eloquence is like a sword in the hands of a madman: it cannot but do great harm.

" 'So,' you will retort, 'no doubt statues are to be prized because of their matter rather than their form; and if Choerilus had sung the same themes as Homer, and Maevius as Virgil, then they too would have therefore been acclaimed among the great poets!' But don't you see the irrelevance of the comparison? We too, hold that a thing is to be judged by its form and not its matter: for the thing is what it is by its form. But the forms which mark one as a poet and another as a philosopher are quite different. Let Lucretius write on nature, on God, on providence, and let one of ours write on the same matters—Scotus, for example, even if he is incapable of poetizing; and what is more, let him write about this in verse, so as to make him all the more awkward. Lucretius will affirm atoms and the void to be the principles of all things, corporeal God to be unaware of our human existence, and everything to occur as a result of the fortuitous clash of corpuscles; but he will say these things in elegant Latin. John Scotus will say that natural things consist in matter and form, that God is a separate mind who knows all and provides for all, that although He sees and regulates everything, even the most minute things, His tranquillity remains undisturbed: He descends, as we say, without yet descending. But Scotus will say this without adornment, crudely, in non-Latin terms. Tell me, if you please, who is the better poet and who the better philosopher? Beyond doubt Scotus is as much the better philosopher as is Lucretius the better poet. And observe the differences: the former's words are unattractive, the latter's foolish; the former does not know the linguistic norms, neither those of the poets nor of the grammarians, the latter is ignorant of the laws of God and nature; the former, though inept in speech, yet understands what mere words are incapable of praising; the latter, although very eloquent, utters blasphemies."

O my dear Ermolao, such—or even more powerful ones if they resorted to sublety—are the arguments which these men might present in defense of their barbarism. I do not, of course, fully share their opinion, nor do I believe that a man of broad and liberal culture can do so. Nevertheless, it has given me some pleasure to deal with such vile stuff, like those who praise a fever, both to strengthen my own abilities and to do as Plato's Glaucon, who praised injustice, not to convince himself by his own arguments but to spur Socrates to laud justice. In the same way, just to hear from you some defense of eloquence, I have polemicized against it, even against my own inclinations and nature. If, indeed, I really believed that the barbarians were correct in their neglect of eloquence, I would never have almost wholly given up studying their writings; nor should I, as I recently have, taken up the study of Greek and your never sufficiently praised "Themistius."

Still, let me express my frank opinion: certain grammarians give me a profound feeling of disgust; those who, having learned the origins of some few words, strut around with such ostentatious display, such arrogance and presumption that, as compared to themselves, they would have no philosopher esteemed worthy. "We do not want," they go about saying, "these philosophies of yours." And I believe there to be nothing curious in this: neither do dogs know how to appreciate Falernian wine!

With this, let me close my letter: if those barbarians have merited some glory only for their knowledge of things, it is not easy to say what glory belongs to you who are most eloquent among the philosophers, and most philosopher among the eloquent.

Florence, June 3, 1485

MARSILIO FICINO

MARSILIO FICINO, *who heavily influenced the history of culture, was born at Figline in 1433 and died, after a life completely devoted to scholarship, at Careggi in 1499. He was trained in the humanities, philosophy, and medicine, studying in Florence and Bologna. In 1462 Cosimo de' Medici made him the gift of a small villa at Careggi, and it was here that Ficino began translating the ancient literature of Platonism. For at least a century, the whole of learned Europe read Plato in Ficino's version. In addition to the enormous body of translations, Ficino published commentaries, digressions, and arguments which themselves constitute impressive treatises. He composed as well a number of original works. Of these, we may cite as being particularly significant:* De voluptate; Theologica platonica de immortalitate animarum; De vita; *and a carefully edited collection of letters, among which are contained many smaller philosophical treatises. The* De sole, *one of his smaller works, was originally published together with* De lumine *in 1493. Ficino's* Orphica comparatio solis ad Deum *is devoted to the same topic.*

Concerning the Sun

CHAPTER I

Words to the reader: this book is allegorical and anagogic, rather than dogmatic.

MAGNANIMOUS PETER, it is truly a divine Pythagorean maxim that "without light one should not speak of sacred things or the mysteries of God." With such words, in my opinion, that wise man Pythagoras meant to teach that concerning God, one should say not only what God's light reveals to inspired minds, but also that one should not attempt to grasp and state the hidden or occult light of God without noting its resemblance to the sensible light: namely, that of the Sun. For it is within our power to ascend from this sensible light to that of God; not however by arguments, but by analogies drawn with light.

Therefore you, very careful reader, whom I would hope to be also full of indulgence, must remember the solar and Apollonian poetic promise: do not ask for more penetrating insights, nor that I present them in Greek, that is, dogmatically. I promise only an allegorical and anagogic exercise of the kind underwritten by Phoebus. The Muses do not argue with Apollo: they sing. Mercury himself, the inventor of disputation, even while treating of grave questions with Saturn and Jove, jests with Apollo. However, he does not play merely for amusement, but sports divinely. Would that we too could play thus!

Let us now bring to focus our thoughts on light and hope that our undertaking may prosper. May God, the Supreme Good, happily inspire us.

CHAPTER II

In what way the light of the sun is similar to God, the Supreme Good.

NOTHING reminds us of the nature of Good more than light. In fact and initially, light appears in the sensible order as the most eminent and pure thing. Second, it is that which most readily spreads, diffusing itself instantaneously. Third, it splays out over everything and penetrates all in a manner that is most gentle and mild, without harming any being. In the fourth place, it carries with it a vital heat which warms everything, generating and moving them. Finally, it has everything in its presence immediately; it is not weakened by anything; nor does it mix with any other substance.

Analogous to light, the Good exceeds in itself the whole of reality; it is spread everywhere, soothing and enticing, forcing nothing. It has love as its constant companion, almost like warmth, by means of which it attracts individual things in different ways, while these happily embrace the Good. Although it penetrates everything to its most intimate depths, it nevertheless mixes with nothing. In short, just as the Good itself is incomprehensible and ineffable, so also is light. No philosopher, in fact, has ever defined the light in such a manner that clarity and obscurity are not at the same time involved in his explanation—like the Good, which is at once the most known and unknown of all things.

Thus the Platonist, Iamblichus, finally concludes that light is action and visible image of divine Intelligence in the same way that the rays which shine are representations of light itself. Perhaps light is the sight of the celestial soul, or that act of vision directed beyond, which moves at a distance and does not leave the sky. Always united with itself, it does not mix with external things even while acting through sight and touch. We sometimes call light a trace of mundane life which offers itself to sight in a certain proportional relation, and appears as an intermediate, vital spirit between the body and the soul. However, of this phenomenon I have already sufficiently spoken in my *Theologica.*

But I shall not become involved in the toils of endless refinements, when all I want to affirm is that above the heavens are many angelic minds which are like lights, "exemplifying their relation with one another and with God, Father of Light itself." Turn your eyes to the sky, you citizen of the heavenly Fatherland, to that sky which God created with admirable and visible order for the purpose of making all creation manifest and open. If you turn your eyes to the sky, the rays of the stars, almost as clear hints, will quickly inform you of the Glory of God. The firmament will tell you of the work of His hands. Yet, the Sun alone can indicate to you God himself. The Sun will give you clear signs. Who will dare to say that the Sun lies? Also, the invisible creatures of God and the angelic spirits are rendered visible by the stars; but it is the Sun that declares His eternal power and divinity.

CHAPTER III

The Sun is the Illuminating Lord and Regulator of the Skies.

THE SUN regulates and guides all things celestial, like a veritable lord of the sky. I will not speak of its immense size; however, it is believed that it is one hundred sixty-six times the size of the earth. It gives light to all the stars, whether these have, as some think, a weak light of their own or, as is more generally believed, lack light of their own altogether. The Sun brings to life the twelve signs of the Zodiac, which is thus truly alive, and was considered so by Ali and Abraham. Two of these signs are, in fact, so filled with power by the Sun that the Arabs call them *Thrones of the Sun* when the planets pass into them. In some way they avoid being incinerated and acquire a marvelous power, especially at the time when the greater planets rise before the Sun, and the lesser ones after it. The sign in which the Sun reigns, Aries, becomes for this reason the prince of constellations, and represents the head in all living creatures. The constellation which is the *House of the Sun*, that is, Leo, is the heart of the constellations and controls the heart of all living things. Thus, when the Sun reaches Leo, it extinguishes epidemics in many regions, almost like serpent's venom.

The annual fate of the world always depends on the entrance of the Sun into Aries. Springtime derives its own proper nature from this beginning; whereas the entrance of the Sun into Cancer signifies the quality of summer. Its entrance into Libra signifies the quality of autumn; and that into Capricorn, the nature of winter. Once the configuration of the heavens is established, time depends on their motion. The Sun then distinguishes the four seasons by means of the four mobile signs. Thus the return of the Sun to the degree and the minute of the birthdate of each person renews his fortune for one year. In addition it should be noted that the motion of the Sun, prince of planets, is extremely simple; it never moves away from the center of the Zodiac, nor retreats from it, as is the case with other planets.

CHAPTER IV

The relation of the planets to the Sun.

THE SUN determines definite spaces in the heavens through which the planets pass and change their own movement and character. Thus Saturn, Jove, and Mars change movement quickly and go forward or backward when they enter the third part of the sky and find themselves in a triangular aspect with respect to the Sun. They move backward if to the east of the Sun, and forward if to the west. Venus and Mercury run shorter but nevertheless well-defined courses with respect to the Sun. Venus cannot move away for more than forty-nine degrees, nor can Mercury for more than twenty-nine.

The Moon changes aspect and nature with every change

of relation to the Sun. She has four seasons, and represents the four seasons of the year like a second sun. Every time there is a conjunction with the Sun, the degree of conjunction and the configuration of the heavens determine the nature of the following month. Whenever the various planets touch the heart of the Sun, they dominate the other planets during that time, no matter how brief. When they come near to the Sun in other ways, they perform their usual function. When Saturn comes near the Sun, it abandons its usual rigor. Even Mars puts aside its customary ferocity. When the Sun comes near the greater planets, they rise; but when, instead, it goes away from them, they fall. Joined to the Sun, they have the greatest epicycles; and when opposed, the smallest. In the quadrant, they are medium in altitude. In both cases the Moon reaches the highest point of the deferent, but in the quadrant it falls. When Venus and Mercury are conjoined to the Sun, while they are progressing, they are large. If they conjoin to it while returning, they are very small. Also, it is not permissible for the planets to make their epicycles without first recognizing the Sun, their lord and master.

From what has already been said, we can see that when the greater planets change their movement in a triangular aspect in relation to the Sun, they pay their tribute to the regal bearing of the Solar Diety. When they are in conjunction with the Sun, they are at a summit and move in straight lines because they are in harmony with their king. The opposite occurs when they are in discord: that is, in opposition. They then become retrograde and very small. When Venus and Mercury touch the Sun and proceed by a straight motion, they ascend sublimely, obeying their lord. Nevertheless, even if they proceed by oblique motion, as if rebellious, they are still subject to the Sun's command.

In considering the Moon, we should not be astounded if she moves up even when in opposition to the Sun. Indeed, what in fact is the light of the Moon, if not the Sun's own light, reflected by the mirror of the Moon? It is light which, when the Moon is full, reflects that of the Sun directly from its face. Furthermore, we see the Moon descend in the quadrant when it looks upon its lord with disdainful eyes. Thus, when the Sun does not withdraw, so also the Moon does not recede, for the velocity of the epicycle prevents this regression.

Finally, by virtue of the Sun, the Moon brings an increment to the constellations situated west of the line of the Sun where resides the great Head of the Dragon. Indeed, when it turns south, there is a diminution of the strength because of the projecting of the Tail of the Dragon in this region. All the planets, depending in every case upon whether they are to the east or the west of the Sun, change character and condition. All, especially the inferior planets, fear the way of the Sun called the ecliptic. The Moon and Venus fear it most, for which reason they move farthest to the side. Moreover, all are thought to change their condition depending upon whether they are on that path or moving away from it, proceeding toward the west or the east. The Moon, matron of generation, has no other light than that belonging to the Sun. When it is in a perfect relation to the Sun, it derives from the Sun all its celestial powers, as Proclus says, and transmits analogous powers to our world.

CHAPTER V

Of the efficacy of the Sun in generation; in determination of times of birth; and of all else.

Now, IN THE BIRTH of each man, the position of the Moon represents the master of generation and the moment of conception. The conjunction of the Moon with the Sun, or its opposition immediately preceding the birth of a man, shows the truth concerning that birth and determines its horoscope. In the celestial configuration the part of the sky in which is found Fortune's Outcome is called the *Demon of Birth* by the ancients. It reveals, or as the Egyptians maintained, produces, the entire character of life. Fortune's Outcome is read in the space observed between the Sun and the Moon, and is therefore calculated in relation to the ascendant degree. Thus the astronomers find and measure the motions of the planets by the motion of the Sun, which is already determined.

Therefore, it is the Sun which determines the days and nights, the hours, the months, and the years with its movement. With light and heat it generates, gives life, moves and regenerates everything, spreading warmth and gladness. Things which were hidden, it makes manifest. Also, by its motion it determines the four parts of the year.

The regions which are distant from the Sun are likewise distant from life. Springtime is thus the most beautiful of the seasons, because it proceeds from Aries, which is the domain of the Sun. Autumn is the worst, because it has its origin in Libra, which is where the Sun falls. Finally, birth during the day is commonly preferred to night birth, principally because a night birth is under the influence of the Moon which is only as a mirror to the Sun.

Astrologers usually divide the configuration of the heavens, as regards nativity, into twelve parts, of which the ninth is assigned to the Sun, and the third to the Moon. The former they call God, and the latter Goddess. They believe that each indicates the greatest gifts, which are, wisdom, faith, religion, and eternal glory. The Sun, in fact, signifies all these things and more—every truth, prognosis, and reign. Again, when the Sun rises to the highest point of the sky, it warms our vital animal spirits in a marvelous way. Conversely, when it descends, our vital animal spirits weaken. For this reason, David, the trumpet of omnipotent God, getting up at dawn to play the pipe and sing, exclaimed: *It is useless to get up before sunrise*. He wished to declare that the rising Sun brings every good, and that our spirits, excited and illumined by the Sun, come thus wonderfully to be called sublime things.

It is commonly believed that the Sun, almost as a

prophet, engenders in sleepers prophetic dreams. Also the Moon, bride of the Sun, which Aristotle calls the mirror of the Sun, in a similar manner restores the spirit and the natural humors of the body when it increases, and weakens them when it decreases. Thus, the more things abound with solar light, the more they are benefited.

I shall omit the matter of how the aspects of the Moon in relation to the Sun are considered when the latter's light does not fail, and how we refer to different parts of the human body, depending on the constellation in which the Sun finds itself. In fact, in this way, by means of the Moon, all the celestial powers come to be transmitted for the restoration of bodily members by using medicines made according to proper time configurations. However, of this matter I have already said enough in my *Book of Life*.

CHAPTER VI

The praises of the ancients to the Sun. In what way the powers of the heavens are all found in the Sun from which they derive themselves.

FOR THESE REASONS Orpheus called Apollo the *Living Eye of the Sky*. From the Orphic hymns I shall now summarize: *The Sun is the Eternal Eye which sees everything, the supereminent heavenly light which rules over the things of the sky and of the world. It guides and rules the harmonious course of the world, since it is the Lord of the Universe, immortal Jove, Eye of the Cosmos, which controls everything and possesses the seal which makes all earthly forms. However, the Moon has all the stars in her bosom; she is Queen of the Stars*. In this way spoke Orpheus.

In Egypt, on the temple of Minerva, one could read this golden inscription: *I am all the things that are, have been, and will be. No one has ever torn my veil. The first generated by me is the Sun.* From this statement it appears that the Sun is the issue, the flower, the fruit of Minerva, that is, of divine Intelligence. According to the testimony of Proclus, the ancient theologians used to say that Justice, Queen of the Universe, penetrates everywhere, directing all things from the throne of the Sun. Thus they practically held that the Sun itself is the regulator of everything. Iamblichus expounds the doctrine of the Egyptians in this way: *All the good that we have, we have from the Sun*—that is, from the Sun alone. Also, even with the participation of others, it is still the Sun which brings good to perfection, or it is the Sun which produces it through other things. Thus the Sun is lord of all the powers of the elements, and the Moon is ruler of generation by power of the Sun.

Albumasar says, therefore, that all things have their life from the Sun and the Moon. Moses holds that the Sun is the lord of celestial things by day; and by night, the Moon is mistress, almost as if she were a nocturnal sun. Thus, all have placed the Sun as lord at the center of the world, even if in different ways. The Chaldeans, indeed, placed it at the center of the planets; whereas the Egyptians put it at the central point of the two poles of the world in such a way that the five planets would be above, and the Moon and the four elements below. They believed that Providence placed it closer to the earth than to the firmament because, with its fervid spirit and fire, it shed warmth on the humidity of the Moon, the air, and the water, as well as on the gross materiality of the earth.

According to still another doctrine, it is the prosperity of the planets which reveals the Sun's centrality; for this is disposed to them in relation to their distance from the Sun. Saturn, Jove, and Mars rise ahead of the Sun. Afterward, Venus, Mercury, and the Moon come up in such a way that the Sun resides regally in the middle. Those proceeding otherwise are weaker. Most powerful among the planets are those which their lord, the Sun, has ordered to go ahead or in front. But let us return to the ancients.

The first Physicists called the Sun the *Heart of the Sky*.

Heraclitus called it the *Source of the Celestial Light*. Very many Platonists place the soul of the world in the Sun which, filling the entire sphere of the Sun, radiates its own rays through the fiery globe as through a heart. By means of these rays, which are almost spirits, it distributes life, sense, and motion throughout the universe. Probably for this reason, the majority of astrologers think that as only God gives us the intellectual soul, He gives it to us only under the influence of the Sun, after the fourth month following conception. However, this matter concerns the astrologers alone.

On the other hand, Mercury, which stands for the motion of our mind, moves but little away from the Sun. Saturn, standing for the condition of the separate mind, stays close to the plane of the ecliptic. Jove and Mars harmonize by means of Sagittarius and Aries, and are respectively in accord with Appollonian Leo, having attained the function of standing for religious justice, civil wars, and prosperity, in the case of Jove; and for magnanimity, strength, and victory, in the case of Mars. The Moon, Venus, and Mercury are called *Companions of the Sun*; because their moving together with the Sun and their nearness to it lead them to deserve this title. Thus they have obtained dominion over universal generation.

The Moon, more humid when in conjunction with and facing the Sun, rekindles the vital warmth. It diffuses in things that are generated a warm, vivifying humor. Mercury mixes with musical proportion all the parts in things which are generated. Venus adds to the mixture beautiful forms, grace, and joy. Just as the Sun distributes light gathered altogether in itself by way of the various stars differing in aspect from one another, so also it spreads a multiplicity of powers with myriads of lights. From all these facts it is permitted us to conjecture that in the Sun there are at least as many powers as there are stars in the sky.

In Chapter VII Ficino continues to expound on the arrangements of the planets and of the constellations in relation to the Sun.

In Chapter VIII Ficino argues that the planets which are in harmony with the Sun and the Moon are happy; while those not in harmony are unhappy. He goes on to describe how the planets "salute" the Sun and the Moon.

CHAPTER IX

The Sun is the Statue of God. Comparison of the Sun with God.

HAVING contemplated all this with extreme care, our divine Plato declared the Sun to be the visible source of highest Good. He also thought that the Sun was the Visible Image of God, put by God himself in this temple of the world so that everybody, everywhere, would admire it above all else. As Plotinus says, agreeing with Plato, the ancients venerated the Sun as God. The ancient Gentile theologians placed all the gods in the Sun: Iamblichus, Julian, and Macrobius attest to this fact. Furthermore, whoever does not see that the Sun is the Image and Vicar of God on earth has, no doubt, never considered the night; has never turned his eyes to the Sun's rising; nor has he ever thought how much the Sun exceeds every sense; and how suddenly it renders alive all things which, far distant from it, appear dead. Such a one has not noticed the gifts of the Sun which make manifest what the mere totality of stars could never accomplish. As was said by Dionysius and the Platonists, let us conclude then, that the Sun, that is, Phoebus, lord of the Muses or of Intelligence, is the Visible Image of God.

Also in this tradition, Phoebe, the Moon, is an image of Phoebus in the same way that Phoebus is the image of God. As Hipparchus says, she is the mirror of the Sun which reflects upon us the light of the Sun that falls upon her. I need not here again take up that Platonic comparison which I have already treated elsewhere.

The Sun creates both the eyes and their colors; and gives to the former the ability to see and to the latter the capability of being seen. It joins both by means of light. God also acts thus in respect to all intellects and to all intelligible beings. In fact, God creates the intelligible species of things, and also the intellects, giving them the rational power which is proper to them. Then He surrounds them continuously with a common light by means of which He excites the powers of the intelligible and those of the intellects to act, joining them in action. This light is that which Plato calls truth with respect to comprehensible things, and science with respect to the mind. He thinks that the Good in itself—that is, God—transcends all these things just as the Sun transcends the light, and as eyes transcend colors.

However, when Plato says that the Sun goes beyond all that is visible, he alludes without doubt to something beyond the corporeal. He alludes to a Sun which is incorporeal—that is, to the divine Intellect. Since, however, one can ascend from the image to the model, eliminating all that is less perfect and adding what has value, one can take away from the Sun, to which Averroës denied matter, every determinate quantity. Yet power, in addition to light, can be left with it; so that the light can remain endowed with a marvelous power; not encompassed within any definite quantity or figure; extended in an infinite space, while yet filling the macrocosm with its omnipresence.

Now think of this light as surpassing intelligence in the way in which that light here below surpasses vision. You will have thus, in some fashion according to your capacity, reached the Solar Deity who has placed His tabernacle in the Sun. Also, as nothing is farther away from the divine Light than formless matter, nothing is farther away from the light of the Sun than the earth. Thus the bodies in which the terrestrial condition prevails, opaque as they are to the light, do not receive any light. This failure is not because light cannot deeply penetrate them. For light, indeed, which does not illumine the inside of wool or parchment, yet instantly penetrates crystal which is otherwise so difficult to pass through.

In the same way divine Light shines even in the darkness of the soul, although the darkness does not understand it. Is this action not also similar to that of God whose Light shines in angelic and blessed minds? It first spreads the science of divine Things, thus lighting the flame of love. Therefore, it lights here below in believers the love which purifies and converts, before giving intelligence of divine Entities.

Thus the Sun illumines instantaneously those natures which are already pure, harmonious, and celestial; whereas those that are opaque and material, it warms first with light, enlightening and purifying them so that they can be illuminated. Having been made light and transparent by warmth and illumination, they are then lifted by the Sun and made sublime. It is in this manner that Apollo pierces, purifies, and breaks up the mass of Python with his arrows, the rays.

Finally, we must not forget that just as we hope Christ, reigning in the end, will awaken from the earth all human bodies with the splendors of His Body, so every year, after the deadly winter, we await the Sun, lord of Aries, who recalls to life and to beauty the seeds of all things and all hibernating animals, hidden in the earth as if dead. For this reason it is said that Mercury, as if a messenger of the Sun, awakens sleepers with his caduceus. Even Plato describes a similar resurrection in his book, *On the Kingdom*.

CHAPTER X

The Sun was the first to be created
and was placed at the center of the sky.

WE ASK: what did God first create? Moses answers: light. Thus, rightly: for the light emanates as more than intelligible from the divine Light and is more like God than any other thing. This assertion is true for the Intelligible Light in the corporeal world above—that is, the Light of Pure Intellect. It also holds for the sensible light in the corporeal world—the light of the Sun. However, light in its first degree, which is to say, its first day, possesses only one property: to shine in itself and to illuminate from the outside. In the second degree, it empowers all things with its heat-giving life. In the third degree, it propagates itself in matter by its own power and by God's commandment. Finally, in the fourth degree of nature and of order, which is almost the fourth day, it has the power of spreading its mass in the world, just as the light of divine Intelligence from which it derives and which it reflects in itself. Thus Moses says that on the first day of creation light alone was manifested. Then, on the fourth day, it became endowed with the figure of the Sun and was made circular.

Also on this topic, Plato refers twice in the *Timaeus* to the constitutions of the Sun: the first time, ranking it almost as if it were just another among the planets; and the second time, providing it with divine Will, a truly marvelous light, and a regal authority. The majority of astrologers place the Sun at the beginning of the world, on the horizon in Aries, which is its own proper realm in the center of the sky. It sits, as if occupying a rock in the center, in the manner of a king. Even Moses, when he says that a day of creation was accomplished not with a morning and the sundown, but with sundown and a morning, indicated that after midday, when the Sun had ascended, the day already born and declining toward evening would have to complete itself the following morning. He confirmed without doubt the regal authority of the Sun, assigning to it the *Day of the Lord*, the solar day. In fact, if God created the world in six days and rested on the seventh, without doubt He must have started His work or begun the world on the same solar day, under the auspices of the same solar power.

In the same way, for His ultimate purposes, He placed Saturn, which is very distant from the Sun, as adverse to generation and to action. He also ordered that we must abstain from acting on the day of Saturn. Yet Christ, source of life, upon the occasion of whose death the Sun had covered his face and mourned in the heavens above, arose from the dead in the hour and the day of the solar ascendance. He will return to us the Intelligible Light, as the Sun gives us that which is visible light.

CHAPTER XI

That the Sun has two lights. The task of Apollo. The degrees of the light. That the Sun has in itself all things divine.

IF WE CONSIDER that creative property of the Sun's nature which was given to it at the first moment of its creation, speaking of it as but one among the other planets, we see that its first light was not so great at the beginning as it became later. In fact, it was, at first, not greater either in size or in light than the other stars. Now, however, in size it is somewhat less than the double of Jove whose light it exceeds a hundredfold. The diameter of the planets can be measured in relation to the earth. Indeed, we have already said how many times the Sun contains the earth, whereas we know that Jove is some ninety-five times the size of the earth.

The immense splendor which is added to the natural light of the Sun must therefore be different in kind and come from a different source. All heavenly bodies, in fact, brought with them at birth their own proper light; but this was feeble and unseen by us, either because of its special subtlety or clarity, or for some other reason. A similar light, or one a little greater in accordance with its size, the Sun would seem to have possessed in the beginning. Yet, to that first and native light which I shall call dark by comparison, God quickly added another, very clear to the eye—almost an image of the divine Intelligence and of the Infinite Goodness. As our theologians say, God has given our minds a double light. The first is naturally lighted in them; the second is added to them according to their merits and grace, filling them with esteemed, blessed goodness.

Since the stars are images of minds, we can by analogy suppose that they too have received two lights. In the same way that God has admirably added this immense Light to the first illumination of the Sun, so also the Sun, Vicar of God, soon added to the native light of the stars its own brilliance. In the sense in which we ordinarily say the light of the Moon is not the Moon's own light, but the Sun's light reflected toward us by it, we can further say on the basis of secret Platonic teachings that this immense splendor of the Sun does not come from it, but from God through it. Hence, this Light, manifested to the eyes, belongs not to the solar globe but to God himself.

Without any doubt, when God endowed the solar sphere with so much splendor, giving to such a small part of the sky so great a power that its singular glory poured over the whole. He meant to declare with supreme evidence that the small mass of the Sun did not derive from itself, but from a Higher Source. It is His incomparable gift: for all the energies and materials of the Sun derive from this single Godhead and are promulgated from Him. Just as the sensible light of this Sun illumines, gives life and form, and turns toward the heavens every creature of sense, so, in the same way does the Intelligible Light in the very soul of the Sun illumine, engulf, and call unto itself the intimate eyes of the soul.

Because of this phenomenon, I believe that the ancient theologians called Apollo *the Sun*; and considered him *Author of every Harmony* and *Leader of the Muses*. Apollo liberates souls from disturbance and confusion. He does this service not so much with manifest powers, but with the hidden influence of his rays, harmoniously regulating them, and guiding them finally toward intelligence. Therefore, it is important that we not believe that this Light which is greatest, most efficacious, the best and most perfect gift in the world, draws its first origin from the weak light of the mass of the Sun. We know it splays out from the Good itself, which is the Father of Light, in which every light is more than intelligible and transcends every intelligence. From this height, descending into the divine or angelic Intellect, it becomes intelligible but not yet comprehensible to us. Then, coming into the earthly mind of the soul, it becomes intellectual and comprehensible to us. Finally, passing to the sky, it becomes both sensual and sensible; until at last, precipitating in lower things, it seems almost to divide, becoming sentient to the eyes of living beings and to sensible objects, preserving both of these characters in a few who see it at night.

But let us return to the beginning. According to the Platonists the principles are three: the *Good in itself*, the *divine Intellect*, and the *Soul of the World*. The light which openly refers everything to itself is one. It reveals in fact the *Good in itself*; since while it admirably exceeds all things, it spreads in everything, sublimating them while maintaining intact its own proper intelligence. It expresses *divine Intellect*, because it declares, distinguishes, and adorns everything. And further, the *Soul of the World* generates, moves, and warms everything by its vital heat. In the same manner through the three supercelestial principles, descending in and underneath the sky, manifesting them, it represents the *Good in itself* through the Sun in the sky. The *divine Intellect*, the fullness of ideas, becomes manifest through the firmament full of stars. Finally, the *Soul of the World* symbolizes the changeable light of the Moon. On earth the first of these is represented through fire, the second through air, and the third through water.

As the greater stars are illuminated immutably by the Sun, and as silently the Moon receives its light from the Sun, so are the angels and human souls immutably illuminated by God.

CHAPTER XII

The similarity of the Sun with the divine Trinity and the nine orders of angels. The nine divinities that are in the Sun and the nine orders around the Sun.

NOTHING can be found in the world which resembles the divine Trinity more than the Sun. In the single substance of the Sun, there are to be found in fact three things which are united and yet distinct from one another. First of all the *natural fecundity completely hidden from our senses;* second, the *manifest light* which pours forth from its fecundity and is always equal to it; and third, the *calorific virtue* which derives from both powers and is equal to both. The *fecundity* represents the Father; the *light* similar to intelligence represents the Son conceived according to intelligence; and the *heat* represents the Spirit of Love.

Regarding the divine Trinity, our theologians posit three hierarchies of angels, each of which contains three orders. The first is consecrated to the Father, the second to the Son, and the third to the Spirit. Analogically, we find a ternary and a tri-ternary connected with the solar trinity. From the *fecund nature* of the Sun proceed in fact three natural fecundities: the *celestial nature,* the *simple nature of the elements,* and the *nature of mixed entities.* Again, a threefold life is propagated from the *vital heat* of the Sun: *vegetative,* in plants; *sensible but motionless;* and *sensible with movement,* as in more advanced animals. Finally, from the *light of the Sun* come three kinds of brightness, which are found in the sky or under the sky: *white, red,* and *mixed.*

Indeed, light is in every way self-identical, almost an embryonic consciousness, and above all the beginning of sense experience. It is so called quite rightly, for to the three species of light there seem to correspond also three species of sense: to the *red* the *corporeal sense,* that is, touch and taste; to the *white* light the *incorporeal sense*, imagination and sight; to the *mixed* light the *intermediary senses*, hearing and smelling. Up to this point, the Sun's light is not merely image, but also cause. Of Pure Intelligence it is only the image; but just as Pure Intelligence it operates in an instant, penetrating at depth, illuminating, and not mixing with anything. Thus light spreads instantaneously on all beings, revealing single things while remaining everywhere invisible, not mixing with anything. When the Sun disappears, light does not remain in the air even for an instant, accompanying Lord Phoebus away.

However, because we are under this Apollo, we are almost turned into poets in a way that I cannot clearly express. Even if we are not good poets, we are allowed to become inventive and inspired with heroic tales. We are stimulated first of all, as Plato has it, by the higher gods, and then by the nine Muses.

The ancients placed all the gods in the Sun. This is understandable because we can, in fact, even now realize the substance and the power of the Sun. In the substance we can see *the essence, the life,* and *the intelligence.* We call *the essence* the sky, Thea *the life,* and Saturn *the intelligence,* respectively. If, after the substance, we contemplate the powers of the Sun, we shall call its *fecundity* Jove and Juno; its *light,* we would call Apollo and Minerva; and its *heat* Venus and Bacchus. The ancients always represented Phoebus and Bacchus as young, and dominant in the Sun. Indeed, if one knows how to appropriate for his own use the light and the heat of the Sun together with the purity and the properties which these have in the Sun; he will attain eternal youth, or will live for at least one hundred solar years.

Now after these nine gods which are internal to the Sun, let us pass to the nine Muses around the Sun. What, in truth, are the nine Muses that surround Phoebus, if not the nine kinds of Apollonian divinities, distributed in the nine spheres of the world? The ancients knew only eight skies; yet under the celestial fire, there is a ninth sky in which they placed pure air, celestial in its quality and motion. In each one of the spheres they then placed divine spirits, invisible to the eye, devoted in orderly fashion to the single stars which Proclus calls *Angels*, and Iamblichus calls *Archangels and Dominations*. The spirits that are everywhere properly solar by their very nature were called *Muses* by most of the ancients. These were assigned to all the sciences; and to poetry, music, and medicine in particular, and also to the Dominations and Powers and Prophecies.

But let us return to the Sun. Small things, just so they be rare, we admire too much; ordinary things, even if great, we have long ceased to admire, out of blindness and ingratitude. No one admires fire, which is as fervent as the sky and the Sun, pure and unmixed, perennially mobile, magnificent, and which from nothing can quickly become very great, reducing everything to itself. Hence, no one sufficiently admires the Sun, which is incomparably greater than anything else, Father and Regulator of all things—that same Sun which makes happy what is sad and brings to life the things that are dead. If once a year the house of the omnipotent Olympians were opened, and many great splendors were suddenly shown, everyone would admire the Sun above all else. All would adore the Sun as a Supreme God, or at least no one would ever doubt that the Sun is a divine Messenger. To the hidden God, they would render daily thanks for such a great gift. To make this point, Iamblichus, Julian, and all the Platonists invite us to imagine a night completely devoid of light from the Moon and the stars, both of which are manifest gifts from the Sun itself, so that we may better understand what life would be like without the Sun, and how much we owe to it.

CHAPTER XIII

That the Sun must not be adored as the Author of Everything.

MORE THAN ONCE did Socrates remain transfixed, contemplating the rising Sun on the battlefield, standing astonished with set eyes like a statue, in order to salute the return of the Star. The Platonists, led by these and similar signs, will probably say that Socrates, inspired since his childhood by a solar daemon, was in the habit of venerating the Sun above all else; and that it was for this reason that the oracle of Apollo proclaimed him the wisest among all Greeks. I will not here discuss the question of whether Socrates' daemon must be thought angel or genius. However, I shall affirm with confidence that Socrates, in his ecstatic seizures, contemplated not this Sun but the Other. Since only novelty surprises us, why would he be amazed by the Sun he saw everyday, whose movements and powers had long been calculated by mathematics and physics? According to Plato, he did not call on the Sun, but the Son of God. Not the first Sun of God, but the second, and therefore almost visible. The true first Son of God, in fact, is not this Sun manifest to our eyes, but that Intellect so far superior: the first and only Intelligible Intellect.

Hence, Socrates, caught by the celestial Sun which was pointing to the Supercelestial One, contemplated its majesty and admired in rapture the incomprehensible Goodness of the Father. This illumination the apostle James called the *Father of Light*: of the Light, I say, which is more than celestial, the Light which knows neither change nor setting.

Those things, in fact, which are Supercelestial are naturally immutable. Celestial things are susceptible to rising and setting, and the things under the sky become obscured daily. Therefore every Good which is naturally inherent in the mind, every perfect gift beyond natural endowments, does not come from the Sun and the mundane stars, but from Higher Sources—from the Father of all Light. With the power of intelligence at a scale which is not celestial but Supercelestial, we can rise beyond the skies—to where we can know, love, and venerate Things which are superior to the heavens themselves. Above all, we can worship the Maker of the Sky. In any case, if our intelligence came to us only from the sky, we would not be able to understand incorporeal beings beyond the sky. Therefore, so that no one be led to admire or to adore the Sun, the Moon, and the stars to excess, venerating them as Author, and as Father of intellectual gifts, we are wisely admonished that this Sun is not the Principle of the Universe.

I shall not on this occasion expound the reason according to which in our theology the Principle of the Universe can be neither body, nor soul, nor intellect, but must, rather, be something infinitely higher from which the Sun of the heavens is very distant, and represents rather more a shadow than it does an Image of the Original. Instead, I shall summarize briefly James's argument. Since immobility or quietude is the principle, the rule, and the end of motion, and is more perfect than any motion, therefore God, Sustainer of All, cannot be in motion. The power of the Principle, being infinite, touches everything and is held back by nothing. The power of the Sun, on the contrary, operating as it does through rays, is impeded in various ways by whatever obstacles are opposed to them. Its strength is weakened by the opposition of the Moon, and it is also many times held back by the clouds. Furthermore, it is stopped by the density of the earth, and its rays are lessened by spatial distances. The Sun itself is nothing but a small part of the world, enclosed within a narrow space, drawn in every way by its own sphere, and is constantly pushed back by the higher sphere against the motion of its own. It is impeded by contrary signs and adverse stars, and is at times, if I may say so, weakened by malignant configurations.

Finally, the Principle of the Universe works in its entirety in every place and in everything. But the Sun does not produce the globes of the world, nor can it make by its own power cold, humid, dense, and similar things. Such powers, if they are in the sky, cannot have their origin in the Sun. Nevertheless, although the Sun is very different from the Creator of the world, all heavenly things are by divine Law related to the one Sun, lord and measure of the Sky.

I say these things so that we may be warned that all that is in the sky, under the heavens, and above the firmament, must ultimately be referred to the Principle of All Things. Considered thus, we must venerate the Single Principle with the same devotion that all the celestial beings of the sky have for the Sun.

GIOVANNI PICO DELLA MIRANDOLA

Oration

ON THE DIGNITY OF MAN

I HAVE READ, most reverend Fathers, in ancient Arabic writings, that upon being asked what it was that seemed to him most marvelous upon the world stage, as one might call it, Abdala the Saracen replied that nothing to be seen was more wonderful than man. This opinion is echoed, as well, in that famous remark of Hermes Trismegistus: "What a great miracle is man, Asclepius."

Still, as I pondered upon the grounds given for these estimates, I was not particularly struck by the different reasons advanced by different people for the assignment of such pre-eminence to human nature. It is said, for example, that man is intermediate among creatures; that he is the equal of the gods above as he is master over the beings beneath; that he, set midway between the eternal and the temporal, is the interpreter of nature by reason of the acuity of his sense, the light of his intellect, and the probing of his reason; that he, as the Persians have it, is a living unity, the world's very marriage hymn; and but a bit below the angels, according to David.

Now without doubt these statements are all quite powerful; still, they do not go to the core of the matter to touch upon the principal grounds which might justify man's unique right to such boundless praise. I asked, why should we not admire the angels and the heavenly choir more than man?

At last I feel that I have come to understand why it is that man, the most fortunate of all living things, deserves universal admiration; of what his proper place is in the hierarchy of beings that makes him the envy not only of brutes, but as well of the astral beings and the very intelligences which inhabit the world's outer limits—a being beggaring belief and smiting the soul with awe.

And why should this not be so? Is it not precisely on this ground that man, with full justification is considered to be, as he is called, a great miracle? Hear then, O Fathers, just what the condition of man is; and grant me, in the name of your humanity, your gracious hearing, as I develop this theme.

God the Father, Almighty Architect, in accord with His mysterious Wisdom had already created this sensible world, this cosmic habitation of divinity, this most revered temple; He had already dressed the supercelestial arena with intelligences, informed the celestial spheres with the life of immortal souls, and set the dung-heap of the inferior world into ferment, swarming with every form of animal life; but when all this was accomplished, The divine Artificer still felt the lack of some creature capable of comprehending the meaning of so great an achievement—a creature which might be stirred with love at its beauty, and struck with awe at its grandeur. Thus, after the completion of all else—as both Moses and Timaeus witness—finally, He conceived of man's creation.

However, in truth, there was left to Him no archetype according to which He might form this new being. His treasures, all but spent, contained nothing fit with which to endow a new son; nor among the seats of the universe was there left a place from which this new creature might comprehend the world. All space was already taken; all beings had been relegated to their proper high, middle, or low order. But the Father's Power was such that it would not falter in this last creative urge; nor was it in the nature of the Supreme Wisdom to fail through lack of counsel in this matter; nor, finally, was it in the nature of His Beneficent Love to create a creature destined to praise the divine Generosity in all other things, who lacked it in himself.

The Super Maker, at last, decreed that this creature to whom He could give nothing uniquely his own, should share in the heritage of all other creatures. Taking this creature of indeterminate image, man, He therefore set him in the center of the world and spoke to him thus:

O Adam, We have given you neither visage nor endowment uniquely your own, so that whatever place, form, or gifts you may select after pondering the matter, you may have and keep through your own judgment and decision. All other creatures have their natures defined and limited by laws which We have established; you, by contrast, unimpeded by any such limits, may, by your own free choice, to whose custody We have assigned you, establish the features of your own nature. I have set you at the center of the world so that from that position you may search about you with the greater ease upon all that is in the world contained. We have made you a creature neither of heaven nor of earth, neither mortal nor immortal, so that you may freely and proudly make yourself in the form which you wish. It will be in the orbit of your power to descend to the inferior and brutish form of life, just as it will be within your power to rise, through your own choice, to the superior orders of divine life.

O boundless generosity of God the Father! O admirable and unsurpassable happiness of man to whom it is given to have what he chooses, and to be what he wills to be! From the moment of their birth or, to quote Lucilius, "from their mother's womb," the brute creatures carry with them all that they will ever possess. Again, the highest spiritual beings, from the moment of their creation, or soon thereafter, were fixed in the mode of being which would be theirs throughout eternity. But it was to man alone, at the moment of his creation, that God bequeathed seeds laden with all potentialities—the germs of every form of life. Whichsoever of these a man cultivates will mature and bear fruit within him; if vegetative, he will become a plant; if sensitive, a brute; if rational, he will discover himself a heavenly being; if intellectual, he will be an angel and the son of God. Again, if he should draw himself to himself alone, because of dissatisfaction with the lot of all creatures, he will there find and become united in spirit with God: and within the solitary darkness of the Father who is above all, he will himself transcend all.

Who then will fail to look with awe or will look with greater admiration upon any being other than this, our chameleon? For man is the creature whom Asclepius the Athenian correctly observed to be symbolized in the Mysteries by the figure of Proteus because of his mutability—his nature capable of self-transformation. This is the origin of those metamorphoses or transformations so celebrated among the Hebrews and the Pythagoreans. For in the hidden theological teachings of the Hebrews, holy Enoch at times is transformed into that divine angel which is sometimes called *Mal 'akh Adonay Shebaoth,* while at other times other personages are transformed into other named divinities. The Pythagoreans transform men found guilty of crimes into brutes, or—if we are to believe Empedocles—

even into plants; while Mohammed, following them, was known to have said on many occasions that the man who forsakes divine Law becomes a brute. What is more, he was right; for it is not the bark that makes the tree, but rather its nonsensitive and unresponsive nature. Neither is it the hide that makes the beast of burden, but rather its brute and sensitive soul; nor is it the bowl-like form which makes the heavens, but rather their harmonious order. Finally, it is its spiritual intelligence, rather than its freedom from a body, which makes the angel.

Should you see a man devoted to his appetites crawling along the ground, you see then a plant and not a man. And should you see a man enchanted by the vain forms of imagery, as if by the spells of Calypso, and seduced through these empty wiles into becoming slave to his own senses, you see then a brute and not a man. If, however, you see a philosopher, judging and considering all things according to the rule of reason, you see then a creature worthy of veneration—for he is a creature of heaven and not of earth. And if, finally, you observe a pure knower—one who, unmindful of the body, is wholly withdrawn into the inner chambers of the mind—here, indeed, is one who is creature of neither heaven nor earth, but some higher divinity draped about in human flesh.

Who now will not look with wonder upon man? Upon man who, with good reason, is sometimes called "all flesh" and sometimes "every creature" in the holy Mosaic and Christian writings, because he shapes, forms, and transforms himself into the likeness of all flesh and takes on the characteristics of every creature. This is the reason why Euanthes the Persian writes in his exposition of the Chaldean theology that man has no single innate and fixed nature but, rather, many which are external and contingent. Hence, the Chaldean maxim: *Hanorish tharah sharinas*—"Man is a being of varied, manifold and ever-changing nature."

What is the point of all this? That we may understand that since we are born creatures who may be what we choose ourselves to be, we are responsible, above all, for seeing that it could never be said of us that being born to this high estate we failed to recognize it and descended to the condition of brutes and stolid beasts of burden; and for seeing, as well, that we verify the saying of Asaph the prophet: "You are all gods and sons of the Most High"; and, finally, that we may not, through abuse of the Most Indulgent father's generosity, pervert the free choice which He has granted us by forging a tool of damnation out of His gift of salvation.

Let a species of holy ambition capture our souls, so that, disdainful of mediocrity, we burn after superior things and —since it is in our power to do so—direct all of our energies to their acquisition. Let us despise the things of earth; let us not overevaluate even the astral; let us, putting all the things of this world behind us, hasten to that arena beyond the world which is closest to the Most Exalted Godhead. There, as the sacred mysteries have it, the Seraphim, Cherubim, and Thrones occupy the first places; still, while contemptuous of any secondary place and unable to yield first to them, let us emulate their dignity and glory. In this way, by willing it, we shall be lesser than they in nothing.

How are we to proceed, and what shall we do in order to realize this ambition? Let us see what they do; what sort of life they lead. For if we lead this kind of life—as it is in our power to do—we shall then attain the same noble estate as they. The Seraphim burns with the fire of love; from the Cherubim there bursts forth the brilliance of intelligence; and the Throne is resolute with the steadfastness of justice. So, in our lives, if we rule over our inferiors with justice we shall be as firm as Thrones. If, devoting ourselves to intellect we meditate upon the Creator in His creature and the creature in its Creator, and free ourselves from external activity, we shall burn with the light of the Cherubim. And if we are consumed with love for the Creator only, His all-embracing fire will at once transform us into the fiery likeness of the Seraphim. God, Judge of Ages, is above the just judge—above the Throne, that is. Higher than the Cherub—he who contemplates, that is—God flies and cherishes him in watching over him. For the spirit of the

Lord moves upon the waters—those waters, which are above the Firmament and which, according to Job, praise the Lord with hymns before the dawn. Whoever is a Seraph —a lover—is in God, and God is in him; it may even be said that God and he are one. Great is the power of Thrones, which we attain by using judgment; and most high the sublimity of Seraphim, which we attain by loving.

But how is it possible for one to judge or to love that which he does not know? Moses loved a God whom he saw and, as judge of his people, he administered among them that which he had first seen upon the mountain. The Cherub is, therefore, intermediary, and by his light prepares us equally for the fire of the Seraphim and the judgment of Thrones. This is the bond which binds the first minds, the Palladian order, the master of contemplative philosophy. This, then, is the bond which we must emulate, embrace, and understand above all else; the bond by means of which we may ascend to the heights of love, or descend, well instructed and ready, to the tasks of the practical life. But surely, if we are to pattern our life on the model provided by the Cherubim, it is worth the effort to have constantly before our eyes both its nature and quality, as well as its offices and functions. Since, flesh as we are, and in possession only of knowledge touching on earthly things, it is not granted us to acquire such knowledge by our own efforts; let us seek the counsel of the ancient Fathers. They can provide us the fullest and most authentic testimony concerning these matters because they were familiar and conversant with them.

Let us ask the apostle Paul, the chosen vessel, in what activity he saw the armies of the Cherubim engaged when he was transported to the third heaven. According to the interpretation of Dionysius, he will answer that he saw them first being purified, then illuminated, then, at the last, made perfect. We, therefore, emulating the life of the Cherub here on earth, may likewise purify our souls so that her passions may not rave at random or her reason be deranged by restraining the impulses of our passions through moral science; and by dissipating the darkness of reason through dialectic, thus washing away, so to say, the filth of ignorance and vice. Next, let us fill our purified souls with the light of natural philosophy so that it may be brought, at the last, to final perfection by knowledge of things divine.

But lest we be satisfied to consult with those of our faith only, let us have recourse to the patriarch Jacob, whose likeness, carved on the throne of glory, shines out before us. This wisest of the Fathers, who, though asleep in the lower world keeps watch on the upper, will guide us. He will advise us, however, in a figure: for all things appeared in figures to the men of those times. A ladder rises by many rungs from earth to the peaks of heaven, and at its summit sits the Lord; over its rungs move the contemplative angels, descending and ascending by turn.

Now, if this is what we who wish to emulate the life of the angels must do, then who, I ask, would dare place filthy feet or soiled hands to the ladder of the Lord? As the mysteries teach, it is forbidden for the impure to handle what is pure. But these hands and feet of which we speak—what are they? The feet of the soul, to be sure: the soul's most despicable part—that by which the soul is held to the earth as a root to the ground. Its nourishing and feeding part, that is, where lust boils and voluptuous softness is fostered. And is not the hand of which we spoke the soul's irascible power? That which struggles in its behalf, fighting and foraging for it in the filth and in the sun, seizing for it all the things which it will devour while slumbering in the shade? Let us purify ourselves—our hands—in moral philosophy as in a living stream: the whole sentient part, that is, in which the body's lusts are seated and which, as the saying goes, holds the soul by the scruff of the neck—lest we be flung from the ladder as profane and unclean. But even this, if we wish to be the familiar of the angels who climb the ladder of Jacob, will not be enough unless we are first taught and rendered able to advance, step by step, on that ladder without deviating and without failing to complete the ascents and descents in their proper turn. When by the art of discourse or reason we shall have been properly prepared, then, inspired by the Cherubic spirit, employing philosophy through the steps of the ladder—the ladder, that is, of nature—we shall penetrate all things from center to center. We shall at one instant descend, sundering the unity of the many, like the limbs of Osiris, with Titanic power; at another instant, we shall ascend, collecting by the power of Phoebus those same limbs into their original unity. At the last, in the bosom of the Father who reigns above the ladder, we shall find perfection and peace through the felicity of theology.

Of just Job who made his covenant with God even before he was born, let us also inquire what it is, above all else, that the Supreme God wishes of those scores of beings which surround Him. Without a doubt he will answer, "Peace." For, as is written in Job, "He establishes peace in the high vaults of heaven." And just as the middle order interprets the warnings of the higher for the lower orders, so the words of Job the theologian may well be interpreted for us by Empedocles the philosopher. Empedocles teaches that there is a dual nature to our souls: one bears us upward to the heavenly reaches, while the other drags us to the nether regions, through friendship and discord, war and peace, as he testifies in those verses in which he makes complaint that he is being driven into the sea-depths, goaded as he is by strife and discord into the semblance of a lunatic and a refugee from the gods.

It is clear, Fathers, that many forces contend within us in deadly intestine war, worse than the civil wars of states. It is equally clear that if we bring about that peace which will place us at last among the elect of God, this will have been accomplished through philosophy alone. To begin with, if we seek only a truce with our enemies, moral philosophy will halt the unreasoning drives of the many-sided brute, the passionate violence and anger of the lion within us. If, acting on wiser counsel, we seek to achieve a lasting peace, moral philosophy will still be available to abundantly fulfill our wants. After both beasts are felled, like a sacrificed sow, an inviolable covenant of peace between flesh and spirit will have been accomplished. Dialectic will soothe those disorders of reason engendered by the anxiety and uncertainty of conflicting hordes of words and captious reasoning; natural philosophy will compose the conflict of opinions and the endless disputes which vex, distract, and tear at the spirit from all sides. Natural philosophy will assuage this conflict, however, in such a way as to remind us that nature, as Heraclitus wrote, is generated by war, and, for this reason, is repeatedly called "strife" by Homer. Natural philosophy, therefore, cannot assure us a true and inviolable peace; the bestowal of such a peace is rather the privilege and office of the Queen of the Sciences, most holy theology. At best, moral philosophy only points the way to theology—it may even accompany us along the path—but theology, seeing us hastening to draw near to her from afar, calls out: "Come to me ye who have labored and I will restore you; come to me and I shall give you the peace which the world and nature cannot give."

Summoned so comfortingly, and invited with such kindness, we shall fly, like earthly Mercurys, on winged feet to greet that most blessed mother, and there enjoy the peace for which we have yearned: that unbounded friendship through which all souls will be at one in that one Mind which transcends all others; and, in a manner which beggars description, we shall attain true unity in the most profound depths of being. It is the attainment of this friendship that, as the Pythagoreans say, is the aim of all philosophy. It is this peace that God established in the high places of heaven, and which the angels, descending to earth, proclaimed to men of good will, so that men, ascending by means of this peace to heaven, might become angels. This is the peace that we would wish for our friends, for our age, for every home into which we enter, and for our own soul, so that it may, through this peace, become the dwelling place of God. So also, when the soul shall have purged herself of all stain by means of moral philosophy and dialectic, and adorned herself with the many disciplines of philosophy as with princely raiment, and crowned her portals with the wreaths of theology, the King of Glory may descend and, entering with the Father, domicile with her. Should she prove worthy of so magnificent a Visitor, she will, through His boundless clemency, draped in the golden gown of the many sciences as in bridal vesture, welcome Him, not as a guest but as a spouse from whom she will never be parted. Indeed, rather than part with Him, she will prefer to leave her own people and her father's home. Mindless of her very self, she will wish to be dead to herself in order to live in her spouse, in whose eyes the death of His saints is infinitely precious: I mean that death —if the very fullness of life may be so called—the consideration of which wise men have asserted to be the end of philosophy.

Let us cite, as well, Moses himself, who is but at a little remove from the living fountain of the holy and unutterable wisdom with whose nectar the angels are drunk. Let us harken to the venerable judges as he proclaims his laws to us who live in the arid loneliness of the body: "Let those who, still profane, have need of moral philosophy, dwell with the herd outside the tabernacle under the open sky until, like the priests of Thessaly, they shall have purified themselves. Those who have already ordered their conduct may enter into the tabernacle: but they may not yet touch the sacred vessels. Let them first, as zealous Levites, in the service of dialectic, minister to the holy offices of philosophy. When they shall have been admitted to those offices they may, as priests of philosophy, gaze upon the multicolored throne of the higher God: the stars. Let them then behold the heavenly candelabra aflame with its seven lights. Let them then behold the fur tent, that is, the elements, in the priesthood of philosophy, so that, at last, having been granted entry to the innermost bosom of the temple through divine theology, they may be made glad in the glory of the Godhead, viewed with no veil before His image." Clearly, this is what Moses commands: admonishing, urging, and summoning us to prepare for ourselves, while we may, by means of philosophy, a path to heavenly glory to come.

Now the dignity of the liberal arts, which I am about to discuss, and the value that they have for us, is testified to in the Mosaic and Christian religions as well as in the most ancient theologies. What else can we understand by the degrees through which the initiates must pass in the mysteries of the Greeks? These neophytes, after their purification by the sciences which we might refer to as expiatory—moral philosophy and dialectic, that is—were granted admission to the mysteries. What else could such admission portend but the interpretation of occult nature by philosophy? Only after they had been prepared thus, did they receive *epopteia*—the direct vision of divine things by the light of theology. Who would not wish to be initiated into such mysteries? Who could not consent to put behind him all human concerns, scorn the gifts of fortune and reject the goods of the body, in order thus to become a guest of the gods, drunk with the nectar of eternity, and receive the gift of immortality while still an earthbound mortal? Who would refuse to be so inspired by those Socratic frenzies celebrated by Plato in the *Phaedrus*, that swiftly fleeing this place, this evil world, by the oars, so to say, of both feet and wings, he might attain swiftly to the heavenly Jerusalem? Let us, O Fathers, be thus driven: driven by those Socratic frenzies which elevate us to such ecstasy that our intellect and our very being become one with God. Indeed, this will be our lot if we have previously done all that lies within us to do. If we shall have restrained our passions with proper controls—moral philosophy—so that they achieve harmonious accord; and if—by dialectic—our reason shall have progressed by rhythmic measures, then, stirred by the frenzy of the Muses, we shall drink in the heavenly harmony with the ears of the spirit. Then Bacchus, leader of the Muses, revealing to us in our study of philosophy, through his mysteries—the visible signs of nature—the invisible things of God, will dazzle us with the richness of the house of God; and there, if like Moses we prove wholly faithful, most sacred theology will supervene to swell our ecstasy. For, risen to her lofty height, we shall from that vantage survey all that is, shall be, and has been in seamless eternity; and marveling at their pristine loveliness, like the seers of Phoebus, we shall become her winged lovers. Finally, roused by ineffable love as by a sting, and, like the Seraphim, born outside ourselves, drunk with the Godhead, we shall be, no longer ourselves, but He himself who made us.

To anyone who grasps their meanings and the mysteries involved in them, the sacred names of Apollo clearly show that God is a philosopher as well as a seer. Ammonius has amply discussed this theme, however, and there is no need for me to develop it anew. Yet, O Fathers, we cannot fail to remark those three Delphic teachings which are so basic for one about to enter the most holy and august temple of the true Apollo who illumines every soul as it enters this world. These, you shall see, give us no advice other than that we should with all our might embrace this tripartite philosophy which we are here discussing. The saying *meden agan*, that is, "Nothing too much," prescribes a standard for all the virtues through the Doctrine of the Mean, which is that of which moral philosophy treats. Again, that other saying, *gnothi seauton*, that is, "Know thyself," urges and encourages us to the study of all nature, of which the nature of man is both connecting link and, so to speak, the "mixed potion"; for he who knows himself knows all things in himself, as first Zoroaster, and then Plato in the *Alcibiades*, wrote. At last, lighted in this knowledge through the aid of natural philosophy, being already close to God, employing the theological greeting *ei*, that is, "Thou art," we shall blissfully address the true Apollo on intimate terms.

Let us seek also the opinion of Pythagoras, that most sage of men, known as a sage precisely because he never deemed himself worthy to be so called. He will first advise us "Never to sit on a bushel"—never, that is, through disuse to lose our reasoning power, that faculty by which the mind proves, judges, and measures all things, but, rather, by the constant use of dialectic to guide and keep that faculty vital. Then he will admonish us concerning the two things which are to be eschewed at all costs: neither to make water facing the sun, nor to pare our nails while offering sacrifice. But only after we have, through the agency of moral philosophy, both voided the debilitating appetite of our too abundant pleasures, and cut away, like nail-clippings, the prickly points of anger and wrath in our souls, can we finally begin to take part in the sacred rites, that is, the mysteries of Bacchus of which we have spoken, and to dedicate ourselves to that contemplation of which the Sun is correctly named father and guide. Finally, Pythagoras commands us to "Feed the cock": to nourish, that is, the divine part of our soul on knowledge of divine things, as if on solid food and heavenly ambrosia. This is the cock at whose sight the lion—all earthly power, that is—cowers in fear and awe. It is this cock to whom, as we read in Job, intelligence was given. At the crowing of this cock, erring man comes to his senses. This is the cock which, in the morning twilight of each day, raises a *Te Deum* to heaven along with the morning stars. This is the cock which Socrates, at the time of his death, when he hoped that he was about to merge the divinity of his spirit with the divinity of the higher world, and when all thought of any bodily illness was gone, said that he owed to Aesculapius, that is, to the physician of souls.

Let us also review the records of the Chaldeans and, if we can trust them, we shall see the road to felicity opened up for mortals through these same arts. The Chaldean interpreters tell us that it was a saying of Zoroaster that the soul is a winged being, and that when her wings are shed, she is plummeted into the body; but when they have grown again, she departs for the heavenly regions. And when his disciples inquired of him how they might obtain well-plumed and swift-flying souls, he is said to have replied: "Refresh ye your wings with the waters of life." And when they pressed him concerning whence they might obtain these waters of life, he replied, as was his custom, in a parable: "God's paradise is washed and watered by four rivers. From these founts you may draw the waters which will be your salvation. The river which flows from the north is called *Pischon,* which means 'The Right'; that which flows from the west is *Gichon,* that is, 'Expiation'; the river which flows from the east is called *Chiddekel,* that is, 'Light'; while the last one, flowing from the south, is *Perath,* which may be understood as 'Piety.'"

Now consider, O Fathers, what these doctrines of Zoroaster might mean. Clearly they mean that we should wash the filth from our eyes by moral science as by western waves; and that our aim must be correctly directed by dialectic as by a sighting taken on the North Star. Then, that we should develop the habit of bearing, in the contemplation of nature, the still feeble light of truth, like unto the first rays of the rising sun, so that finally we may, through theological piety and the most holy worship of God, be enabled, as heavenly eagles, to bear the most dazzling splendor of the noonday sun. It is these, perhaps, which are the "morning, midday, and evening thoughts," which David first sang and St. Augustine later developed. This is the noonday light that inspires the Seraphim toward their goal and illumines, as well, the Cherubim. This is the promised land toward which our ancient father, Abraham, was ever journeying; this is no place for impure spirits. And, if it be permissible to say anything in public about the deeper mysteries, even in the guise of a riddle—since man's sudden fall from heaven has left his mind in a dizzy whirl, and since, according to Jeremiah, death has come in through the windows to plague our hearts and vitals with evil—let us implore Raphael, the heavenly healer, to release us by moral science and dialectic, as with heavenly drugs. When we shall have once again attained health, Gabriel—the strength of God—will dwell within us. Guiding us through the marvels of nature and showing us the power and goodness of God in everything, he will consign us at last to the high priest Michael who, in turn, will reward those who have successfully completed their term in philosophy's service, with the holy office of theology, as with a crown of precious stones.

These, most reverend Fathers, are the reasons which led —nay, compelled—me to the study of philosophy. I set them forth only to reply to those who would condemn its study: not only those in high office, but those, as well, in modest situation. For the whole study of philosophy—and it is the misfortune of our time—is now regarded as contemptible and vicious rather than honorable and glorious. This lethal and monstrous conviction—that philosophy ought not be studied at all, or, at best, by very few—has taken over practically all minds; as though it were valueless to have before our eyes and at our disposal the causes of things, the ways of nature, the plan of the universe, God's counsels, and the mysteries of heaven and earth, unless by such knowledge one might procure some profit or benefit. We have reached, thus, the point, alas, where no one is deemed wise unless he can prostitute the pursuit of wisdom; and chaste Pallas, who dwells among men only by the generosity of the gods, is scorned, derided, and whistled off the scene, with no one to love or befriend her unless, by making money, she is able to recompense her lover with the foully procured price of her deflowerment.

I direct all these complaints, with the most profound disgust and indignation, not against the princes of our times, but against the philosophers, who believe and insist that philosophy should not be pursued because it brings no material reward. They are mindless that by this alone they disqualify themselves as philosophers. As their whole life is dedicated to gain and the fulfilment of worldly ambitions, they never embrace the knowledge of the truth for its own sake. This much I will say for myself—and I feel no embarrassment for praising myself on this point: I have never studied philosophy except for the sake of philosophy; nor have I ever desired or hoped to secure any profit or fruit from my studies and lamplighted researches other than the cultivation of my mind and knowledge of the truth—things I value more and more with the passage of time. I have been so keen for this knowledge, and so in love with it, that I have neglected all my private and public affairs to spend myself fully on contemplation, from which no disparagements of those who hate me, no curses of the enemies of wisdom, have ever been or will be able to divert me. Philosophy has taught me to depend on my own convictions rather than on the opinions of others, and to be less concerned with whether I am well thought of than whether what I do or say is evil.

I was not unaware, reverend Fathers, that this disputation of mine would be as acceptable and pleasing to you who favor all good sciences and who have consented to honor it with your presence, as it would be annoying and displeasing to many others. I am aware, as well, that there are many who have condemned my project before this, and continue to do so, for a number of reasons. But it has always been so: well-meant works, those genuinely intended for virtuous ends, have always had rather more than fewer detractors as compared to those works directed at questionable ends and undertaken for devious reasons. Some persons disapprove of the present species of disputation in general, as well as the method of publicly arguing learned matters; they hold that they serve only to exhibit cleverness and biases rather than to add to the stock of knowledge. Others, while not disapproving disputations in general, resent the fact that at my age, a mere twenty-four years, I have presumed in proposing a disputation dealing with the most abstruse mysteries of Christian theology, the most subtle points of philosophy, and the most exotic branches of learning; and that I have done so here, in this most celebrated of cities, before a large body of the most learned men, in the presence of the Apostolic Senate. Yet others have yielded that I have the right to dispute, but not nine hundred theses; for they hold that such an undertaking is too much, overambitious, and well beyond my powers. To these objections I should have bowed willingly, and at once, if the philosophy which I espouse would have permitted me to do so. Further, if I believed that this disputation were motivated by mere purposes of altercation and litigation, I should not here have undertaken to respond to them, as my philosophy urges me to do. Therefore, let all intention of denigration and annoyance be cleansed from our minds, and with it that malice which, as Plato says, is wholly absent in the heavenly choir. Let us decide, as friends, whether I am to be allowed to proceed with my disputation and whether I may venture to treat of so great a multitude of theses.

To begin with, I shall not have much to say against those who disapprove this species of public disputation. If it be criminal, it is a crime in which I participate with all of you, most excellent Doctors, who have yourselves engaged in such bouts on many occasions to the glory of your reputation, as well as with Plato and Aristotle and all of the most respected philosophers of every age. Philosophers of the past thought that naught would repay them more in their search for wisdom than frequent participation in public disputation. Just as the body's powers are strengthened through gymnastic, so the powers of the mind wax in strength and vigor by this manner of learning. I am inclined to the belief that when the poets sang of the arms of Pallas, and that when the Hebrews called the *barzel,* that is, the sword, the symbol of men of wisdom, meant nothing else by these symbols than this species of combat, so honorable and so necessary for the attainment of wisdom. Possibly this is also the reason why the Chaldeans cast a horoscope in which Mars confronted Mercury from three distinct angles at the birth of a man who was to be a philosopher; as if, that is, they wished to say "if these assemblies, these disputations, should be discontinued, all philosophy would become lethargic and dormant."

Now against those who claim that I am unequal to this task, I have a more difficult time defending myself. If I maintain that I am equal to it, I shall appear to entertain an immoderately high opinion of myself. If I admit that I am unequal to it, while yet persisting, I shall certainly merit the charge of being rash and imprudent. You see the difficulty of my position: I cannot, without censure, promise something about myself; nor can I, without equal censure, fail in what I promise. Perhaps I can remark the saying of Job: "The spirit is in all men"; or take consolation in what is said to Timothy: "Let no man despise your youth." But to speak out of my own conscience, I might say that there is nothing either outstanding or singular about me. I am, I admit, wedded to study and avid after the good sciences. Still I neither assume nor arrogate to myself the title of "learned." Consequently, if it is the case that I have assumed such a tremendous burden, it is not owing to ignorance of my own limitations. It is, rather, the case that I understand that in this kind of learned contest the real victory lies in being defeated. Hence even the weakest ought not to shun them, but should, indeed, seek them out as best they are able. For he who is overcome receives a benefit, and not an injury, from his conqueror. He returns home richer than he left—more learned, that is, and better armed for future combat. Inspired by such hope, though myself but a feeble soldier, I have never feared to enter so dangerous a contest against even the most strong and vigorous man. Whether, by acting so, I have been foolish, or not, may be judged best from the outcome of the battle and not from my age.

Third, I must respond to those who are shocked by the large number of theses and the variety of topics I have proposed for dispute, as though the onus, however great, rested on their shoulders and not, as it does, on mine. Surely it is unbecoming and immeasurably captious to want to set the limits for another's endeavor and, as Cicero says: "To desire moderation in a matter which is the better for being on a large scale." In undertaking this venture, but one alternative confronts me: success or failure. If I succeed, I do not see how it would be more honorable to succeed in defending ten theses than in defending nine hundred. If I fail, those who hate me will have proper grounds for disparagement, while those who love me will have occasion enough to forgive me. In so grand and important an undertaking it appears that a young man who fails through paucity of talent or learning deserves indulgence rather than chastisement. For, according to the poets: "If strength fails, surely there shall be praise for daring; and it is enough to have striven for great things." And if in our time many, in imitation of Gorgias of Leontini, have been accustomed to dispute not merely nine hundred questions, but the whole range of questions concerning all the branches of knowledge, and have incurred praise for doing so, why should I not, then, without incurring criticism, be permitted to discuss a large number of questions indeed, but questions which are at least clear and well defined? This, they answer, is unnecessary and ostentatious; I reply that in my case no superfluity is involved, but that all is necessary. If they consider the purpose of philosophy, they will then feel compelled, even against their instincts, to recognize this necessity. Those who are disciples of one or another of the philosophers—of Thomas or Scotus, for example, who today have the widest following—can indeed make trial of their particular doctrines with a few questions. I, by contrast, have trained myself so that I am the disciple of no one man. I have examined all the masters of philosophy; perused all their works; become acquainted with all schools. Consequently, I had to speak of them all in order that while defending the beliefs of one I might not seem committed to him at the cost of deprecating the rest; thus, while setting forth a few theses from some one school, I was led inevitably to set forth a great number concerning all the schools together. Nor am I to be held culpable because "wherever the gale blows me, there I remain as guest." For it was a practice among all the ancient writers never to leave unread any commentaries which might be available. Aristotle, in particular, observed this so religiously that Plato called him *anagnostes*, that is, "the reader." Clearly, it is a mark of mental narrowness to restrict oneself to a Porch or an Academy; nor is anyone justified in being the disciple of one school or philosopher unless he has first acquainted himself with them all. There is, further, in each school some unique position which is not shared by others.

Now when we turn to the men of our own faith, to whom philosophy came after all the others, we find in John Scotus both vigor and subtlety; in Thomas, solidity and consistency; in Aegidius, clarity and precision; in Francis, depth and penetration; in Albert, a sweeping sense for ultimate issues; in Henry, as it seems to me, a sublimity which inspires reverence. Among the Arabs, there is something solid and deep-rooted in Averroës; in Avempace, as well as Alfarabi, something serious and profound; in Avicenna, something divine and Platonic. Among the Greeks, philosophy was always brilliant and, above all, pure: in Simplicius, it is rich and overflowing; in Themistius, elegant and comprehensive; in Alexander, learned and consistent; in Theophrastus, well thought-out; in Ammonius, graceful and pleasing. If you look to the Platonists, to name but a few, you will, in Porphyry, be charmed by the wealth of material and by his preoccupation with things religious; in Iamblichus, you will be awed by his knowledge of occult philosophy and barbarian mysteries; in Plotinus, you will find it impossible to point to any one admirable thing, since all is admirable. The Platonists themselves, laboring over his writings, understand him only with great difficulty when, in his abstruse style, he speaks divinely about divine things, and far more than humanly of human things. I shall not remark the more recent figures, Proclus and those others who follow him, Hermias, Damascius, Olympiodorus, and several more in whom there flame that *to theion*, that is, "the divine," something which is the special mark of the Platonists.

It should be added that any school which attacks the true doctrines, and makes sport of true causes by means of clever slander, strengthens rather than weakens the truth itself, which like a glowing ember is encouraged to flame rather than die, by being thus agitated. These considerations have motivated me in my determination to bring the opinions of all schools, rather than, as some might have preferred, those of any particular coterie, to the attention of mankind. For it appeared to me that by the presentation of many schools, and the argument of many philosophical systems, that "effulgence of truth" of which Plato speaks in his *Epistles* might illumine our minds the more clearly, like the sun rising over the sea. What should our plight have been if only the philosophy of the Latins—say, Albert, Thomas, Scotus, Aegidius, Francis, and Henry—had been broadcast, while that of the Greeks and the Arabs was neglected, as all the thought of the barbarian nations was inherited by the Greeks and from the Greeks transmitted to us? In philosophy our Latins have always based themselves on the thought of foreigners, and simply perfected their work. What value would there have been in discussing natural philosophy with the Peripatetics if the Platonic Academy had not also taken part in the exchange? Indeed, the Academy's philosophy, even where it touched on divine matters, has always been esteemed as the most lofty of all philosophies, as St. Augustine bears witness. And now, for the first time, so far as I am aware—and there is nothing invidious in my saying so—this philosophy has been brought by me, after so many centuries, to the test of public disputation. And what would be the worth of all this if, having simply discussed the opinions of innumerable authors, we—like free-loaders at a banquet of wise men—should contribute nothing of our own: nothing conceived and worked out by our own mind? It is, indeed, the earmark of the impotent, as Seneca writes, to have all their learning inscribed in notebooks, as though the discoveries of our predecessors had blocked the road to us, as though the power of nature were lacking to us and could bring nothing forth which, if not capable of demonstrating the truth, might at least point to it from afar. The rustic hates sterility in his field; the husband, in his wife: much more, then, must the divine mind hate the sterile mind to which it is yoked, because it desires in vain from that dam to have noble offspring.

These are the reasons why I have not been satisfied to mouth well-worn doctrines, but have proposed for disputation, instead, many points of the early theology of Hermes Trismegistus, many theses drawn from the doctrines of the Chaldeans, Pythagoreans, the occult mysteries of the Hebrews, and finally, a large number of propositions concerning both natural philosophy and God, which were discovered and studied by me. First, I have proposed a harmony between Plato and Aristotle. Many before have believed this harmony to obtain, but no one has ever established it. Among the Latins, Boethius promised to establish such a harmony, but he never carried his proposal to the end. Among the Greeks, Simplicius made the same promise, with like outcome. St. Augustine also writes, in his *Contra academicos,* that others had attempted to prove it, and with the most subtle arguments. John the Grammarian, for example, held that Plato differed from Aristotle only for those who did not understand Plato—but he left it to posterity to prove that their philosophies were identical. I cite, moreover, a great number of passages drawn from Scotus' and Thomas' writings, as well as from Averroës' and Avicenna's, which, traditionally regarded as irreconcilable, I prove to be wholly in accord with one another.

In the second place, along with my own expansion of both the Platonic and the Aristotelian philosophies, I have set forth seventy-two theses in physics and metaphysics such that, if I am not completely wrong—and this will become clear in the course of the disputation—anyone who subscribes to them will be able to answer any question put to him on the subject of natural philosophy or theology: and this based upon a principle entirely different from any contained in the philosophy that is current in the schools or taught by any contemporary master. Nor should anyone be surprised that I, in my early youth, at such a tender age that I should barely be permitted to read the works of others, as some have hinted, should wish to propose a new philosophy. Rather, if it is well defended, they ought to praise this new philosophy; or if it is refuted, reject it. Finally, since it will be their duty to evaluate my discoveries and my scholarship, they ought to look to the merit or fault which these show, rather than to the number of their author's years.

In addition, I have introduced a new method of doing philosophy—a method based on numbers. This approach, in truth, is very old, having been cultivated by the ancient theologians: first by Pythagoras, and then by Aglaophamos, Philolaus, Plato, and the earliest Platonists. However, like so many other noteworthy achievements of the past, it has fallen into such disuse, owing to the carelessness of subsequent generations, that hardly any traces of it are to be found. Plato writes, in the *Epinomis,* that the science of numbering is supreme, and the most divine among all the liberal arts and theoretical sciences. In another place, asking why man is the wisest of animals, he replies: "Because he knows how to count"—a view in which Aristotle, in his *Problems,* concurs. Albumazar writes that a favorite saying of Avenzoar of Babylon was: "He knows all things who knows how to count." These opinions are devoid of any truth if, by the art of number, they intend that art in which merchants are most proficient. Plato confirms this, warning us emphatically not to confuse divine arithmetic with the arithmetic of the marketplace. I therefore promised, when I appeared, after many long nights of study, to have discovered that arithmetic which is so highly regarded, that I would myself, in order to put it to the test, respond in public through the art of number to seventy-four questions considered of prime importance in physics and metaphysics.

I have proposed, as well, certain theses concerning magic, in which I have indicated that magic has two forms: one consists entirely in the operations and powers of demons, which, as God is my witness, appears to me to be a distorted and monstrous business; and the other, as it proves when thoroughly investigated, is nothing other than the highest realization of natural philosophy. The Greeks knew both these forms. But as they considered the first form to be wholly an aberration, they named it *goeteia*, reserving the term *mageia* for the second form, and understanding by it the highest and most perfect wisdom. The Persian term, *magus*, according to Porphyry, means "interpreter" and "worshiper of the divine" in our tongue. What is more, Fathers, the disparity and dissimilarity between these arts is as great as one could possibly imagine. Not only the Christian but all religions and every well-structured state despises and condemns the first; while the second, by contrast, is approved and respected by all the wise and by all peoples solicitous of heavenly and divine things. The first is the most meretricious of arts; the second, an exalted and holy philosophy. The first is empty and frustrating; the second, firm, well founded, and gratifying. The disciple of the first tries to conceal his practices because they are shameful and unholy; while cultivation of the second has always been the source of highest glory and renown in the arena of knowledge. No philosopher of merit, eager in the study of the beneficial arts, ever devoted himself to the first; but to command the second, Pythagoras, Empedocles, Plato, and Democritus crossed the seas.

They, in turn, returning to their homeland, taught it to others and deemed it a priceless possession, well worth watching over. As the first can be supported by no true arguments, it is never defended by reputable thinkers; the second, esteemed by the most celebrated fathers, so to say, has in particular two proponents: Zamolxis, who was imitated by Aboris the Hyperborean, and Zoroaster—not him of whom, perhaps, you are thinking, but he who is the son of Oromasior.

Should we turn to Plato and inquire after the nature of each of these magic forms, he will reply, in his *Alcibiades*, that Zoroaster's magic is naught else but that science of divine things in which the Persian kings had their sons educated so that they might learn to rule their state on the model of the universe-state. In the *Charmides*, he will reply further that Zamolxis' magic is the medicine of the soul through which temperance is brought about in the soul, just as through temperance health is brought about in the body. In the footsteps of these men, there followed Charondas, Damigeron, Apollonius, Osthanes, and Dardanus, as also Homer—of whom I shall prove at some time in a *Poetic Theology* which I plan to write—who concealed this doctrine along with other doctrines, symbolically, in the wanderings of his Ulysses. These same two men were followed also by Eudoxus, Hermippus, and practically all those who delved into the Pythagorean and Platonic mysteries. Of later philosophers, I find three who had ferreted it out—the Arab, al-Kindi, Roger Bacon, and William of Paris. Plotinus gives certain signs that he was not unaware of it: particularly in the passage where he shows that the magician is a *magus* of nature, and not merely a charlatan. This most wise man lauds and supports this kind of magic, while so detesting the other, that once, when asked to participate in rites involving evil spirits, he replied that they ought rather to come to him than he to them. Surely he spoke well: for just as that first form of magic makes man a slave and a pawn of evil powers, so the second form makes him their ruler and lord. That first form cannot lay claim to being either an art or a science; while the second, filled as it is with mysteries, comprehends the most profound contemplation of the deepest secrets of things and, ultimately, the knowledge of the whole of nature. This beneficial magic, in coaxing, so to speak, the powers which God's generosity has sown and planted in the world from their hiding places into the light, does not so much perform wonders of itself as serve a wonder-working nature. Gazing, with keen insight, upon that universal harmony which the Greeks, with their rare facility for such terms, called *sumpatheia*, and seizing upon the mutual affinity of natures, this second form allows us to apply to each thing those inducements—called the *iugges* of the magicians—most suitable to its nature. Thus it draws forth for public scrutiny the miracles which lie hidden in the secret recesses of the world, in the womb of nature, in the storehouse and secret vaults of God, as though it were itself their creator. As the farmer weds his elms to the vines, so the *magus* weds earth to heaven—the lower orders, that is, to the endowments and powers of the higher. Hence it is that the second form of magic is as divine and beneficial as the first is monstrous and harmful. But the most profound ground of the difference between them is the fact that the first, delivering man over to the foes of God, separates him from God; while the second, benevolent magic, rouses him to an admiration of God's works which becomes, quite naturally, faith, hope, and charity. Nothing so surely directs us, that is, to religion and the worship of God, as the diligent contemplation of His miracles; and when, by means of this natural magic, we shall have profoundly scrutinized these works, we shall all the more avidly be led to love and worship Him in His works until, at the last, we are compelled to give voice to the paean: "The heavens and all of the earth are filled with the majesty of Thy glory." So much of magic: I felt it necessary to say even this much because I know that there are many who—just as dogs always bark at strangers—condemn and despise it despite the fact that they do not understand it.

I come now to those matters which I have elicited from the ancient mysteries of the Hebrews and have cited to confirm the inviolable Catholic faith. Lest these matters be thought mere fancy and charlatanry by those who are not conversant with them, I want everyone to understand what they are; what their true nature is; whence they came; who the famed writers are who testify to them; and how mysterious, divine, and necessary they are to men of our faith for the defense of our religion against the gross misrepresentations of the Hebrews. Not only famous Hebrew masters, but such men of our faith as Esdras, Hilary, and Origen, write that Moses, when on the Mount, received from God a more secret and true explanation of the Law than is contained in the five Books which he handed down to posterity. They write further, that God directed Moses to make the Law known to the people, but not to write its interpretation down or to divulge it to any but Jesu Nave who, in turn, was to reveal it to succeeding high priests, all of whom were to be similarly pledged to silence. It was sufficient to relate, through simple historical narrative, God's power, His wrath against the wicked, His mercy toward the good, His justice toward all; and to enlighten the people, by divine and benign commands, to live well and happily, and to worship in the true religion. To have explicitly revealed to the people the hidden mysteries and the secret plans of the highest divinity, which lay hidden under the shell of the Law and the rough garb of language—would this not be tantamount to casting holy things to dogs, or pearls among swine? Consequently, the decision to keep such things hidden from the rabble and to make them known but to a chosen few, among whom alone, as Paul says, wisdom speaks, was not a decision made by human prudence, but by divine fiat. And the philosophers of antiquity maintained this safeguard: Pythagoras confided but a few trifles to his daughter, Dama, on his deathbed. The Sphinxes, carved on the Egyptian temples, reminded them that the occult doctrines should be kept inviolable from the vulgar by means of the knots of riddles. Plato, writing to Dion concerning the most divine substances, explained that he had to write in riddles "Because the letter might fall into other hands, and others come to know the things I have meant for you." Aristotle used to say that the books of the *Metaphysics* in which he treats of divine matters were both published and unpublished. But need I multiply instances? Origen maintains that Jesus Christ, the Teacher of Life, revealed much to His disciples which they feared to commit to writing lest the vulgar come into possession of it. Dionysius the Areopagite gives strong support to this when he writes that the most secret of mysteries were transmitted by the founders of our religion *ex nou eis moun dia meson logou*—that is, by rote learning, without any writing, through the medium of the spoken word alone. As the true interpretation of the Law given to Moses was, by God's fiat, revealed in precisely this same way, it was called *cabala*, which in Hebrew means "reception." The point is that the doctrine was received from one man by another as a hereditary right, not through written records but through a regular succession of revelations.

Now after the Hebrews had been released by Cyrus from their babylonian captivity, and after re-establishment of the temple under Zerubbabel, the Hebrews directed themselves to the restoration of the Law. Esdras, then head of the church, amended the Book of Moses. He says clearly that because of the exiles, massacres, flights, and captivities of the Israelites, the practice of transmitting the doctrine by word of mouth, which had been established by the ancients, could not be continued. They had to be committed to writing, or else these heavenly teachings, divinely revealed, must surely perish, as the memory of them was rapidly dwindling. Hence he decided that all of the sages who were still alive should be convened, and that each should communicate to the assembled body all that he remembered of the mysteries of the Law. These communications were then to be inscribed in seventy volumes—about the number of elders in the Sanhedrin. But, Fathers, there is no need to take my word alone for all this; listen to Esdras: "After forty days had passed, the Most High spake unto me, saying, 'the first things which thou hast written, publish openly, and let the worthy and unworthy alike read it: but keep ye the seventy last books, that thou may deliver them over to such as be wise among the people: for in them is the fount of understanding, the stream of wisdom, and the river of knowledge.' And thus did I." These are Esdras' words to the letter. These are the books of cabalistic lore. In these books, as Esdras clearly tells us, there dwells "the fount of understanding"—that is, the ineffable theology of the supersubstantial deity; "the stream of wisdom"—that is, the precise metaphysical doctrine concerning intelligible and angelic forms; and "the river of knowledge"—that is, the best-grounded philosophy of nature. Pope Sixtus IV, the immediate predecessor of our present pope, Innocent VIII, under whose reign we are fortunate, indeed, to be living, took all possible steps to guarantee that these books would be translated into Latin for the general good of our own faith. By the time of his death, indeed, three had already appeared. Among the Hebrews of today, these books are treasured with such reverence that no man is so much as permitted to touch them who has not attained his fortieth year.

When I purchased these books, at no small expense, and had read them through from cover to cover with the most rapt attention and unwearying labor, I discovered in them—as God is my witness—not so much the Mosaic as the Christian religion. Therein I found the mystery of the Trinity; the Incarnation of the Word; the divinity of the Messiah. Therein one may read as well of original sin; of its expiation by Christ; of the heavenly Jerusalem; of the fall of the devils; of the pains of purgatory and of hell. Therein I encountered the same things which we read every day in Paul, Dionysius, Jerome, and Augustine. As for philosophy, it is as though one were listening to Pythagoras and Plato, whose doctrines are so closely related to the Christian faith that our Augustine offered infinite thanks to God that the books of the Platonists had fallen into his hands. In brief, there is absolutely no controversy between ourselves and the Hebrews, on any matter, with regard to which they cannot be refuted and convinced out of the cabalistic writings, so that no corner is left for them to retreat to. With regard to this, I can cite a witness of unimpeachable authority: the most learned Antonius Chromicus. On the occasion of a banquet at his home, which I attended, he heard, with his own ears, the Hebrew, Dactylus, a profound cabalistic scholar, come over completely to the Christian doctrine of the Trinity.

But let me return to reviewing the chapters of my disputation. I have also set forth my conception of the way in which the poems of Orpheus and Zoroaster should be interpreted. Orpheus is read by the Greeks in an almost complete text; Zoroaster they know in a corrupt text, while in Chaldea he is read in a form more nearly complete; and both these men are considered as the authors and fathers of ancient wisdom. I shall pass over Zoroaster, who is cited frequently by the Platonists, and always with the most profound respect. But of Pythagoras, Iamblichus the Chaldean writes that he took the Orphic theology as the archetypal model after which he shaped and formed his own philosophy. It is for this reason that the Pythagorean maxims are called holy—because, that is, they derive from the Orphic. For it is from this original source that there followed that occult doctrine of numbers, and everything else that the Greek philosophy has of greatness and sublimity. Orpheus, however—as was the case with all the ancient theologians—so interwove the mysteries of his doctrine with the veil of poetry that one reading his hymns might well take them to be but vain fables and the veriest commonplaces. I say this so that one might appreciate what labor and difficulty was involved in my ferreting out the occult meanings of the hidden philosophy from the intentional knots of riddles and the obscurity of fables in which they were submerged. This task was made all the more difficult by the fact that in a matter so profound, abstruse, and unplumbed, I could look for aid to the work of no other interpreter. And still, like dogs, some growl that I have heaped together a great quantity of pointless drivelings in order to make my display impressive by sheer numerical weight. As though all did not concern subtle questions, subjects of vicious controversy, over which the principal schools confront each other like gladiators—at dagger's point. As though I had not contributed many things heretofore unknown and unsuspected by the very men who are even now striking at my repute while styling themselves the masters in philosophy. I am, in truth, so innocent of the fault with which they charge me that I have striven to limit the disputation to as few chapters as I could; had I wished—as others are wont—to divide it into parts, and to cut these into bits, their number might well have increased to infinity.

To pass in silence over other things that I might mention, who is not aware that one alone among my nine hundred theses—namely, that concerning the reconciliation of the philosophies of Plato and Aristotle—might easily have been expanded, without anyone suspecting that I was seeking mere quantity, into six hundred or more chapters? How? By simply enumerating, one after another, in proper order, those points on which others think that these philosophies differ, and I that they agree. But speak out I shall—though in a manner which is neither modest in itself nor truly characteristic of me—because my detractors, those who envy me, force me so to speak out. I wished to make clear in this disputation, not so much that I know a great deal, but that I know a great deal which others do not. And now, reverend Fathers, in order that this claim may be verified by the fact; and in order that my oration may no longer delay the gratification of your desire—for I see, excellent Doctors, that you are prepared, girded up, and even pleasured in anticipation of the contest—let us now, with the hope that the outcome may be fortunate and favorable, as to the sound of war trumpet, join in battle.

LEONE EBREO

THE PHILOSOPHER *and physician Leone Ebreo (Leo Hebraeus), was born in Lisbon about 1460. Very little concerning his life can be established with certainty; it is doubtful that he is to be identified with Abarbanel* (or Abravanel). *It appears that he studied in Seville in the 1480's and that he fled to Naples in 1492, when the Jews were expelled from Spain. In Naples he became personal physician to the viceroy. Some years later we find him in Florence, where he joined the brilliant circle which centered around Ficino. He is last heard of in 1521. It is not known for sure whether he died in Naples or Ferrara. His* Dialoghi d'amore, *written in Italian, were most influential. They were translated into French, Spanish, Latin, and Hebrew, and were to leave their mark upon all subsequent* Trattati di amore. *It is held that a copy of Ebreo's* Dialoghi *was found in Spinoza's library, and that the latter's notion of the "intellectual love of God" is not unrelated to his reading of Ebreo.*

On Love and Desire

A DIALOGUE BETWEEN PHILO AND SOPHIA

Philo. Having met you, O Sophia, has awakened within me both love and desire.

Sophia. It seems to me, Philo, that your response to

having met me is contradictory. But perhaps it is your passion that makes you speak in this way.

Philo. They are contradictory, all right, but only so far as you are concerned, since you have no similar feelings for me.

Sophia. No: I mean that they are contradictory in themselves. Love and desire are incompatible affects of the will.

Philo. Incompatible? How so?

Sophia. Clearly because we love those things which we possess and own, while we desire only those which we do not have. Consequently we love that which we at first desired, but when we have obtained the desired object, we then love it, and desire is at an end.

Philo. How did you arrive at this position?

Sophia. By examining instances of things which we love or desire. You see, don't you, that when we do not have health, we desire it? Yet we would scarcely say that we love it. And when we have gained it, we love it, and then do not desire it. So long as we do not have them, wealth, inheritances, jewels and such are objects of desire, not of love. Once acquired, however, they are no longer desired but loved.

Philo. It is true that we cannot love health and wealth when they are not ours simply *because* they are not ours; still, we love having them.

Sophia. This is abusing the language: one does not speak of "loving" when he means "wanting possession" of something. Here what we should say is that we "desire" it. The object of love is the beloved thing itself, while the object of desire is the possession or acquisition of the thing. Love, then, does not seem compatible with desire.

Philo. These arguments, Sophia, speak rather more for the subtlety of your mind than the truth of your position. Consider: if we could not love what we desire, we should then desire that which we do not love or, to put it another way, what we abhor and detest. Now this is a real contradiction in terms!

Sophia. I am not wrong, Philo. I desire that which I do

not love only because I do not have it; still, the instant I have it, I shall then love and not desire it. But this is not to say that I ever desire what I hate any more than it is to say that I desire what I love. We love, you see, what is ours, and desire what is not. What better example than the case of children? For he who has none cannot be said to love them, but rather to desire them; while he who has children, does not desire, but rather loves them.

Philo. Ah, but consider the case of the husband, and not just the children. Before he, the husband, becomes ours, he is both desired and loved; and, once he is ours, he is no longer desired—indeed, in some cases he is not even loved, although in others he not only continues to be loved, but the love increases. The same, too, is applicable with respect to wives. Doesn't this example seem to you to speak for my position more effectively than yours spoke against it?

Sophia. In part, your argument does satisfy me—but only in part. For your illustration seems to me to be as questionable as the whole problem we are discussing.

Philo. Let me then generalize. Love, you know, is of things that are good, or considered to be good; for only a good thing is worthy of love. Now just as there are three sorts of good—the profitable, the pleasurable, and the virtuous—so too there are three sorts of love—one of profit, one of pleasure, and the third of virtue. Once virtue and profit are ours, they must be loved forever—both before we have acquired them, that is, and after. But pleasurable things are not loved after they have been acquired; for whatever things delight our gross senses are of such kind that their possession breeds loathing rather than love. It follows from here that you must yield that such things are loved before they are possessed and are simultaneously desired. And as desire dies once they have been possessed, so too does love. Consequently you must allow that it is possible for love and desire to obtain simultaneously.

Sophia. As I see it, you have validly established your initial thesis. Still you have not done damage to mine. But is it possible that the truth can conflict with the truth? This troubles me. Can you resolve this difficulty?

Philo. I am here, Sophia, to seek from you a cure for my own troubles—and you ask me for a resolution of yours! Perhaps you do this in order to make me direct the topic away from one that displeases you. Or is it that you dislike the workings of my mind as much as the workings of my affections?

Sophia. Sweet and candid reason have more power to sway me than any affliction of the heart, I assure you. But I do not feel that I am wronging you in fixing upon that which is most precious in you. And if you, as you insist, do love me, you should seek rather to gratify my mind than to arouse my emotions. Please, then, forget all else and direct yourself to resolving my doubts.

Philo. I do have an argument ready at hand for not complying with your wish; still I shall yield to your will—such is the power of the triumphant beloved over her poor, spent lover! Very well, then: I say there are some who maintain an opinion wholly in conflict with yours. It is their opinion that love and desire, in essence, are the same. It is their claim that whatever we desire, we also love.

Sophia. Clearly they are wrong. Even if we were to grant that we love whatever we desire, it is yet the case that we love, as well, many things we do not desire—as in the case of those things which we already possess.

Philo. You make a good point. Still, others hold that love includes both that which we desire without having it, and that which we have obtained, possess, and consequently no longer desire.

Sophia. I disagree here too. Many things are said to be desired which are yet not loved, as they have no being. Love pertains to things that have being; desire, to those which do not. How is it possible to love children or health while we do not have them? And yet, may we not desire them? Hence I maintain love and desire to be contrary affections of the will. Still you insist that the two can coexist. How can that be?

Philo. If love is only of those things that actually have being, why should not desire be of the same?

Sophia. As I said: just as love presupposes the being of things, so desire presupposes their nonbeing.

Philo. How is it that love presupposes the being of things?

Sophia. Love, you see, must be preceded by knowledge. We could not love anything which we had not first known to be good; and we cannot have knowledge of anything before it is, actually, in being. Our mind is a mirror, a model, or more precisely, an image of real things; hence it is impossible for us to love anything unless it has real being.

Philo. Granted as true: yet it is for the very same reason that desire must always be desire of things in being; for we desire only those things which we have previously known to be good. Hence the Philosopher has defined the good as *that which all things desire*. Since knowledge is always of that which *is*, the objects of desire must exist equally as the objects of love.

Sophia. Granted: desire is preceded by knowledge. But I would point out further that knowledge is not only of that which *is*, but as well of that which *is not*. The mind judges things which *are* what it judges them to be, and it judges also things which *are not* to be so. And since it is the function of the mind to distinguish between what things *are* and what they *are not*, it must be able to know both those which are and those which are not. Consequently I would say that love presupposes knowledge of things which *are*, while desire presupposes knowledge of things which *are not*—things which we lack.

Philo. Prior to loving or desiring, we must know that the object of love or desire is good. It is impossible that we should know the object as other than good, for if it were other than good, then knowledge would produce utter loathing for it, rather than love or desire for it. Love and desire alike, then, presuppose the existence of their objects—existence in being no less than in knowledge.

Sophia. Now it would follow that when we judge a thing to be good and desirable these judgments would be always veridical if it is the case that desire presupposes the existence of things. But don't you see that these judgments are quite often false? That the reality does not always correspond to the judgment? It seems, then, that desire does not always presuppose the being of its object.

Philo. But this objection holds for love as well as desire! Quite often that which we judge to be good and worthy of love, is evil and despicable; and even as our judgments of things, when they are true, give birth to right and virtuous desires, from which spring all goodness, temperate acts, and meritorious deeds, so such judgments, when false, issue in evil desires and loves, from which spring all human vices and errors. Both alike, then, appear to presuppose the existence of their object.

Sophia. I cannot follow you, Philo, on these flights into such rarefied regions. Let us stay here upon earth. I still fail to see how any of the things we most desire are truly loved.

Philo. It is true that we always desire that which we do not have. Yet this does not imply that the object *is not*—desire, rather, is usually of things which *are*, but which we do not have.

Sophia. Only too often desire is of that which *is not*, which we yet desire *to be;* and yet, not necessarily that they should come *to be ours*. We desire rain, for example, when the weather is fine; or we desire fine weather, the arrival of a friend, or the conclusion of some business. These things do not exist, and it is our desire that they come to be so that we may derive some benefit from them, but not so that we may possess them. Nor would it be correct to speak of loving them.

Philo. That which *is not* is nothing; and clearly *nothing* can be neither loved, desired, nor possessed. But the examples you have cited are instances of things, which—although not actually present or existent at the time they are desired—have the possibility of coming to be. And it is their potential existence that we desire to actualize. In the same way we may desire that such things as *are* but are not *ours*, should, to the degree that they *are*, become ours. Hence this is the way it is with all objects of desire: either those which *are not* should come *to be*; or that we may possess that which we lack. How can you justify the position that every desire presupposes existence, in part, and privation, in part, and then assume that its object is the actualization of whole and perfect being? It is true: desire and love are rooted in the being of things, not in their nonbeing. It is true further that the object of desire must have three qualities, and in this order: first, being; second, truth; and third, goodness. These alone make it an object of love and desire. It could not become such an object if it were not first judged good—for otherwise it would not be loved or desired. And, before it can be thus judged, it must be recognized as true; and, as it is truly present to cognition, so it must actually *be*. A thing, that is, is first in being before it can imprint itself upon the mind, and only after this can it be judged to be good. Finally, it is loved and desired. Hence the Philosopher says that being, truth, and value are not three, but one. Only that being *is* in itself: truth—when it has impressed itself upon the mind; and value—when the mind and will, led by love and desire, come to seek possession of things. So that desire as well, and equally with love, presupposes being.

Sophia. Yet we desire a multitude of things which are not only not in our possession but, in fact, absolutely *are not*. Health and children, for example, when we do *not* have them; and clearly these are not loved, but only desired.

Philo. Even if the object of desire is lacking to the one who desires it, and even if it *were not*, it is yet not wholly without being. It must exist in some sense, else it could not be known as good, or desired, even though it lacked existence in the proper sense. This holds for health in respect of the sick man who desires it—for it exists in the healthy, and existed, as well, in the sick man before he became ill. The case with children is similar: though they do not exist relative to those who desire them because they lack them, yet they do exist relative to others—since all men are, or have been, someone's children. Hence he who has no children, still knows them, judges them to be good, and desires them. Such modes of being are sufficient to give the sick man a conception of health, as well as the childless man a conception of children. Thus love and desire are of things which in some sense have real being and are known to be good. Love, however, appears to encompass many goods, irrespective of whether they are ours or not, while desire is only of such things as we lack.

Sophia. You are implying that we love whatever we desire—an opinion which you cited as being held by some—and that love encompasses the entire class of things judged as good: both such things as we lack and desire; and such as we possess and do not desire. All of these, as you say, are objects of love. But in the case of things which we lack entirely—as in the examples of health and children—it does not seem right to me that we who lack them can love them, although we may desire them. For that being which they have, as you say, relative to others, is not sufficient to make us knowledgeable about them; and consequently this cannot make us love them. We do not love the children or health of another, but our own; and when we do not have these things, although I can understand how we can desire them, how can we love them?

Philo. Now we are hovering at the very edge of the truth! Although we say in the vernacular that we "love" things because we judge good those things which we desire, yet more precisely speaking, we should not say that we "love" those things which have no proper being—such as the health or the children which we lack. I speak of *real* love: *imaginary* love may be felt for any object of desire as this has being in the imagination. The very imagining of it gives rise to a certain "love"; but its object is not the real thing itself—for that has as yet no proper being in reality—but is only the idea of the being abstracted from the general being. Love of this variety has no proper object as it is not real love—it is not real because it lacks a real object—it is only an imaginary and fictitious love, as the desire of nonreal objects cannot involve real love. But let us arrange things in one of the three classes involving love and desire: some are both loved and desired—such as truth, wisdom, and a true friend, when we lack them; others are loved but not desired—such as all goods which we have and own; and others are desired but not loved—as health and children when we lack them, as well as all other such things which have no real existence. Consequently the things we both love and desire together are those that we judge good which have no proper being, which we yet lack; the things we love but do not desire are those which come into being and become ours; and the things we desire but do not love are those which we not only lack, but which have not themselves the proper being to serve as objects of love.

Sophia. I understand you, and your explanation pleases me greatly. Still there are many things which I see—which have real and proper being—which we desire when we lack them, although we do not love them until they become ours, and then we do love them without desiring them. Riches, for example, a house, a vineyard, a jewel—these we desire when they belong to others, although we do not love them because they belong to others; but, once they belong to us, desire comes to an end and love takes its place. Before their acquisition, then, they are desired without love; but once they are obtained, they are loved but not desired.

Philo. That is quite true. But I do not claim that every object of desire which has proper being is also loved—what I affirm is that whatever objects are desired must have proper being equally with the objects of love; otherwise they could only be desired, not loved. It was for this reason that I cited examples not of a jewel or a house, but of virtue, wisdom, or a true friend—for when these are lacking, they are both loved and desired.

Sophia. How does it come about that there is this difference among the objects of desire which have proper being? How is it that some can be loved at the same time that they are desired, while others cannot?

Philo. This owes to the difference that we find between the objects of love. These, as you know, are of three kinds: useful, pleasurable, and virtuous—and they differ in their relation to love and desire.

Sophia. But what is the precise nature of the difference

between them? I mean, between love and desire? So that I may grasp this more clearly, please define love and desire in such a way that they encompass the three kinds of objects.

Philo. It is more difficult than you suppose to set forth a definition of love and desire which embraces all their facets; for their nature manifests itself differently in each of these facets. The books of the ancient philosophers do not propose any such wide definition of them. For our present purposes, however, it is adequate to define desire as *an affect of the will directed at the coming to be, or coming to be ours, of a thing which we judge good and lack.* Love, we would define as *an affect of the will to enjoy, through union, the thing which we judge to be good.* From these definitions you will come to understand the difference between the two affects of the will; you will also see that the object of desire is what is not, while the object of love may either be or be lacking; for the will may be directed toward enjoyment through union with things that we lack as well as things that we possess. Such an affect, that is to say, does not necessarily involve either possession or privation, but is common to both.

Sophia. I shall accept these definitions provisionally, although actually they require a more thorough analysis. Still they do seem to provide an initial key to my problem about the reason for the difference between love and desire in respect of the three kinds of objects you mentioned: profitable, pleasurable, and virtuous. Please continue.

Philo. Profitable things, such as wealth, and personal possessions which we have ourselves acquired, are never loved and desired simultaneously. While we lack them, rather, we desire them; but we do not love them, because they are the possessions of others. Once we have acquired them, however, we no longer desire, but love them, as our own; they are enjoyed as being united to us in the sense that they are our property. Nonetheless, even though desire for the particular riches we have acquired comes to an end, it yields immediately to new desires for yet other things belonging to others; and those whose wills are driven by love of gain, have various and numerous desires, of which, when one is gratified, another, more powerful and driving replaces it. So that the will is never sated in one with such desires: as possessions grow, so, too, do the desires; it is as if one should attempt to gratify one's thirst with salt water—the more one drinks the more the thirst grows. This—the desire for profitable things—is called *ambition* and *cupidity*. In a more moderate form it is called *gratification* and *satisfaction of our needs*, and *sobriety* because it manifests contentment with necessities. Wise men agree that he is truly rich who is content with what he possesses. While, in a word, one extreme of this virtue is avaricious grasping of the superfluous, the other is cessation of desire for even the necessary—or *sloth*.

Sophia. What is it that you are saying, Philo? Aren't there many philosophers who advocate the rejection of all wealth? And didn't many, in fact, actually do this?

Philo. Yes—some of the Stoics and Academics maintained this view. But in their case it was not sloth which took the place of desire to gratify their needs; what they did was to surrender the pursuit of these objects in order to turn to the contemplative life. They regarded riches as an obstacle to deep and serene contemplation, since riches tend to preoccupy the mind and distract it from that contemplation wherein consists its perfection and its happiness. The Peripatetics, on the other hand, disagree. They hold that, though riches are not virtues, they are at least instrumental to virtue, since without adequate means no one could practice generosity, or altruism, or almsgiving, or any other such charitable act.

Sophia. But wouldn't good intentions, plus readiness to perform deeds of virtue like these when the means *are* available, be sufficient as regards such deeds of virtue? If so, a man might be a good man even if he lacked wealth.

Philo. No: the mere intention without the action is not enough. Virtue consists in a habit of acting well, and is acquired only in the actual and continuous performance of good works. And since such works as those I have cited cannot be performed without means, it follows that without means we must lack in such virtue.

Sophia. How did it happen that the Stoics did not see this? And, for their part, how can the Peripatetics deny that wealth distracts the mind from contemplation?

Philo. The Stoics never denied that certain domestic as well as civil virtues absolutely require means. But do not, from this, be lead to believe that happiness consists in means rather than in the intellective and contemplative life, for the sake of which we ought to abandon wealth and guard against the possibility that the virtues that stem from wealth be perverted to vices instead of growing into other virtues more exalted and closer to supreme happiness. Nor do the Peripatetics deny this. The real difference between them and the Stoics is that the latter, desiring only the highest virtue, despise wealth, which they yet recognize as necessary for the attainment of certain virtues. These, as men of great nobility, feel that if they have the light of the sun this is preferable to the light of a candle; especially as they see such wealth to be more often a source of vice than virtue. The Peripatetics, however, while admitting that wealth is not absolutely requisite for such exalted spirits, yet insist that there are other great virtues which, although possibly inferior, still require that they be acquired by means of wealth. So both schools agree that sloth consists in ceasing to desire what is necessary for the attainment of those virtues which do not spring from intellective contemplation. Sloth, thus, is considered a vice at the other extreme of cupidity; while the mean between these two extremes is the sobriety of the man who desires only the necessary, which represents the height of virtue in respect of the desire of profitable things.

Sophia. Is it the case that there corresponds to this virtuous mean and two sinful extremes in respect of the desire of profitable things, similar means and extremes in respect of profitable things which we already possess?

Philo. There certainly are; and they are equally easy to grasp. For intemperate love of riches which we have gained, or possess, is *avarice*—a vicious and monstrous sin. When we love our own wealth more than we should, we are thereby driven to hoard it, our duties notwithstanding, instead of dealing with it as reason and virtue direct. A moderate love of our possessions, and their appropriate use, is a virtuous and noble mean, and it is known as *liberality*. The total absence of any love for what we possess, and its wanton dissipation, is the extreme in opposition to avarice, and is known as *prodigality*. Thus the miser and the prodigal are alike sinful, as their love of profitable things takes an extreme form. That man is virtuous and liberal who adheres to the mean between the two. I have just expounded to you the forms, moderate and immoderate, in which we find love and desire in respect of profitable things.

Sophia. I am fully satisfied by this explanation. Now will you expound the modes of love in respect of pleasurable things? This seems to me to be nearer to our present purpose.

Philo. Even as in respect of profitable things, love, in the proper sense, is found united with desire, so also in respect of pleasurable things love and desire are united. For whatever pleasurable thing is lacking to us lays claim to our love equally with our desire or appetite, until it becomes wholly ours and we have become sated with it. The toper both loves and desires his wine before he commences to drink and until he attains satiety; the glutton desires and loves his sweets before eating them, and until he is stuffed. In general, he who is thirsty, while he desires, also loves, to drink; and so for the hungry man, and the man who desires and loves woman (and woman, the man). Moreover, these pleasures are such that, once enjoyed, not only is desire for them quieted, but in most cases love also—which, as we know, quite often changes to disgust and abhorrence: as he who has glutted his hunger, or thirst, has no further desire of food or drink, but rather draws back from them. The case is the same with other material pleasures—when desire of them ceases because of satiety, a like revulsion ensues; so that, in respect of pleasure, love and desire flourish together and perish together. Some, it is true, are immoderate in their pursuit of pleasure, just as others are in their pursuit of gain—they are neither sated nor do they wish to be; such we call gluttons, drunkards, and libertines. These fear and avoid satiety and soon return to love and desire of the same things, or of others of the same variety. Desire of such pleasures is properly called *appetite*, even as desire of gain is called ambition or cupidity. Immoderate desire and pursuit of such things as give ourselves pleasure, we call *lust*—which may be carnal, or lust for food and drink, or of other unnecessary delicacies or unseemly luxuries. Those who are dedicated to such vices we call *lustful*. Those whose reason offers a certain opposition, although they are ultimately overcome by lust, we say display the sin of *incontinence*. While those who are utterly abandoned, and who do not even seek to offer any resistance to their vicious dispositions, we call dissolute. As this extreme lust corresponds in respect of pleasure to avarice and cupidity in respect of gain, so at the other extreme of this vice, corresponding to prodigality, is immoderate *abstemiousness*. The one surrenders a fortune in a way incompatible with a good life, while the other resigns the pleasures necessary to support life and maintain health. The mean between these extremes is the admirable virtue called *continence*. And when, in response to the prod of sexual desire, we repress it by reason and virtue, that is called *temperance*. When, however, sensuality no longer plagues our virtuous reason, but augments it in a temperate reaction to pleasures—neither avoiding the necessary nor pursuing the superfluous—this virtue is called *fortitude*. It is truly predicated, as they say, of him who conquers himself; for pleasure has a greater power over human nature than gain, being, as it is, its means of self-preservation. Consequently, whoever is able to be reasonable about such excesses may be said, in truth, to have overcome his most powerful and ineluctable enemy.

Sophia. I am satisfied with your account of love and appetite in respect of pleasure. Still, I feel some uneasiness about your stating that we love and desire those pleasurable things we lack, but cease to do so when we are in possession of them. It seems to me that this holds true only of desire, and not of love. For love is born of possession of these things and not of their lack. The taste of such pleasures, indeed, seems to be the very source of the love of them.

Philo. It may be the source of love, as you say, but it also arouses appetite and excites desire and relish. Yet appetite and desire are always for what is lacking.

Sophia. How is that? Pleasure, as we know, even while we enjoy it, is not only loved but desired. It seems, then, that we should lack, and not possess, even that which we do possess!

Philo. It is true that such things are loved and desired after we have obtained them, but not after we have possessed them utterly, for then satiety follows, and we cease simultaneously to love and desire them. On the other hand, while we are enjoying them, and up until we are sated with them, there always remains some lack. And the merest anticipation of pleasure to come gives strength to our recognition of this lack and adds, thus, an edge to our appetite and a force to our love. This edge and this force are the resultants of a feeling of privation, and they become augmented and sharper as we come upon and begin to taste of the pleasure which we lacked; but when we have partaken of it to the point of satiety, the lack no longer remains, and gone with it are all desire and love, which are then succeeded by aversion and disgust. Desire and love, then, are bound up with the lack of a pleasure, and not with its enjoyment.

Sophia. I am satisfied with this explanation. Now I know how gain and pleasure resemble and differ from each other in relation to love and desire. I understand the cause of their similarity, which is obvious, but I cannot discover the reason why they affect the will in different and contrasting ways—and this I should like to be clear on. Why, I mean, do desire and love not go hand in hand in respect of gain, but one always excludes the other? In respect of pleasure, as we saw, it is the other way round: whatever is desired is loved, and when desire dies, love dies with it. Tell me how it comes about that two such similar kinds of love should display such differences.

Philo. The cause lies in the different ways of enjoying these two kinds of objects of love and desire. Use is implied in the continuous possession of a thing, so that the more complete the possession, the more its use is enjoyed—hence love is not born until the object is ours, and while it is ours this love grows but desire ceases. If, on the other hand, we lose possession and the term of ownership comes to an end, then it becomes possible to speak of desire but not of love. As for pleasure, however, its delights consist neither in possession, enjoyment, nor complete ownership, but in a certain tension connected with privation; and when this is over, pleasure is completely at an end, and so our desire and love of pleasure is completely eliminated.

Sophia. It is quite understandable to me that the lack of pleasure should bring about desire; but why is it that love does not require its presence? And even as there can be no pleasure derived from what we lack, neither can we feel any love for that which we lack—although we may feel desire. Love of pleasure, it then seems, must be possible only to the degree that we enjoy it—not before, when it is lacking, nor later, when we are sated.

Philo. Sophia, that is a most ingenious objection! You are right in saying that there is no love of a pleasure insofar as it is tinged with any lack of fulfillment. Still you must realize that pure desire of pleasure contains an element of pleasure which, although imagined, is not actually enjoyed. This, however, is not the way it is with material things; for their absence saddens the man who desires them. This is the reason why you quite often see that men whose desires are set on pleasure are happy and lively, while the slaves of ambition and gain are grim and melancholy. Pleasure, you see, has more power than gain over the imagination when it is not obtained; whereas the actual possession of profit stirs us more powerfully than pleasure. In the case of pleasure, then, the nongratification of desire is itself both a pleasure and the indispensable condition of pleasure. On the same ground, both the imperfect fulfillment of desire and the pleasure of which it is an element excite both love and desire; only with the difference that—

since the desire is imperfectly fulfilled—desire and appetite are dominant over love: while when the pleasure is realized, love dominates appetite.

Sophia. I see—and agree. For we all know that imaginary dreams of pleasurable things do contrive to bring about real pleasure. Indeed, the same effect may be achieved by vividly imagining them, even while we are awake. But the imagination of useful things does not have the same effect. Still there is one thing that bothers me: when we compare the two kinds of love, which should we discover as the more comprehensive and universal? And is it possible for the two to coexist in respect of one and the same object?

Philo. Love of pleasure is by far the more profound, wide, and universal. Not everything, you see, which is pleasurable is useful—indeed, those things which bring the most sensual delight are of the least possible use to him whom they delight, whether for the rule of his body, his health, or the acquisition of wealth. But that pleasure which is most compatible with profit, when it is experienced in gain, reaches its most intense point in the acquiring of wealth. This, as we acquire it, constantly produces pleasure in the acquisitor, although the pleasure may diminish through continual possession—for it seems as if pleasure of all varieties is but a relief consequent on the acquisition of that which we lack, so that it obtains rather in the acquisition than in the possession of things.

Sophia. What you have told me of pleasure is sufficient. Now it is time that I should understand the other kind of love: love of virtue—which is the worthiest and noblest.

Philo. These—love and desire of virtue—are characteristic of the truly great men. For such men, love and desire are subservient to the excellence of that highest element in man—that in virtue of which he is a man: i.e., the element most remote from matter and from darkness: that which is nearest to the divine light. This is the intellect—which alone among the parts and powers of men escapes the horror of death. Love, thus, and desire of the good, consist in two qualities of the intellect: virtue and wisdom. For these alone are the cornerstones of true goodness. True goodness alone is above the profit of gain and the delights of pleasure. Pleasure resides in our sense of utility and in our imagination, but virtue resides in our intellect—which surpasses all our other faculties. Virtue, moreover, is the end which the other two should serve. Gain is sought as a means to pleasure, since, by the aid of the wealth and possessions that we have acquired, we may pursue the pleasures natural to man. Pleasure serves to re-create the body, which is an instrument of the intellect in its exercise of virtue and wisdom. The purpose of man, then, consists in acting well, virtuously, and wisely—which surpasses in value every other activity of man, all other loves and all other desires.

Sophia. You have demonstrated goodness to be superior to pleasure and profit; but we are primarily concerned with the differences between love and desire in respect of goodness, as well as the manner in which love and desire of goodness resemble love and desire of pleasure and profit.

Philo. I was about to speak of this when you interrupted me. Love and desire of goodness resemble love and desire of both pleasure and profit, to some degree. In part, love and desire of goodness are like love and desire of pleasure and unlike those of profit; and in part, they are like love and desire of profit but unlike those of pleasure. Again, in part, they differ from love and desire of either profit or pleasure.

Sophia. Be good enough to explain each of these points to me.

Philo. In respect of both goodness and pleasure, desire is always of what is lacking. Just as we desire pleasurable and useful things when these are lacking to us, so too we desire wisdom and virtuous acts when we lack them. In respect of goodness, as of pleasure, love coexists with desire. For just as desired pleasures are loved even before they are enjoyed, so too, wisdom and virtue, before they are possessed, are loved as well as desired. But when it comes to objects of gain, they are desired but not loved until they are ours, so that in this, love and desire of good differs from, even opposes, love and desire of gain.

Sophia. How does it happen that goodness resembles pleasure and not profit? At first sight one would think that goods—like virtue and wisdom—could not be loved while they are not possessed. Virtue and wisdom, you see, as long as they are lacking to us, have no true being. They are like health, when it is lacking: or like other such things which have no sort of existence and so cannot be loved.

Philo. The profitable is totally extraneous to the man who desires it so long as he does not actually possess it, and therefore, even though it exists and has being, it cannot evoke love. But objects of pleasure, as we said before, give rise through desire to a certain excitement and pleasurable anticipation, even before they are actually enjoyed; and this provides a proper basis for love, since this state of wanting is itself proper to the lover. Similarly—nay, even to a greater degree—the desire of wisdom and virtue and the good bring about a certain mode of being of these things in the intellect of the one who desires them. To desire wisdom and virtue is truly to desire wisely and virtuously. Now this mode of being of the good, which we both desire and lack, is rooted in the noblest of our faculties; and love, therefore, should follow directly on its appearance. The good, then, as an object of desire, can lay claim to even a greater love than pleasure. And thus it is that desire is bound up with love of both alike while they are lacked—as distinct to what occurs in the case of gain.

Sophia. That seems clear enough. Will you please go on to explain the two which remain.

Philo. The good resembles gain in the kind of love to which it gives rise—the kind, that is, which is engendered when the object of gain is fully possessed. Even as material goods are loved once they are possessed, so it is with all goods; and wisdom and virtue are loved just as greatly once they are attained. The case is quite otherwise with pleasure, which, once fully enjoyed, no longer generates love, but rather disgust and loathing. The good, however, differs from both profit and pleasure in that it is always an object of love—both when it is desired and lacked, and when it is possessed and no longer desired. It differs, moreover, in another outstanding property: while virtue, in respect of the other two, consists in a mean between love and desire (since excess in gain and pleasure are extremes from which stem all the human vices), so far as the good is concerned, the more excessive and uncontrolled our love and desire, the more meritorious and virtuous it is. Its lukewarmness, if I may put it in this way, is evil: whoever is lacking in this love and desire would be not only vicious but inhuman; for moral goodness is the true good—and the good, as the Philosopher said, is that which all men desire; (and this despite the fact that by nature we all desire knowledge).

Sophia. I believe that I have heard this difference explained in another way.

Philo. How was that?

Sophia. In respect of the good, it is held, the greatest excess of love and desire is virtuous—because the more we desire, love, and pursue the good, the greater our virtue. The other extreme—the absence of such love and desire—is evil. There is no greater evil than ceasing to love the good. So far as pleasure and profit are concerned, however, the opposite situation obtains: for in these, virtue consists in the extreme of loving and desiring very little, both profits and pleasures; and vice consists in the extreme of pursuing them too assiduously and lavishing affection on them. So far, then, as the good is concerned, virtue consists in an overflowing love of the good, and vice in the lack of such love; while in respect of profits and pleasures, virtue consists rather in loving them little, and vice, in loving them too much.

Philo. Your analysis is true of some men. For these, that is, virtue in respect of profits and pleasures consists of indifference to them. But this is not universally true. In the moral life of most men, virtue, as regards these two, consists in moderation, and not in any extreme. Just as excessive love of profit and pleasure is wicked, so too it is the case that abhorrence of them—or, more precisely, caring for them less than one should—is, as I said before, a sin. Though it is true that the Peripatetics regard it as a sin in those who live the contemplative and intellective life—in which one attains supreme happiness—to care for profit or pleasures; and not merely to care excessively but even moderately; for poverty is a condition of the most profound thought, which is hindered by the uses of wealth and pleasure. The Stoics, in addition, have shown that the contemplative life requires far less material goods than the ordinary moral life. Thus, in the moral life, virtue is moderation in respect of profit and pleasure, but in the contemplative life it consists in a negative evaluation of these. In the moral life, all extremes are sinful; in the contemplative, only deficiencies are sinful.

Sophia. Now I see the full range of both these definitions. But how does one account for the diversity between the good, profit, and pleasure?

Philo. It hinges on this: that while uncontrolled lust after pleasure, and unstinted greed for gain, debase our intellect, thrusting it into the trough of matter, and all but extinguishing the light of our intellect in the deeps of sensuality; the inextinguishable and burning love of wisdom and virtue makes our mind Godlike and transmutes even our frail body—that vessel of corruption—into an instrument of angelic spirituality.

Sophia. Don't you regard moderation with respect to gain and pleasure to be good?

Philo. Since this is virtuous, of course it is good.

Sophia. If it is good, then why is its excess evil? You said before that the perfection of good lies in an extreme, and not in deficiency or moderation. You said further that moderation, not excess, was virtue in respect of profit and pleasure. There is a contradiction here.

Philo. Would that your mind were rather more wise than subtle! Virtue in respect of profit and pleasure is not such in virtue of their nature—for the delights of sense and the imagined profit of material things are both alien to spirit, or intellect, which alone is the source of greater good. Hence the higher its love and desire, the greater our virtue and goodness. Profit and pleasure, however, participate in intellective reason only to the degree that reason imposes a mean, or moderation, on love and desire of these things; and so this mean, or moderation, is their only virtue and, when it is lacking, evil dominates more or less in relation to profit and pleasure. These passions, when divorced from reason, are wicked and sinful, proper only to brutes—indeed, it is only the mean imposed upon them by reason which elevates them to the status of real love. As regards this mean, you see, it is the case that the more ardently we desire, love, and pursue it, the more true our virtue. Since such desire is neither of pleasure nor of profit, but of the tempering of these by the intellect, it is a true good.

Sophia. I am now aware of the differences in love and desire as these are related to the objects of our will, as well as the causes of those differences. Now I wish to know to which of the three categories we previously demarcated, the following objects of love and desire are to be assigned: health, children, husband or wife, and power, dominion, rule, honor, fame, and glory. All of these, you know, we both love and desire, yet it is not clear to me whether they should be classed with the profitable, the pleasurable, or the good. On the one hand, they certainly appear to be pleasurable—especially when one thinks of the pleasure their possession brings; on the other hand, as they do not cease to delight us, but rather continue to command our love even while they are being enjoyed, it appears that they should be classified among the profitable, or good, things rather than the pleasurable.

Philo. Even though health serves a useful purpose, it is yet essentially pleasurable. It is far from unfitting that some pleasurable things should be utilitarian, as well. Nor is it unfitting that some useful things be pleasurable, and some pleasurable and useful things be good. Thus health, as I say, is essentially pleasurable in view of the pleasure it gives; it is also advantageous and even good; and it is for this reason that an abundance of it will not produce disgust or abhorrence, as do mere pleasures; for these latter are not cared for when they are possessed, but are desired only when they are lacking. There is yet another reason why health does not weary us or pall on us: because the pleasure it affords affects not only our exterior, material senses—as foods, for example, affect our taste or carnal delight our sense of touch, or perfumes our sense of smell—which soon become odious; but it affects, as well, our interior senses, which are less quickly jaded. Although it does not consist in the hearing of sweet music and melodious voices, nor in the sights of beautiful and well-proportioned figures, the joy of health permeates our entire consciousness: our interior senses, our exterior senses, and our imagination as well. In its absence, we desire it—not with the merely sensuous yearning but with our true will, as reason dictates. The joy of health then is a good, even though sustained enjoyment tends to make us esteem it less highly than we should.

Sophia. So much for health. What of children?

Philo. Sometimes children are desired for their use: as when we wish to bestow a patrimony upon them. Still our love and natural desire for them is quite pleasurable—nothing of this kind of pleasure is manifested by the beast, whose pleasures are limited to those which address the five material senses. Parents, it is true, may derive delight in seeing and listening to their children; still this, and the mere possession of the children, is not the goal of a human parent's desire. His chief delight derives from his imagination—his thoughts about his children—from an activity of spirit, that is, and not from the exterior senses. Hence fulfillment does not breed satiety: the more so because this desire is not sensual only, but is of the will subject to that incorruptible mistress of nature, reason. As the Philosopher said, living things which are mortal, and recognize their finitude, desire to live on at least in their offspring; thus mortal creatures seek after immortality. The pleasure which we derive from children is consequently different from all other delights; and it is for this reason that we do not weary of them or turn away from them. In this, then, children resemble health: that love does not end with their acquisition, but grows, and sees to the tending of the children with active concern—for in them is implanted our aspirations for immortality. Hence our pleasure in our children is marked, as is every good thing, by the persistence of love in possession. Such also, as we have seen, is the case with health.

Sophia. Now I understand how it is with children. Tell me next of the love between husband and wife.

Philo. Obviously the love of husband and wife is pleasurable. Yet it must be bound up as well with good. Indeed, it is for this reason that a mutual love survives the enjoyment of its delights, and not only persists but continuously grows through participation in the good. More, the good and pleasurable elements in married love are augmented by that of advantage—for each of the married lovers ever derives benefit from the other, which greatly contributes to the nurture of their love. Thus, married love, being essentially pleasurable, is maintained because of its connection with both advantage and good.

Sophia. Speak now of the desire which men have for power, for dominion, and for rule. What kind of desire is manifest in these? And how should we classify love of these objects?

Philo. Love and desire of power has for object a combination of pleasure and profit. Inasmuch, however, as the pleasure is neither material nor sensual but, rather, spiritual, having its seat in thought and imagination; and inasmuch as this pleasure is bound up with advantage; therefore, the possession of power does not become jaded in men. Rather, it is the case that when they have acquired dominion, command, or leadership, they love and watch over them jealously and shrewdly—not because they participate in the good, (indeed, there is very little good to be found in most of these desires), but because imagination, in which this pleasure is rooted, is not sated like our material senses, but is by nature quite insatiable, and the more so in this case where pleasure is joined with advantage—a combination which nurtures our love of such power once it is acquired, causing us to guard it assiduously, and to long, avidly and with unlimited desire, for its continued growth.

Sophia. In which of the three categories are we to

place honor, glory, and fame? You have not yet touched on these.

Philo. There are two varieties of honor, or glory: one meretricious and false, the other genuine and true. Meretricious honor is that species which is awarded to power; true honor, that which rewards virtue. The first kind, desired and pursued by men in power, is to be placed in the category of pleasure. But because such pleasure springs not from our easily jaded senses but from our insatiate imagination, it never palls on us as material pleasures do. Quite the contrary: although it is not good, as it has nothing in common with goodness, it is, nonetheless, once acquired, kept and guarded with an ever increasing avidity of desire. True honor, however, the reward of virtue, though essentially pleasurable, yet has its pleasure mixed with good. This—and also because it is grounded in the imagination which knows no limits—is why it follows that true honor is loved and its increase is sought after with limitless desire. Nor does the imagination rest content with glory and honor enjoyed merely so long as life lasts, but it desires—and even may obtain—their continuation after death. And this is properly designated, fame. Now though it is true that honor rewards virtue, it should not therefore be viewed as the goal of good and virtuous actions; nor should we behave with a view to winning honor—for the goal of goodness is the perfecting of our intellect, which is formed, purified, and enlightened by virtuous deeds until at last wisdom crowns it with a vision of the Divine. The true end of genuine virtue therefore, cannot lie in the opinion of men; for they measure honor and glory by history and records, which are the monuments of fame; nor can it lie in the pleasures of imagination which any man may draw from his glory or fame. Indeed, honor and glory are entirely fitting rewards for good men, but these should not be the end for the sake of which noble acts are performed. Virtue and goodness should be admired: but virtue should not be pursued for the sake of admiration. Praises, it is true, may tend to increase virtue; but if they are the reason for which virtue was practiced, they tend to diminish rather than increase virtue.

It is, in a word, because of the connection between these pleasures and the good that we eternally cherish and love them, and ever seek after their increase.

Sophia. I am wholly satisfied with your explanation of the problems at issue. I now quite understand that all these objects of desire are what they are because they produce pleasures of the imagination, added sometimes to advantage, or to both; and that it is for this reason that enjoyment of them does not result in satiation, or disgust. But now I should like to learn from you the nature and species of human friendship, and of love of God.

Philo. Of human friendship, sometimes the object is advantage and sometimes it is pleasure. But such friendship is not durable and is not the proper bond uniting two friends; for were the cause of the friendship removed—that is, if it were to cease to afford profit or pleasure—then the friendship itself would end and dissipate together with its cause. True friendship, however, is that which generates good and combines with the virtuous. Such a bond is indissoluble; and that friendship which is predicated upon it is quite stable and wholly perfect. This alone, among the kinds of possible human friendships, is truly noble and praiseworthy. It is this union which welds together in intimate union the souls of true friends. It becomes such that the joy or despair of one is the joy and despair of the other —each feels the other's victories and defeats even more profoundly than his own; each lightens his friend's sorrows by the part he takes in them (for grief divided is lessened by so much). Friendships of this kind are what are meant when the philosopher writes that a true friend is another self—meaning that those linked thus in true friendship have a dual life, as each comprises in himself two lives: his own and his friend's. It is as a consequence of this that Holy Scripture enjoins virtuous friendship: it is written: "Thou shalt love thy neighbor as thyself"—implying a friendship of perfect unity in which a single love unites the hearts of both friends. Such union, such conjunction, must be founded on the reciprocal virtue or wisdom of both friends; and this wisdom, being spiritual and, consequently, alien to matter and unbounded by corporeal limits, transcends the distinction of persons and bodily individuality, bringing into being in such friends a single mental essence, preserved by their mutual wisdoms, loves, and wills, and untouched by distinctions and divisions, precisely as if this love resided in but a single soul and a single being. To conclude, I might say that noble and true friendships make two persons of one, and one person of two.

Sophia. In these few words you have imparted much to me concerning human friendship. Now I should like to hear you speak on the love of God; for this, surely, is the greatest love of all.

Philo. Love of God does more than merely participate in good: it comprises the goodness of all things and of all loves. For the Godhead is at once the source, the means, and the end of all good deeds.

Sophia. But if He is their source, how can He also be said to be their end—let alone their means?

Philo. He is their source, inasmuch as the intellect, through which all human good is achieved, depends on Him. The intellect is a small glimmer of God's infinite splendor, assigned to man for the purpose of making him immortal, happy—rational. The intellect, however, before it can achieve good deeds, must come into communication with the divine light; for even though as a beam of God's glory it is naturally luminous, yet it is dimmed because of its connection with the body. Dimmed thus, by the opacity of matter, it cannot attain to the noble disposition of virtue or to the clear concepts of wisdom unless it is purged by the divine light. For just as our eye, though clear, can see neither colors, figures, nor other such visible things unless illumined by the sun's light, which, obtaining between our eye, the visible object, and the intervening space, is the actual cause of the eye's vision; so it is the case that our intellect, although clear in itself, is yet so blocked in wise and virtuous activity, and so soiled by the gross body in which it resides, that it needs freshening from the divine splendor. This freshening actualizes its potentialities and makes it truly intellectual, prudent, and wise—avid after all good and wary of all evil. This is accomplished by the divine splendor's illumining the ideas and forms of things issuing from the activity of understanding, which is intermediate between intellect and imagination, so that the darkness of the intellect is dispelled, and it shines forth with perfect clarity and reality. It is thus, then, that the Most High is the source of all human goods—both of their potentiality and of their actualization. And as the Most High is supreme goodness, infinite excellence and virtue, all other goods and virtues derive from Him. He is the true source and cause of all perfection.

Sophia. It is fitting that all good things should take their rise in the supreme Creator. Who could question that? But how is He their means and end?

Philo. God, in His mercy, is the means by which all virtuous and splendid deeds are brought about. Divine providence, as we know, especially favors those who partake of the Godly virtues—and favors them in proportion as their role in the attainment of these virtues is greater; so there can be no question but that He aids in the exercise of such virtues—helping good men to achieve and perfect their good actions: for, as all virtues and excellences are contained in Him, He provides the archetype to be emulated by all who seek to attain virtue. What more profound loving-kindness and mercy than God's? What liberality is greater than His, who gives of himself to all created things? What justice so flawless as His rule? What greater goodness, more certain truth, more profound wisdom, more auspicious providence than that which obtains in God? Although we may not directly perceive these qualities in Him, they are yet clearly manifested in His works: in the creatures of the universe which He has fashioned and preserves. Emulation, therefore, of the divine virtues affords a way and means of bringing us to whatever good and virtuous deeds, whatever wise conceptions, lie within our grasp. God has not only shown His fatherly love for us in our creation, but He invites us, by His teaching and blessed ordinances, to reach for those goods of which He provides the clear and brilliant models.

Sophia. It pleases me that almighty God should be both the source and the means of all our good. Now tell me: how is He its end?

Philo. He alone is the ultimate end of all human actions. Gain is but a means to the acquisition of pleasures, and necessary pleasures, as we have seen, serve to support life; but the end of life is the perfecting of the soul. How does the soul attain perfection? First, through disposition toward virtue; and then, by way of that wisdom which aims at the knowledge of God, who is supreme wisdom, supreme goodness, and the source of all good. This knowledge kindles within us a powerful love, made up of all excellence and goodness, as love is excellent in proportion as its object is known to be good; therefore, love of God must transcend all other good loves or noble deeds.

Sophia. But, as I recall, you once said that God, being infinite and wholly perfect, cannot be apprehended by our minds which, in all respects, are finite and limited. Yet, to gain knowledge, we must comprehend; but how can the finite and limited comprehend the infinite and unlimited? And how, without this knowledge, can there be love? The good, you know, must be known before it can be loved.

Philo. We love Him to the degree that we know Him. Since He cannot be fully known by us, nor can His wisdom be grasped by men, it follows that He cannot be loved by us entirely, or to the degree which befits His nature. Nor are we capable of such a degree of love; and our mind is such that its knowledge is limited by the capacity of the knower rather than by the infinite value of the object of knowledge. So we love Him, not as He merits loving, but yet with all the intensity of which we are capable.

Sophia. But is any knowledge possible of that which the knower does not fully know?

Philo. It is enough that we know just that part which we do know. For the object of knowledge is grasped by the knower according to his powers, not according to those of the object. You know, for example, the way the figure of a man is impressed on and received in a mirror, not as a complete human being, but within its limited powers and capabilities, which are capable only of reflecting the figure and not the essence. Our eyes receive the nature of fire, not in conformity with its burning nature—else they would be destroyed—but in conformity with its visible qualities. Again, we apprehend the whole vast bowl of heaven by our tiny mote of an eye—and yet its minute size is such that there are wise men who regard it as indivisible and incapable of being further reduced. Still this eye is able to perceive objects according to its visual power, size, and nature, not according to the condition of things as they are. In this same way, our minute intellect apprehends God in His infinity—relative, that is, to the power and capacity of our intellect rather than to the bottomless deep of His divine essence and wisdom. And it is to this knowledge that there corresponds our love of God, which, therefore, is determined by human capacities rather than by the infinite goodness of God himself.

Sophia. Is desire involved in this love of God?

Philo. Love of God involves the most ardent desire: the desire, that is, to gain knowledge of Him, for the degree of our love keeps pace precisely with that of our knowledge. But as the nature of God infinitely transcends human capacities for knowledge; and as His goodness transcends no less the love that men hold for Him; so men nurture forever a happy desire—as ardent as it is boundless—to increase eternally their knowledge and love of God. Increase of knowledge is always possible in respect of such an object; although so far as human powers are concerned they may be limited and stopped at that point which no man may go beyond. It is possible, however, that even when that point is reached there can persist a trace of desire for that knowledge which man lacks and can never obtain—even though he draws from the nobility of his love's object a state of blessedness far beyond the ordinary faculties and dispositions of men. But for those in this state of blessedness, the desire causes no suffering due to the lack involved, since it is simply beyond human capacities to obtain more—rather, one's acquisition of the limits possible for such knowledge and love yield up supreme gratification.

Sophia. Once this point is reached, what is the nature of this human blessedness?

Philo. Here the opinions of men vary. Some hold that it consists in the profit and possession of the goods of fortune, and the abundance of these so long as life lasts. But this is clearly false: for material goods are good only in virtue of the spiritual good which is connected with them; and happiness must consist of something more excellent. To such happiness as this view involves, all else is a means, while it itself serves no further end, being a final end. Further, such material goods are subject to fortune, whereas the only true condition for happiness must be man himself. Others, who held a different opinion, maintained that blessedness consists in pleasure: these were the Epicureans, who believed the soul to be mortal, and held that there was no happiness for man beyond pleasure of every variety. But the falsity of this view is again obvious: pleasure destroys itself when it is sated, while happiness fosters complete content and perfect satisfaction. Now we have said before that the end of pleasure is the good, while happiness serves no other end, but is itself the final cause of all things. Unquestionably, then, happiness must consist in excellence and in the activities and dispositions of the intellect which are the most worthy and to which all other human activities are but means. Indeed, it is in virtue of this that man is man, and surpasses all other creatures.

Sophia. How many faculties of the intellect are there, and what are they?

Philo. There are five: art, prudence, understanding, science, and wisdom.

Sophia. How are they defined?

Philo. *Art* is the faculty of making things according to reason. It is required that these things be produced by our hands or physical labor. All mechanical crafts, to which our bodies are instrumental are included. *Prudence* is the faculty of acting according to reason. This is the business of human morality which includes all the virtues which have their seat in the will or which spring from the will's two chief affects: love and desire. *Understanding* is the faculty and principle which apprehends those axioms which everyone naturally admits as soon as he has grasped their sense: "good is to be pursued," for example; "evil is to be shunned"; "opposites cannot be predicated of the same subject"; and others of the same kind in which our intellectual faculty manifests its primary activities. *Science* is the faculty of knowledge and inference based on the just named principles. Under science we include the seven liberal arts, in which our intellect exhibits some of its highest activities. *Wisdom* is a faculty concerned with both principles and conclusions touching on all that exists. It alone seeks to attain the highest knowledge of spiritual things, which the Greeks call *theologia*—the science of the divine—and which is also called First Philosophy, as being the crown of all the sciences. It is in this discipline that our intellect behaves according to its highest and most perfect nature.

Sophia. In which of these faculties does happiness lie?

Philo. Certainly not in art or in the products of art. For these hinder rather than aid our acquisition of happiness. It is to be found, therefore, in the other faculties, whose activities aim at virtue or wisdom.

Sophia. In precisely which of these two qualities—virtue or wisdom—does happiness lie?

Philo. The moral virtues are indispensable to the achievement of happiness; happiness, however, really rests on wisdom. But wisdom is unattainable without moral virtue: he who lacks virtue, that is, cannot be wise. Virtue, then, is the road to wisdom—but wisdom is the temple of happiness.

Sophia. But knowledge is of many varieties, and different sciences are formed to deal with the different objects. Now tell me in which, or in how many of these sciences, happiness consists. Does it involve knowledge of all things that are, or of some only, or of a single one? And if a single one, which one is it the knowledge of that can assure our happiness?

Philo. Some wise men have held that happiness involves knowledge of all sciences and of all their objects.

Sophia. How do they support this view?

Philo. They say, to begin with, that the intellect is the power of understanding—a potentiality, that is, undifferentiated in itself and generally able to conform with all objects; or, as Aristotle says, our intellect is essentially a capacity to understand and grasp all things; it is the active intellect, on the other hand, which makes these things intelligible and enlightens the mind. Thus in the light of the active intellect all things are made intelligible, and cast their image or impression upon the intellectual substratum, which thus passes from potentiality to actuality in respect of all existent things; just as it is a power of apprehending all, so its perfection and happiness must lie in actually grasping all, so that no defect or unactualized potency be left in it. It is this, then, that serves for the supreme blessedness and happy end of the human mind; for in this way, they say, our mind becomes wholly freed from potentiality, and is made wholly actual, changing into and becoming one in all things with the active intellect illuminating it, as the potentiality, which previously separated them, is eliminated. Thus our power of intellection becomes pure actuality: and in this union lies supreme perfection and true blessedness. And this is known as the happy marriage between passive and active mind.

Sophia. This seems to me to be rather more high-flown than convincing; it comes rather more near establishing the nonexistence of blessedness than the manner in which it has being.

Philo. How is that?

Sophia. Because if no man is happy until he has knowledge of all things, then he will never be happy. It is impossible for a man to achieve knowledge of all existent things: life is too short, and the contents of the universe too numerous.

Philo. That is quite true: it is impossible for a man to know all things and know them individually. The different parts of earth contain so many varieties of plant, beast, bird, and lifeless elements that no man could possibly explore the whole of earth to see and study them all. Could he do this, and then investigate the seas' depths wherein are many more kinds of creatures than on earth, it would still be necessary to point out that we haven't studied the heavens. Who could possibly tell the number, nature, and properties of all the stars in the eighth sphere where the forty-eight different constellations are: twelve in the Zodiac through which the sun courses; twenty-one between the equator and the Arctic Pole, visible to us in what is known as the Northern Hemisphere; and the remaining fifteen visible in the Southern Hemisphere between the equator and the Antarctic Pole, which is hidden from us? Doubtless, too, in the southern-most zone around the Pole there are many other stars, forming constellations as yet unknown to us because they are always below our horizon. We were ignorant of this for some thousands of years. Only lately, indeed, have we gained some inkling of these things due to the voyages of the Portuguese and the Spaniards. I do not need to enumerate all that we do not know of the spiritual and angelic sphere, and of divine things, concerning which our knowledge is to our ignorance as a single drop of water is to the whole ocean. I pass over, too, all the things we perceive without knowing—even matters pertaining to ourselves—with respect to which there is a saying "ignorant even of our own peculiarities." At all events, we cannot doubt that there are many things in the world which we neither see nor perceive, and consequently, do not understand. As the Philosopher said, there can be nothing in the mind which was not first in the senses.

Sophia. How is that? Spiritual things are known to the intellect and these have never been seen or perceived.

Philo. Spiritual things are all intellect. And the light of the intellect is in our minds. This is not true of the things of sense, however, for they need the activity of intellect to render them intelligible, but intellect admits them as alien things. But inasmuch as they are all material, it is true to say that they cannot enter the intellect except by way of the senses.

Sophia. Is it the case that all spiritual matters are grasped because of their essential similarity with our intellect?

Philo. Not exactly—although that would be the most perfect variety of spiritual union. There is, however, another way: the grasping of spiritual matters through sight, or perception, of their effects. Seeing the perpetual motion of the heavens, for example, we then conclude that they are not moved by a body or by a material power, but rather by an immaterial spirit or mind. But if you had not first sensed the motion which it effects, you could not know this. This way of cognizing spiritual things is then succeeded by another even more perfect: when our intellect grasps the spiritual science inherent in itself, actualized by its identity of nature and essential unity with spiritual matters.

Sophia. I see. But let us not become sidetracked. You said that happiness cannot consist in knowledge of all things because it is impossible to know all things. But if it is impossible, I should like to know how wise men have insisted upon this view.

Philo. But those wise men did not mean that happiness consists in knowing all these particulars one at a time; they meant, by "knowing all things," knowledge of all the sciences which treat of all things according to certain universal notions. These give an account of the essence and modes of all existents, even though not every particular has been sensed by us.

Sophia. Well, is it possible for any one man to amass knowledge of all the sciences?

Philo. Even if it is possible, it is still highly improbable. The Philosopher says that all science is to be found easily, in one sense, and with difficulty, in another. "Easily," he means, in the collectivity of men, but "with difficulty" in any one man. Still, even if the possibility were realized, happiness could not consist in knowledge of numerous and separate things; for as the Philosopher says, happiness consists in the exercise of knowledge, not in its mere possession. The sage is happy while he is employing his wisdom, not while he is asleep. Blessedness, then, must consist in a single act of apprehension; because although we may possess many sciences, and all at once, yet we can but apprehend one object at any given instant—consequently, happiness cannot depend on our knowing all or numerous separate things, but must consist, rather, in our comprehension of a single object. Now it is true that in order to attain happiness we must become proficient in all the sciences, and in the art of demonstrating truth and distinguishing it from falsehood in all subjects and in all areas, which art is called logic; we must become proficient in moral philosophy, which consists in prudence and the exercise of virtue in our activities; also in natural philosophy, the study of all things capable of motion, change, and alteration. We must become knowledgeable about mathematics, which deals with numerable or mensurable quantities. Considered as pure numbers, mathematics embraces the study of arithmetic; studied as the quantity of sounds, it constitutes music; as pure measure, it makes up the science of geometry. When it deals with the dimensions and motions of the heavenly bodies, it makes up the science of astrology. Above all, however, we must become perfect in that branch of learning which comes nearest to perfect conjunction with happiness: First Philosophy, that is, which alone is truly called wisdom, as it has for object all things that have being, and it deals with them particularly with respect to the degrees in which their essences excel that of others in nobility and worth. It is this science alone which treats of spiritual and eternal things. The essence of these spiritual things is of far more value and greater intelligibility than that of material and corruptible things, even though they may seem to us to be less intelligible, since, unlike material things, they are quite outside the range of our senses. Our intellect, in respect of these things, is like the eye of the bat in respect of light and visible objects; for although sunlight is brilliant, bats cannot gaze upon it as their eyes are unaccustomed to such splendor, being adapted to the glow of night which is more proportionate to their powers. It is this wisdom, First Philosophy, which touches on the knowledge of divine things—so far, of course, as these are accessible to the human intellect. Hence it is called *theologia*, which means *study of God*. It is in this way that knowledge of the several sciences is requisite for happiness, although happiness does not itself consist in these, but rather in the most perfect apprehension of a single object.

Sophia. What science and what object is this, the knowledge of which alone makes a man happy? Whatever it is, I cannot help but think it strange that the cause of happiness should be regarded as a function of knowledge of a part rather than a whole. Your earlier argument, you see, from which you drew the conclusion that happiness consists in actual knowledge of all things or sciences which our intellect has the power to apprehend, seemed to me to argue that our intellect, being such a power, should discover its happiness in the actualized knowledge of all possible objects. And if I am right in this, then how can it find happiness, as you maintain, in a single apprehension?

Philo. Your argument is valid: but one truth cannot contradict another, so one of the two conclusions must yield to the other. Now you must accept that happiness consists in knowledge of one thing only. It is not the case that it lies in knowledge of all things individually, but rather in the cognition of a single object which comprises, in itself, everything in the universe. The cognition of this one object, then, will involve the cognition of all others, simultaneously, in a single act—and it provides a more perfect cognition than would be possible even if each were cognized separately and individually.

Sophia. What one thing is this, which, being but one, yet comprises all things together?

Philo. Of itself, the intellect has no fixed essence, but is potentially all things. Its essence, that is, is the power of understanding all things. Intellect in act, however, is pure being and pure form; it contains within itself all being and all forms and acts in the universe. It contains them all in essence, in unity, and in pure simplicity. Now whoever could apprehend this intellect would, in a single apprehension, and with a simple cognitive act, apprehend the full being of all things in the universe; and this would be accomplished with an intellectual vision far more perfect, in terms of clarity and intelligibility, than their own natures would yield—for material things, when understood, approach to the condition of beings more perfect than themselves. In a single apprehension of active intellect, then, man can grasp the whole of the sciences and their objects. In this way, he achieves happiness.

Sophia. What intellect is this that you keep referring to?

Philo. Some call it the active intellect, which, by joining our potential intellect, brings about a conjoined vision of all reality in a single act of the most dazzling apprehension. They hold that happiness comes at that moment. Others, however, hold that we are happy when our intellect, wholly illumined by its union with the active intellect, becomes fully actual—lacking any potentiality—and then recognizes itself according to its most profound intellective essence in which are contained all things, made spirit. In this recognition, the object and the act of intellection become one—inseparable, indistinguishable. Those who maintain this view, add that the intellect, when thus actualized, becomes and remains one, in essence, with the active intellect, with no element of division or duality remaining. The greatest philosophers, indeed, discourse on love in these terms—but it is out of keeping with the present occasion to go into all their arguments for this position. I shall say only that those who meditate most on these matters—and I am in agreement with them—hold that the active intellect, which lights our own powers of understanding, is the Most High God. It follows, then, that they are of the opinion that happiness consists in cognition of the divine intellect, which, in itself, embraces all things more perfectly than any created intellect. These things, of course, obtain within Him effectively, and not merely rationally, but in the sense of cause—for He is the first and absolute cause of all. Thus He is at once their efficient cause, the mind that comprehends them, the form which informs them, and the end which directs them and for which they were created. All proceed from Him; ultimately, all return to Him, as their final and true end and common happiness. He is the first being; all that exists, exists by reason of participation in Him. His is the supreme intellect, upon which all intellect, act, form, and perfection depend. All things tend toward Him as to their most perfect end. All subsist in Him without multiplicity or division, in utter simplicity and union. He is true happiness. He is necessary to all, while none are necessary to Him. In contemplating himself, He knows all; and He both contemplates and is contemplated by himself alone. Were one able to see with His sight, he would see all in perfect harmony. No one, however, is capable of this; but all comprehend to the degree that they are able to do so. According to their capacity, the human and the angelic intellect contemplate; and according as they view things united in the highest perfection, they partake of His happiness; and they become and remain happy, conformable with the character of their being. I can say no more than this, as it goes beyond the scope of our discussion; and besides, human discourse is incapable of fully expressing such experiences of the spirit. Material sounds simply cannot reproduce the spiritual purity of divine things. Let it suffice that you understand that human happiness consists in the knowledge and vision of God in whom we behold all things with perfection.

Sophia. I shall press you no further on this. It suffices, as you say—indeed, it even exceeds—my powers of comprehension. But I have a difficulty: I once heard it said that happiness consists in love and blissful enjoyment of God rather than in knowledge of Him. Can you speak to this point for me?

Philo. God alone is the true object of our happiness; and we adore Him through love and knowledge. Wise men, it is true, have differed on these two activities: does happiness lie in knowing God or in loving Him? Content yourself with knowing that both activities are necessary to happiness.

Sophia. What are the grounds upon which these differing views are based?

Philo. Those who insist that happiness lies in loving

God argue as follows: Happiness consists in that activity of soul which is ultimate, so far as God is concerned; but God is man's ultimate end; and since it is requisite that we know Him before we love Him, it follows that happiness consists in the love, rather than the knowledge, of God. They continue by pointing out that pleasure is essentially bound up with happiness, and that pleasure is an affect of the will, from which it follows that true happiness is of the will—i.e., love, for it is love from which the pleasure derives and not from the activity of intellect, for this latter is less bound to pleasure. Their opposition, on the other hand, reasons as follows: Happiness consists in the activity of the most essential and spiritual faculty of the soul; and as the faculty of intellect is more essential than the will, and more completely abstracted from material things, it follows that happiness—far from being an activity of the will manifested in love of God—is secondary to knowledge of Him in the acquisition of happiness.

Sophia. Both arguments seem to me to possess equal force. How would you decide between them?

Philo. It is not simple to attempt to resolve a problem which has been discussed for so long—by ancient philosophers as well as by contemporary theologians. Nevertheless, I shall say something—even though I am aware that you have directed me into this whole discussion in order to stop me from telling you, as I wanted to, how my soul is in torture on your account!

Sophia. Please do so. Perhaps, when we have wearied of divine things, we can discuss our own human friendship with more open minds.

Philo. The proposition that happiness consists in the ultimate activity of soul is both true and necessary. It is similarly true and necessary that happiness consists in an activity of the most noble and spiritual faculties of the soul—the intellect. That love presupposes knowledge is undeniable. But it does not follow from this that love is the ultimate activity of the soul. Of God, as of all other objects of love and desire, there are two forms of knowledge: one precedes and causes love—but such knowledge is not simply one; the other form is caused by, and follows, love—this knowledge is simply one, and results in the enjoyment of perfect union. If bread, for example, is known in the first way, it is loved and desired when we are hungry; for if we first had not knowledge of it, we could neither love nor desire it. And it is in virtue of this love and desire that we attain to simple cognition of the bread—i.e., we actually eat it—for the true knowledge of bread lies in the tasting. The same holds of the relation between men and women: for from knowledge of them there springs love and desire which lead to the union in knowledge, which is the end of desire. The case is the same with respect to everything else we love and desire; for, as regards them all, love and desire are means of progressing from imperfect knowledge to perfect union, which is the true end of love and desire. Now these are affects of the will, as we know, which transmute dual cognition into enjoyment of perfect cognitive union. When you grasp the essential nature of these two affects of the will, you will then see that it does not differ greatly from that of mental desire and mental love, although when we discussed this matter before we just touched it in a most general way and so we concluded somewhat differently. Love, I think, can really be defined as *desire to enjoy in union an object known to be good*—and this, even though I said before that desire presupposes the absence of its object. Now, however, I shall add that even when the good exists, and is ours, we may yet desire—not the possession of the object, for this is already ours—but enjoyment of cognitive union with it; and such future enjoyment we may desire because it is not yet actual. It is this desire which we call love—a desire to possess things we lack, or a desire to enjoy in union those which we have obtained. Both of these may be properly called desire, but it is more accurate to call the second love. Love, then, we define as *a desire to enjoy in union*—or, perhaps better, *to become one with—the object of love*. Now to return to the subject matter: I say that we must first possess that knowledge of God which it is possible to attain in respect of so sublime, so infinite a subject; and, as we aspire to His perfection—although incapable of apprehending it completely—we love and desire to enjoy Him in the most perfect union of knowledge possible to us. The magnitude of this love and desire of ours ravishes us into such contemplation as expands our intellect until, illuminated by special grant of God, it transcends the limits of human capacity and speculation and attains to such union and conjunction with the Most High God that we may be sure that our intellect is itself a part of the essence of God rather than a mere human form. Then our desire and love are satisfied with a satisfaction which far transcends our first knowledge and our former loves. Yet love and desire may very well persist—no longer for union in knowledge which has already been attained, but for continuation of the enjoyment of this union with God. And this is the most true love. I can't say that we experience pleasure in this blessed enjoyment, except in the moment of its attainment, when the pleasure stems from the obtaining of what we desired and lacked. Most pleasures, as you know, spring from the satisfaction of a need and the obtaining of what we had desired; but the man who enjoys the activity of this blessed union retains no sense of imperfections, but undergoes the complete satisfaction of a union which exceeds all pleasures, delights, and joys. In conclusion, however, I should like you to know that happiness does not consist in that primary act of knowing God which gives rise to love; it consists solely in the conjunctive act of intimate cognitive union with Him, wherein there is to be found the supreme perfection of created minds. It is this which is the ultimate activity and blessed end; it is in this that we become divine rather than human. For this reason, Holy Scripture—after enjoining us to recognize the perfect and pure unity of God, and to love Him above the profits of greed and the pleasures of appetite, as well as all the goods pursued by the spirit and rational will—commands as the ultimate end that we *cleave unto God.* In other places, promising supreme bliss, it is written: *And ye shall cleave unto God*—with no promise of anything further, as life, or eternal glory, or supreme pleasure, delight, infinite splendor, or any other such thing. Conjunction is the most proper and most accurate term to designate bliss. In conjunction, there is comprised all the good and perfection of the intellect—it is its true happiness. It is not easy, it is true, to attain such bliss in this life; or, having gained it, to maintain it forever. This is because while we live our intellect is imprisoned, in a certain way, within the matter of our frail body. For this reason, some who had attained the conjunction of which I spoke could not continue in perpetual enjoyment of it. After conjunction with God, they returned to the recognition of material things as before—but before that, as they reached the limit of life, the soul in the embrace of God wished to abandon the body altogether, remaining in supreme bliss, in conjunction with the Godhead. And the soul which achieves this experience, let loose of its imprisoning environs, enjoys without impediment its happy union with the light, just as the blessed angels and disembodied intelligences, each according to the degree of its dignity and perfection, enjoy it forever. Now, Sophia, this should content you with respect to spiritual things. Would you be so kind now as to return to me, and think about a remedy for the torture which you, my heart's desire, have inflicted upon me? Offer some remedy, please, with which I may keep body and soul together.

Sophia. But not before you tell me the nature of the love which you profess to hold for me. You have grouped in three categories, and expounded upon the nature of the many different loves and desires encountered in man: now tell me, which variety of love do you bear me?

Philo. The love I bear you, Sophia, not even I can understand or explain! I feel its power, but I do not understand it—its strength is such that it has made itself master over my whole spirit. It controls me. It is my sovereign ruler. I, its bondservant, cannot rise to knowledge of it. I am sure of but one thing, however: that the end of my desire is pleasure.

Sophia. In that case, do not request that I, as the remedy, satisfy your longing. And do not reproach me for withholding satisfaction from you: you yourself told me that when one obtains the pleasurable end of desire, it is not only the case that the desire ceases, but love, as well, is destroyed and turned into hatred!

Philo. It is bad enough that you pick from our argument only that fruit which is sweet and salutary to you: must you pick, as well, for me that fruit which is bitter and poisonous! How God must frown at this! You are ungrateful and pitiless if you can thus, with the very arrow which sped from my bow in your service, cruelly stab my heart!

Sophia. But if, as I believe, you count your love for me to be a worthwhile thing, I should be doing it a great disservice if, in the granting of your desire, I brought about the extinction of your love. I would indeed be displaying cruelty if I did this—both to you and to myself; as this would put an end both to your loving and to my being loved. Let me instead be kind to both of us: I shall deny you the object of your passionate desire so that your sweet love may endure!

Philo. But you are fooling yourself—or perhaps you are teasing me in attributing to me a premise both utterly false and totally inapplicable to love: namely, that pursuit of the object of desire extinguishes love and turns into hatred. This is most false!

Sophia. False, did you say? But didn't you previously show that it is an essential attribute of love of pleasure that its satisfaction results in loathing and aversion?

Philo. Not *all* pleasures thus breed disgust when attained. Virtue and knowledge, for example, delight without cloying. Indeed, we constantly seek their increase. And it is not only with such objects that are good in themselves, but others as well, which are not good in themselves—such as power, honor, and wealth—which are pleasurable to obtain and yet never breed disgust. Quite the contrary: the more we have of them, the more we desire!

Sophia. It seems to me that you are contradicting all that you formerly said about pleasure!

Philo. Not at all: what I said before was that those objects generate satiety and loathing which satisfy only our exterior senses or, rather, the material senses, such as taste and touch. But this is not the case—at least, not to the same degree—with the senses of sight, hearing, and smell. Solomon said that *the eye is not satisfied with seeing, nor the ear filled with hearing.* Even less, then, are fancy and imagination sated with the things which gratify them, such as honor, riches, dominion, and such things. These, one never tires of pursuing; but far more insatiable is the pleasure taken by the mind and intellect in the activities of virtue and wisdom. And the more inexhaustible the pleasure, the more noble and better it is.

Sophia. I understand quite clearly that the soul's more spiritual faculties enjoy a correspondingly greater degree of inexhaustible and cloyless pleasure. But what your desire expects of me is satisfaction, in the common sense, of touch. And it is precisely this sense whose satisfaction is most immediately followed by satiety and loathing. It seems to me, then, quite reasonable to deny your desire.

Philo. It is clear that the senses of touch and taste (which two, of the five, serve to maintain the existence of the individual and the species alike, through successive procreation of like kinds, which is the function of touch) have their functions limited by nature to a greater extent than the others. The reason for this is that the other three or four senses are not indispensable to the continued existence of the individual or of the species, but subserve, rather, the well-being of man and the higher animals. Consequently, as their being is not indispensable, they have no need of limitations on their functions; and, as the life of a man does not depend upon his sight, hearing, or smell, neither is it destroyed by too much indulgence in these—unless it be by accident. Touch and taste, however, being necessary to the perpetuation of man, so that their destruction would seriously affect his state, cannot be indulged in excess. Excess of eating and drinking, for example, kill no less surely than hunger and thirst; carnal copulation, as well, if performed in excess, is fatal; and extreme of heat and cold affect us similarly adversely. This is because the bond of pleasure being, as it is, most intimately connected to these two senses—because, as I said, of their responsible position with respect to the perpetuation of the race—it became requisite to set natural limits upon them, so that whenever pleasure goaded them to harmful excess they might be restrained by natural limitations, and so save the individual from destruction. Nature thus showed her wisdom in imposing natural limits and constraints on the senses of touch and taste rather than on any of the others, no less than she displayed her wisdom in their design. And although it may be the case that a lover's appetite is sated by the union of copulation, and that his desire is, as a consequence of this, extinguished, still the love in his heart is not sated. Indeed, it makes possible a closer and more binding union which actually converts the one lover into the other or, rather, fuses them both in one, eliminating, so far as this is possible, any difference between them. Thus the love endures in greater perfection and unity; and the lover remains continuously desirous of enjoying the beloved union, which is the true definition of love.

Sophia. So you admit that the end of your desire does reside in the most material of the senses: the sense of touch! I am astonished that you should place the end of love in so lowly a thing if love, as you say, is so spiritual!

Philo. I did not say that this is the end of perfect love; what I have been insisting, however, is that this act, far from destroying perfect love, proves and integrates it by means of the bodily acts of love, which acts are desired because they give evidence of the reciprocity of love between the lovers. Further, when two spirits are absorbed in spiritual love, their bodies desire to further the union so that no distinction whatsoever may obtain between them, with the union being in all ways complete—the more so, as a corresponding physical union augments and completes the spiritual love, even as prudence is perfected by the congruity of prudent actions. Finally, I wish to inform you that whereas we before defined love in general, the proper definition of the perfect love of a man for a woman is *the conversion of the lover into the beloved together with a desire for the conversion of the beloved into the lover.* And when this love is mutual, it is defined as *the conversion of each lover into the other.*

Sophia. These are subtle arguments, albeit plausible—still I prefer to judge what you are saying by my own experience, which, as I see it, is more credible than any argument! Now in my experience it is the case that many have been seen to love who, after having possessed their beloved physically, ceased not only to desire but even to love them at all! Love in some cases, indeed, being replaced by detestation! This was the case with Amnon, son of David, who so loved his sister, Tamar, that he wasted away to the point of death in his desire for her. Yet, when Jonadab had by wiles and fraud managed to bring about the consummation of his desire, Amnon immediately conceived such a hatred of her that even in the condition that she was in after he had ravished her, he drove her, in the middle of the day, from his house.

Philo. Love is of two varieties: one is engendered by desire or sensuous appetite—a man may love a woman, that is, because he desires her. This kind of love is not perfect; it derives from an inconstant and vicious source: desire. Amnon's love for Tamar was of this kind; and in cases of this sort it does, as you observe, eventuate with the cessation of all love; because when the cause, desire, no longer operates, neither does its effect, love, which may even be converted to abhorrence, as happened in this case. But the other love generates desire of the beloved, rather than the other way around. In fact, we first love perfectly, in this second kind of love, and then the strength of that love makes us desire spiritual and bodily union with the beloved. Thus the first kind of love is the child of desire, while the second is the true begetter of desire. Now when this love obtains the gratification of its desire, it does not therefore come to an end, although the desire and appetite may do so; for the removal of an effect does not bring about the removal of the cause; the more so as there is—and I repeat it now—no cessation of the perfect desire to enjoy union with the beloved—this desire being ever connected with love as an essential portion. What does quit immediately, however, is a particular desire and appetite for the bodily act of love; and that ceases only because of the natural limits imposed on this activity. You have no grounds, therefore, for rejecting the perfect love which I offer you, unless you think of it as an imperfect love. The love I bear you, be assured, is not the child of desire but, rather, the other way round; and if you recall, my very first words to you were to the effect that my acquaintance with you had awakened within me *love and desire*—I did *not* say *desire and love*, because my love is not derivative in any way from my desire, but rather precedes it, as its cause.

Sophia. But if the love which you hold for me does not spring from appetite, and is not begotten of desire, nor, as the saying goes, is it "born of idleness and human abandon," please tell me what *has* brought it about? Undoubtedly, all human love has a beginning and a birth; and everything which is born must be born of another—there can be no son without a father, no effect without a cause.

Philo. Such perfect and true love as I bear you, which begets desire, is born of reason. True reason has engendered it within me. I know you to possess virtue, intelligence, and beauty, admirable and seductive, and my will desired your person, which reason correctly judged to be noble, excellent, and worthy of love in every way. My affection and love has transformed me into you, begetting in me a desire that you may be fused with me, in order that I, your lover, may create with you, my beloved, a single being, with our mutual love making of our two souls, one, which may in the same way vitalize and inform our two bodies. The sensual element in this desire excites a longing for bodily union, so that the union of bodies may match the unity of spirits which wholly mesh with one another. Observe, Sophia, how this sequence of reason and knowledge, which first begot love, and which then begot desire, was implicit in my opening words to you—that my acquaintance with you had awakened love and desire within me. It was the acquaintance which I had with your adorable qualities which caused me to love you; then love, in its turn, urged me to desire you.

Sophia. How can you maintain that true love is born of reason? It is well known that perfect love defies and rejects all reason. Therefore, it is referred to as "unbridled"—it will not submit to the bridle of reason, nor even wear one at all!

Philo. What you say is quite true. Now although I said that such love is *born* of reason, I did *not* say that it was bound or controlled by reason. I say, as a matter of fact, that once having been born of reason and knowledge, love no longer submits to dictation by the reason which sired it, but repudiates its parent, becoming, as you say, so unmanageable as to bring harm to its votaries. For he who truly loves another, loves not himself—which is opposed to all reason and duty. Love, like charity, should begin at home; but the lover disregards this, loving another more than himself: a most remarkable thing! But because love, after birth, is totally lacking in reason, he is always pictured blind, sightless; and inasmuch as love desires beauty and is born of reason as she discerns the beauty, goodness, and love-worthiness of another, Venus, as the mother of love, is pictured with beautiful eyes. Cupid is depicted naked because great love cannot be concealed by reason, nor masked by prudence because of the unbearable tortures it inflicts. Cupid, further, is depicted as a babe because he is quite lacking in prudence and not subject to her demands; he is shown as winged because of the speed with which he enters the soul and urges it in eternal pursuit of the beloved; he is shown as abstracted because, as Euripides says, lovers exist only in the person of another; he is portrayed as an archer because he strikes from afar, aiming at the heart as his proper target, and also because the wound of love is totally unexpected and in every way like that of the arrow—deep-piercing, although the lips of the wound may be close-set; a wound not easy to discern, difficult to tend, and extremely difficult to heal. Seen from the surface, one might account it of no great moment; yet that which is hidden is extremely dangerous and in the form of an incurable fistula. And even as an arrow wound is not healed when one unstrings the bow from which it proceeded, so the wound of true love will not be made whole by any joy which chance may award or which the beloved may sometimes concede, nor by the irreplaceable loss of the beloved in death. Wonder not, therefore, that perfect love, though born of reason, is not subject to reason.

Sophia. Indeed not! I wonder, rather, how it is that love can be admirable when it is not governed by reason and prudence? I thought, as a matter of fact, that it was in this that the difference between virtuous love and wanton love was grounded. I am now baffled as to what sort this perfect love might be.

Philo. You have missed the point. Lack of restraint is not characteristic of wanton love but pertains, rather, to all great and noble loves—good or bad. The only difference is that when the love is good, its excess heightens the virtue, while when it is evil, excess aggravates the fault. Who can gainsay that good love may involve strange and limitless desires? What love is more noble than the love of God? And yet what love is more avid and unrestricted? It certainly is not subject to reason, which guides and tends to the preservation of men, since for the love of God men have held themselves to be worthless and even sought to destroy themselves. Many, indeed, love God so much that they do not love themselves, even as unhappy men love themselves so much that they do not love God. Finally, how many have sought to die and have consumed themselves in the name of love of virtue and glorious fame? But common reason does not condone such self-destruction—it orders things, rather, with a view to their well-being. Need I add that many have paid court to death gladly for the sake of the love they bore their friends? Now although I can cite any number of such examples, in order to avoid prolixity I shall omit them. But all this considered, surely the burning love and limitless affection of a man for a woman is not more deserving of reproach than that of a man for his friend, so long as it is born of true knowledge and judgment that she is worthy to be loved. Love like this is no less noble than pleasurable.

Sophia. And yet I would rather have your love governed by the reason from whence it sprang. Reason governs every person of worth.

Philo. But such a love can never possess a lover and, though we might call it love, such a love would not truly be love. True love controls the reason, as well as the entire being of a lover, with a most wonderful power and marvelous violence. It troubles the mind, the very throne of judgment, more than any other single human condition, canceling from it the memory of all other things with which it might concern itself, and utterly splitting a man in two, making him, in truth, an adjunct of the beloved. True love makes the lover an enemy of society and its pleasures; he is a lover of solitude and melancholy; he is filled with passions, girded with sufferings, tormented by doubts, crucified by desire, nurtured on hope, swept by despair, weighted by thought, harassed and cruelly afflicted by suspicion, stabbed by jealousy; he is without respite in his distress, without rest from his labors, attended always by sorrow and filled with sighs, never freed from anxieties and wrongs. What more can I say except that the lover's is a continuing death within life, and life within death? But what is even more astounding is that no matter how overwhelming and unbearable his burden, the lover yet never hopes, wishes, or plans to escape it; and he regards as his mortal enemy whoever wishes to advise him on how to ease his lot! Does it seem rational to you, Sophia, that a man caught up in such a web cannot be made to abide the laws of reason or the rules of prudence?

Sophia. Please, Philo, soften your words. I know only too well that lover's pangs are as nothing compared to his protestations!

Philo. Your not believing them proves only that you have not experienced them. Only those who love can credit the immensity of a lover's suffering. If my malady were only contagious, then you would not merely believe every word I say, but much more. For I can neither articulate what I feel, nor can I maintain silence. My words cannot convey the least part of what I suffer. How could you imagine that a lover's tongue might remain free to invent his passions while he is at the same time plunged into such utter darkness and confusion that his reason is blasted, his memory preoccupied, his fancy distraught, and his sense overcome with infernal pain? What I do manage to utter is only that which words can convey and my tongue control. The rest I leave to him to understand who has himself experienced what I suffer; who has himself drunk of the bittersweet of love and could not—nor would he—had not the wit to—refuse its spiced poison when it was first offered. In truth, I can find no way to communicate it. My soul burns; my heart blazes; I am one all-consuming fire! Don't you think that one who finds himself in this condition would, if he but could, extricate himself? Yet he cannot. He is not at liberty to free, or even try to free, himself. How can he who is unfree then be governed by reason? Corporeal bondage leaves at least the will free; but love's bondage first binds the lover's will and then subjects his whole person to this captive will.

Sophia. That lovers undergo torment until they obtain their heart's desire is a truism; but directly after, the ship of love lies completely becalmed. Their suffering, then, proceeds, it would seem, rather from desire of what they lack than from any true love.

Philo. Again you speak out of the depths of your inexperience! For if the lover's torments cease with the carnal possession of his beloved, his love springs not from reason, but from simple bodily appetite; and, as I told you before, his sufferings and passions would be carnal, not spiritual, like those profound and exquisitely poignant ones which lovers feel whose love springs from reason. For these, the torment is not relieved, nor the love dulled, by carnal possession of the beloved; rather, it is the case that if they suffered greatly before, after such union they will suffer far more painfully!

Sophia. But why should their passions swell after they have achieved their heart's desire?

Philo. Because their love is a desire for perfect union of the lover with the beloved; which union involves complete dissolution of one within the other. Their souls can accomplish this, for they are spirits, and incorporeal spirits can interpenetrate, unite, and come together as one. But in their bodies, which are distinct, each with a spatial location of its own, there remains after such union and interpenetration—by contrast with what it is that they both desire—an even more avid longing for that union which they can never perfectly achieve. And as the mind strives ever for complete fusion with the beloved, and even abandons the person of the lover in the attempt to accomplish this, the very incompleteness of the union, occasioned by the corporeal limitations, causes the continuation of torment and suffering which no reason, will, or prudence can restrain or resist.

Sophia. My soul is prone to accept your arguments. But there is one thing which I find it difficult to comprehend, and that is that any good in man, or in the world, for that matter, should not be subject to reason. Quite evidently reason is the ruler and mistress of all good and admirable things, since the value of things is determined as a function of their participation in reason; how then can you maintain that perfect love is not ruled by reason?

Philo. As this appears to be your last doubt, let it also be the last problem which I shall deal with in this discourse. There are, you must know, two sorts of reason found in man: one we may call *common,* the other, *uncommon.* It is the function of the former to sustain and preserve men in the good life—all other things, hence, are subordinated to this end, and whatever stands as an obstacle to the good life of man is, by this common reason, scorned and refused. This is that reason, which, as I said before, has no place in perfect love; for such love in its pursuit of the beloved injures and afflicts our own person, life, and welfare with insufferable dis-eases. It is the purpose of the uncommon reason, on the other hand, to attain the beloved; and it is no respecter of our own interests, but prefers, before them, possession of the beloved, even as the best is to be preferred before the good. As the philosopher says, the beloved is more perfect than the lover; for it is the beloved which is the end, and the end is always more perfect than that which serves as a means to its attainment. Further, it is quite reasonable to labor for an article of high value as the following natural and moral illustrations will demonstrate: first with respect to nature: a man about to be wounded in the head you will see strive to guard it with his arm—the head being the more valuable and worthy part. Just so in the case of the lover and the beloved interpenetrating as one: the beloved is the more important, and the lover the lesser factor in the union. As a consequence, it is entirely natural for the lover to avoid no affliction or suffering to possess the beloved; but he should, indeed, follow her as his true end with every possible diligence and fervor, disregarding all that pertains to himself, because he is, to tell the truth, not his but another's. The example from moral philosophy is this: common reason enjoins us to conserve our possessions against the time when we may have need of them; but the higher reason bids us to utilize these possessions well and fittingly with respect to others—to, that is, the more noble end of acquiring the virtue of liberality. The former enjoins us to seek our utility and virtuous pleasure; the latter has us rather labor and burden both body and mind for a nobler end—judged a worthier love by reason.

Sophia. And which of the two do you feel that we should follow, Philo?

Philo. It is the second which is the more worthy and the higher in rank, even as the prudence of the liberal man in spending his money is more worthy than the prudence of the miser in hoarding his wealth. For, although it is true that he who acquires wealth is prudent, yet he who liberally dispenses this wealth is both greater and more noble in his prudence. But the man who, guided by reason, perseveres in a good and worthy love without enjoying it, is like a fine tree, which, although evergreen and many branched, yet bears no fruit—it is, in a word, sterile. And he in whom there dwells no good love at all is attended by the fewest virtues. But he who seeks his pleasure in women and a formless love, such as stems from bodily appetite unsupported by reason's evaluation of the merits of the beloved, is like a tree bearing lethal fruits, the rinds of which are sweet-tasting. The first-named love, however, ordained by reason, displays a great sweetness, not only to the bodily appetite but to the immaterial mind as well. And when you, Sophia, learn the important part played by love throughout the entire universe, not only as it obtains among bodies but even more among spirits; when you see how, from the primordial cause to the last created thing, there is not one but which loves; you will then hold it in greater esteem—then, indeed, you may attain to a greater knowledge of its true origins.

Sophia. If it is your wish to bring me utter peace, expound this to me as well.

Philo. It is late—very late—for such a story. It is time, indeed, that you sought your bed, while I, as usual, shall keep my tortured vigil. But believe this: though my mind remains alone, you are with it always; and so the torture of its vigil is relieved with joy. Goodnight.

Suggested Readings

MARSILIO FICINO

COPLESTON, F. C. *A History of Philosophy*, vol. 3. London, 1953.
DELLA TORRE, A. *Storia dell'Accademia Platonica di Firenze*. Florence, 1902.
FICINO, M. *Commentary on Plato's Symposium*, ed. and trans. S. Jayne. *University of Missouri Studies*, vol. 19, No. 1, 1944.
———. *Five Questions concerning the Mind*, trans. J. Burroughs, in E. Cassirer *et al.*, eds., *The Renaissance Philosophy of Man*. Chicago, 1948.
HÖFFDING, H. *History of Modern Philosophy*, vol. 1. New York, 1950.
KLIBANSKY, R. *The Continuity of the Platonic Tradition during the Middle Ages*. London, 1950.
KRISTELLER, P. O. *Eight Philosophers of the Italian Renaissance*. Stanford, 1964.
———. *The Philosophy of Marsilio Ficino*, trans. V. Conant. New York, 1943.
MAURER, A. A. *Medieval Philosophy*. New York, 1962.
NELSON, J. C. *Renaissance Theory of Love*. New York, 1958.
RANDALL, J. H. *The Career of Philosophy*. New York, 1962.
ROBB, N. A. *Neoplatonism of the Italian Renaissance*. London, 1935.
SAITTA, G. *Marsilio Ficino e la filosofia dell'umanesimo*. Bologna, 1954.

GIOVANNI PICO DELLA MIRANDOLA

ANAGNINE, E. G. *Pico della Mirandola*. Bari, 1937.
COPLESTON, F. C. *A History of Philosophy*, vol. 3. London, 1953.
DULLES, A. *Princeps Concordiae: Pico della Mirandola and the Scholastic Tradition*. Cambridge, Mass., 1941.
GARIN, E. *Giovanni Pico della Mirandola*. Florence, 1937.
HÖFFDING, H. *History of Modern Philosophy*, vol. 1. New York, 1950.
KIBRE, P. *The Library of Pico della Mirandola*. New York, 1936.
KRISTELLER, P. O. *Eight Philosophers of the Italian Renaissance*. Stanford, 1964.
PICO, G. *Of Being and Unity*, trans. V. M. Hamm. Milwaukee, 1943.

———. *Oration on the Dignity of Man,* trans. E. L. Forbes, in E. Cassirer *et al.*, eds., *The Renaissance Philosophy of Man.* Chicago, 1948.
———. A *Platonick Discourse upon Love,* trans. Thomas Stanley, ed. P. G. Gardner. Boston, 1914.
RANDALL, J. H. *The Career of Philosophy.* New York, 1962.

LEONE EBREO

BRÉHIER, É. *The History of Philosophy; The Middle Ages and the Renaissance,* trans. W. Baskin. Chicago, 1965.
COPLESTON, F. C. A *History of Philosophy,* vol. 3. London, 1953.
NELSON, J. C. *Renaissance Theory of Love.* New York, 1958.
RANDALL, J. H. *The Career of Philosophy.* New York, 1962.
ZIMMELS, B. *Leo Hebraeus.* Leipzig, 1886.
———. *Leone Hebreo, Neue Studien.* Vienna, 1892.

III

RENAISSANCE ARISTOTELIANISM

PIETRO POMPONAZZI

Born in Mantua in 1462, Pietro Pomponazzi studied philosophy and medicine at the University of Padua. He stayed on at Padua after obtaining the degree, accepting a professorship in 1488. He left only after the university was shut down because of the war of the League of Cambrai in 1509. Pomponazzi resumed teaching at the University of Ferrara; finally, he accepted, in 1512, a professorship at the University of Bologna. He remained at this post until his death in 1525. He was a layman, and married three times. Of his writings, only a few were published while he was still alive. Among the most famous and philosophically significant of his works are De immortalitate animae, De incantationibus *and* De fato. *The latter two works were published posthumously in Basel, in 1556 and 1567 respectively.*

On God's Foreknowledge and Human Freedom*

BOOK IV

CHAPTER I

In which the intention is posited and certain arguments are adduced which try to show that divine providence and free will cannot obtain simultaneously.

Previously we considered free will and the providence of God in themselves and not compared with each other. In

* Translated by Frederick Scott especially for this volume.

this book, however, we intend to investigate whether free will and divine providence can obtain together. As Boethius says in Book V of his *De consolatione*, this is a most ancient problem, a problem which Cicero raises also in his *De divinatione*. The difficulty owes to the fact that knowledge and opinion are distinct: as is said in the *Prior Analytics*, knowledge is with certitude, which is something perfect, whence it cannot be removed from God; opinion, however, is with fear, which obviously cannot be but imperfect, whence it can in no manner be attributed to God, since thus God would be imperfect. Therefore, this providence ought to be with certitude, which cannot fail or vary. On the other hand, true free will is contingent and undetermined. How, then, can free will, which is variable and undetermined, be subject to divine providence, which is most certain and unchanging?

Now the Stoics and the followers of Cicero thought that these two could not coexist or stand together, although the Stoics spoke otherwise than the Ciceronians about the two parts of this difficulty. For the Stoics granted providence but denied free will, while the Ciceronians granted free will but denied that divine providence extended to the sphere of human action. Both of these positions are opposed to the truth and the Christian religion. Moreover, later writers have argued the same way as the former. If God knows now, and knew for a thousand years in the past, all that will be—since upon the knowledge of a thing it follows that the thing is, as is stated in the *Posterior Analytics*—it follows that, if God knew all things which will be, they will be. Therefore, since the antecedent is necessary, so is the consequent, as is shown in Book II of the *Prior Analytics*. But the antecedent is necessary simply, because the past cannot not be past, as Aristotle writes in Book VI of the *Ethics* where he approves the dictum of Agathon: *For this alone is lacking even to God, to make undone what once was done*. Thus it is necessary that all those things which will be, will be; because they will not be able not to be. Since human acts will be, and necessarily, free will is eliminated. Necessity and such liberty exclude one another.

Again, what is known by God must be; otherwise His knowledge would not be certain but changeable, which is repugnant to His perfection. But whatever is going to be, is known by God, since these things are under His providence. Wherefore, all future thing of necessity will come about. But human actions will come about; therefore, they will come about not by free will. These are the better arguments which, it is thought, can be adduced.

CHAPTER II

In which are posited the common responses to these arguments, and doubts concerning these responses.

BOETHIUS, in the said Book V of his *De consolatione*, subtly and ornately intending to respond to these doubts, gives two or three replies which hardly differ, as it seems to me. The first reply, over which he hesitates quite some time, is that nothing prevents knowledge from being certain in itself, although what the knowledge is about is uncertain in its own nature; knowledge does not necessarily follow the nature of the known, which he shows holds in us with respect to sense and the sensibile, imagination and the imagined, and understanding and the understood. This holds, then, much more for the divine understanding. Wherefore, he says that there is nothing untoward in the fact that human actions are uncertain in their own nature, while God is certain about them. Whence it happens that a certain providence in God is not repugnant to the indeterminacy of free will in itself.

In the same book he gives a second reply which I judge as barely differing from the first. There is nothing, he holds, repugnant in the fact that something related to one thing has an opposite disposition when compared to another thing. Hence it is not repugnant that human actions, as related to the divine knowledge, are necessary, whereas related to themselves, or to their contingent causes, they are contingent. For the most part, this reply is followed by modern theologians in their examples of a conclusion which follows, although only contingently, from a necessary major premise and a contingent minor premise. Aristotle discusses this in the *Prior Analytics*. Thus, although this effect is necessary with reference to the major premise, since it has a necessary cause, with reference to the minor premise it is contingent. Because an effect follows more the proximate cause than the remote cause, it is contingent absolutely speaking, even though it is said to be necessary. They cite the example of a plant which, although produced by a necessary cause—namely, the sun—and by a contingent cause—namely, seed—is nevertheless said to be a contingent effect rather than a necessary one. Wherefore, although the knowledge of God is necessary, and with reference to it a human action is necessary, in itself however, and as produced by the will, the human action is contingent. Nor do these two factors in simultaneous conjunction encompass any incompossibility.

Boethius' third response holds that it is not repugnant that something be contingent absolutely which nevertheless is conditionally necessary: e.g., it is contingent that I have a ship, but it is necessary if I am to take a trip across the seas. Wherefore, human actions are simply contingent, but necessary as they stand under divine providence. Further, it is not repugnant that contingency and indetermination stand with necessity and determination if both are not taken in the same manner: namely, contingency simply, and necessity conditionally; indetermination simply, and determination conditionally. For as is stated in the *Sophistical Refutations*, a contradiction is to the same through the same and according to the same.

Boethius does not reply to the second argument, nor does he even mention it. Again, he neither replies to nor mentions the third. Later writers, however, as Thomas

Aquinas, do so. Neglecting for the moment some replies which it is not now necessary to review, Thomas holds that the consequent is not necessary absolutely, although the antecedent is simply necessary, because things under the control of the activity of the intellect and will are necessary just to the extent that they are, and as they are, under the control of the intellect and will. Hence future things are not necessary unless, and to the extent that, they are foreseen by God. Whence it is by all means conceded that future things will be of necessity not simply, but only as foreseen by God.

To the third argument, Thomas replies by marking a distinction in the propositon: *Everything known by God must be*. According to the divided sense, the major is false; according to the composite sense, the major is true. But he does not say whether the minor is true or false, or whether the conclusion follows. I think that he meant that the conclusion does not follow, because the minor may be contingent, and from a necessary major premise and a contingent minor a necessary conclusion does not follow.

These are the more common replies which, had they not been discovered or approved by very serious men, I would certainly say are absurdities and puerile illusions. Indeed, the authority of these men intimidates me; nonetheless, I shall say what gives rise to my doubts concerning their responses.

The first reply of Boethius seems in no way tolerable. For he says that what is from its nature undetermined is yet determined with God. Now if this could be, there is no reason why God could not know the impossible, which, however, is not possible. For what is known, is; what is, can be; and thus the impossible would be possible. The inference is evident, since the impossible can be known by God only insofar as the impossible, by its nature, cannot be (if, indeed, the impossible can have a nature; here "nature" stands for the intrinsic concept). Since indeterminacy belongs to the very intrinsic meaning of a future contingent, how can it be determinately known? For it is understood thus under a condition repugnant to its own principle. Further, if it is determinately known by God, the divine intuition is directed to one determined part; and not only is it directed determinately to that part, but it also knows it determinately to be true and the other part determinately to be false. If God knows, for example, A to be true determinately, A is therefore determinately true, and a determined truth is therefore in the nature of A. But this is opposed to what was conceded. Neither is the guiding principle of Boethius true. For he says that knowledge does not follow the nature of the known, whence the knowledge is determined and the known undetermined. But, as we have said many times in the previous book, adequation and representation involve likeness; otherwise there would not be true knowledge nor would truth consist in adequation. Wherefore it is necessary that the principles which are in the known be represented in the knower. If the opposite are represented, the knowledge is not true. If, therefore, the known principles are undetermined—and indeed indeterminacy belongs to the very concept of a future contingent—the knowledge is false; if determined principles are represented in God, understanding that determination belongs to the concept of the contingent. To know that this is determinately true is to know that the undetermined is determined, which implies a contradiction. Nevertheless it is true that the disposition of the known does not determine the disposition of the knower in matters other than representation and adequation: e.g., that the knower be a cause or an effect. It is obvious that these are outside the nature of adequation and representation.

The second reply is dismissed by practically the same arguments. What in its nature is contingent, in the nature of the divine knowledge is necessary or, related to the divine knowledge, is necessary; related however to a contingent cause, it is contingent. For if it is necessary, as it is in the divine knowledge—since, in general, knowledge of a thing implies the thing—if the knowledge is necessary, the thing itself will be necessary. Whence the thing in its nature will be necessary and not contingent, which is opposed to what was conceded.

Moreover, when it is said that the contingent, as it is in the knowledge of God, is necessary, either it is to be understood that the contingent of necessity follows upon the knowledge of God, and thus this follows: *God knows* A, *therefore* A *exists*, and thus there is the necessity of the consequence and not of the consequent, as is commonly said; or, that it is necessarily, since it is represented in the necessary because in God; or, it is concerning a necessary object which is proper to necessary knowledge. For it is called necessary since it is impossible that what is known be otherwise. If the first alternative is granted, certainly the contingent is no more necessary as known by God than as known by Socrates. This is a correct inference: *God knows* A, *therefore* A *exists*, and *Socrates knows* A, *therefore* A *exists*. If, on the other hand, it is claimed that what is said to be necessary is so because it is represented in the necessary, then both opinion and indetermination will be necessary because they are represented in the necessary. Since this is not proper (as the contingent is not said to be determinately known because in the determined: for thus doubts which are in our intellect would be determined because in the determined), it remains therefore that it be said to be necessary in the knowledge of God, because that knowledge is about a necessary object, as if the proper manner of accepting necessary knowledge. For knowledge is said to be certain, not because from knowledge there follows the absolutely known, nor because it is in the certain, but because it represents the certain and the determined. Wherefore, Aristotle in Book I of the *Posterior Analytics*, said: *Hence, of whatever there is knowledge simply, that cannot be otherwise than it is*. He does not say: *That thing of necessity follows from the knowledge, not as it is represented, for it is represented in the certain*. Knowledge is called necessary, or certain, because it is about a necessary object. Similarly, opinion is called uncertain because it is about an uncertain object, and not from another cause properly and according to its nature. Although we may have an opinion about what in itself is certain, this is due to our shortcomings. Opinion is properly concerned with the uncertain in itself. If the contingent is known by God with certitude—since certitude takes on the nature of certitude from the object and not from the subject in which it is, nor because it represents something of necessity—then if the knowledge of God is certain, the object is certain. To say that the contingent in itself is uncertain, and as known by God is certain, is to say that certain knowledge is about an uncertain object and that immutable knowledge is about a changing thing. Aristotle would have been dreaming had he written the above statement. For in general, the certitude of knowledge, and the lack of it, derive from the object, as all philosophers know. It is contradictory to say that as it is in knowledge it is something necessary or certain, while in itself, nevertheless, it is contingent or uncertain.

Now as concerns the examples: *From a necessary major premise and a contingent minor premise a necessary conclusion does not follow;* and that: A *plant related to a heavenly body is necessary while to the seed it is contingent* —to the first it is replied that the contingent conclusion related to the necessary major is by no means necessary, nor does the major imply the conclusion absolutely without the minor, as is obvious. If the major without the minor would infer the conclusion beyond doubt, the conclusion would be necessary. But a thing known by God is inferred simply from the knowledge of God. If God knows the present, future, or past, necessarily it will follow. But a false assumption was made: because the conclusion related to the major is not necessary, nor does the major imply the conclusion without the minor.

With regard to the second example, it is falsely assumed that anything contingent in its intrinsic nature is necessary as referred to another. The necessary and the contingent are opposed, and the intrinsic principles of a thing cannot be opposed; because thus opposed they would obtain together, since intrinsic principles are in the principle. Opposed conditions, however, can be successively in the same subject as well as opposed or diverse relations—as likeness and unlikeness or large and small. For the same thing is both like and unlike, or large and small, in comparison to different things; but the same thing is not man and non-man either in itself or in relation to the diverse. If some man compared to one man is sometimes called a man, but compared to another man is called a beast and not a man, this is not with reference to nature and intrinsic principles, but with reference to accidents or a certain likeness or a metaphor, and not according to the truth. What is contingent by nature never becomes necessary, no matter what it be compared to, unless by a likeness. Otherwise, one nature could be changed into another; and thus a man could become an ass, which is impossible—although an ass can become from man, as matter carried over into itself. Nor for this reason do we deny that a contingent cannot always exist; because God by His power can keep a corruptible thing in existence, but He cannot keep the corruptible, incorruptible. Corruptibility and incorruptibility are among the intrinsic principles, or consequent upon them, which God cannot vary. God cannot make a man without matter, upon which corruptibility follows. However, according to faith, He can suspend the act of corruption, although not according to philosophers, since according to them God acts of necessity.

In conclusion, we say that what in itself is contingent, compared to God is not of its nature necessary. Whence, if the contingent is certainly and determinately known, since knowledge takes its certitude from its object just as it takes its necessity (knowledge is said to be necessary knowledge because it is about a known necessary object, just as it is called rational or intentional knowledge from its object and not from the subject in which it is) and if the knowledge of God is certain about some object, it is necessary that that object be certain. By knowing the contingent and indeterminate certainly, the contingent must be certain and determined. Nor for this reason do I say that if the known is certain and determined, the knowledge which is had about it is certain and determined; because there can be opinion about what is certain and determined in itself. More is required that knowledge be certain and determined. Knowledge must be through determined principles. It is a fallacy of the consequent to argue from the certitude of the object to the certitude of knowledge. Another proof is that from a thing uncertain in itself, certain knowledge cannot be had. Certain knowledge can be had concerning a thing which has causes and principles when we are certain that it has them, as is said in the beginning of the *Physics*. If, therefore, certain knowledge is had, this is by reason of the certitude of the principles of the thing. But the principles of the contingent are uncertain; this is of the very nature of the contingent. Hence certitude cannot be had about the contingent qua contingent. Another fact which strengthens this point: it is certain knowledge to know that something is, which cannot be otherwise than as it is known; this is of the very concept of certain knowledge. If God certainly knows one alternative of the contingent, it cannot be otherwise than as He knows it. The opposite part cannot be. But in the contingent, each alternative can be. Thus the same part simultaneously can be and cannot be. We are left then with the conclusion that it is impossible that something is contingent in its very nature and yet is certainly known.

Boethius' third response, no less than the previous responses, seems to be invalid. He says that human action is simply contingent but necessary by supposition. Inasmuch as it falls under divine knowledge, it is necessary; simply, it is contingent. Now in the first place, this can no more be said of God than of man. Although it is contingent that you are running, inasmuch as I know that you are running it is necessary. God has as much difficulty here as any other knower.

Second, if a future human act is simply contingent, to say that we understand its contingency to consist in the fact that it is not necessary that it always be, although true, is not to the point; because we are talking about the necessary, i.e., the inevitable, in the same manner in which we say that *yesterday will be necessary*, not, indeed, because it will always be, but because it is inevitable that it be according to the common course of nature. If, however, it is said that a human act is contingent because it cannot be, granting the knowledge of God that it will be, this is impossible;

because if the knowledge is certain, it is about what cannot be otherwise. How, for example, can A, if it is an object of knowledge, be otherwise and simply not be? Because the knowledge, which God has of one part of the contradiction, is intuitive, which demands the presence of the object, if the thing is present, how can it not be for the present instant? Indeed, inasmuch as it looks to the future it will be able not to be, but not for the present. By no power can this occur. Thus there is no contingent which totally cannot be.

Thomas' reply to the second argument also does not seem able to stand. First, because the conclusion should not be inferred thus: *God knows that you will be, therefore you will be*, but thus: *Therefore you will be as God knows that you will be,* which is false. In the *Posterior Analytics* Aristotle writes: *The true must be, because it is impossible to know nonbeing.* He says "true" without conditions: not *inasmuch as it is known to be, the true must be.* It is impossible in a valid inference that the antecedent be absolutely necessary and the consequent conditionally, or from a supposition. Take away the supposition and the consequent will not be; take away the supposition and the antecedent will be, because it is absolutely true. The inference was not valid, because the antecedent requires verification as long as the consequent has not been verified.

Thomas' reply to the third seems as well to be an illusion and an involution; nor is it true in itself. For he denies that the proposition, *Everything known by God must be,* is true in the divided sense. But this proposition is true. If A is known by God and it is not necessary that A exist, as was said against Boethius' third response, the object of most certain knowledge can be otherwise than as had through the knowledge, which is against the very notion of the object of knowledge. Therefore, if A is the object of God's knowledge, it cannot be otherwise than as represented through the knowledge of God. Moreover, such knowledge is intuitive; and what is intuited, for the time or degree to which it is intuited, cannot not be. Hence the assumed proposition is most true. Thus it seems to me that these responses are involutions and litigations rather than proper arguments, granting that truth and modesty have been preserved in this discussion.

CHAPTER III

Other replies to the first doubts.

SINCE THE USUAL REPLIES do not satisfy me, I have conceived another manner of replying which may, perhaps, appear strange, owing to its unique character; nonetheless, I shall not desist from stating it. If it be a good method, thanks be to God from whom all truth and goodness proceed; if false and bad, I believe that its falsity will be pointed out to me. I shall, indeed, confess my indebtedness to those who show me its falsity.

God has a perfect and most exact knowledge of the future, the present, and the past as well as of the possible, not only with regard to knowledge of the species, as I judge was held by the Peripatetics, but with regard to the very individuals themselves. God has knowledge of all future things. As future, they fall under the knowledge of God; otherwise, they cannot be. The object of knowledge cannot be otherwise. According to the *Posterior Analytics: Of that which is known absolutely it is impossible that it be otherwise*.

However, there is a difference among future things. Some futures, before they exist, have determined causes. Not only God, but also the created intellect, indeed even the human intellect, can know determinately and with certitude such futures before they actually exist, since their causes are determined and certain. A good astronomer can predict exactly a future eclipse, even though the eclipse does not actually exist. Such facts are more truly called inevitable than necessary; or, if the name *necessity* be admitted, they should be called *necessary for such a time*, but not absolutely. Such, I think, are whatever is not under the control of the will. As I said in Book I of this treatise, I cannot see how such cannot be determined in themselves by reason of their causes, and that they are inevitable.

The outcome of some futures depends on the power of the will, and does not have natural determined causes. Their determination is in the will and depends upon the will. In regard to these, no created intellect can have certain knowledge of them before they actually exist, although we might conjecture more or less. A more informed man can offer a firmer judgment on the outcome of a war than a less knowledgeable man, although neither man can offer a certain and firm judgment. Since, however, they exist actually, because they are determined, they can be known certainly and determinately by the created intellect.

Now when such acts or actions are in potency and in their causes, they cannot be known by God with certitude and determinately, unless the time in which these acts will exist is present to God. If in eternity, which by its definition is simultaneously whole, God knows them when they are in potency and in their causes; He thereby knows because time, e.g., the first future year, is present to eternity. On the other hand, if in the same eternity He sees and knows that they actually are, He sees and knows them because the time in which they will be determined is also present to the same eternity. If in eternity He sees both parts of the contradiction, He does not see them according to the same notion of time. For He sees one part of the contradiction because the time in which that part is verified is present to eternity; the other part He sees according as the time in which the other part of the contradiction is verified is also present to eternity. Although times are not simultaneous in themselves, nevertheless as they are in eternity they are simultaneous. Where our will or knowledge requires a real diversity of time, in eternity a diversity of reason suffices. This should not seem unusual and strange, for what diverse natures do in creatures, one nature does in the creator.

Among creatures one thing warms, another freezes; fire heats and water freezes, and these are distinct. However, the heavenly body does both; not, however, according to the same part or according to the same disposition. A star heats differently from the way in which the star freezes—according, that is, to nearness and distance. God does both through the same thing, since in God there is not real but only conceptual diversity. If the human intellect is uncertain about a future event, and again is certain, it cannot be really certain and uncertain according to the same time, for these diverse dispositions really require different times. God, who is not measured by time, in His eternity, which is simultaneously whole and embraces all time, at the same time sees both, not according to the same but according to a different aspect, as has been said abundantly and sufficiently.

We may now respond easily to the doubt and the other alleged data. Recall the argument: *If God sees all things and with certitude sees the future effect, the effect cannot not be; but what cannot not be, must be; and the existence of what must be, is not contingent, as Aristotle says in* II Perihermenias. *Therefore, what exists contingently does not exist contingently, which is a contradiction. Whence free will is destroyed, for necessity is not consistent with free will, as we are here speaking of free will.* In reply to this argument, according to what we have aleady said, if God is not certain about that future event as future, and considers the time in which that effect will be in its causes, He only knows and can know what can be and what cannot be. But if He truly is certain about that future event, it is to the extent that the event is outside its causes, and God considers that time in which it will be outside its causes as that time is present to eternity. To the extent that God is certain about such an event, the event cannot not be. The thing which is independent of its causes either actually is or actually was. If it was, it cannot not have been; if it is, it cannot not be to the degree that it is. For at that time it is inevitable that it be. In either case, therefore, God knows the thing itself; and according to that manner of knowing the object cannot be otherwise and is inevitable. As God knows the future event as future and in potency, the event can be or not be, and is undetermined. Of necessity, that effect will be able to be and not be, since God's knowledge regards it as such. As, however, God knows it determinately, since as such it is outside of its causes, to that degree it cannot as such either not be or not have been. Since each knowledge is most certain, it most certainly and inevitably implies its object according to the appropriate proportion: namely, when He knows something as future and in potency, He most certainly knows what can be and not be, and it is inevitable that such a thing, under such knowledge, can be otherwise. But when He knows the thing as outside its causes, that thing, as it is outside its causes, cannot not be or not have been.

That argument, therefore, that is usually employed in this difficulty is empty. This is the usual argument: *If God is certain about a future contingent, e.g., that Socrates will sin, therefore Socrates will be able to sin or not to sin; if he will be able, of necessity he will sin, for not to be able not to sin is convertible with it is necessary to sin; if, however, he will not be able to sin, how can it come about that God is certain that Socrates will sin?* To this argument I respond: God is not certain nor can He be, granting the freedom of Socrates, that he will sin, from the very point of view that Socrates will sin, and He considers the future as future and the time in which Socrates will be in potency to that sin. He only knows that Socrates can sin or not sin. To the extent God considers the time in which Socrates actually commits such a sin or has already committed it, to that extent He is certain, and as such Socrates is no longer in potency to such a sin, because it has been committed—although perhaps Socrates is in potency to another sin. As long as there is certitude about Socrates as a future sinner, he is no longer in potency to that sin; but Socrates is said to be in potency only when the sin is in its causes and, as such, God neither knows nor can know the determination of the part of the alternatives, as long as freedom of the will stands. Certitude cannot be deceived, nor otherwise than as He sees and knows.

This supplies us with an answer to the second doubt and to the statement: *If God knows that Socrates will sin, Socrates will sin; but the antecedent is absolutely necessary; therefore, also the consequent.* I say that the antecedent in its formal understanding or meaning includes the future. God does not know the future as future except as it is contingent. Whence if God knew or knows Socrates just inasmuch as he is a future sinner, He knows that he will sin only contingently. Thus, God knows that Socrates will sin contingently. But from that antecedent it does not follow that Socrates will sin absolutely, but contingently; actual existence does not follow from contingency and possibility. The argument, then, is of no moment so long as we are vigilant and consider that it can be replied to in this manner. It need not capture our minds, since it obviously does not conclude. If it is objected: *Assume that Socrates will sin to the extent that God knows that the very act of sinning is outside its causes and known with certitude,* we need not be taken in. It is obvious that as such the inference is that Socrates has actually sinned or sins, not that he will sin. Whence, as such, it includes necessity, as is said in *II Perihermenias.* As such also, it is not opposed to our position.

With regard to the third doubt, we say that whatever is known by God must be, in whatever sense it is taken, whether in the divided or the composed sense. For the future event either is known by God as future, and thus when it is known it is known that it can be or not be, hence it will have to be contingently; or it is known by God as it will be outside of its causes. In this condition also it cannot not be; and this is convertible with it must be. And thus in the divided sense the proposition is true. It is manifest that it is true in the composed sense.

From all of this it is clear that those illusions or involutions or intricacies which are usually uttered in this matter —namely, concerning the composed and divided sense, and the necessity of the consequence and not of the consequent

—are not necessary in this matter, nor do they bind the intellect, but represent words and bran rather than things and true flour. I have never been able to understand what these words mean and how they solve any difficulty. Rather, these subtleties seem to hamper and perturb the mind, and one grasps them only by words, not by the understanding of words.

CHAPTER IV

A doubt and a response.

THERE ARISES HERE a difficulty, not too easy of solution, against what I have said. It was said that God does not determinately know future contingents as future, but only inasmuch as God views the time in which either they will be in act, or the time in which they have already become actual. For example: Socrates is in potency to perform sin A in the first future hour; in the second future hour the sin has already passed. According to the given response, the first hour is present to God and as He views it He does not know determinately that Socrates will sin. However, as He views the second hour, He knows that Socrates sins. As for the rest of the time, He knows that Socrates has sinned. Whence, during the two latter times, God has determined and certain knowledge.

Still there seems to me to arise an arduous difficulty: for example: When our Savior, before His passion said to Peter: *Peter, before the cock crows, three times you will deny Me,* either the Savior said this to Peter to the extent that He considered the time of the denial (or after he denied), or He considered the time in which Peter was in potency to deny. If the first alternative, then it follows that Peter did not sin in denying Christ. Given this first alternative, the Savior knew determinately and inevitably, since the present and past are inevitable. But where there is inevitability, there is neither sin nor virtue. Therefore, Peter did not sin. This, however, contradicts the truth of the Gospel: *The Lord looked at Peter and Peter went out and wept bitterly*—from which we may assume that Peter was sorry for the sin he had committed. For his penance, sorrow, and bitterness of mind, Peter merited pardon. All the doctors agree that Peter sinned, although there seems to be some dispute between Augustine and Jerome as to whether the sin was mortal or only venial. It is not our intention to enter into this debate. But it follows that the freedom not to sin was taken away from Peter by the words of the Savior, and that God, thus speaking, was the cause of Peter's sinning. All this is impossible and contradicts the holy doctors. It is impossible because God can neither sin nor be the cause of sin. It is opposed to what the doctors have said, because Origen, Chrysostom, and the rest say that Peter sinned not just because the Savior predicted he would sin, but the Savior predicted it because Peter was about to sin. Hence it seems that the Savior predicted this in no manner as regards His consideration of the times as determined. If, on the other hand, it is assumed that the Savior said this to Peter inasmuch as He considered the time in which Peter was in potency, and God only knew that Peter was about to sin contingently, no fewer inconveniences seem to follow. First, the Savior was no more able to say this to Peter than to John; for it is manifest that just as it was in the power of Peter to deny the Savior, so also it was in the power of anyone else. Moreover, such a prediction does not argue or prove that the Savior was divine or admirable, since even a mere man could make such a prediction. If the disciples had not believed Him, they would not have been accused of infidelity. But this does not seem to be true, since it appears that if they did not believe the word of the Savior, they would not have believed that He was the Son of God and thus, if they did not believe, they would have despised His words. Further, this explicitly contradicts the Gospel truth. Matthew and the rest add to the word of the Savior, *Amen*, which signifies something certain. Matthew says: *Amen, I say to you, before the cock crows, three times you will deny Me.* Consequently, that knowledge was certain and therefore infallible and inevitable. Whence from all sides there arises perplexity and inextricable difficulties.

Adhering to this doubt with neither rashness nor pertinacity, but submitting to the truth and the holy Roman Church, I say, as it seems to me, that God spoke thus to the extent that He considered the time in which Peter did not sin, but was only in potency to sin. Nor was it fitting that the Savior should speak or understand otherwise. Indeed, He was not able to understand otherwise in order to manifest that to Peter. For if He had considered the time in which Peter actually sinned or in which he had already sinned, then thus it was inevitable and it would be no longer in the power of Peter. Since the Savior spoke these words to Peter while Peter had not yet entered into sin—indeed, Peter firmly believed the opposite, as we can see from the following words: *Even if I would have to die with You, I will not deny You*—those words could not be true unless Peter had sinned under compulsion, and then God would have been the cause of the sin. But each of these is impossible; for neither can sin be compelled, nor can God be the cause of sin.

There is further confirmation that God said this to Peter as a future contingent. He spoke to Peter in the same way that He spoke to Judas when He said that he would betray Him. But this was a warning and a seeking to avert betrayal. When the Savior said: *One of you will betray Me,* he added, to arouse fear: *It would be good if that man had not been born.* Now threats are not directed to the inevitable. The Savior wanted to prevent Judas from sinning.

There is further evidence for this interpretation. The Savior often made similar statements. While washing their feet He said: *You are of this world but not all of you,* also, *What you do, do quickly.* It is evident that the Savior spoke thus as an admonition. It is unlikely that the Savior would have spoken otherwise, because His speech would not have been words of salvation but of perdition, and thus not every action of Christ would have been for our instruction, which is manifestly false. Consequently, we conclude that no wayfarer can be certain of his future status given his free will and power of sinning. These latter, it seems to me, imply alternatives which do not fall under divine providence. If the wayfarer is certain of his future state, it is impossible that it be otherwise. Certitude is to be considered not only from the point of view of the believer—that he in no manner doubts, but also from the point of view of the object—that it cannot be otherwise. Speaking about certitude in the first way, those who will be damned can be certain about their salvation because some of those who will be damned believe without any doubt that they will be saved. But this is not true certitude. True certitude is the case where that about which certitude is had cannot be otherwise. Whence that sentence: *Before the cock crows, three times you will deny Me,* encompasses opposite alternatives. God is above time, nor is His action measured by time. He is certain of the future, but not as future, nor under the aspect of the time in which the contingent is in potency, but to the extent that the contingent has passed into actuality, which is present to God by reason of His eternity which views all things. But no creature can be in eternity nor can its action be measured by eternity. What belongs to God cannot belong to another.

To return to the point at issue, I say that when the Savior spoke to Peter, or to anyone else about the future which depends on the will which can choose either alternative—as when He said: *One of you will betray Me,* or: *It is necessary that scandal come,* or: *They will scourge and crucify Me,* and in general about all such statements—although to eternity these were certain and inevitable facts inasmuch as they were done, nevertheless as Savior He spoke and communicated to men, disciples, prophets, and whomsoever else, to the extent that He considered that something as contingent and uncertain. In no other way could He communicate to men existing in time if freedom to sin or not to sin were to be preserved, as has been said.

In responding to the objections one must keep in mind that although acts of the will are not necessitated by another, as has been abundantly shown in Book III of this work, nevertheless an act of the intellect necessarily precedes the act of the will, since it is impossible to wish or not to wish the unknown, as is said in the *Ethics,* Book III. Now we may consider the relation of intellection to the will in the following manner. Although the will is not necessitated by the act of the intellect, the will follows the operation of the intellect or imagination, except perhaps once in a million times. It has been said that given an opinion about the universal and the particular, action follows immediately unless an impediment arises. If we think that everything sweet should be tasted, and that this is sweet, immediately we taste, as is held in Book VII of the *Ethics* and in *De motibus animalium,* unless an impediment arises not only extrinsically—e.g., someone takes away the wine from the power of the will, which seems to me to be what Aristotle means by "obstacle"—but also with regard to the elicited act of the will, because the will can suspend willing, as we said in the third Book. Similarly, in the case where the mind is not actually but only habitually attending to the proposition: *No one shall commit adultery,* and a vehement passion is aroused for this woman, the will does not necessarily elicit the act of willing adultery. Indeed, in both cases it most rarely happens that given those circumstances the act is not elicited. But the wise man will not put himself in such danger, for what happens most rarely is practically considered impossible. What happens in one out of a million times is scarcely considered necessary. Hence, Scipio Africanus is more to be commended than Alexander of Macedon because, after the city was captured, Scipio did not wish to gaze upon the beautiful women, while Alexander, who did want to look at the daughters of Darius, yet restrained himself. For Alexander exposed himself to great danger with respect to a bestial habit; something which Scipio by no means wished to do. The antecedents of the act of the will induce a strong disposition, indeed they almost necessitate the act of the will. The antecedents of the act of the will are natural. To the extent that they are in their causes, certain knowledge can be had about them, just as in the case of a future eclipse. Thus the Savior saw Peter's inclination to deny Him. Although this disposition did not necessitate Peter's denial, it almost completely compelled him to deny, because he feared death or capture or that some other punishment would be inflicted upon him. However, not for that reason did Peter necessarily deny. He was able to choose death rather than sin, just as he had previously promised. All this the Savior saw in their causes, since they were not subject to an act of the will, which will alone He wished to be free.

To the first objection it can be replied that the Savior spoke as He did only to Peter because He knew that the other disciples would not face that decision. Whence He forewarned Peter and not the others, although He forewarned all when He said: *All of you will be scandalized in Me this night*. When it is objected that such a prediction does not imply any divinity or marvelousness, I reply that it does. For if something is foreknown by dreams, visions, and prophecies, it is foreknown as sent by God. Although men can offer judgments about human acts, they cannot do so with so great a certainty, since their intellections and understandings are not open to them as to God. Nor do men understand well human nature, the celestial movements, inclinations, and in general the motives to sin or be virtuous, as God Himself knows them. Dreams, prophecies, and divinations in general come about through these factors. They do not impose necessity, but an inclination and a most proximate disposition, and are scarcely avoidable by the human will. When afterward it was said that if the disciples had not believed the word of the Savior they would not have been reproached, I say that to believe more or less than is fitting is to be conceived as a fault. If the disciples had believed that one of them would inevitably betray the Savior they would have sinned and would not have adhered to His words. They had it on the word of the Savior that the sins would be ours. Otherwise the admonitions of the Savior would have been in vain. If, on the other hand, they had not believed that a great danger threatened, they would have scorned Him. In addition, it has been further objected that this reply of mine is opposed to Gospel truth and to the statements: *Amen*, which carries the meaning of certainty: *You will deny Me*, said absolutely and without any opposition; the remark of the evangelist: *For He knew who would betray Him*, and: *Knowing all that was to come upon Him*, and many others. To this I reply again that what almost never fails and scarcely meets opposition is usually announced absolutely; and, as is said in *Physics II*, *a miss is as good as a mile*.

Taking these circumstances into account, it is most rare that man does not sin. Whence the Savior, seeing the nature of Peter, His own capture and abandonment by all, the insolent and joyful ministers of the Jews, their proud questions, and the great terror, said absolutely: *Peter, you will deny Me*. Not that Peter had to deny Him, but with, as it were, recognition of inevitable danger. His absolute statement was more to warn Peter not to sin, and to become more attentive lest he fail. We are thus accustomed to speak when we wish someone whom we especially love to avoid a fall; we speak unqualifiedly to him in order that a greater fear be instilled in him, for we know that the fall can be avoided. Otherwise the warning would be in vain. When we see someone about to fall, we say: *You will fall*, with the condition understood: *Unless you are on your guard*. We speak thus absolutely in order that he take greater notice. Although the Savior said with certitude: *Amen, I say to you Peter, the cock will not crow until you will deny Me thrice*, he meant: *Unless you take most diligent care, certainly you will fall into a denial of Me, since I see so many and such circumstances that you will scarcely escape unless you proceed most cautiously*. I say all this not rashly, but always ready to yield to a superior understanding and to the decision of the Church.

CHAPTER V

In Chapter VI, Book II, of the present work, four arguments were brought forward against my opinion which might, perhaps, cause some difficulty for some people, so that I intend now to reply to them.

In the first argument it was said that God does not determinately know future contingents as future, i.e., He does not know which of the alternatives is determinately true. A doubt was raised against this argument: *Either that determination is from God himself or from the will; if from God, the acts of the will are God's and not ours. Whence it is foolish to say that He does not know determinately when the determination is from Him. For thus He would not know what He Himself would do, which is ridiculous. If, however, the determination is from the will, then it follows that there is some effect of which God is not the cause, and thus God is not the cause of all things. Further, this effect is not known by God, because God knows nothing outside Himself unless He is the cause of it, as is commonly held.*

Although much has been said above in answer to this doubt, nevertheless briefly and to the point we shall repeat what is pertinent. I say, therefore, that God is not absolutely and totally the cause of that determination; nor does it follow that there is something of which God is not the cause absolutely but only accidentally; for this is not fitting. God is not properly said to be the cause of sin, though sin does not escape altogether the causality of God. Our Savior, when Pilate said to Him: *Do you not know that I have the power to crucify You and the power to let You go?* replied: *You would not have any power over Me, unless it were given to you from above.* Nevertheless, Pilate, in crucifying the Savior, was not without fault. Thus God is the cause of sin according to a fitting manner. Much more so is He the cause of virtue and the good. This suffices to show that God knows, because such a fact falls under His causality.

The following constitutes a keener objection: *Granted the foregoing, God would determinately know even when He knows the future as future, for God is said to be a cause just at the moment when the volition is actually produced.* In answer, it was stated above that that act of willing or not willing ought to be actual, not because God then makes that act more than before, since that act is elicited by the will, nor because God receives anything. The act is required as determining the certitude of God; because the act was not determined before, nor was God certain about such an act before. If it is insisted that: *Therefore from eternity God was not certain about such an act, since such an act did not exist from eternity,* the reply is the same as before: such an act was present to God from eternity, and the time in which such an act takes place is in eternity present to God; as such, therefore, it is eternal. But as enough has already been said concerning this matter, I shall not discuss it further, although I do experience great difficulty with this argument.

Here is the second argument: *We find among the precepts of the Savior: If any should see anyone in error and could rescue him from error and does not, he is a murderer. Now since God knows all things and can rescue anyone in error from that error, why does He not prevent such people from sinning? Why is this a sin for man but not for God? Since the more one knows and is able, so much the more is he culpable for not rescuing those in error.* To this I reply first of all that the comparison is quite inappropriate. The creature is under the law of the Creator; the Creator is subject to no one. Whence what is ascribed to the creature should not be ascribed to the Creator. Second, man is bound to correct his neighbor and to remove him from sin, not by taking away free will (since he cannot), but by exhortation, counsel, and other deeds which are not in the power of the sinner, if the corrector himself has the power of performing such tasks, e.g., if he is a father or teacher or leader or something of this kind. Now God is not deficient in what He has done. First of all, He deliberated and took counsel to enable all to discern good from evil; He sent the prophets, He gave the Law to Moses; finally, He sent His only begotten Son; the holy apostles; and the martyrs and confessors. Nor are there lacking priests, preachers, advisers and others of this kind who can guide the will to a good choice. God has not been deficient. Just as He has charged one man to correct another, with free will intact, so has God himself done. But if God were totally to remove man from sin, He would not preserve the nature of the free will. He would be rather a corruptor of nature than a preserver. God removes man from error in the same way as men are bound to do. Just as men *do not* force free will, neither does God. He has, in removing sin, done as much as is consistent with preserving the freedom of the will.

Here is the third difficulty: *God not only does not remove delinquents from error, but puts before our eyes every inducement to err. He gave us a will liable to sin and an intellect which is clouded with mist; He made sins delightful, and virtues to be obtained and maintained with sorrow and labor; He made it difficult to flee desires, and to embrace sorrows. For the most part He has given temporal goods to sinners, and almost always no good is given to those who abstain from sin and are upright; but rather they are persecuted with needs, labor, intolerance, the cross, torture, and the rest. It is almost as if God were jealous that men follow virtue as not befitting them, but only the gods; and as if He wishes men to follow vice as proper to men. Men who pursue virtue are looked upon as thieves and robbers, as if they usurp what belongs to the gods. Those who follow vice are considered as just, because they pursue what is their own.*

I reply that if God had given all these things enumerated to man in order to induce him to sin and to attract and remove him from virtue, the argument would be insoluble. Actually, it is quite different. If God gave a corruptible will, He gave it not that man sin, but since he could sin, that by not sinning he may attain more merit. The Church celebrates the just man *who while able to transgress did not transgress*. The reason for having given a clouded understanding is because the human intellect requires this, since it is the lowest of the intellects; if it were naturally more clear, the human intellect would not remain but it would be an Intelligence. Though beclouded, it is not so clouded as not to be able to discern good from evil. All conditions for right operation were given. Although God made vice come with pleasure and virtue with sadness, He didn't do this so that vice and pleasures overcome us, but that we overcome them in order to win greater joys. To the extent that the soul is more noble than the body, and eternal things than the temporal, just so much are the pleasures of the virtues better than the bodily and temporal pleasures. He did not strip virtues of pleasures, but adorned those virtues with the most excellent pleasures. If virtues are acquired with sadness and labor, we enjoy them with gladness and rest. If, however, vices are acquired with pleasure and rest, their end is crowned with sadness and labor. Whence, since a thing takes its value from its end and not from its beginning, the condition of the virtues is far better than that of the vices. Since the good attracts and evil repels, and the good of virtue is far better than the apparent good of vice, God did not wish to repel men from virtue and lead them to vice, since the good of virtue is much better than the good of vice. Nor does God envy those who pursue virtue and love those who pursue iniquity, since God "loved justice" and the other virtues and "hated iniquity"; and He does not let iniquity go unpunished or virtue without reward. If evil is so easily acquired, and good with such difficulty, this is for the greater good of virtue, whose nature demands this, since virtue deals with the difficult, vice with the easy, which most of all shows the cheapness of vice. What quickly arises, quickly perishes; what arises with difficulty, endures longer, as is evident in plants, animals, and everything else. The position—vices are proper to men, virtues are foreign—is wholly false. Man as man is intellectual and rational. Reason is for the best, and for virtue. To the extent that man pursues vice and pleasures, he is a beast and only an animal, since he follows what is alien to his nature. *God made man in His own image and likeness*—i.e., according to intellect and will, and wanted man to be zealous and rational. He gave man a figure and physical constitution fit for reason and not for a beast as the argument alleged. Nor does what was adduced at the end of that argument follow, namely, in vain were demons posited as tempters. Although perhaps it cannot be proved by natural reason that there are demons, as we wrote in our *De incantationibus,* nevertheless their existence must be admitted, because the Church holds this doctrine. Temptation by them is permitted for our greater victory. God, through His Son, gave many aids to resist and overcome their snares.

This is the fourth difficulty: *This order which we perceive in the universe either is better or worse than if all men, or at least the great majority, were assiduous. If better, it was intended and willed by* God. *Since, however, this order could not be unless there were so many sins, it seems that* God *wishes sins. But whatever* God *wished He made; therefore* God *is the cause of sin. If on the other hand this order is worse, there still remain difficulties. If this order is worse, it is not willed by* God. *Just, then, as whatever He wished He made, so whatever He did not wish is not made or done. Further, since this second order is possible (since it is willed by* God *who, as the apostle says wishes all men to be saved, if it were not possible, it would not have been willed by* God*),* God *and nature bring about from the order of possibility what is better,* God *therefore ought to upset the present order and introduce another. Third, the virtues which presuppose sin, as pardon and mercy, were intended by* God *either* per se *or* per accidens. *The latter does not seem to be the case since these are most noble virtues and one should entrust himself to* God *most of all for mercy. Therefore, the former. But the end cannot be intended unless the means to the end are intended. Thus, sins are intended by* God *and consequently* God *is the cause of sin. Finally, if* God *knows future things because they are future, they would not be future, because He* *would know the future. This is the error of Origen condemned by Boethius and, in general, by others.* I wanted to repeat all of this in order to make my reply appear the more clear. I shall now respond to this doubt together with its confirming evidence, without prejudice to the truth.

As I see it, my reply to the first difficulty is that absolutely it would be better if all, or many, men were good than if all men were not good or many were evil, all other things being equal. As to: *If it is better, and possible to be, why does God not do this, since He and nature do what is better among possible alternatives?* I say that the order of the universe (taking "universe" not only for the substances in it, but also as it includes all operations, human acts and the rest) depends on two things, namely, God and human wills. To the extent that they depend on God, all things are disposed in the best manner so that, if they should vary, harmony would be destroyed. Just, that is, as happens in melodies: if all the strings were of one sound the harmony would not be present. With regard to human acts, of which God wanted human wills to be in control, the disposition is the opposite. For the human will in most cases does what is worse. If it be asked: *Cannot God bring it about that the human will always wills what is better and does not will what is worse?* I say No—not so long as free will stands. Since the order of the universe requires this grade of perfection, if God wishes this grade to exist, He should leave the will free. If God were to move the will always to the good, the will's freedom would not be maintained, although God aways by the light of reason inclines the will itself to the good. If it is asked: *Whether the human will can always wish the good?* I believe that it can, although with the greatest difficulty. Again: *Why does not the will always do this?* I say because the will does not will to, nor do I think any other reason can be adduced. Again: *Can God bring it about that the will does not sin, although it is in the power of the will to sin?* I say No, properly speaking. The act of the will belongs to the will and not to God. If God should bring it about that the will not sin, the act would be God's and not the will's. Still God can induce the will by an inclination, even though the free will be inclined to the opposite. Further, it is said: *If God wishes all men to be saved and none to be damned, what He does not will happens, and what He wills to happen does not happen.* To this I reply: God wishes all men to be saved rather than any be damned. He wishes all men to be free rather than all men to be saved without their freedom. If then He wishes all men to be saved, He wishes this with their freedom remaining; which, so long as it remains, since men take a fall for the worse, He does not wish men to be saved universally. One will of God is absolute and will be fulfilled; the other is conditioned and will not be fulfilled. What God wills and does not will absolutely and determinately, happens and does not happen; what God wills conditionally and not determinately, does not happen absolutely. He wishes Judas to be saved, if he acts rightly. He does not absolutely and determinately wish that Judas be saved. Whence also he will not be saved absolutely. When then it is said: *God wishes all men to be saved, therefore all men will be saved,* the antecedent *God wishes* involves a condition, i.e., if Judas acts rightly. Similarly, to the saying: *God does not wish this order which exists, because there are many sinners; therefore, this order does not exist, since what God does not wish to happen does not happen*; I reply: God does not wish this order, not because absolutely and determinately He does not wish this order to exist, since nothing happens against His will, but He does not wish this order because He does not approve of it; indeed, this order displeases Him. However, He permits this order to exist, since He determinately wishes the will to be free. Thus the will is free.

When further it is asked: *Are the virtues which presuppose sins to be said to be principally and by a first intention intended by God?* I reply: It seems not, for the reason above cited which convinces me. God, the most prudent artist, made the will free and saw that sometimes it will elect the good, other times, evil. Although a good choice is better than a bad choice, nevertheless He permits a bad election since by accident good follows from it. Although the will of God does not directly fall on the bad election, since however from it a great good follows, therefore He permits it to happen. If God wills pardon, He wills it to the extent that it includes the good, not insofar as it presupposes sin. Although He does not will sin by approval, He wills it by permission. From evil God brings forth good, since nothing but good can proceed from Him. When it is said: *It seems that such virtues are primarily intended because they are the highest virtues, for martyrdom seems to be the most illustrious virtue,* I reply: I see no repugnancy, indeed it is a fact that someone who is not actually a martyr could be more perfect and have greater charity than an actual martyr. Since perfection is measured by charity, I maintain that the virtue which is martyrdom would not be lacking in the universe, for, although there would be no actual martyrdom, the virtue of martyrdom would not for this reason be absent, since virtue principally consists in choice. Whence all Christians ought to be ready to die for Christ and to do everything to avoid sin. And perhaps it might be granted that if everyone were good, virtues would not be so perfect intensively; extensively, however, they would supply or make up for any defect on the part of intention. When it is said: *Then God would not be merciful and forgiving, for where there is no sin there is no pardon,* I say first of all that in the case that no one would sin, mercy would not, for this reason, be taken away from God. He made us from nothing, and without mercy we would not have been prevented from sin, nor would we have received all the other benefits we obtain through His mercy. What, however, is said about pardon is true; but this does not argue defect in God. The fact that God does not pardon the blessed and most glorious Virgin is no defect on God's part or on the part of the blessed Virgin—indeed, it is to her praise. If, on the other hand, the will falls into sin and God is merciful and pardons it, this well argues perfection in God, although even if He were not to be merciful this would not argue imperfection. Therefore, there is no imperfection if there is no pardon where there is no sin; indeed, there is a greater perfection. There is perfection if there is pardon where there is sin.

With regard to the last inference: *If God is not the cause of virtue and sin, but the will, then the will would be the cause of the knowledge of God,* we have spoken at length above. There is nothing unfitting in that God's knowledge is in some way dependent and in some way not. Also we have spoken about how the saying of Origen and Chrysostom (no one doubts that he was a saint) is to be understood, because that saying contains truth if it is properly understood.

CHAPTER VI

Since in Book II, Chapter VII, of the present work, in defending the fifth opinion—that of the Christians—many motives opposed to this fifth opinion—indeed, the truth—were incidentally brought forward, we now will reply individually to each one of them.

1

An effort was made to approve the opinion of the Stoics and to show that the fifth opinion was to be preferred to all others. Against, it was urged: *Either that opinion contradicts itself or the more it tries to destroy fate the more it builds it up*. Neither of these is true.

The reason for the first alternative is this: The opinion in question asserts that everything which is going to happen is known by God with certitude, and yet we are in command of our own acts. Further, all agents besides the first agent are instruments of the first agent and are not moved unless moved by the first agent, and then only according to the manner in which the first agent moves them, and yet it is within our control to thus move or not move. Third, future contingents by their intrinsic nature are undetermined, and yet God knows them determinately. This our understanding does not grasp. Finally, Socrates must sin, if God knows his sin; whence that Socrates will sin is necessary with the necessity of the consequence and not of the consequent, and yet God with certitude knows that Socrates will sin and absolutely. The opponent inferred that all these propositions are mutually repugnant and that they are illusions and involutions.

Now we have already seen that these statements are not repugnant; nor are they illusions or involutions. We do not approve of the distinction between necessity of the consequence and of the consequent; nor have we followed the mode of replying pursued by others. We need not here repeat what our mode is, but simply refer the reader above.

In replying to the first doubt raised against the Stoics, a great effort was made by the disputant to show that the same consequences followed from the Christian position: *Either God would be the* per se *cause of sin, or there really was no sin, but one only judged it to be a sin.* The supporting argument was based on the inequality existing in the universe, since there could not be two species of essentially equal perfection, and even within one species, especially the human, there appears such inequality that one individual necessarily is less perfect than another and one species less than another. This does not argue defect in the universe or in God; rather, it argues a greater perfection in the universe and God. If the Stoics held this to be a defect, so also must the Christians hold that it is a defect in God and the universe. Whence the disputant wished to have it that if in the human race are found both good and evil men, and God should be the cause of all, then either this does not argue defect in God or, if it does argue defect according to the Stoic view, so also it does according to the Christian.

Now the Christians do not doubt that the universe is so disposed by God that there is a great diversity. So, just as the Christians hold that it is not a sin for the wolf to eat the sheep, it is not a sin for the wealthy to crush the poor. Just as the eating of the sheep by the wolf contributes to the perfection of the universe, so does the crushing of the poor by the rich; because the universe and the state do not stand up well without the rich, just as the universe cannot do without wolves. Just as you cannot have wolves without their destroying sheep or some other innocent animal, so you cannot have a wealthy person unless he robs the goods of the poor. Whence either both must be considered sin by God or neither is a sin.

To this I reply that the similitude does not hold. For one is an evil of custom, the other of nature. An evil of nature does not argue defect in God or in the universe; but an evil of custom, which proceeds not from God but from the will, argues defect in the efficient cause and in the universe. Whence God cannot be the cause of it, although He is the cause of the evil of nature.

2

SINCE INNUMERABLE arguments were given against this response, and my reply to them can be gleaned from what was said in the previous chapter, I shall not delay in answering each one but shall handle them in the manner of a few summary points.

The first adverse argument was this: *The will is a mere instrument of God and is related to God as a hatchet to a carpenter, whence the total action will be God's and not the will's.* Second: *God gives to the good people as habits and occasions, all that conduces to good and the opposite to the evil. God seems to do this just that there might be diversity among men. God thus seems like a bird-catcher who uses nets to catch many and different birds. If we run through the men themselves, this is apparent. Some, God made naturally lascivious, others temperate; some mild, others crude; some benevolent and lovers, others wicked and hateful; and similarly as regards the rest of the opposed virtues and vices. Also He gave the external occasions,* e.g., *the lustful to meet with the beautiful and intemperate in the halls of the princes, and so for the rest. Also He made them by nature sinful, whence if they had not sinned, His power would be vain. Since God and nature make nothing in vain, these people naturally sin.* Third: *The virtues which presuppose sin are most intended by God; therefore also the sins. Such virtues are not intended by God, like the sixth finger, since they are as far more perfect than the other virtues. They are not like monsters, since a monster is not more perfect than a nonmonster. This is confirmed by the following: either it is better that these virtues not be than be, or vice versa. If the first, why did God bring them to be, since among the possibles He does what is better? But if it is impossible that they not be, neither is it possible that sins not be. If the second, God therefore wishes sins to be, since He wishes what is better, if it is possible.* Fourth: *If it is said that God gave men the power of sinning, not that they sin but that they overcome vice, and that their virtue would be more excellent, it would be strange and cruel if, since God would know that they would sin and be overcome by vice and condemned forever, He made men such and then placed so many snares in their path. God seems like a father who gave to his son robbers and cutthroats as companions; which argues either stupidity or cruelty.* Fifth: *The Stoics better avoid the unbefitting consequences of their theory than the Christians. According to the Stoics, if God seems to work poorly, He is likened to someone lame from birth who cannot act otherwise. According to the Christians, God is likened to one who is voluntarily lame, for God can prevent evils and does not, although He knows everything, as this opinion holds. Whence, not to prevent sin when able, especially when he who does not prevent it says that he loves that person, seems equally sinful, or a greater sin, than to perform the very sin, especially when he openly says that he wishes to do it. For the first is more deceitful.* These are the arguments against the Christians. Now for the replies.

That the will is an instrument and moved as a hatchet is moved by a carpenter—this was denied in the previous chapter. Compare this chapter for the manner in which the will is moved by God.

To the second: It is true that men differ and show different dispositions to virtues and vices; but not that there should be vices and that men should pursue them. God gave men the power of overcoming vices—a will and a reason to direct it—the Law given to Moses—and finally He sent His only begotten Son. Whence that there should be so many and such diverse dispositions in men was not that there should be vices but virtues. He made some lustful from birth, not that they be lustful but that they be chaste and continent. If He gave the stimulus of the flesh, it was that virtue be greater, because virtue is perfected in weakness and deals with the difficult. The other virtues are to be understood in the same manner. The foundation of that argument is false, because this diversity is ordered toward good and not evil. Nor does the inference *such sins are natural,* hold. The sins in question are not from nature but from the will. Though nature inclines, it does not necessitate. These inclinations are given by God and nature, not that the will be overcome by them, but they by the will. Reason, which directs the will, is more powerful than inclination: inclination is corporeal and material, while reason is immaterial and eternal.

With regard to the third difficulty: It has already been stated how those virtues are intended by God which cannot come about without preceding sins, and also that they are not principally intended. For God does not absolutely wish that men repent of their sins; He did not wish His Mother to repent of sins; He wishes only the sinner to repent. Nor does God absolutely wish to pardon man, because thus He would have pardoned His Mother and His only-begotten Son and our Savior. He wished to pardon the penitent, which repentance presupposes sin. Nor, absolutely speaking, is repentance better than not to repent, for thus the Savior and His Mother would have repented, which is false. For the sinner to repent is better than not to repent. Nor is it absolutely better that God should pardon than not to pardon, for thus He would have pardoned the Savior and His Mother. But it is better that God should pardon the sinner who is sorry than that He should not pardon. Likewise, it is better that God lift up the fallen sinner than not, always however keeping to himself the power of lifting up or not. Nevertheless, absolutely it is better that He should not lift up than lift up; since to lift up presupposes sin, whereas not to lift up, does not. Therefore, these are not simply intended but according to the intended occasion and presupposition. Mercy, on the other hand, does not absolutely consider sin, since God created and preserved out of mercy what had no sin. The further consequences are handled according to these answers.

It was alleged that these virtues are supreme and most perfect, and what is most perfect cannot be intended in the second place and after what is less perfect is intended, as what is not monstrous and is perfect cannot be intended by nature after what is monstrous. In reply: Although the monstrous is not primarily intended, there is nothing to prevent the clarity and excellence of nature from appearing more in the monstrous than in the nonmonstrous, just as we see in artificial things. It is not as marvelous if an artist makes a beautiful and perfect work from good material as from bad material, even if not as beautiful and perfect as in the work from good material, all things else being equal. The marvelousness of God shines forth more if He elicits good from evil than good from good, although absolutely it is better to elicit good from good than good from evil. These virtues are most outstanding, not because they are better, but a greater marvelousness is seen in them, for they draw forth good from evil, which is a great marvel.

Further, I think that even if there were no sin, these virtues and perfections would not be absent from the universe, on the part of neither man nor God, because virtue principally consists in choice and not in the external deed, except to manifest the choice. Whence actual sorrow presupposes sin. A person can still have the virtue of repentance, even if he is not actually sorry for sins either committed or omitted, as long as he is bound to be of this intention that, in case he should sin, he would be sorry and repent. Likewise, although one does not pardon another who would have offended him, since no one has offended him, still such a person is resolved firmly that, if offense should occur, he would pardon. Indeed, I think that one who does not actually pardon because no one has offended him can merit more in the line of pardon than the one who actually has pardoned and been offended, since such a one can call forth the act of pardon with greater charity than the one who has been offended. Many who have not actually suffered martyrdom were able to have, and perhaps had, greater merit from martyrdom than those who actually suffered it, since their will for martyrdom was with greater charity than those who suffered it. As in the Gospel it is said of the little old woman who contributed only a denarius that she merited more than those others who deposited more money. Although we are more certain about those who were actually martyred, it is not the same with God to whom alone our wills are known. A creature judges about the external. Therefore no virtue of whatever kind would be lacking to man, even if there were no sin, as long as man wished to have virtue. The virtue of pardon would not be lacking to God even on the supposition that there was no one to pardon for sin, because He is of such and so great goodness that if someone sinned and repented He would pardon such a one. God prefers that men not sin and, if they should sin, to have the firm intention of not sinning, rather than that they sin and repent. Therefore, such actual virtues, i.e., that anyone actually repent of sins committed, are not primarily intended. What is primarily intended is that if sin happens, there be a resolution to repent. Each Christian should have this resolution. The same holds for martyrdom and other things of this kind. Before God created the world He had all the virtues He now has, although He would not manifest any of them by an external act. It does not follow that the universe is imperfect if there are no sins; indeed, if there were no sins the universe would be more perfect and none of the virtues would be lacking. If there were not any virtues according to the manner which now obtains, there would be according to a more perfect manner. For, as we said, virtue is by far more perfect if there is no repentance for sins committed, with the intention however to repent if sin should occur, than if sins had been committed and repented. It pleases God much more if He does not pardon enemies because He does not have any, with the firm intention however of pardoning if there should be any enemy, than that He should have enemies and pardon them.

In reply to the fourth difficulty: God is neither cruel nor stupid, since, if God gave man the power of sinning and many incitements to sin, He did not give them in order that man sin, but that he gain merit by overcoming them. God acted out of love and not from hate or deceit. Nor did He make man without aids to overcome sin, since He gave reason, law, the sacraments, and other things by which man can overcome temptation. He performed the work not of someone ignorant, but of the most prudent founder. The father who joins his son with robbers and thieves does this either out of knowledge or out of ignorance. If out of ignorance, he cannot be accused of being imprudent; if out of knowledge, he either wishes the perdition of his son, or not; if he wishes it, he is cruel; if not, he is stupid. This cannot be said of God, however; He does not wish the loss but the happiness of man; nor does He act stupidly, because He fortified man in the best way to conquer adversity. But a son left in the hands of robbers cannot defend himself from them.

Here, it might be objected: *A wise man does not expose either himself or another to danger. A prudent father removes his son from danger as much as he can. It seems then that God should not offer such incitements, since there is the great danger that man may be conquered by those enticements.* To this it may be said: God does not will anything impossible or inordinate in the universe. To those who see that they are unable to resist, God gave the power to flee; to those who see that they are able, He gave war and victory. Just as the father removes a weak son from dangers, so God gave man reason by which he can avoid dangers. There is the further objection: *The father's warning is useless since the son has God's warning.* But this does not follow. First, because the son is not yet an adult and hence does not use reason well; second, because the father is bound to this by a divine precept. The warning of the father is also that of God. He imposed the law on parents to take care of their children. A father sins in a twofold manner if he does not correct his sons: first because he does not love his sons, and second because he does not obey the divine law.

The fifth difficulty maintains that: *If God, as the Stoics say, is like one who naturally falters, God is defective and consequently is not God;* whence the opinion of the Stoics is foolish. According to the Christians, however, neither does God falter by nature nor voluntarily. He is entirely free of defect. When it is further said: *There is a sin of omission as well as of commission,* I reply that this is so, but neither of these modes is found in God. It is obvious that there is no sin of commission. None of omission can be shown. For he who simply omits something is not thereby said to sin. For one who omits to kill an innocent tyrant would thus sin. This is manifestly false. But one who omits to do what he is held to do, sins. God, however, if He permits anyone to sin, is not held to remove him from sin. But a neighbor is bound to remove from sin another neighbor as much as he can. It is sufficient if God give the power and many aids to avoid sin. A subject is bound to one thing, and a king to another. But if it should be asked: *Why does He preserve some from falling, although they are in danger, and, if they fall, raise them up; others, however, He neither preserves, and if they fall, abandons them?* Certainly, I would reply, this is beyond human investigation. I believe that ultimately the divine will is the only reason which can be assigned. For, although God allows a sinner from some serious sin committed to fall into a greater sin and does not lift him up as a punishment for the first sin, God nevertheless sometimes lifts a sinner up in some sin after another sin has been committed. In this we can look, it seems to me, to nothing other than the divine will: *The judgments of God are a great abyss.* As I see it, this displeased the Stoics. They wanted this to happen from nature because the perfection of the universe demanded it, and not from the free will of God. This seemed to them more impious than if it happens naturally, just as it seems a lesser defect if someone limps naturally than voluntarily. They held this opinion because they did not realize that God is not so bound as a creature is by divine precept.

3

IN THE SAME RESPONSE an argument was brought forth against Aristotle's opinion that sins are necessary and natural. First, according to Aristotle, *There must be outstanding virtues, which cannot be without sins; Therefore, there must be sins.* Second: *The power of sinning or not is from nature; therefore, also the acts, since act is proportioned to potency.* Further evidence: *If a man should never sin, the power of sinning would be in vain and thus something would be in vain in nature. Also, there is no man who does not sometimes sin and sometimes not sin, if he is of the right age and has the use of reason. Therefore, it is natural for man to sin and not sin, and it is necessary that at some time he sin.* Third: *Everything corruptible of necessity is corrupted; therefore, everything which can sin at some time necessarily sins.* The inference is proved: *Just as matter is related to corruption, so is nonbeing to sin. For the cause of corruption is matter, and the cause of sinning is to be from nothing. If matter necessitates corruption, so does nonbeing necessitate sin.* My reply is not undertaken to defend Aristotle, but because these objections seem to operate also against the Christian opinion.

Now with regard to the first I say that if Aristotle seems to hold that these virtues are necessary inasmuch as they actually presuppose sins, to this extent I do not agree with him. It seems to me that such was the opinion of Aristotle; and yet I must hold that these virtues can be such that they do not actually include sins. Just how this can be, I have stated above.

In reply to the second difficulty, I say that sin is natural as distinguished from the violent, since it is voluntary. However, sin is not intended by nature. It belongs to the will, not nature. *Act is proportioned to potency* is to be understood as follows: That which can do something is that which does it, and conversely. Still it is not necessary that, if potency is from nature, act is also from nature. For the will, which is a potency, is not in our control; yet to will is in our power. Whence, if that which wishes is that which can wish, and this comes from nature, then to will comes from nature; not, however, if the potency to will, as indicating the essence of the potency, is from nature. The point of the confirmation alleged that: *If men were never to sin, the power to sin would be in vain*, and this must be conceded; at least so it seems to me according to the principles of Aristotle, since nothing is in vain in nature. Hence, monsters are necessary according to him, since, unless nature were to fail at times, it would have been granted the power to fail in vain. Whence there are added extrinsic impediments to assure that nature not be in vain, as the Commentator says in Text 48, Book II of the *Physics*. But whatever be the opinion of Aristotle, I say that for us this does not follow, since, if God had made a peccable will in order that it sin, the argument would follow; but He did not make the will peccable in order to sin, but He made it such that although it could sin, it would not sin, for its own greater perfection: as is said of the just man: *Though he was able to transgress, he did not transgress*. The statement that *Everyone sins* is not so, at least morally. Venial sins are not in our power nor, properly speaking, do they occur according to election. Nor does anyone sometimes act rightly according to election, because if he were to seem to act rightly sometimes, he rather does this from nature or some other circumstance than from a right election or choice.

With regard to the third difficulty, the similitude is denied. Just as the corruptible is necessarily corrupted, so also the peccable necessarily sins. Corruption is not in our power, but nature's; while to sin is in our power. Corruption is subject to celestial motion; to sin is not. When it is further said that: *Just as matter is the cause of corruption, so is the will the cause of peccability, because the will is from nothing and intellectual,* the reply is that this is not true. That what is material is corrupted is due to celestial motion and mutually contrary agents. If matter did not have an agent, it would not be despoiled of its form. But actual sin is from the free will, which, though it can sin, also cannot sin. But the heavens and the contrary agents, given the order of the universe, cannot not corrupt. God can change this order, so that He can bring it about that the corruptible is never corrupted. To the objection: *Nature gave the power of sinning; potency is related to act; therefore God ordained this power to this act. If then the power never becomes actual, this potency is in vain and the work of nature is thus in vain,* I reply: This argument seems to me to have some evidence according to Aristotle, but none according to us. The power of sinning looks to the act of sinning not as ordained by God and nature, but refers to the act of temptation and struggle. For example: He gave to the choleric person the ability to be angry, not that he actually become angry and actually sin, but that he be easily aroused to ire and at times moved to anger, without sinning. If someone does not get angry because he has not been aroused, this is not virtue. It is virtue when, though aroused, he restrains himelf. Therefore, the power to sin is not ordered to sin but to the act outside of the sphere of sin, so that virtue, which has the difficult for its object, be elicited.

4

In reply to the third doubt: *To will is not in our power, since sometimes we will that we will something which we cannot will and we would wish not to will what we cannot not will,* I say that these two facts are not simultaneously conjoined, and are not in the same time. For example: someone is a gambler and accustomed to play and suffers a loss in his goods and honor from play. Certainly, considering the loss and shame, especially when he loses money, he is sorry that he likes gaming, nor does gaming please him for the length of time during which he is sorry; indeed, he detests the habitual pleasure he takes in gaming. When however he is playing, he does not believe that he suffers loss from play and then he is pleased. Hence under different circumstances and at different times he has opposite acts of the will. No one should doubt that, if he wishes, he can refrain, although it is very difficult for one used to something. Admittedly, this argues difficulty but not impossibility.

In reply to the fourth doubt: the difficulty was touched upon that the will is subject to the heavenly bodies such that astrologers know how to judge acts pertaining to the intellect and will; and that the laurel trees (which Suetonius mentions in his *Life of Galba*) were born and died at the same time as the Caesars who descended from Aeneas, whether they died of their own fate or by another fate, as Gaius Caligula and Nero. This could not happen unless human wills were subject to fate; and that the sting of the spider lasts just so long as the spider, whether it is killed by another or dies of itself.

To these and the like, it is replied that the Christians do not deny that wills are subject to celestial bodies indirectly and by accident, but only directly and *per se*. Since the will presupposes the intellect, and the intellect as joined to the body presupposes the senses, so the will to this extent is subject to the celestial bodies. Celestial bodies and constitutions account a great deal for the inclination of the will, yet they do not necessitate it. Since to fight vice is hard, and to follow it, easy and delightful, the heavenly bodies seem to hold sway over our wills; because for the most part men follow their senses and constitutions which *per se* are subject to celestial bodies. Whence astrologers many times make true predictions about voluntary acts. And it is not impossible or against reason that the laurel trees died at the same time as those Caesars, since to the extent that it depended on the heavenly influences, the laurel trees had the same period as the Caesars. But "wisdom rules the stars": that they died together is because Caligula and Nero, bestial and sensuous men, followed their senses which are *per se* subject to the celectial bodies. If reason had dominated them, the opposite would have happened. If the spider story has any truth in it, the reply is the same, since their will follows the celestial motions and they are rather led than leading.

Lastly, in the same chapter, evidence was brought forth concerning the following Stoic opinions: *Different regions of the universe give different customs, virtues, and vices to men. Many cannot, by any skill, escape fate to whom it is granted by the stars to be happy or unhappy. The four ages alternately vary according to the diversity of the stars. Thus just as spring, summer, autumn, and winter succeed each other in order according to infinite time, so the golden, silver, copper, and iron ages continually succeed each other, according to the dispositions by which men vary in virtues and vices. The stars do not vary according to the virtues and vices. Thus all of these facts give evidence that everything is governed by fate.* It was added that: *Aristotle held that all sublunary bodies vary according to the nature and disposition of the stars. Where there is now a desert, there was a sea; kingdoms perish and others arise; the proud are humbled and the humble are raised up; opinions die and are born and continuously return in an infinite circle; nothing is which was not, nothing was which will not be, nothing will be which was not. All these things have a* per se *and unchangeable cause. It seems necessary that everything happens by fate.*

It is by no means true that we attribute to fate and the stars what proceeds from our fault and defect. Many regions have temperate air and food and yet men sin more there than in other regions having opposite dispositions. The reason is the evil will and habits of men; especially of the civic leaders. For the most part, and almost always, the malice of the citizens comes from the malice of the leaders. Wherefore, the assumption is not universally true. Nevertheless, we do not deny that the appearance of the stars exercises much influence. Yet, either the appearance of the stars takes away from men the use of reason or it does not.

If it does, there is neither virtue nor vice, since, if reason is removed, there is no free will; but if it does not take away the use of reason, the will is master of its own acts, since the stars do not coerce though they dispose and incline. Yet such a disposition is for greater merit. Aristotle, in Book II of the *Economics*, says that if Alcestis and Penelope had not suffered so many adversities their virtues would not have shone so much. The stars do not give vices, rather, they intensify the virtues to the utmost.

To the statement: *The many, to whom it is given by the stars to be happy or unhappy, in whatever they do follow the stars*, I say that for the most part this is so, since men follow the sensitive part and their constitution, which *per se* are subject to the celestial bodies. Whence they have followed fate. Others, however rare, have overcome the stars. And if they have not been able when they tried to avoid a pre-announced fate, this perhaps comes about from the fact that by a judgment they are being punished for a previous sin, or to incur this fate is better for them than not to incur it. It was better for Socrates that he died a violent death, as it had many times been foretold, than that he should perish by his own fate. He would not have been so famous or acquired such great virtue although simply he could have avoided that fate, as is evident in his life.

The third remark was: *The four ages occur naturally in which men are diversified according to virtue and vice and not the ages according to virtue and vice*. Perhaps this assumption is false. The ages are more diversified from the customs of men than the customs from the ages. It is a common saying that "then the age was golden when men were like gold," comparing good men to evil, as gold to the other metals. The true cause of such goodness was the good will of men and especially of the leaders on whom depends the rule of the citizens. Further, not only are ages called good or evil from the goodness or malice of men, but also because they vary in abundance and fertility, temperateness and intemperateness. We read in the *Old and New Law* that God, since He sees good and evil men, acts against the order of the celestial bodies. Nor ought one to agree with the Peripatetic impiety that God cannot vary this order. We have said also that although the stars and motions of the celestial bodies induce different dispositions to human mores, nothing is to be attributed to them as regards sin. For they either take away the use of reason or they do not; if they do, there is neither virtue nor vice; if they do not, man can studiously work to see that the inclination is ordered toward the good and not toward evil. That this contains truth is manifest, since there was no age so golden in which the wicked were not found, nor any so iron in which the good were not found. After Adam, there was Cain who slew his innocent brother. Whence, Augustine said: "The first thorn-bushes were drenched with fraternal blood." And in this our age, which is called an "iron age," are also found some good men; which can be ascribed only to good and bad will as its cause.

There was the further statement about the changeability of the regions of the universe, where first there was dryness, then moisture; where first there was the proud, then the humble. This is true according to the common course of nature. This can be truly predicted by the astrologers, as long as there remains always the divine will which can change this order which we see in the universe and has changed it at times. This order and this vicissitude has a *per se* cause, which is the heavenly bodies. However, when it is inferred that these bodies are also the cause of human acts, the inference is denied. Human acts depend on the will, which *per se* is not subject to the celestial bodies, but only by accident, as we said.

This series of questions was raised: (1) *Why evils all the time? Why virtues all the time? Why are the same things renewed in human acts? Why is philosophy again and again renovated?* And so forth. Since the will was always free, it will always be free until the universe stops, and if free, then not necessitated. (2) *Could not every will not sin?* Answer—Yes. (3) *Why then does it sin?* Answer—Because it wants to. (4) *Why at least does it not sin less rather than more?* Answer—It is more pleasurable to sin than not to sin, and easier to follow the senses than the understanding. Yet this is not the essential cause but the occasion; the essential cause is because the will pleases to do so. (5) *Why does it please to do so?* Answer—There is no further cause to look for. That opinions are repeated, sins and virtues renewed, is not immediately due to celestial bodies, but to the will, and no other cause should be looked for. Still we do not deny that these cannot be done by men without the celestial bodies, but we say that these are not immediately brought about by the celestial bodies such that these bodies compel, as in things not subject to the will. For we have said many times that as long as the order of the universe remains, whatever happens, inevitably happens, except voluntary acts and whatever is under the dominion of the will.

The following argument is raised in the form of an objection: *What always are, are necessary; sins and virtues always are; therefore they are necessary. But this is repugnant to the notion of virtue and vice, since they are ours and in our power; therefore, the position contains opposites. The major premise is proved: everything which is, either is necessary or contingent. The contingent is divided into the contingent for the most part, for the least part, or equally; but none of these is always, thus no contingent always is; therefore, nothing which always is, is contingent. But what is not contingent is necessary; therefore, every being which always is, is necessary, for what always is, is necessary. And thus the major premise is evident.*

A reply is called for here, though it is very difficult. That division of the contingent is to be understood of the natural contingent which in some part should be reduced to act, since nature does not operate in vain. That whose possibility to be, and not to be, depends on the will need not be reduced to act for this reason: it ought to be reduced to act either by our will or by another; not by another, because this is against what has been granted, i.e., we are speaking of what depends on our will; if, however, it be demanded that of necessity it be reduced to act by our will, the will will not be free. It is not necessary then that the contingent, to the extent it depends on our will, sometimes fail or sometimes come about. Indeed, if free will be granted, it can always determine itself to one part of the alternatives. Whence God gave the power to sin or not to sin that it be in the will's freedom to do either, though His principal intention in giving it was that the will not sin, yet leaving it up to the free will. If man will never sin, the ability to sin will not be in vain, because it was not given to be used to sin, but not to sin, even though it can sin. And if it will always sin, the ability not to sin will not be totally in vain, since justice will follow to which sin is ordered, not from the intention of the sinner who hates justice, but from the intention of God who punishes. Also the ability not to sin will not be totally in vain, because God gave it that it be used according to the good pleasure of man, and accordingly the sinner has used it. Wherefore in no case will it be in vain, no matter what follows.

In following the principles of faith it seems to me that I must answer as follows. I have not seen these (opinions of the Stoics) in Aristotle, nor do I recall having seen them in any author. Hence I believe that they are repugnant to the doctrine of Aristotle. I say that, as I said before, either Aristotle held fate as the Stoics did, or he contradicts himself. If we hold free will, then it follows that there always will be something which nevertheless is not necessary. This contradicts what he said in Book I of *De caelo*. I do not see how it is possible to combine the two facts that virtues and vices are necessary and yet are in our power. Nor do I see any repugnance in the idea that no man sins, in that presumably God would be willing the impossible when He wills that all men be saved, just as there is no repugnance in the idea that every man sins.

In the same chapter it was said that the activity of men of the world seems to be a certain kind of game: for if anyone would inspect all the sublunary bodies, he would either laugh or cry. This indeed seems to be a game according to all other opinions besides that of the Christians. For the world has a beginning and an end and all this activity was made for man, at least secondarily, that he may enjoy beatitude. God ordered all corporeal things for man that he might use them well, and having made good use of them that he might enjoy the Trinity forever. Nothing more beautiful, nothing more useful can be imagined. But no matter what others say, it seems to be a game. Whence, the Stoics and the Peripatetics, who say that God acts of necessity, are accustomed to say that God's goodness demands that He communicate His being to the extent that it is communicable and, since it is communicable according to the many degrees and modes which we see in the universe, so does He communicate. What is subject to generation and corruption by comparison with what is eternal seems to be smoke and nothing. They seem of little value, and indeed a game, in comparison with those supreme values. Yet, however corruptible they be, they still include some perfection. Since for whatever being it may be, to be is better than not to be; and since God makes what is better from among the possibles, God makes these corruptible things and conserves them. Thus, although human life in comparison with the eternal is, as it were, nothing, it is of great value in comparison with other things subject to generation. And each thing subject to generation is of great value in comparison with nonbeing. Since it is better to live one year than never to live, a life of one year is not to be despised, since the appetite is drawn toward the good and also the greater good. If there is such great variety in the universe, life should not be deemed a game. The nature of the universe requires this variety. So much then for this chapter.

Much else was said in Book I in defense of the Stoics which seems to be opposed to this opinion. For much could be drawn from that book which could be directed against the opinions of the Christian religion. However, as I judge, from what has been said here in Book IV, if they are well and attentively considered, an easy and obvious solution to these difficulties will appear. Whence I shall abstain from that task. Thus terminates here Book IV, *On Fate*.

TORQUATO TASSO

TORQUATO TASSO *was born at Sorrento in 1544. Educated in Naples, Tasso mastered both Greek and Latin by the time that he was ten. He later studied philosophy at Venice and at Padua, where he listened to Sigoni's lectures on Aristotle's* Poetics. *Tasso firmly believed that his studies and writing would bring him glory; and, in truth, by 1575 he was riding the crest of a superb career. From about 1576 to his death in 1595, Tasso suffered from a mental illness characterized by profound depressions, delusions of persecution, hallucinations, and the persistent fear that he was guilty of heresy. He is known chiefly as a poet; his philosophical writings have not been seriously studied. Aside from his poetry, he wrote numerous plays, dialogues, and tracts. Of particular interest are his six discourses* De poema eroico; *and the three* Discorsi dell' arte poetica.

On the Art of Poetry

FIRST DISCOURSE

To Lord Scipion Gonzaga

ANYONE who intends to write heroic verse must observe three rules: (1) to select material capable of receiving the most excellent form the poet can possibly give to it; (2) to give it this form; and (3) to add to it the exquisite embellishments appropriate to its nature. The present discourse will be divided according to these three themes. I shall begin with a discussion of the judgment which the poet must make in the election of the material; I shall then pass to the art which, if he have it, the poet must employ to form this matter; and, finally, I shall discuss the adornment of the work.

Naked matter (and I mean by "naked matter" that which has not yet received any form, either by an orator or by a poet), falls under the consideration of the poet in the same way that iron and wood fall under the consideration, respectively, of the blacksmith and the carpenter. Just, as I might say, as those who build ships are obliged to know not only what the form of the ship will be, but also what kind of wood is best suited to receive this form, so also it is proper to the poet not only to employ art in the formation of his product, but judgment in the selection of its matter. He must choose it so that it is, in its own nature, capable of every perfection. Naked matter is offered to the orator always by chance or necessity; to the poet, however, it comes by choice. It is for this reason that often while such or such a matter is commendable in the orator, it is not so in the poet. The poet must create sympathy for a character who, let us say, has voluntarily stained his hands with the blood of his father; but concerning the same event the orator has the opportunity to evoke supreme sympathy, directly, by his own speech. In the one, we may possibly condemn the choice of matter; while in the other, although we may deplore the necessity to deal with it, we may yet praise the ability demonstrated in its handling. Now there is no doubt but that the power of art can, in a significant way, exploit the capacities of any subject matter in such a way that things which are different can be made to appear similar to one another, and those which are made to evoke sympathy are yet those which, in themselves, are not properly pitiable, while those which are made to seem marvelous are yet those which are truly not. Similarly, there can be no doubt that such qualities as these can more easily, and in a more sublime degree, be extracted from those subject materials which are naturally apt to produce them. Thus we can assume that by employing the same artistic devices, and the same eloquence, some can arouse sympathy for Oedipus who killed his father in ignorance, while others can do so for Medea, who, quite conscious of evil intent, butchered her children. Yet, in truth, the story constructed around the accidental slaying by Oedipus would turn out to be more capable of arousing pity than that other which dealt with Medea; the first wiill inflame the soul with pity, the second will hardly warm it: and this, mind you, even if the artistic construction in the one and in the other are not just similar but equal. In the same way, the form of the signet ring leaves its impression much better in wax than in some other material, more fluid or more dense. Again, a statue made of marble or of gold will be more worthy than one made of wood or of an ignoble stone: and this, even if equally, and in both, we can see the admirable workmanship of Phidias or Praxiteles. I have broached this only to italicize how important it is for the poet to elect one subject material rather than another. We must now see from where this matter must be drawn.

The subject materials which can, without disagreement, be considered as appropriate for the selection of a plot may be either fictional—and so it would seem that the poet has a part not only in its choice, but also in its very invention—or else it may be taken from history. In my opinion, it is best that it be taken from history. For the poet must everywhere seek verisimilitude (I presuppose this as a very well-known principle), and only an illustrious action can have the requisite verisimilitude. For the purposes of the heroic poem, I would suggest that it is best for the story to have been set down in a written history, rather than transmitted by word of mouth to posterity. Great events cannot remain unknown; but where they have not been recorded, men are prone to argue about their accuracy. Should these be regarded as false, they lose their capacity for moving men to ire, or terror, or pity; they can not move men so easily, now to be happy, now sad, now suspended in their feelings, or enraptured. In short, if not documented, these plots can not arouse the same anticipation, or cause the same pleasure, as they would do if they were wholly, or in part, known to be historically factual.

For this reason, because the poet must impress his readers with a semblance of truth, and not only convince them that the things he treats of are true, but submit these truths to their very senses so that they feel they are not merely reading about them, but are present at them—seeing them and hearing them—it is necessary to impress their souls with the conviction of truth; and this, with the authority of history, can most easily be accomplished. I speak, here, of course, of the poets who imitate noble actions, such as those treated in tragic and epic poetry; with the comic variety, however, which imitates ignoble and common actions, it is always permissible for the poet to fabricate his plot. These need not, however, be repugnant to verisimilitude, for all men are as familiar with individual foibles as they are with the city in which they live. And if we read in Aristotle's *Poetics* that invented tales please the public on account of their novelty—as was the case among the ancients with Agathon's *Flower,* and as it was among us with the heroic tales of Boiardo and of Ariosto, or with those tragedies written by some who are more modern—we must nevertheless not be persuaded that any inventive tale is worthy of as much commendation as is a noble poem. Indeed, we have shown this in our discussion of verisimilitude; and many others have done so, as well, by means of quite conclusive arguments. Further, the novelty of a poem does not consist principally in the fact that its matter is fabricated; it consists rather in the novelty of structure and in the unfolding of the plot. The plots having to do with Thyestes, Medea, or Oedipus, were treated by various ancient writers; but they always wove them a bit differently; and by constantly adding to them they constantly invigorated them. A poem, that is, will be new in which the plot is structured anew; in which the resolutions are new, and the episodes which it contains are new—even if the actual matter is very well known and has already been treated by others. On the other hand, we can not call "new" that poem in which the characters involved in the plot are fabricated, when the poet has structured the poem in the same way that others before him had done. And this is what has happened in some modern tragedies: tragedies in which the material and the names are fictitious, but the plot is constructed and developed in the same way as was done by the ancient Greeks. These, consequently, lack doubly, in that they contain neither the authority which history affords nor the novelty afforded by fiction.

The plot of the epic poem, therefore, must be drawn from history. History, however, is either of religion that we consider false, or of religion that we consider true—true, that is, such as is the Christian religion, or such as was the Hebraic. Nor do I feel that the actions of the Gentiles offer us a proper subject for perfect epic poetry. For in these poems, we either appeal to deities which were adored by the Gentiles or we reject appeal to them. If, on the one hand, we do not appeal to them, the poem will lack the marvelous; and if, on the other, we do appeal to them, the poem to that degree will be lacking in verisimilitude. A poem which does not exploit these Gentile marvels is truly disappointing: for such events move not only the souls of the ignorant but even those of the learned. I speak here of those rings, of those enchanted shields, of those flying horses, of those ships changed into nymphs, of those larvae which turn into warriors, and of other such things. These are occurrences which the author needs in order to adorn his poem, and give it spice. With these, he not only easily arouses and gratifies the taste of common men, but he satisfies as well those who are more understanding. Since these marvels of which I speak cannot be effected by natural power, it is necessary for us to turn to supernatural power; and when we turn to the deities of the Gentiles, verisimilitude immediately ceases. For that cannot be taken as real by the men of our own time which is impossible in itself, and is known to these men to be so. It is quite impossible that from the power of those vain idols, which are not true deities and never were, there could proceed things which can far surpass the powers of both nature and humanity. As for just how far those marvels (indeed, if they deserve this name) are from any factual reality, any man of even mediocre intelligence can easily see for himself by reading those poems which draw upon the falsities of ancient religions.

Signor Scipione, these two natures, the marvelous and the verisimilitudinous, are very different; so different, in fact, that they are almost contraries of one another. Nevertheless, both are necessary in the poem, although the poet's art must be of such excellence that it can succeed in bringing them together. Now the precise manner of doing this—though it has been, in fact, accomplished by many—has not, to my knowledge, ever been taught. Men of supreme wisdom, indeed, recognizing the mutual repugnance of these two natures, have opined that that part of the poem which has verisimilitude is not marvelous, while that part of the poem that is marvelous has no verisimilitude. Still, they say, both being necessary, we must employ now verisimilitude, and now the marvelous, in such a way that neither is neglected to favor the other, but one is tempered by the other. I, for my part, do not share this view. I do not feel that any part of the poem should lack verisimilitude. This is the reason that makes me think so: poetry is, in its own nature, nothing but imitation. Who can doubt this? Imitation, moreover, is not separated from verisimilitude, since to imitate, and to make similar, are one and the same thing. Therefore, no part of the poem can be separated from verisimilitude. Verisimilitude, consequently, is not one of those conditions required by poetry for its greater beauty and adornment; but it is, rather, intrinsic to its very being: indeed, it is the most important feature of any of its parts. While I tie the epic poet to this obligation of always observing verisimilitude, I do not at the same time exclude the other part: the marvelous, that is. I say, in fact, that an action can be true and marvelous at one and the same time. I believe, further, that there are many ways of combining these seemingly discordant parts. But I shall postpone treatment of these ways until I come to speak of the nature of the plot, at which point it is most properly discussed. For the moment, I wish to discuss only imitation.

Give the poet license to speak of certain operations

which by far exceed the powers of men, of God, of His angels, and of demons; or of those to whom God and the demons concede this power, such as our saints, magicians, and fairies. These operations, considered in themselves, will appear marvelous: in fact, as we commonly refer to them, these are known as "miracles." Now these, if we have cause to admire the power of the poet who employs them, will be judged as verisimilitudinous; for the men of our time have drunk the milk of these opinions while still in their swaddling clothes. To these men, having been confirmed by those who teach our sacred faith in the view that God and His ministers—and the demons and magicians, with His permission—can do marvelous things which transcend the limitations of nature: to these men, I say, reading and hearing every day newly remembered examples, it will not seem incredible but it will seem, instead, to them, that often such occurrences have taken place, and that they can again take place. To the ancients, who lived in the error of their vain religion, in the same way such miracles must not have seemed impossible. And not only did their poets invent stories about their gods, but also about their history. Even if the scientists were to judge such things, properly, as impossible, it was still grist for the poet's mill. In this manner, as in many others, the poet must be sensitive to the opinions of the multitude. Many times, indeed, he has to adapt himself to these, and put aside the exact truth of things. An action, then, can be at the same time marvelous and verisimilitudinous: marvelous, when looked at in itself, and referred to natural limits; verisimilitudinous, when viewed apart from these limits and referred to supernatural powers.

But those poems in which the Gentile deities are introduced, lack the proper manner of joining the verisimilitudinous and the marvelous. Those poets, however, who found their poetry on our religion, can successfully manage such a marriage. This reason alone, as I see it, is enough to show that the plot of the epic must be drawn from histories which are not Gentile, but Christian and Hebrew. Further, our religion lends a different greatness, different dignity, a different majesty to celestial as well as mundane counsels—

as in prophecies or ceremonies—than that which the Gentile faiths possibly could. Finally, whoever wishes to form the perfect idea of a knight, as seems to have been the intention of certain modern writers, should not, as they do, eliminate the virtue of piety and religion: for this tends to characterize him as idolatrous and evil. If Theseus, Jason, or someone like them cannot be imbued with the zeal of true religion without impropriety, then Theseus, Jason, and the others, should be left alone; others, instead, like Charlemagne, Arthur, and men like them, should be elected. I shall say nothing, for the moment, regarding the fact that the poet must have much concern for the good; not, mind you, insofar as he is a poet (for this is not the end of poetry), but insofar as he is a civilized man and a part of the Republic. He will, indeed, much more effectively inflame the souls of our men by providing examples of faithful knights, than examples of those who are infidel; he will better stimulate by employing examples of men similar rather than dissimilar to ours; and to employ native rather than exotic heroes. The plot of the epic poet must, therefore, be drawn from the histories of religions that we believe to be true. But the incidents in these histories are either sacred or venerable: such incidents as are essential to the faith it would be impious to alter; those, however, which are not sacrosanct in nature—which contain no article of faith—are open to treatment by the poet. For he will not be accused of audacity or of faltering belief if he thinks that something might be added or withdrawn from these histories without in any way changing its essentials. Upon historical incidents of the first kind, our epic poet must not dare to lay hands. These are to be left inviolate, in the pure and simple truth, to pious men. Fiction is not permitted here. Yet he who fabricates nothing—the poet, that is, who simply stays with the particulars that are contained in these histories—would not be a poet but a historian. Let him, yet, in the epic eschew treatment of the sacred as set forth in the histories of true religion, regarding these as something altogether unalterable.

Now the histories properly available to the poet, either

contain events chronicling our own times, those of very remote times, or events that are neither very modern nor very ancient. The histories of distant centuries give the poet his greatest opportunity for fabrication. For these things are so deeply buried in the bosom of antiquity that not even the weakest or most obscure memory of them remains; hence the poet may cast and recast them at will, and narrate them as he thinks fit. But with this convenience there comes an inconvenience which is far from inconsequential; because, with the antiquity of the age represented, it becomes necessary to parallel, in the poem, the antiquity of custom. The ways of the ancients during war, as with all their customs, cannot be read except with difficulty by the greater part of the men of our epoch. An example of this is provided in the books of Homer, which—however divine they may be—are nonetheless extremely tedious. In large measure, this is due to the antiquity of the customs cited therein, which customs—to those accustomed to the taste, the gentility, and the decorum of modern times—appear as something foul and rancid. The recitation of these is most tiresome. He who attempts to imbue antiquity with contemporary customs, on the other hand, will appear like the injudicious painter who clothes Cato and Cincinnatus in the manner of Milanese or Neapolitan fops; or who tries to take away from Hercules his lion-skin and cudgel, painting him, instead, dressed in doublet and helmet.

In this regard, the more modern histories offer greater opportunities; for they involve modern customs and habits. But they tend to deprive the poet of his liberty to invent—and this license is most necessary to poets, and particularly to epic poets. The poet who would depict the deeds of Charles V in any way different from the way they actually happened—in a way, that is, other than that which many who are still alive have themselves seen or experienced—would appear brazen. Men will not tolerate distortion concerning the things that they have themselves been involved in, or have been told by their immediate progenitors. But the histories of times neither too modern nor too remote do not present us with the inconvenience of bizarre customs, nor do they deprive us of freedom to fabricate. Such are the times of Charlemagne, Arthur, or those that shortly preceded or followed them—hence it has come about that their feats provided material to so many writers. The memory of those ages is not so fresh that if some lie were told, or some anachronism of custom were introduced, it would appear as impudence. Indeed, even if in some measure the customs of those times did differ from ours, our poets yet know how to make them familiar and acceptable to us. Let the subject of epic poetry, therefore, be taken from the histories of true religion; but not from those events which are so sacred as to be unalterable; let it deal, moreover, with an epoch neither too remote nor too near to the memory of those who are now living.

All these conditions, Signor Scipione, I believe are to be sought in the naked matter. This does not mean, however, that if one of the conditions is lacking, the matter becomes, therefore, incapable of receiving the form of the heroic poem. Each condition, by itself, has some effect—some more and some less—but, generally, these conditions are such that if none of them obtains, the matter in question is not amenable to any perfection. But above and beyond all of these required conditions, one is the most fundamental of all: that the actions presented in the epic be noble and illustrious. This condition is the *sine qua non* of the epic; and in this, both heroic and tragic poetry differs from comic, which, as we know, imitates ignoble actions. But we must consider more carefully the common opinion that the tragic and the epic do not differ from one another in the things imitated—since both imitate great and noble actions—but that their specific difference is based upon a difference in mode.

In his *Poetics*, Aristotle states three essential and specific differentiae (so to say), by which differentiae, the one is marked off and distinguished from the other. These differentiae are: the things imitated; the mode of imitation; and the instruments employed in imitating them. The things imitated are the actions; the mode, the manner in which the actions are narrated and represented. In narration the person of the poet appears; in representation the part of the poet is hidden, for here the actor makes his appearance. The instruments are speech, harmony, and rhythm. By rhythm I mean both the measure of the movements, and the gestures employed by the actors. Aristotle, having set forth these three essential differentiae, then seeks to understand the distinction between the species of poetry. He says that tragedy resembles comedy in the mode of imitation and in its instruments. Both represent, and both use, verse, rhythm, and harmony; but what makes them different in nature is their diversity with respect to actions imitated: tragedy imitates noble actions, and comedy, ignoble ones. Now the epic conforms with the tragedy insofar as things imitated are concerned, both imitating noble actions, but the mode makes them different: the epic narrates, while the tragic represents; and with regard to the instruments, verse alone in the epic, while the tragic, in addition, uses rhythm and harmony.

Because these things were stated by Aristotle but briefly and obscurely, as is usual in his writing, the tragic and the epic have come to be construed as similar in the things imitated. This opinion, however, although generally accepted, I cannot share. Here are the grounds which lead me to disagree: if the actions of the epic and the tragic were of the same nature, they would produce the same effects. From the same causes, that is, the same effects will follow. But they do not produce the same effects; hence it follows that their natures are different. That they do not produce the same effects is quite clear. Tragic actions move us to terror and pity; and where this terror and pity is lacking, the actions are not tragic. Epics, however, are not constructed to arouse in us either pity or terror; nor is this required of them as a necessary condition; and even if, occasionally, one finds in heroic poems an episode arousing terror and pity, one does not, for this, seek for terror and pity in the whole tale. In fact, this is accidental to the epic, and appears only as an ornament. Consequently, we say that while the actions involved in both tragedy and the epic are equally noble, their nobility is yet different in nature. The nobility of the tragedy consists in the unexpected, sudden change of fortune, and in the magnitude of the events dealt with: these, properly, bear with them terror and pity. The nobility of the heroic, on the other hand, depends upon supreme enterprises of a warlike nature, on matters of courtesy, of generosity, of piety, of religion. Such actions, proper to the epic, are in no way relevant to the tragedy. It follows that the characters introduced in both kinds of poem, even if possessed of the same regal stature and supreme dignity, are nevertheless not the same in nature. Tragedy requires characters who are neither good nor evil, but of a middle condition—such as Orestes, Electra, and Iocastē. This middle condition of which I speak, Aristotle marks in Oedipus more than any other character; he himself judges such a character as most suitable for the tragic plot. The epic, on the other hand, requires characters of supreme strength; in fact, it is this which gives them their name. In Aeneas, for example, we find the excellence of piety; in Achilles, of military strength; in Ulysses, of prudence; and, to speak of our own epics, we find the excellence of loyalty in Amadigi, and of constancy in Bradamante; indeed, in some of these characters, we can find combined all of these virtues. And even if in a tragedy and in an epic the poets were to take the same character as subject for their poems, he will be considered under different aspects in each of them. The epic poet sees in Hercules and Theseus their excellence and valor in battle; the tragic poet sees them as guilty of the sin of pride, for which reason they have fallen into misfortune. In the epic, moreover, we find displayed not only the pinnacles of virtue, but as well the depths of vice—and this with much less danger than in tragic poems. Examples are: Mezenzio, and Marganorre, the famous misogynist in *Orlando furioso;* also there is Archeloro, a character in *Orlando innamorato*, and Procrustes, Diomedes, and other similar characters.

From what has been said, it is clear that the difference between tragic and epic poems does not grow merely out of a diversity of instruments and modes of imitation; it derives much more fundamentally from the difference between the actions imitated—which difference is much more deep-rooted, internalized, and essential than the others. If Aristotle does not make specific reference to this, it is because it was his purpose merely to indicate that the tragic and epic do differ—which he was able to indicate sufficiently well for his purposes by simply indicating those differences which are now quite well known, without going into this one. Now this nobility, which we have attributed to heroic poetry, can be more or less illustrious depending upon whether or not the material contains within itself events which are suitable to the highest form of the poem. I do not deny that the heroic poem can be shaped out of less magnificent events, such as the loves of Florio, or those of Teagene and Caraclea; but in such cases the most perfect form of the poem is not being sought by the poet. Nonetheless, in general, I say that the matter must be, to begin with, noble and excellent. Of the appropriate degree of excellence is the arrival of Aeneas in Italy; for, in addition to the plot, he is himself very great and noble. Furthermore, this greatness and nobility is connected with that of the Roman empire which had its origin in his entrance into Italy; and for this event the divine epic poet had particular consideration, as we may derives from the beginning of the *Aeneid*, where he writes: *Tante molis erat Romanum condere gentem*. In the same way, properly, the liberation of Italy from the servitude of the Goths furnished suitable matter for Trissino's poem: those deeds, undertaken either for dignity of empire, or for the exaltation of the faith of Christ, have in themselves great power over the souls of readers, and are capable of arousing incredible pleasure and anticipation; and when the art of the poet is added to this, the themes become irresistible, gripping forces.

I have put before you, Signor Scipione, the conditions which a judicious poet will seek in naked matter; which (to recapitulate briefly) are these: the authority of history; the truth of religion; the freedom of invention; the character of the times treated; and the greatness and nobility of the events. But this, which before coming under the hand of the artificer who shapes the epic, is called "matter" is no longer matter after the poet has treated it, formed it, and turned it into a tale: rather, it is the form and soul of the poem, and it is so judged by Aristotle. Even if it is not simply form, we should judge it at least as a composite of form and matter. At the beginning of this *Discourse* we likened this matter which we have called "naked" to that which the naturalist thinkers call "first matter." I wish to further this analogy: I wish to say that just as first matter which, although lacking in any form, yet, according to the philosophers, has quantity as its perpetual and eternal accompaniment, such that it obtains in matter before the birth of form and remains after the form's corruption; so also the poet must, in this, our matter, consider the quantity. It is necessary, that is, that he, in selecting his material, select it along with its quantity, since this is a condition which always accompanies it. Let him be warned, therefore, lest the quantity he selects be too great. For if this is the case, then in the texture of his tale, he cannot properly treat many episodes, nor can he adorn and illustrate things that require such artistry; for if he were to do this, the poem would swell to such an extent that it would appear improper and out of balance. The poem, that is, must not exceed a certain prescribed magnitude, as we shall show in its proper place. If the poet takes on too much, then, if he wishes to avoid this excess and lack of measure, it becomes necessary for him to omit digressions, and other such adornments, which are yet requisite to the poem. This, indeed, is what happened to Lucan and Silius Italicus: both these poets attempted to embrace too much matter; for the one took as his subject not only the whole of the conflict of Pharsalia, as his title denotes, but the whole civil war between Caesar and Pompey; while the other chose the entire African war as his subject. These matters, being in themselves very broad, occupied all the available space which is proper to the greatness of the epic. There was no room left for the genius and invention of the poet. Many times, as a consequence, when one compares the same event as treated by Silius the poet and Livy the historian—who writes, as is proper, much more dryly and with less ornament—there yet seems to be more ornament in the historian than in the poet: precisely the contrary of what the nature of things would seem to require. The same flaw is to be noted in Trissino, who chose as the subject of his poem the whole expedition of Belisario against the Goths. As a consequence, he is as flat and arid as the desert, which is wholly unsuitable in a poet. If Trissino had cut so little as even a single episode, the most noble of the expedition's exploits might thereby, by accident, have been made to appear artistic. Anyone, in short, who proposes to himself too great a subject matter is forced to lengthen the poem beyond its proper limits (which excess length could have ruined the *Innamorato* and *Furioso* if the author had attempted to treat their matter within the scope of a single poem). At the least, such a poor selection would force the poet to omit the very episodes and ornaments which are so necessary to his poem. Marvelous, indeed, was Homer's judgment in this respect: for he, having proposed to himself a rather brief matter, then lengthened the episodes and enriched the ornaments in every way, bringing his poem to a laudable and proper magnitude. Virgil selected a somewhat larger subject matter—like one who might take the subject matter of both of Homer's poems for a single work. Still his selection was not so broad as to fall under one or other of the two vices which the poet must avoid. With all this, Virgil often restricts himself. He is very spare in ornament; so that his purity and brevity are marvelous and distinctive, albeit his work of necessity lacks the florid abundance of language utilized by Homer. I remember, in this connection, hearing from the lips of Sperone (whose private apartment I frequented more often and more willingly than the public schools when I was studying in Padua, for it seemed to me that these rooms smacked of that Academy and Lyceum in which the Socrateses and the Platos used to dispute)—I remember, I was saying, hearing from him that our Latin poets are more like the Greek orators than the Greek poets, while our Latin orators are more like the Greek poets than the Greek orators. The orators and the poets of Greece had each achieved the virtue proper to their own art; whereas the Latin orators and poets had each, rather, usurped the excellences proper to the art of the other. Indeed, anyone who carefully studies the style of either of them will see that the copious eloquence of Cicero comes close to the broad abundance of Homer; while in acumen, scope, and noble brevity Demosthenes and Virgil appear quite similar.

To recapitulate, then: The quantity of the naked matter must be not more than is sufficient to permit the inventiveness of the poet to add to it, without, by so doing, exceeding the appropriate magnitude. As I have already spoken of the judgment that the poet must exhibit in choosing his subject matter, I shall proceed, in the next *Discourse*, to speak of the art by which means this matter is to be properly ordered and formed.

End of the First Discourse

Suggested Readings

PIETRO POMPONAZZI

ALLEN, D. C. *Doubt's Boundless Sea*. Baltimore, 1964.
BRÉHIER, É. *The History of Philosophy; The Middle Ages and the Renaissance*, trans. W. Baskin. Chicago, 1965.
CASSIRER, E. *The Individual and the Cosmos in Renaissance Thought*. New York, 1964.
COPLESTON, F. C. *A History of Philosophy*, vol. 3. London, 1953.
DOUGLAS, A. H. *The Philosophy and Psychology of Pietro Pomponazzi*. Cambridge, 1910.
HÖFFDING, H. *History of Modern Philosophy*, vol. 1. New York, 1950.
FIORENTINO, F. *Pietro Pomponazzi*. Florence, 1868.
MAURER, A. A. *Medieval Philosophy*. New York, 1962.
POMPONAZZI, P. *De immortalitate animae*, trans. W. H. Hay, in E. Cassirer *et al.*, eds., *The Renaissance Philosophy of Man*. Chicago, 1948.
RANDALL, J. H. *The Career of Philosophy. New York*, 1962.

TORQUATO TASSO

BLACK, J. *Life of Torquato Tasso; with an historical and critical account of his writings*, 2 vols. Edinburgh, 1910.
BOULTING, W. *Tasso and His Times*. New York, 1907.
DONADONI, E. *Torquato Tasso*. Florence, 1946.
FLORA, F. *I discorsi del poema eroica di T. Tasso*. Naples, 1951.
SOZZI, B. T. *Studi sul Tasso*. Pisa, 1954.
WEINBERG, B. *History of Literary Criticism in the Italian Renaissance*, 2 vols. Chicago, 1961.

IV

THE PHILOSOPHERS OF NATURE

BERNARDINO TELESIO

BERNARDINO TELESIO *was born in Cosenza in 1509. He was initially educated in Milan and Rome by his Humanist uncle, Antonio Telesio, and then went on to study philosophy and mathematics at the University of Padua, obtaining the doctorate in 1535. In Cosenza he founded the Accademia Cosentina, dedicated to the study of natural philosophy according to his principles and methods. Telesio died in the city of his birth in 1588. His most important work is* De rerum natura iuxta propria principia, *which he first published, after many hesitations, in Naples in 1565. A revised and expanded edition appeared in 1570, and a much enlarged third edition in 1586.*

[Note to the reader: Telesio is concerned to establish three principles as being basic to all things: (1) an incorporeal active principle, or *hot* and *cold;* (2) a corporeal, inert, and recipient principle, or *matter;* and (3) a conflict of *natures* which are the products of *heat* and *cold* (or *earth* and *sky*) operating on permanent, inactive matter. *Hot* and *cold,* moreover, are themselves in eternal conflict. Note also that when Telesio speaks of "enjoyment," "abhorrence," etc., he is not being merely metaphorical. Rather, he is introducing a vitalistic, pan-psychistic, or even animistic principle into his cosmology. Cf. the selection from Campanella.]

On the Nature of Things According to Their Own Proper Principles

CHAPTER I

That the construction of the world of nature, and the magnitude of bodies therein contained, should be investigated not by reason alone as the ancients believed, but by sense experience.

IT APPEARS that those who before us diligently investigated the construction of the world and the nature of things only imagined what they thought they knew: for it is clear that they achieved no certain knowledge. What they said is filled with internal contradiction. These investigators are not even in substantial agreement among themselves. Overly confident of themselves, as if competing with God himself in wisdom, they neither looked upon the things of nature in the light of nature's own laws, nor did they see them in relation to the powers with which things come naturally endowed. Thus, in their daring to search for the principles and causes of this world by the use of the unaided reason, and in their strong desire to succeed in this endeavor, they only invented a world according to their arbitrary will.

To the bodies of which this world is composed they conceded neither the magnitude which properly belongs to them, nor the position which they have come to occupy, robbing them of the dignity and the power with which they come naturally endowed. They ascribed to the things of nature only those characteristics which their reason dictated they ought to have. I say that it is not proper that men should be so proud as to attempt to take precedence over all nature and emulate thus not only the wisdom, but also the power of the Almighty.

We, not so confident of ourselves, endowed with a slower intelligence, and less ambitious lovers and students of all human knowledge, desire more humbly to investigate the nature of this world and every part of it, together with the passions, actions, and operations of the things contained therein. Our knowledge will have reached completion when the things that sense experience now displays are shown to be conformable with things already known. Only then will we have attained perfect knowledge. Indeed, if we really attain to this condition, the magnitude and the form of each thing will be revealed to us; and with these, the property, power, and nature of all things.

If these writings do not show anything of divine worth or great subtlety, we hope the reader will not be offended or hold this against us. We shall follow nothing but our observations, sense experience, and natural powers as they operate naturally and in harmony with one another.

CHAPTER II

That the whole world appears to be composed of sky, earth, ocean and air in addition to large bodies. That the sky is of the same substance as the sun and the stars.

At first view, the world-universe would seem to be composed of sky, earth, ocean, and air: the latter filling all of space and obtaining between the earth, ocean, and sky. We cannot by means of our senses attain to the farthest reaches of this great expanse of air, but only to that portion which, contiguous with the earth, thrusts itself against us when it is slightly stirred, entering into such things as bellows, wineskins and, indeed, into our very bodies.

That portion of the air which includes the distant sky,

and which is very remote from us is quite unknown to us as it is wholly hidden to sense. Nevertheless, these facts can be drawn from what we know by experience: that all the space between the earth's atmosphere and the stars, and even the sky beyond, must contain some kind of body that is similar to and compatible with those bodies to which it is contiguous and neighbor. It is quite evident that nature is propelled by self-interest. In fact, nature can tolerate neither a vacuum nor anything without purpose. All things enjoy touching one another, and maintain and conserve themselves by this mutual contact. Indeed, they so hate being disjoined and separated, that if some body is pulled away from its neighbor in such a way that neither air nor any other substance is allowed to replace it, its divorced partner will immediately follow it even if it is immobile in its own nature or its own proper motion is contrary to that which it thus pursues.

We cannot believe that the outer reaches of this air of ours can of itself be that which prevents stars and other bodies from touching. Rather we should say that continuous and contiguous bodily being obtains between the air and the stars. The diverse and simultaneous movements of all the stars shows that they are fixed onto a single body about which they wheel. Indeed, if they moved of their own accord, since they are all of the same nature, those with great paths to traverse and those with lesser paths would never be juxtaposed, as we often observe them to be. This must follow from the fact that they are contained and carried in one body. Otherwise, all would revolve eternally about the same center with the same velocity.

We must concede that the body on which the sun and the other stars are fixed must be of the same substance as they are. We cannot conceive of this body as being contrary or dissimilar to them since they are neighbors and contiguous. Also, we cannot believe that they oppose or exclude one another but, rather, that they must be similar and compatible. Indeed, we believe that they aid, mutually embrace, and conserve one another. Nor can we believe that the observable, fixed wheeling could ever characterize the motion of the stars if they and their neighbor bodies were not of the same nature and endowed with the same powers. Those things which entities accomplish, they accomplish not by means of alien powers; nor do they receive their proper powers from any foreign source.

The sky is of the same substance and, in every way, of the same nature as the stars. Not that like them it heats, sheds light, or is wholly visible; but because in the stars, light and heat have become extremely lethargic and sluggish. Indeed, it is evident that the sky is endowed with an extreme tenuity and subtlety. The sky neither changes nor diminishes our view of the dense stars which are situated in that rare and fine vapor. These visible star-flames clearly demonstrate that heat and light diminish as they become more tenuous, rarefied, and weak. By contrast, in the dense and aggregate, they swell and increase in power. Heat applied in things more dense will quickly make them appear hotter and brighter. By contrast, in the more rarefied and subtle, heat is sensibly weakened and diminished. Thus, no matter how close heat and light may be, in a tenuous and subtle medium they appear neither luminous nor clear. Hence it must be the case that the sky is endowed with the same forces and the same form as the stars; but only when these forces are more numerously collocated and dense do they become manifest to us. The world-universe is composed, like the great bodies, of sky, earth, sea, and air; and the sky is of one and the same substance as the sun and the stars.

CHAPTER III

That the world-universe is composed only of sky, earth, and large bodies.

IF NOW WE consider the matter carefully, it becomes clear that neither the air nor the seas are the principal parts of the world-universe, but, rather, only the sky and the earth. Nor can we believe that everything between the sky and the earth is air, and that it is completely homogeneous. We ought perhaps to regard all of the air in our immediate and contiguous skies in terms of that air which obtains on the summits and above the mountains. Although the upper sky touches directly our own lower air and is one with it, this latter is yet contained in the vast and immense sky. We must admit that the whole is identical. All the air must be similar and conforming, since it is all quite naturally hot, like that substance which becomes sky when it becomes excessively hot or earth when excessively cold. This matter, air, has in its upper part entirely become hot.

Therefore we do not doubt that the further the air moves from the earth, the more thin and warm it naturally becomes. From this phenomenon, it appears manifest that all the upper air is endowed with the nature and the power of the sky. When it is compressed, it becomes as we see it, lighted and stunning, as is clearly shown by the stars which run through the firmament, and by the comets which Aristotle thinks are generated in the air. But these comets are not generated in the air. It is more likely that they are made of something that is a little more dense than air, so that, by nothing really contrary to their nature, they are brought to their condition. Beyond this, we conclude from the fact that the air in the sky turns into or performs the same operation as the sky, that it is of the same nature as the sky. The motion of the comets themselves shows that the air moves with the sky and the stars. Each comet turns or faces the fixed stars and moves with them. We must conclude that they are of the same nature. But this is not to say that the lower air which remains, and can be observed, does not move with the sky and is not one with it.

Now all this expanse of lower air together with the oceans stretch for such tremendous reaches that they can be located from any part of the world. But even if the two were conjoined, they would still be greatly surpassed in size not only by the sky, but by the earth as well.

The truth of this may not be immediately apparent; still it may be safely assumed. For the sea, which is superimposed upon half the earth, does not descend to its center, or even to its deeper parts. The sea lies in such a way that it is a shallow whole, its depth not to be compared with that of the earth upon which it rests. According to some mathematicians, the total area is only twenty-eight thousand stadii. Others think it to be much more. According to the usual measurements, the depth of the ocean hardly extends a single degree at its greatest depth. At this depth, cerulean color is generally manifested; when deeper, the water appears darker and more obscure. But even in the Strait of Sicily where it appears very deep and very dark, the water's depth does not exceed two degrees; and it is as deep at this point as anywhere in the ocean. Clearly, the ocean cannot be compared to the greatness or the extension of the earth upon which it is superimposed.

Leaving the sea for a moment, the air which is contained amidst the mountains is seen to obtain in very little space. The highest mountains, according to some expert mathematicians, rise not more than ten degrees in height. Therefore—even assuming that they exceed this measure—the space which remains between them is nevertheless in proportion to the ambit of the earth's circuit at any moment. Thus, as was said, the magnitude of the ocean and air taken together is greatly surpassed by that of the sky and the earth. Indeed, they are not to be compared either in quantity of material or in weight.

Meanwhile, having compared the oceans and the air to the earth and the sky, we can now consider the parts of the world in a larger context. The earth cannot be considered very large in comparison to the great sky. Not because it is far surpassed by the totality of the bodies in the sky taken together, but because of their superior space and magnitude, quantity of matter and weight. The earth cannot be considered as being any part of the sky. Hence, if the earth became rarefied and its density were diminished, or if the sky itself became glutinated, restricted, or made more dense, then perhaps on these grounds the earth would greatly increase to the extent of appearing a larger part of the world-universe. For it would then contain, if not greater space, at least greater density of material.

CHAPTER IV

That the sky and the earth alone are the principal bodies of the world-universe.

WE CAN SEE then that the sky and the earth are not merely large parts of the world-universe, but are of primary—even of principal—rank. We mean to say that they transcend all other parts not only in magnitude, but also in power and in strength. They are like mother and father to all the others, and are that from which all the others are constituted and made. Not only are all things below the surface of the earth made by them, and manifestly composed of earth by the sun; but also the air and all the waters including the sea are similarly constituted. Certainly the sky and the earth present themselves always the same. It appears that neither of them is constituted or corrupted by the other but remains always unchanged. Only the uppermost parts of the earth seem to be altered by the sun, while nothing appears to change the sky. Nevertheless, the sun's operation and the operation of those things which are greatly similar to it are changed by the earth. Also, those things which are made in the depths of the earth, or those which derive or grow therefrom: the metals, the broken sulphuric, bituminous, or nitrogenous rocks; and, furthermore, those sweet and gentle waters, as well as the plants and animals—if these are not made of earth by the sun, one cannot imagine of what else or by what other agent they could be made.

The ancients doubted not that everything is made of earth. Some, however, thought that the quantity of the sea and the air take precedence and are endowed with supreme powers. They also believed that these depended on nothing else, and were converted and reduced to the nature of earth, bringing about all changes out of their own substance. It is a fact that no amount of earth mixed with any quantity of water or air has ever been observed to become either of these. However, it may be seen that the air in water, even marine waters, is transformed into crystal and ice, thus taking on the nature of earth. But it cannot be that cold is the sole characteristic of any of these substances, for the air, the water, and the sea are all corrupted by cold and reduced to earthlike matter. We cannot doubt that all those things would be finally reduced to earth if the power of the cold were not impeded or turned back by the sun.

Considering primary things and their constitution, it would appear that they are all made of earth by the sun; and that in the constitution of all things the earth and the sun enter respectively as mother and father. From this observation we can see that all the waters, and the ocean itself have been made by the sun out of the earth, since they never cease to run and never become sweeter or more diffused. If they were not made of earth long before the rest, and particularly from the earth's uppermost parts, so many fountains of water would not be emanating, but all would long since have disappeared—including stagnant pools and deep-filled crevices. Furthermore, we would not be able to understand, contrary to opinions of the ancients, how those currents could return to the sun from the earth; since, of the lands from which rivers flow into the sea, those which seem to be lowest are yet higher than the sea. Grow as they may by the flux and reflux of waters, no matter how much freedom they be given in their course, they will still always flow into the earth. That which has already run downward will be elevated, and will in this way surpass the altitude of the sea; because if the entire ocean has need for a larger place it will seek it as a whole, and not merely raise its separate parts. Also there can be no doubt that the rivers return from the sea; for if they did not, then they would no longer spring abundantly from the higher places, as we see happening in all lands but, rather, proceed from the lower ones. Therefore, as we said, since the sources of water never cease, we must admit that they are all made by the sun out of the earth, including the sea, because it never ceases or diminishes.

As can be verified by the sense experience of everyone, the ocean is continually diminished by the sun, becoming less salty and less dense, its salinity and density continually diminished. Thus when ocean water is reduced to vapor by some degree of heat, and then reconverted into water, it becomes sweeter. Clearly this shows that when the ocean is made less dense it becomes sweeter. Now the ocean is constantly being reduced to vapors which then return to the sea; hence there is forever pouring into the sea an immense quantity of soft and sweet waters. Because therefore, always, and in many ways, the density and salinity of the seas are continuously being diminished, it is clear that these properties come to the sea from some other source, or doubtless it would have long ago all become soft and sweet.

We cannot doubt that such great quantities of water can be drawn from the earth by the sun. Nor can we doubt that the salt which is reduced to sea water originates owing to the deprivation of whatever heat obtained in its more rarefied parts. Again, considering the lesser quantity of ocean as compared to earth, we may well raise the question as to whether the earth, when deprived of so much of its waters and vapors, will not in the end come to lack them altogether. Having become supremely arid and dense, it could no longer be softened and converted by the sun. Again, although the sea is continually augmented by so many waters, we may well inquire as to why it does not increase to infinity.

Now the more rarefied parts of the sea—those which continually flow into the earth—cause rarefaction in the mass of which the earth is continually divested, and return it thus to the sea. In this manner the sea takes away that from itself which is continuously added to it. It cannot be that the waters which flow in and out of the sea and which are continually made by the sun, enter the earth and are carried to its uppermost parts. Nor can it be observed, in any way, that these return again to the ocean. Such is not the property or the nature of waters. They cannot be attracted by the earth from their lowest depths to its uppermost parts. Nothing presses us to say that if the sea and the waters did not flow back, there would be nothing to make them return. Nor can we deny that the earth can be converted into water: for any dense earth, and even rocks, are resoluble by heat into vapor. This fact, indeed, was known to the ancients.

The sea can be reduced into extremely hot and rare vapors, and can become something very dissimilar to water. It is clear that the sun, drawing all the waters from the earth, can also pull the air from it in the same way. We can thus see that all the waters are resoluble by a small amount of heat. From them, and particularly from the oceans as we have said, we see vapors rising. These vapors are commonly denser than air, but in no way different, although they are carried a little higher by it and become thus more rarefied when they pass into the nature of air. Vapors do not appear as higher parts of the earth from which the sun daily derives its vapor. Also this diffused substance does not manifest itself to us, because it is made of a denser stuff and by a heat that is not so strong. Yet in reality it is more rare than that substance which can be seen breathed forth. Thus it can be understood, if we seriously seek to comprehend those things which are between the sky and the earth, that they, as all others, are made by the sun. This fact will be made more clear when we look at the sky, the earth, and beyond; and at every other thing: at actions, passions, the species of both, and of all.

The earth and everything else is changed by the sun. Things are also observed beginning to interpenetrate; and all are reduced almost to the same nature. Supreme heat, whiteness, light, and motion are found in the sun. By contrast, there is in the earth supreme cold, darkness, and immobility. Also, in exactly the same way, in all other things there is nothing but hot and cold, light and dark, power and impotence for self-motion. There obtain contrasts of such a kind that the form and the powers of all things are like those of the sun and of the earth; differing only in that they are not supreme and entire in these other things, but are rather diminished and subdued. They are diminished by contraries, and reduced to being something between one and the other. We mean to say that all entities are either hot or cold, light or dark, mobile or immobile. None of them, however, except perhaps fire, which may be considered as one with the sun, is equal in heat, light, or mobility to the sun. None, moreover, is equal in cold, darkness, or immobility to the earth; none, again, appears to be all earth or to be made the same as the sun; but all derive change from these into their own nature, power, and form.

The parts of which we have been speaking are to be considered as the primary and most important parts of the world-universe; preceding all others in power, dignity, and time. But in truth, only the sky and the earth can be so considered. Not being constituted by anything else, they do not depend on anything other than themselves. They are self-constituted. They are changed solely by themselves, while they generate and undo everything else. Therefore, the air, the ocean, and all other things are secondary parts: made, like all the others, from earth and sun. It is by these that they are continually changed and corrupted.

In support of these observations, the sacred and divine letters testify that the sky and the earth were the first bodies: saying that in the beginning they were those that God first created.

CHAPTER V

That all things are constituted of two natures: of one that is made and unmade and of another which remains unchanged. That from the latter is given the mass and the body of things, and from the former the form and the property.

BASIC AS SKY and earth may be said to be, the underlying substance which makes up everything is neither sun nor earth but something else. Those entities which become corrupted are not destroyed, but are really converted into different substances. Thus they do not show up in the generation or corruption of anything or everything, although they are involved in the thing's change or mutation. The being that is newly generated is constituted in such a way that it remains what it was, but takes on a new form. Hence that which is corrupted does not altogether perish. Only its form and its properties perish, while its body and mass remain the same. Hence, properly speaking, all entities are composed of a certain corporeal mass and of a certain other feature, but are not made of numerically the same mass or of the same nature. Each thing is constituted more or less on its own. Substances are very different—sometimes even in opposition to one another. Further, we can see that this same matter is arranged and modified in different ways. Although it may be compressed in itself and reduced, and then decompressed and dilated, it nevertheless neither perishes nor reduces to nothing. Nothing comes to take its place. However, natures differ, and some perish altogether, becoming nothing; and other natures succeed in their place. Sometimes these latter natures are very opposed to those whose place they take.

Now the earth appears to be a certain corporeal mass, very much compressed unto itself and confined: entirely dense and cold; full of darkness and obscurity; immobile and lazy—almost as if dead. Fire also is truly a certain corporeal mass; but it is supremely expanded and dilated; endowed with heat, whiteness, light, and with a supreme capacity for self-motion. When the earth becomes fire, nothing else but earth appears, and the things of which it is composed disappear, becoming nothing. Its whole mass remains, that is, but its arrangement and other characteristics perish absolutely.

In place of the density, cold, darkness, obscurity, and immobility, there succeed opposite natures: rarity, heat, whiteness, light, and mobility. Therefore earth, sky, the sun itself, or any other being, however much it may appear homogeneous and simple, is never constituted by one and the same nature. Rather, any being whatsoever which fluctuates between creation and extinction, however endowed or composed of whatever number of natures, displays its own nature. It follows then, that if there are two works of a single nature, one of which is matter, the latter never perishes or dies but perpetually remains in all beings. The other brings or induces in things their arrangement, their form, powers, and capacities. It is one nature alone which induces all changes, and brings into being the things that really perish and are really born.

CHAPTER VI

That the nature which appears and disappears
is not one and the same, but
multiple and endowed with active powers:
and that it is incorporeal.

WE SEE THAT the inducing nature which comes and goes in bodies brings them form, properties, and power; and that these natures are not only different in different entities, but are, as well, opposites, tending to destroy one another. We must not think this nature to be one and the same, lazy, dead, or inactive; but rather as being multiple—such that whatever portion and species of it be endowed with active virtue, this part throws all other parts out of their own proper place. By itself this active part dominates and constitutes things, and works in those already constituted. We must not think, however, that because the heat, rarefaction, whiteness, light, and mobility are the nature and condition of the sun and of fire, they are of the same substance as the others that are in the earth, such as cold, density, darkness, obscurity, and immobility. They are not of the same nature in the same way. We have no objection to the idea that those things which are not endowed with opposite powers, or which differ not in powers but vary only in degree of power, are all made up of the same nature. It can be understood from this observation that their structure is so closely related as to be almost one and the same. In fact, they mutually support and conserve one another, in no way offending or offsetting one another, so that where one thing is made, the others also come about immediately.

This is not the case with the things that are in the earth. They perpetually oppose one another; forever disturbing or destroying each other. They do not desire to be together, nor can they remain together in any way. While one of these is being made, if all others do not perish, at least those which are opposed to it either quickly perish, run out, or suffer diminution. These are made of opposite natures. Moreover, those which are of a nature similar to that of the sun, but which yet are not endowed with identical powers, appear to be constituted, though not entirely, by a single nature. Still these are endowed with different powers; and for this reason and in this respect they are differently constituted and hence entirely different from the substance of the sun.

The natures and conditions of things which are in the earth differ from those which are in the sun, even as they differ from the sun. The conditions of any such substance, in whatever bodies they may be found, come entirely from the earth of which they have been constituted and made. Furthermore, no thing is of a nature different than that of the thing which has constituted or made it. Natures cannot, and do not, introduce themselves into the beings in which they are found. These facts are true for anything whatsoever that is made in nature. However, sometimes the natures and conditions of things which seem to be made of the same substance do differ and greatly disagree with one another, so that they mutually offend and persecute each other to the point of destruction.

That there are things in the sun and the earth which are not homogeneous substances, but are composed by one of them as mixed entities, does not mean that the nature which comes and goes in a thing is double. It is really one and then the other. That from which each thing is constituted is divided in many—distinct in species. Thus, as was said, things make one another reciprocally. If they did not mutually disturb one another, and occupy one another's place; and if each did not constitute itself, they would never convert into one another as we constantly see them do. However much we would wish to see them come together and to join with one another, each tends to conserve itself in its own nature.

We have seen that only those natures which are active introduce themselves into the things in which they operate. Hence those which never perish, never become altogether extinguished or turn into something else, but only change into their opposites. Those, moreover, which are of a nature that partakes of both, are correspondingly altered, diminished, and reduced to their opposites. These fly only from those things which are opposed and disturbing. Opposites act in this manner as a counterforce.

It must therefore be admitted that the natures which are generated and corrupted are endowed with the power of insinuating themselves into their contraries, and destroying them. They also suffer, and are destroyed by them in turn, and by all constituted things as well, so that they may operate in the things already existing. Having discarded the nature which was first there, the same matter and the same mass remain; and another nature enters into the same mass. Another operation is thus born, which characterizes the newly acquired nature. It also appears that this nature is incorporeal; and that in itself it could not be hosted by any body whatsoever. We can see that things have not changed entirely into other things by virtue of any corporeal-acting nature which changed them, influenced them, or added to their matter. The active agent only structures them differently: that is, it makes them more rare, more diffuse, more dilated; or more dense, more compressed and restricted. All this is accomplished according to the property of the active nature as it enters afresh into the thing.

Since it was this agency that made the thing what it is to become—changing neither its mass, its particular appearance, nor anything else that can be seen—it seems endowed with a different nature and with different powers. This nature, as we said, is incorporeal. Things are made different by its coming and going, in response to which they take on individual natures and distinct powers. Nothing would be truly one or perfectly whole, or endowed with the same virtues, if the nature it had received were not incorporeal. Indeed, if that nature were corporeal, it would not enter into that mass. It could not mix with it, becoming one with it; nor, as we can observe, would it appear homogeneous with the whole. As corporeal, it could never make itself one and the same with the substance into which it enters. If it were not thus, it would be impossible to distinguish between the received nature, the original nature, or the newly mixed nature.

It is the case, then, that the nature which comes into things and departs from them is indeed multiple. Thus, whatever its quantity and species, it is incorporeal and endowed with active powers—powers which drive out some things from their own place and destroy others, producing themselves in their place. These forces change and constitute substances, and are operative in bodies already formed.

CHAPTER VII

That the remaining nature is corporeal, all one, without action and operation whatsoever. That it receives and conserves the active natures which operate.

THE NATURE which remains must be taken to be entirely corporeal and one and the same throughout. Although all things manifestly become corrupted and change into other things, or take on other arrangements and other forms, nevertheless, the mass and the body remain. If it were incorporeal we should not be able to comprehend the way that a body is constituted, or how incorporeal natures become bodies. Not even the Peripatetics, although they inquired into the matter very diligently, were ever able to discover how this could occur. The very best of them thought this nature to be corporeal. If it was not all one, proper and common to all active natures, joining equally with all; or if all things were not constituted from a single matter, but were made of various entities by different substances; then no active nature whatever—which we see happening—would introduce itself into matter. Nothing could be made of a common matter, but only certain kinds of active natures would enter into certain kinds of matter. In this case all things could be made only of certain entities, and would not be able to enter into a heterogeneous mixture with any other substance. Indeed, only those things could be made which are mutually interchangeable with one another, because they happen to have a common matter.

The said receptive nature, that is, matter, does not appear to be endowed with any active virtue, but seems entirely passive, as if dead. We can thus see that action does not derive from anything except that to which it properly belongs and from which it takes its origin. When another nature supervenes upon the same matter, another action and another operation succeed. There is received in that matter another nature which remains, and in which the action and the operation cooperate, rendering this nature capable of action only in the matter in which active natures operate and conserve themselves. Being incorporeal, these natures cannot be entirely for themselves, or subsist in themselves. We have this knowledge from observation: that in all things which are made by nature which we seek to understand, no action and no operation depends on any corporeal substance whatsoever. It is the case then, that the remaining nature, that is, matter, is corporeal, all one, and without any action or operation whatever. It only receives and conserves the natures which are active and which operate.

CHAPTER VIII

That the active natures contend with one another because each desires to occupy the whole of matter. Yet in the same matter there cannot be contained many natures together.

It is not blind and senseless chance, then, that brings the active natures into perpetual conflict. They all desire in the highest degree to preserve themselves; they strive, furthermore, to grow and to reproduce in their individual subjects, all of which are capable of every variety of growth. But a multiplicity of natures operating together in a single subject could not move in a single direction.

Now, not any subject selected at random would be a fitting host to any nature, but only to that nature which is proper and adequated to it. It does not happen in living beings that the nature which comes upon a particular material becomes indistinguishably and numerically one with it. Indeed, if such were the case, this nature could not manifest its activity in more than a single subject.

Further, it is necessary that the nature be proper and adequated to the action. It is important that the instruments and organs involved be not artificial—because the subject, host to the nature which operates in it, must be wholly in accord with its manner of functioning. The activity of such a nature depends upon the whole, is attached to the whole, and is entirely unified; so that those operations which characterize it cannot be intrinsically more active than the capacity of the matter which contains it.

Thus we see that any nature which supervenes and renders the matter into which it enters capable of its proper action and operation is neither capable nor desirous of being alien to that matter. In this way, in the quarrel and strife of the active natures, one nature will at times win over another, defeating it; and on yet other occasions it will become defeated by the other and lose out.

CHAPTER IX

That rarity, denseness, light, darkness, motion, and immobility are not endowed with the power of operating actively on themselves.

WE SEE, THEN, that the sun and the earth operate actively, not in the mass or the body of the whole, but in those natures which are generated and corrupted in things. If we realize that these agents are all actively operating in relation to those which are opposed to them, and which in turn suffer opposition, thus constituting themselves in the subject of their opposites, it will become evident that all things are endowed equally with active power and with passivity. If we see that only one nature is of this kind and that all the others are constituted by it, it will clearly be the case that only this one is active and the maker of all the others, and that all the others are merely passive, the work of one agent.

Rareness, however, whiteness, light, and mobility—insofar as these are in the sky, in the sun, and in things that are generated—we see constantly made and unmade. It is evident, then, that they are not endowed with active powers. Nor is it clear that these dispel any of the opposites of subjects, producing in them their own substance and taking their place. Indeed, notwithstanding that rarefied and fine things are opposed to thick and dense ones, the rare do not become dense and the dense do not become rare. Only in those cases where the mixture of two things is accomplished such that both are changed can we find two agents obtaining in an opposite.

However, it is not admissible that those things which are extremely rarefied, thin, and apparently ready to move, depend for their motion upon the rareness. The rareness is itself the work of that same nature which also produces motion as subject-act proper to itself, as we will later show in detail. It is also the case that light actively operates in darkness and obscurity, and that it renders the air—which in itself is invisible and dark—visible, making it shine. Light spreads by means of darkness, and in it makes itself visible. Those things which are dark and obscure and opposed to light, illumination casts away and prevents from occurring. As we have shown elsewhere, this character is the virtue, the action, and the property of all light. It can in a flash reach over to any other thing, no matter how rare or dense it may be.

Nevertheless, it is not evident that darkness and obscurity disturb the light from its own subject, constituting themselves in it as do the active natures. Neither does the light which comes to occupy the place of darkness and obscurity chase these latter from its own place. Light does not perform this action by its own operation, nor could it even accomplish this if it were joined with a little heat, for great heat is requisite. As we said, the light of the sun, even before it is great and splendid, does not constitute itself, but performs this act only after its power has become almost that of fire.

Certainly it is not for the reason that it is shiny that light produces itself and the other things which we see generated by it but, rather, because it is hot. Thus, if the light, powerful and whole, is not seen as being endowed with power to activate in the darkness or to generate subjects by itself, it must be very far away and possessed of a diminished and weak light. Indeed, as long as light does not appear, it is nothing else but a living whiteness, visible only as such. Whiteness glows as a light not visible in itself, but diminished and weak. Yet when it is placed against things which are howsoever black, it does not appear that black affects it, or that it in any way changes anything in the black. Where one and the other are mixed, it is the case that color is produced between them. It is because the one, that is to say, when it is mixed with the other is changed by it from its own proper subject, that they can be seen together. If, furthermore, one could be separated from the other, it would be evident that neither had suffered any changes whatever, but that each had preserved its own proper nature.

But to expand: mixed things do not eliminate mobility, nor does immobility change them in any way, in cases wherein they respectively constitute themselves in place of one another. Also, moving beings do not lend the power of motion to immobile ones; nor do the immobile diminish the mobility of those that move and render them static. Even the sky which is supremely mobile and is perpetually turning around the earth has never made it move, but transforms it from a distance. We also can observe that the sky and the air which turns with the sky not far from the earth are never divested of the power to move.

CHAPTER X

That hot and cold operate actively within one another. That from this depends rarefaction and denseness, light, darkness, motion, and immobility.

IT IS EVIDENT that hot and cold are active in and of themselves and that they continually fight and displace one another, the one occupying the subject of the other. Also, from these, rareness, whiteness, light, and motion come about, as also density, darkness, obscurity, and immobility. But not all are equally made by hot and cold; some, rather, by cold, and some by hot. The actions, aspects, and operations of all opposites depend ultimately upon these contrary natures.

We see that rarefaction is engendered by heat, follows it, and is properly its very own. Indeed, where there is heat in active operation, capable of converting, there is also, if the heat be great and overpowering, rarefaction in its extreme forms: smoke and very fine vapors. But where the heat is not great or not continuous, minute particles will remain. Even very dense and very hard things, such as stones, iron, and earth itself are converted by great heat and are finally resoluble to vapors and smoke.

On the contrary side, we see that all things that become cold become dense, frozen, and in every way solid and hard. Also, very fine vapors become water and snow, and water—even the sea itself—becomes ice and crystal. Finally, if the cold is extreme, these vapors are reducible even to earth. Such an event, however, cannot occur in the uppermost parts of this earth, as these are kept warm by the sky and the stars.

Anything which is hardened or made dense appears to be the work of heat. Some things, however, which are not wholly homogeneous are not wholly made dense by it. Only their rarer and thinner parts become converted into smoke and vapors and seem to disappear. But having thus had the parts consumed which were softest and most liquid, those which remain become more dense and hard, so that these, not having been converted by the heat, are then free to perform the operations proper to the things they have become.

Nevertheless, that material which has been overcome and converted by heat and is already exhausted in rareness would be converted even more dramatically if the heat were stronger and more continuous. But in the case just discussed this conversion does not take place with respect to the solids which remained.

Even light, doubtless, belongs properly to heat and manifestly follows it, since it is generated by it. However, that heat which is in the highest degree powerful and pure, that which exists in rarefied things and in that which is made up of great quantities of heat, is seen only in fire. Therefore, it is this power which is in those substances that are supremely hot and supremely rarefied and in those that are so formed as to be resplendent and to cast light.

Not only smoke, but also anything tinged with sulphur, when put close to the flame becomes luminous and splendid. Thus it is only when the heat which it lacked before is added to the sulphur that it can become flame. Cold, on the other hand, is completely and entirely in opposition to the nature of light. The flames demonstrate this observation when they are set in the deepest parts of the earth where obtains the greatest cold. There we see flaming bodies extinguished. They become extinguished because the cold is stronger and can smother and destroy the heat which is followed by light. From this fact we can see that whiteness is made from heat. Indeed, it cannot be that the diminished and soft can be made from any other nature than this whiteness from which light itself in all its power derives. Moreover, whiteness is entirely proper to rarefaction which stems from this principle and perpetually follows it, as shown in the treatise *On the Generation of Color*. Whiteness, even as rarefaction, is the work of heat.

Finally, it can be noted that motion is exclusively the

work of heat; and conversely, immobility is altogether due to cold. All things moving and immobile prove this point clearly. All cold things appear to be made of earth and its constituents. The others, on the contrary, are warm—like the sky, fire, and the animals. Also those beings quick to move are still warmer. We cannot conceive that rarefaction or density, light or whiteness, darkness or obscurity, or motion and immobility operate actively, even by their opposites. Rather, all of these are born from hot and cold. We must attribute the entire power of activity to these two principles. However, it may seem that motion creates heat and other things that appear, indeed, to be made by heat. Thus we have next to consider whether motion is made by heat, or heat by motion, and also whether both interchangeably make things, and are therefore of the same status and dignity.

CHAPTER XI

That heat is prior to motion in nature, time, and dignity. That motion is wholly the work of heat. Why motion makes heat.

THOSE WHO SEARCH for the excellence and the dignity of heat and motion and of whatever is prior to them must properly consider the nature and properties of the one and the other. They must also note the way in which they reciprocally generate one another. Furthermore, things which concern their substance and their powers must not be overlooked. Let us then consider the condition of both, and what belongs to each in particular, and to their reciprocal generation. We intend to establish that heat is the substance of those things in which it is found. We will also show more clearly, in its proper place, that heat remains perpetually the same in eternal things, and that heat which obtains in things that are not eternal remains only so long as the things last and are able to maintain themselves. In fact, heat is the very cause of the duration and conservation of things. Everything whatsoever conserves itself in its own proper nature only so long as the heat remains within it. As the heat diminishes or increases the thing dissolves and changes into something else. Indeed, although heat cannot obtain by itself or sustain itself, it is fixed in a certain way in the subject in which it is found so as to seem one with it.

It must not be thought that motion is a substance of things, nor that it is any substance at all; for it does not remain the same in any moment of time. That motion which appears continuously one and eternal, actually perishes as it is made, and would disappear completely if it did not receive other motion to replace it. The substance that it is and of which it is made, is manifestly different and can, at least in imagination, be separated from it. Thus motion appears to be some kind of operation belonging to heat itself, since it follows it perpetually and obtains only where there is heat. Motion appears thus to stem wholly and exclusively from heat. Heat introduces itself into all things, and in making them warm it causes them to move.

Motion, however, does not operate in this way. Those things which are agitated and are set in motion by outside powers, eventually become mobile by themselves because heat first endows them with the power to move. Therefore we must conclude that in nature, in dignity, and even in time, heat is prior to motion. In the same way, substance is prior to operation. Thus, when the substance is born, the operation quickly follows. Since the operation follows on the substance, it must also succeed it in time.

We must not be seduced into looking for the cause of heat in motion, or come to believe that the two cannot disjoin and separate, or reciprocally become one another by the similarity and conformity that they have in common. We cannot doubt that motion is born out of the substance and nature which is proper to heat; nor can we believe that it can possibly be born out of any other substance. Indeed, we see that wherever there is heat, there also is motion in operation. Furthermore, this operation is not common to other natures in the same way, nor is it contingently attached to heat. Heat does not produce this operation by chance, nor does it in some irrational way cease to effect it. Coming solely from heat, motion is joined to it, and dependent on it in such a way that heat and motion are indistinguishable.

That the nature of heat must be considered as highest and most rarefied and as entirely perfect for its subject, we must concede. In fire, for example, it is evident that heat is in no way conserved and vivified by motion, but is preserved solely by its own nature which, if not actively in motion, would lead the fire to be extinguished. Motion so depends on heat that it is not born from any substance which is not constituted by heat. Who can say that the operation which we have seen, belonging to heat itself, and constituted by the sky, is not in accordance with the natural properties of heat and what it produces? All the elements in the sky are gathered and conserved by heat. This heat-force operates perpetually, without surcease. It is seen to be born from nothing else, and derives simply from the nature and property of heat, never being dependent on another nature.

It is for this reason, then, that heat makes motion: because it is born of heat's substance and nature. Motion cannot derive from any other nature, for wherever motion appears, there also must be heat. That thing, therefore, which is agitated and forced to move itself must necessarily be set in motion by the nature and property of moving entities which are hot. The earth, however, remaining always the same, will not effect those operations which depend on the nature of the sky and of fire, but is itself converted into sky and fire. It cannot be denied, then, that earth assumes the property and the powers of sky and fire, whose operation it is to effect.

CHAPTER XII

That heat produces rarefaction, so that it is fit for motion, and that motion derives enjoyment from it. That cold, on the contrary, makes density because it enjoys the immobility which preserves it. Also, why they fight among themselves. And in what way rarefaction, light, and motion belong to heat—the opposite of cold.

WE SEE THEN that heat expands and that cold contracts, conglutinates, and condenses. Heat, producing motion, renders the affected subject proportionate to itself, so that it can raise and transport it. Heat's power makes the subject thin and light, such that it is oppressed and impaired in its self-motion only by the remaining traces of matter. Indeed, flames lighted in denser things remain motionless, retreating from their own nature. Only those parts of these things which have become more rarefied rise. Therefore, heat rises and moves, having made itself proportionate to the light subject. By contrast, cold thickens the things that it occupies, since, enjoying this immobility, it organizes the subject to its most dense capacity.

Thus it is evident that hot and cold strongly abhor one another, and are contrary to one another. The one and the other desire the same matter and the same subject, but want to organize it very differently. The dense, which is most in accordance with and favorable to the nature and the operation of cold—if we speak of immobility as an operation rather than as the cessation of functioning—is extremely unfit and ill-adapted to the workings of the sky, which embraces and conserves heat. Notwithstanding the fact that rarefaction, light, and motion belong to heat, while density, darkness, and immobility belong to cold, they are not to be thought of as dynamically unrelated forces. Rarefaction is proper arrangement for the subject of heat. Light is the proper aspect of perfect heat. Motion is heat's operation. It is precisely the opposite with respect to cold.

CHAPTER XIII

That heat and cold are the first acting principles of all things.

It appears that only the sky and the earth are the first and principal parts of the world, and that from these everything else is made. It is also true that of the substances in the sky and in the earth, respectively, only heat and cold operate actively. Furthermore, all other conditions of the one and the other do not act at all, but are brought about entirely by heat and owe wholly to its operation. Thus everything in the sky is made from heat and constituted by the sky. Everything is actively made by heat or by those substances which heat actively engenders. The earth itself contains nothing that acts, or makes anything, except those things which are made and constituted by cold. It therefore must be admitted that the sky and the earth are composed respectively of hot and cold. There is in the sky and the earth no other natural agent; and without these everything would remain inoperative and inactive.

If any greater proof is needed that the sky is made by heat, we need only to observe that all things that we see produced by great heat become like sky. Pure fire and flame, which are made by extreme heat, may be observed to be very rarefied, white and light, like the stars. The sun is the first among all things formed by heat. From this fact, we see that the sky is distant from earth and is opposed to it, not perhaps so much in space but in operation. It follows that the sky is constituted by an opposite nature from that of the earth. As we have said, all other things are made by the action of the whole sky, especially that of the sun on the earth, and are derived from the earth by this action of the entire firmament. There is nothing in the macrocosm which is not of the sky and the earth. All is akin to them, is composed of a mixture of their natures, or is entirely made from one of them. Those, however, which are heterogeneous in nature are not entirely potent and whole, but are subject to diminution and alteration by one or the other.

Since we are not able to discover any other natures except those which are actively produced by heat and cold, and which are affected and changed by these two principles, we must say that everything is made by them. It is incomprehensible that any other nature could be operating in anything except that nature which is self-constituted. Further, it can be seen that the thing that changes, although it may be endowed with diverse powers, is not altered by any agent except that which is contrary or similar to it. Moreover, no catalyst or active nature which obtains in a subject either abandons its own composition or ceases its own proper action. Those substances which are not similar to it and do not conform with it, it opposes and seeks to change. It thus extends itself into the internal nature of these while always preserving its own equilibrium, and perpetually expands, conserving itself, with all other subjects.

In conclusion, it can truly be restated that the principal agents of all things are heat and cold.

CHAPTER XIV

That from two active natures many entities are constituted. That their powers vary greatly. That these, having become different, have diverse natures and that their

proper subjects become unlike.
Also that before one becomes transmuted
into the other, it is necessary that
all those in between be converted.

THE SKY actively operates on the earth, converting it into its own nature. It enters into the production of many different substances during this process. Thus the powers of the sky and the earth are not indivisible. Since these substances are altered by others, they fail and perish, instantly turning into their opposites. But they are also endowed with broader and larger powers which cannot be destroyed, either altogether or separately. These are such as are diminished little by little. Since they are being replaced by different powers, they become different, and compose different entities.

It is evident that neither the powers of heat nor those of cold, however great and whole, can generate or destroy instantaneously. They generate gradually, and modify slowly. Also, it may happen that both powers operate in a single subject, even as it is generating. It can be observed that each of these substances is opposed by its opposite and destroyed by it. Nature therefore converts itself into many things, and truly creates itself in this way. Finally, the heats, which are different and converted into opposites of one another, each form their own entities, whatever they may be. Not only do they desire and struggle to conserve this equilibrium, but they try also to occupy, spread, and diffuse themselves throughout the entire subject they seek to occupy.

Although the sky and the earth, the original sources of nature, are very far apart, those natures which gave to the sky and the earth their peculiar qualities and arrangements are not so distant from one another that they are not convertible into one another. The graded heats are no more distant from one another in location than is the earth from the sky. Thus they convert into others, passing through the whole space between them. Thus the acting nature does not evolve by leaps and bounds, but has a continuous or flowing quality. It does not cover that space between the things that are made and those that disappear in a single step without affecting bodies between them: it runs through all of them. Those things that it changes, it first takes over by all the means which it possesses, and afterward changes their form. Extreme density and hardness is transmuted into intense rarefaction and softness only after the rare and soft substance lying in between these limits is transmuted. Deep darkness and obscurity must become purple, cerulean, red, and all the other colors before it can pass into extreme whiteness and light. This action will occur if the color is uniform and heat is actively operating in a uniform way. Thus, although the sun is much more powerful than the earth, it cannot by an instantaneous action convert the things of the earth into its own substance. Also it cannot instantly change cold, condensed, black, and obscure substance into sky and earth.

Only very slowly can the sun change the substances of earth and introduce into them its own nature. Thus, before the earth can be converted into the form of the sun and the sky, it must first be converted into many other forms and natures.

CHAPTER XV

That the earth is first converted into those things which are more akin to its nature, and then into those which appear to be more remote; not, as the ancients believed, that things are first converted into vapors, water, metals, and stones.

The sun changes the earth into something other than its own substance and only gradually clothes it with the sun's own arrangement and form. It is reasonable, therefore, to believe that those things are first converted into one another which are most similar to sky and sun, nearest to the earth, and closest to each other. Thus we find it impossible to believe, as the ancients believed, that the earth was first converted into vapors, the uppermost of which came to constitute the sublunar ether, and the lowest of which remained congealed by cold in the concavities of the earth, turning into stone. We hold, instead, that gradually the substances of earth were stripped of their own proper nature and arrangement. They became endowed with those powers and features that are halfway between sky and earth, converting first into many things, and finally into air.

The earth, which is very dense and very cold, must become tepid and soft before it can become rarefied and hot. The vapors cannot be converted into metals unless they are first changed into states that are in between and are no longer compressed and solid or liquid and flowing. Earth, as such, cannot be changed into metals without intermediate changes. These latter are constituted entirely by liquid and flowing substances. Vapors, therefore, need not first be formed which afterward become liquid and moving substances that finally, being greatly compressed, are constricted to metals. Metals, we believe, are made by the sun as something between vapor and earth, much nearer to the nature of earth than to that of vapor. From these, vapors are born.

Now Aristotle denies that earth and the vapors that are derived therefrom are converted into water, since the earth is arid and dry. Neither this material of the earth, as he sees it, nor the things that are made from it, are capable of constituting things that are humid. He thus found it necessary to place Plato's Tartar in the earth. Indeed, if this substance does not administer certain currents of water in certain amounts, that is, if it does not afford vapor to all the waters, we could never discover how or where so many vapors could arise. It is not reasonable, according to Aristotle, that bodies of water be contained in the earth, be cause all the waters are placed on its outer surface. If this were the case, the waters would long ago have evaporated and disappeared.

The Peripatetics' doubt that the continuous action of the sun is needed to convert earth into water, and that the currents of water are not constant, is not justified. The heat introduced into the earth from which the waters are particularly made does not actively operate in the whole of the earth. Only a certain portion of the heat melts and liquefies that part of the earth which it turns into water; but the heat which remains is yet not inactive. Similarly, when the flow of waters is diminished only a little, this is because not all of the heat is operating upon it; but it cannot be said that the heat which is not operating upon it is wholly inactive.

Now heat, in this way, is continuously changing the entire earth, although not uniformly, nor all at once, because the earth itself is of a mixed composition. Whereas certain parts of the earth are conformable only with water, those that are more dense and further from the nature of water are, in the meantime, being softened and brought closer to the liquid state. From this it follows that once the waters begin to flow, they will run unceasingly, granting only that there is no surcease of agency and matter. Note that during the summer the waters appear to be more shallow because of the stronger heat, even though there are more such bodies of water present. In turn, these variegated matters, after being converted into water, are then quickly converted into vapors.

During the winter, the waters in no way diminish. Instead, the rivers that flow from the earth—as even Aristotle agrees—are received, gathered together, and steadily augmented. In periods of the greatest heat we ofttimes observe that the strongest flow of waters, even those which are nearest the sun and have run all summer, disappear the moment the sun is gone. Again, all during the springtime, the waters continually increase, even when they are not augmented by snows or rains as they are in the winter.

The Peripatetics, then, have said nothing to show that the waters which derive from the earth are not generated from the sun, earth, and the heat working therein. They also do not deny that the earth first converts into things which are most like it before it converts into those things which are at a further remove and quite unlike it. We can no more deny, therefore, that vapors are not changed into water by the cold than that the cold congeals and condenses all fluid things.

Those things which are made humid by the heat, and which are soft and rarefied, are not reconverted to hard, stable, and dense entities by the cold. They change to this state only because the sun does not operate steadily and with the same action. As we will show, the sun operates with varied power, and makes different things in their proper order. As regards the earth, cn the other hand, it actively performs in a contrary manner, making hard and more dense those things which are made soft and liquid by an oblique and moderate sun. Thus, when the sun gets closer and stronger, the substances become soft; but when it departs, they become congealed and thickened by the nighttime cold.

Were it not for this evidence, we might heedlessly believe that the earth first converts into those things which are most remote from its own nature, these in turn changing into others which are closer and more akin to the earth's nature. But in this case the arrangement which is in bodies would not appear to be derivative of the nature of the entity from which it is made. Yet, as we saw before, this is not true; the earth generally changes in an ordinary way.

Now we will return to our starting point in search of the cause of the diversity of things.

CHAPTER XVI

That since the sun actively operates with very different and heterogeneous heat on a varying and divergent earth, it converts the earth into many things, not all necessarily or continually rare or hot.

THE EARTH is converted by the sun into many and various things. It is very far from the sun; and it is evident that because it is penetrated variously it receives many different forms and becomes endowed with many diverse properties. Perhaps it even becomes converted in many more and diverse ways than those of which we are aware. These conversions do not occur in some prescribed order; nor do they constitute a continuous operation governed by the same order which determines things closer to and similar in nature to the sky. Things which are shaped by the sun do not constantly become rarefied and hot. Some, indeed, are formed in the opposite way. These, becoming more dense and cold, acquire still other natures and become different things. In some instances, indeed, certain parts of them become endowed with many different natures.

The sun operates actively but with varying degrees of heat. It works on an earth which has been previously altered and made diverse by it. Thus, since the earth is itself not only extremely dissimilar to the sun but is also quite heterogeneous in its own constitution, and since also it is one entity in itself, it is understandably converted into things composed of very dissimilar parts. The sun, turning continuously around the earth, does not always actively operate on it. Sometimes it ceases to do so, conceding the earth a certain latitude so that it thus utilizes its own action to form things, rather than operating to corrupt or destroy the sun's produce. It slows down the motions of the sun and impedes them, converting them in this way into other things. Again, because the sun does not use its own action directly upon the earth, either continuously or for any steady length of time, since it changes both angle and place constantly, it performs its activities with many different powers. Indeed, direct-angle light differs from oblique-angled light, as is sufficiently demonstrated by the difference between the summer and winter sun, and even by the light reflected from mirrors. Thus oblique light is not felt to be warm; whereas the same light, focused directly, can be made to create warmth of any degree.

Furthermore, we can see that the sun actively operates not only with the heat which emanates directly from it, but also with that which it has for a long time daily introduced into the earth, not only in the earth's higher parts, but in its lowest depths. These latter parts suffer very little change. The sun hardly affects them at all. They can be influenced only by the heat which strikes the highest parts of the earth and descends gradually into its interior, diminished and diluted, greatly compressed, and unlike its former self. In fact, the sun, operating as it does on the surface of the earth, does not affect the whole of it; nor does it even affect the earth's nearest and most contiguous parts with the same force. This is a fact because the earth is divided not only into mountains and hills, which, being heated, reflect the sun in different ways, but even those parts of the earth which appear most spherical and flat are pocked with unequal but small irregularities which sense observation can detect.

Now everything on the earth is thus marked with minute changes in elevation. In this way it happens that the great mountains do not all receive and reflect the same light, but gather it strongly and directly on one side, and weakly and obliquely on the other. Also certain parts, such as depressed places, that is, valleys and the like, separate and further scatter this reflected light. Mirrors clearly show that light suffers from these inequalities: dense air will cause shadows; and other such causes work also to diminish its splendor and power. Hence it follows that mirrors, if not clean and flat on the surface and cleared of every blemish, do not reflect full strength, but weakly, although they may be capable of profound reflecting power. The light is in some manner obscured by blemishes and impeded or aborted.

Therefore, not being able to reflect light whole and united, the mirror is no longer endowed with the same powers as the light. Furthermore, although the surface of the earth has been basically the same from the beginning, it has been altered in different ways, because it received the sun in different ways. It follows, hence, that its higher parts have acquired a different nature and arrangement from its internal parts, and those parts which have been exposed to the direct sun have become different from those upon which it shone but obliquely. Again, the same differentiation occurs with respect to even those parts that are close and contiguous to one another on the surface. It appears therefore to be the case that the sun converts these earth parts in the same way into different things, in that its light is alternating and varied. Indeed, if the diversity and lack of uniformity of heat and of matter are seen by themselves as capable of constructing different entities, then adding these deviations together makes them capable of making an immense variety of species of things. Some of these will even appear to have been entirely made from one or the other nature.

TOMMASO CAMPANELLA

TOMMASO CAMPANELLA *was born in Stilo in 1568. He entered the Dominican order at fourteen years of age. His zeal and acuteness in disputing Aristotle soon gained him the reputation among his fellow monks of possessing occult powers. In order to avoid the consequences of the enmity he was arousing, he traveled first to Rome, and then to Florence and Padua. The hostility with which he met at every turn led, in 1600, to accusations of heresy, and of holding views inimical to the state. Subjected to the most inhumane persecution, Campanella was detained in prison for twenty-seven years. Even the indescribable horrors of his incarceration were not enough to break his spirit; while in prison he wrote, meditated, and studied. Finally he was freed and sent to Rome. The last years of his life were spent peacefully in France. He died in 1639. Among his most important writings are his* Apologia pro Galileo, Civitas solis, *and* De sensu rerum et magia.

On the Sense and Feeling in All Things and on Magic

BOOK I

On that wonderful part of occult philosophy where it is demonstrated that the world is a living image of God and, therefore, that it is sentient and knowing in all its parts large and small, all of which have sense and feeling sufficient in degree for their preservation and the conservation of the whole in which they obtain, and in which may be discovered the reasons for all the secrets of nature.

CHAPTER I

That there can be no more in the effect than there is in the cause, and that, therefore, the elements and the world as a whole have sense and feeling.

In a work of ours that many already know, we have shown that no entity can give to another what it itself does not possess. Experience more than proves this. No one has ever seen light produce darkness, heat produce cold, a thorn to caress, or weight to produce lightness. This is a matter of common observation. It is true that a hot mass can become cold, but it is certainly not the coldness in the heat which produces the cold any more than it is the coldness of the mass which makes it hot. And when heat is kept contained, increasing thereby, it is not the cold which gives it greater heat, but rather it becomes hotter on its own, being by its own nature diffusive and self-increasing. This is something which could never happen if things were unproductive or inactive in themselves.

Now if animals have, as we all agree, what is called sense or feeling, and if it is true that sense and feeling do not come from nothing, then it seems to me that we must admit that sense and feeling belong to all the elements which function as their cause, since it can be shown that what belongs to the effect belongs also to the cause. Consider then, the sky and the earth and the whole world as containing animals in the way in which worms are sometimes contained in the human intestines—worms or men, if you please, who ignore the sense and feeling in other things because they consider it irrelevant with respect to their so-called knowledge of entities.

CHAPTER II

That there can be no argument against our first proposition.

IT IS said that the sun is neither animal nor plant—yet it makes animals and plants. It is said that the sun is subtle, noble, and white—yet it hardens and condenses the mud and darkens the Ethiopians who dwell under Cancer and Capricorn, where the sun stays the greater part of the year. It is said that fire heats; and that the cold snow heats the hands and enriches the earth; that saltpeter cools hot drinks; that fear, which is not hot, nevertheless heats a man. It is said that what is alive kills what is alive and that, in brief, the similar produces the dissimilar, and that everything is made out of what it itself is not. It would thus appear that sensible and sensitive things can arise from things insensible and insensitive. My position is that, between sun and earth, all things that are receive all they possess from these two elements. Animal nature, however, is not made directly of sun but of earth in which the sun, operating from within as a spirit, laboriously produces it. Not being able to free itself, or exhalate itself from within, it organizes matter into bodies, each adapted to its own life. But this we will demonstrate later on: for the moment, let it suffice to note that plants and animals derive their spirit, heat, subtlety, and motion from the sun and their matter from the earth, in which the organizing sun operates. But note that these things possess nothing more than is to be found in their cause, even though the form in which they manifest it may differ from the way in which it appears in the cause.

The varied modes of things arise from the opposition that one contrary receives from its contrary. These owe, then, to the opposing actions which the blessed Lord has ceded to active causes so that they might serve as instruments proper to the coining of various models based on the first Idea. In this way, in everything, there is reflected the goodness of the First Cause. This is not to say that either the sun or the earth intends to bring about its produce: but the sun is fire and the earth is mass, and so they oppose one another and thus bring about mixed images of the primordial Ideas of which they are instruments and models. Sense, however, and feeling are not models but, rather, things essential to every active virtue; and this we shall see in the sequel.

That the sun and the earth feel is undeniable. Now the sun does not harden mud in the sense that it gives it dryness and hardness; rather, it uncovers the hardness of the earth which was already present in the earth but which was hidden and mixed under the softness of water. Mud, as we know, is made of earth, hard in itself, and water which is soft; and when the fire acts, it first converts the water into vapor and then into air and then into sky. Water, which is always similar to itself, does not resist its own proper action, and so the earth alone remains, manifesting its own proper dryness—a dryness which can itself be liquefied by intense fire and made to produce great fumes, as we observe in the furnaces where metal and salt are melted.

Elsewhere we have demonstrated, against Aristotle, that the sun, which is hot, produces heat which conforms with or, as is said, "is univocal" with common fire. However, when the sun is weak it produces less. In the same way as with our example of mud, if the mobile part is taken away from any substance the rest of that which was involved in the motion remains unmoved. Thus the sun darkens—not producing darkness—but making manifest that material darkness which was hidden under the whiteness. If you burn this paper which is white, you will see a white flame, which is the tenuous part of the paper, issue forth, while the gross and black matter remains behind. Still a greater heat acting will turn it into glass; and if the heat is further increased, it will turn into white, thin air—even though it is said that all matter is inert and black. In philosophy we show that inert and inactive blackness resides in things as does coldness—subject, that is, to the operation of heat.

Now from these arguments it follows that in mud and coal there is nothing which is not in the sun or in the earth and matter; and that it is of fundamental importance to observe the action of the sun—which action is always subtle, fine, and white. It is true that there are many dark clouds: these are not, therefore, to be viewed as things entirely deprived of the sun's whiteness. For the sun always whitens, rarefies, and moves, even if not always in the same way or to the same degree. Snow, for example, does not directly warm the hand, but the heat which is native to man, feeling the cold which agitates its native state, gathers itself, swells, and goes out of the hand in order to combat the cold. Similarly, the snow feeds the earth, as it too has a bland, native heat appropriate to itself; and saltpeter cools because the extrinsic coldness of wine, sensing an adverse motion and unfriendly odor, becomes concentrated and increases—although if a very long time elapsed it would destroy itself and heat the wine. Fear is similarly to be understood as the fight of the warm, vital spirit from the inferior parts, undertaken in order to evade the attack of a vengeful enemy. This comes about in such a way that the extremities become almost cold, with air entering into them: they then commence to tremble as there is no longer enough spirit, but only air, to support them.

Now it is accidental, and not essential, action that occurs when the living kills the living; and in all such actions that take place by art, rather than by nature, there is no similitude to be found between the effect and its cause. Thus my writing is made by me, and I am not the writing but the writer. Still, I have the similitude of the writing in mind and am thus able to convey it to this paper. The effects of such actions, therefore, are not properly to be ascribed to the instrument but to the agent. What I am writing resembles my mind; while the pen and the ink which contribute to the color, thickness, and thinness of my written characters, since they are instruments of this mind, are more important than I am to the writing, although not to the meaning. Again, when one kills another, death resembles the mind of the killer and not his being as such, while the width of the wound he inflicts depends upon the blade. Thus, when heat kills cold, driving it out of the wood which it destroys, or when a ball of snow is flung into a great furnace, we must not say that the death grows out of the heat but, rather, from the nonbeing of the cold; since, even while killing the cold, heat does nothing else but heat.

In this way, what gives heat to wood can be only what already possesses heat; and if it happens that cold perishes and cannot remain together with the heat, this comes about accidentally. Being killed, which represents a lack of power, as I have said in the *Metaphysics*, happens to the cold because it is not hot and therefore cannot stay with itself. Thus destruction depends upon some nonbeing; and, consequently, upon the common nothingness from which things derive. As we have said before, there is no gainsaying the principle that nothing can come to be from a cause in which it is not already contained.

CHAPTER III

Lucretius was wrong in denying sense to things; Galen was also wrong; and what wiser men have said.

BEHOLD Lucretius the Epicurean attempting to show, with Democritus, that insentient and inert things can give rise to things with sense and feeling! Maintaining that from nonweeping, nonlaughnig elements, men, who weep and laugh, can come into being! Anaxagoras sets forth many similar views. I, however, persist in maintaining that there is laughter and weeping in the elements—though not in the way that they are in men—for laughter is a dilation of spirits, and this dilation obtains in all things that are rarefied. Thus, when fire feels occasion to conserve itself, it dilates, and is, in its own way, happy. Weeping is a compression of the spirits, resulting in the elimination of the water which is in the membranes and in the cavities of the head—it is as when we press wet earth and it exudes water. Everything is in the cause, although, as we said, perhaps in a different way.

We must be careful here to note that Lucretius not only denies sense and feeling to the first principles of all things, but says, with Democritus and Epicurus, that everything under the sun is made from the minglings of atoms; and, according as these take on various configurations in their minglings and joinings, they manifest varied appearances and forms. In themselves they are held to be neither hot nor cold, black nor white—and they lack entirely in sense. It is held further that from these couplings, heat is born from those atoms which are sharper, and cold from those which are obtuse, while the soul is born of the round ones. From empty space, as they see it, interspersed with air which becomes much condensed, water was made; and from further comminglings, the earth. This view, which we have refuted in the *Physics* and *Metaphysics*, we shall not here stop to examine further. I wish only to say that if men have reason and counsel, and the very leaves on the trees display that they are the produce of reason, as do flowers and thornbushes, and bees have sense together with ants and other such creatures, we are compelled to admit that there is a first wisdom, called God, in which all participate; and that pure accident cannot, by any tossings of the letters of this book together an infinite number of times, produce this book as it is, while art makes it with a single try. Thus we must not attribute the ordered construction of the world to anything but the First Art.

Hot and cold, I say, understood as active, and wholly free of atomic passivity, are not born without active power. An infinite number of prickly things and thorns could never heat anything, nor could gross powders cool. Moreover, why does not the sun, which so diffuses its substance, not destroy itself, unless it be that it is an active, diffusive, and incorporeal power? But Lucretius holds that the sun is born every morning, a new sun being made of atoms every day, which then proceeds around the earth by chance, to die, finally, in the west. But that this should happen with such order and precise division of times due to mere chance is unthinkable; and the experience of those who, since Columbus, have gone around the world proves the utter stupidity of this view.

I do, however, admire Galen and many of the Peripatetics who, as opposed to Democritus, place the active powers in the elements—although they deny these elements feeling and sense. But feeling and sense arise out of the relation between things united and adjusted in a similar way, and there could be no vital and sensitive power except as other things respond to the unity and adjustment. The strings of the lute, for example, are of a hard matter, which, when adjusted, can make music; yet the music is not one thing, but different percussions of the air made by the unison of the different strings; and the strings contain no more nor less music than the one with the art and power to play the strings can give to the strings upon which it plays. Thus the united qualities could never feel, or cause feeling, if sentient feeling were not in them to move them and bring them to life. But as these philosophers concede that sentient things move themselves, they ought also to affirm that they feel, in themselves.

Now I do not say, with Anaxagoras, that everything is in everything actually; though the food we eat does divide into flesh, nerve, bone, and hair, with each similar part going to its similar, so that each thing is basically the same in the world, for everything is made of every other thing in succession. What I do affirm is that this constant becoming derives from the varied dispositions of one and the same matter; such that some part is now adapted to become bone, another flesh, another water, and another smoke. And these dispositions have always, since the beginning of the world, varied, by reason of the various actions of active powers.

Anaxagoras' argument that everything which is made cannot be made of that which it is not, but only of that which it is, is of course true. He was wrong only in saying that it had to be made in one particular way. For fire is made of wood, which is not fire but something else; and it is made more of wood than of stone, which is not as cordial to fire. Yet stone, when it is rubbed, as we rub wood, will yield fire; and flint more than another stone because it has more fire hidden in it, as is proved by the sulphuric odor of its ashes and sparks. Aristotle is wrong in saying that motion accounts for this. Because with still other stones, even great blows will not produce fire. In matter where heat is dormant, heat takes on vigor in manifesting itself when the matter is struck, erupting in ignitable bits. Nothing, I repeat, can give that which it does not have. St. Augustine affirms that the seeds of all things are hidden, so that it would seem that he is in agreement with Anaxagoras; yet one must understand this ultimately in connection with the most primordial disposition of things. Now if sensitive things are made, it is necessary to say that they are made of sentient elements; and that all things are produced by them, as the good Telesio wrote, and as Thales of Miletus proved with his lodestone experiment. Hippocrates, in his book on human principles, grants sense to heat, and indeed, every cognitive power. St. Clement the Roman cites St. Peter as saying to Simon the magician that where there is order and reason there is sense; and since every plant, stone, and animal is made with order and reason, they are all possessed of sense. And all creatures laud the Creator and obey Him, as is written in Wisdom; and David exhorts them to laud Him whom they know by natural sense, which is intrisic to everything, and they take delight in being, and in living, while abhorring nonbeing. Happiness, says St. Paul, is testimony of a very happy God. But in order to understand how things are really moved—whether, as Anaxagoras believed, by mind; or, as Avicenna held, by necessity; or, as Alexander believed, by the active intellect —we must first understand what sense is and how every form is sensitive.

CHAPTER IV

Sense is the perception of passion
joined with a thing existing in act,
and not in formation of pure potency;
and of the difference between them.

IT SEEMS THAT sense is passion, because when we feel heat or cold, we become the cold or warm that we feel. Thus, when the man with a fever touches someone whom I, being healthy, consider warm, he feels instead the sensation of cold. But when one touches another who is as warm as he, he has no sensation of the other's heat. Therefore, we feel as we feel: the thorn pricks us, the sweetness sweetens us, the sense of odor is reflected in our nostrils, and color gathers or ungathers our sight as we feel with it. Sense then, is passion—but of two different modes: for the sensible either delights or displeases us, or else it is neutral with respect to pleasure and pain. Those things delight us which are commensurate with the sense in those organs to which they are addressed; while those which destroy—like fiery iron—displease us. And so for all objects; if they serve to conserve our being, they please us; if to destroy our being, they displease us. Sense, therefore, is not only perfective passion, as Aristotle thinks, but corruptive as well. Moreover, when we feel anything, we do not take all of the power and form from it; we do not take on its form when we see a stone, for it cannot yield up its whole form. It is merely the tinted light of its surface, so to speak, which enters through the eyes, touching and moving our spirit, which, by this means, feels; whereas if it actually took on the form, it would become a stone.

Thus sense is not made by information, as Aristotle maintains, but rather by confrontation. For if it were by information, it would be requisite that the total destruction of the preceding form take place, and be replaced by the introduction of a new one. Again I know the fire in the sun when I am altered by it, although the alteration, of course, is not total. For were it total, it would mean my becoming fire not to some small degree, but wholly. And from this little alteration, my sentient being approximates the balance of the fire's power. And from many such experiences it attains knowledge of fiery things. Thus sense is not only passion, but it is self-expressing to the sentient being. It is expressed in this sense the moment it arises; and when we see what we have seen before, or anything similar to that which we have seen before, we immediately experience the same—as one who, being present at a feast, remembers another like it and is gladdened thereby; or as one who, when he sees a ship, remembers the nausea that he suffered while on the sea and vomits anew.

So sense is passion; and memory is sense anticipated and renewed; and speech is sense of like for its like; and just as many kinds of similitude as there are in the world—of essences, of qualities, of actions, of places, of times, of operations, of cause, of quantity, of sight, of figure, and of color —there are as many kinds of speech and syllogism. And all those animals that have spirit free in their cavities have also memory and speech—and this includes plants, despite the fact that they appear to be dumb.

Soul is already spirit which is warm, subtle, and mobile. It is capable of receiving feeling, and of feeling quickly as the air, as we shall see in Book II. Hence spirit is not pure potency, like matter, but something capable of being open to everything which is similar to it, although not of being open to everything about the things which are similar to it. And the mind of God, which permeates man, not only possesses this same sensitive animal speech and memory, but is as well higher and more divine, as we shall later show.

Now if sense is passion, and if all the elements and everything composed of them are, as we say, open to everything, they must feel. It often happens, however, that man is open as well to that which he does not feel—as in sleep, or when he is bitten by lice. Hence sense is the perception of passion; and if the perception be destructive, resistant, and opposed to the percipient, it is unhappy; while if it be pleasing and conserving, it applauds it, pursues it, and loves it.

CHAPTER V

Of the actions and passions of things; that it can be shown that they all feel and sense, and that without sense the whole world would be chaotic; nor would there be any generation and corruption.

COLD AND HEAT are such enemies that the one persecutes the other even unto death. The one that is unable to repulse the other, flees; and whichever of the two finds itself surrounded by the enemy gathers itself together, swells, and increases in strength, as does the warmth in winter, or when it is enclosed within clouds, and as does the cold in hail. These two mainfest all the activities of animals and behave, in general, just as fire and earth which, with eternal enmity, strive to kill one another.

We must admit, then, that the one knows the other to be its enemy, and that in trying to preserve itself, it is led to destroy the other; and that from this unceasing warfare there proceeds not only their own debilitation, but as well the generation, transmutation, and corruption of mixed entities. Now as all physicists are agreed, there would be neither generation nor corruption in the world were it not for contrariety; and were it not that one contrary could recognize its contrary, it would not oppose itself to it. Let all then hear me: the greater the fire which wins out over earth, the more the earth becomes attenuated and ascends into the fiery sky which it comes to resemble; then the earth, raised thus on high, strives with all its might to get back down; and just as every animal flees its contrary and gravitates toward its kin and den, and just as men live with men, wolves with wolves, and fish with fish, so it is also with the great bodies—the planets. All of them feel: were it otherwise, the world would be utterly chaotic. Fire would not rise, water would not flow to the sea, stones would not fall, but everything would remain forever in its present state, as nothing would feel any sense of peril from its contrary, nor any need for conservation by what is like itself. Therefore the argument which concerns the sense and order of all things in the world, and the view of the whole process of things according to which it is regarded as similar to sentient animal life is more than credible. We must, in fact, admit that the first animal bodies possessed this power of feeling; and that it is very crude of Averroës to refer to simple bodies, as well as the composites made up simple bodies, as weak, half-consumed, and lacking in any superior qualities. For if the elements are mixed with their contraries, they react violently to them in such a manner that they feel both internal and external unhappiness. Unmixed elements, on the other hand, feel only external unhappiness.

CHAPTER VI

That the opposing views of other scientists, on the sense and feeling in things, contain egregious errors.

MANY SAY that God governs all things by His own act. Anaxagoras seems to regard chaos as unmixed with mind; and he therefore holds that fire ascends and heavy things descend because mind orders and makes these distinctions. Also this mind creates generations and corruptions and performs separations and joinings. Gabriel Theologo appears to agree with this view. He says that the sun does not shine, but God shines in the sun; that man does not speak, but God speaks through him; that fire does not move, but God through fire. Others maintain that these activities are performed by angels; and it seems that St. Augustine feels this way, for he tells us, in his *De cognitione verae vitae*, that storms and gales are moved not by themselves, but by demons and angels. And Themistius, with other Peripatetics, also has recourse to Intelligences. Alexander and Avicenna seem to agree with Anaxagoras; and Galen, in his *De formatione foetus*, expresses admiration for this mind which gave the world the formation of an animal, as do the Platonists, Basil and Augustine. Many theologians, indeed, attribute all of this to the First Wisdom.

I say that these opinions have all been misunderstood, and that, in addition, they are erroneous; for if the works of God (as Moses says) are perfect, then God must have endowed everything with powers sufficient to conserve them; and since no faculty is more necessary to this end than the knowledge of one's similars—which knowledge saves us from the enemies who would destroy us—it is necessary to recognize that there is feeling it all natural things. We all know from our own experience that the flight from pain and the search after pleasure derives from our sense of these, since no one seeks to avoid pain that he does not feel. Animals do not avoid the snare that they don't see; nor do sheep run from the wolf that is not seen; nor he from the dart which is not felt. Thus also, neither fire, earth, nor anything else would pursue or flee if it did not feel. There is in everything desire and love as well as hatred and abhorrence. No love is born of a thing which is not loved: and so it is with natural love and natural knowledge.

Now if fire seeks to ascend, this is because it knows what conserves it, and that descending would destroy it. Whereas it would be contrary to nature and to the forms of things to hold that God ascends with the light of the sin. Further, it is the cause of frequent errors to confuse reference to forms with reference to God. From such a confusion, it follows that it is not our souls that want and feel, but God who feels and wants in our souls—both good and evil—which view goes even beyond the impiety of Calvin who says that God can force the soul to do evil, and that although He himself does no evil, He does it through us. Further, if one being is similar to another by its form, then it is by this form that it will feel the other, and not through, or by, anything else. And certainly Anaxagoras, by postulating unmixed mind, sets conditions which require that the order of all things be explained by their obeying themselves. It is thus requisite that all things have feeling to obey, since this is the nature that God has given to them. Either this is the case, or we must admit that God alone is the form of things and operates himself in place of the forms. But this is perverse error; and Anaxagoras understood very well the nature of this error, even if he did make the mind separate. God operates in everything as First Cause, giving to all things the being, powers, and operations which mesh with all other things, as regards being and nonbeing. Things tend to nonbeing, as I have proved in my *Metaphysics*, because of lack; for sin, as lack, is not a sufficient but a privative cause. Nevertheless, it is true that forms operate—that heat makes things warm, while earth makes them cold and heavy—and this is sufficient to demonstrate that things act by themselves, and that the soul of the world, or the common nature of things, provides for everything, having learned from God. But with regard to particular actions, we must seek particular agencies. God created the world, and He created things, and He gave them the power to conserve themselves and to change themselves in time; and that power will remain, as nature, until at the last the universe comes to an end. And nature is participant in Eternal Law in the way in which, as St. Augustine says, the light which is in our home is participant in the sun.

Thus, to attribute to angels the operations of natural forms is an error. I believe that St. Augustine, in the example which I cited, has in mind only extraordinary events requiring supernatural forms. More usually, in the event of storms and gales, the sun and the moon expand and the winds then move in order to find more space for their subtlety—for being restricted to a small place would mean destruction for them. Similarly, water makes itself move because of its sense and feeling, as I shall show in the following books. I shall show too, in what follows, that animals are formed by nature necessarily; and that everything is thus brought about according to the form which God has ordained. But to say that the stone falls to earth not because of its own power, but because it is thrown by an angel, or that fire avoids its enemy because an angel leads it to do so, is to speak nonsense, wholly unworthy of the Creator—as if He had neglected to give all the necessary vitality to everything. It is, moreover, an offense to the angels to regard them as deputies responsible for natural acts: as servants to every lowly thing as its form: an offense, because men and animals have forms more lowly than the straw or clay which angels would have to serve. Furthermore, the angel is not, like God who moves everything without violence, intrinsic to things despite the fact that He remains extrinsic. If we were thus to insist upon purely extrinsic forces, every motion would be violent. Now if you wish to say that fire or earth obeys a certain order, what you must say is that they obey their commandments, for no corporeal instruments compel them; and nothing responds to any commands except those of God, as He alone, who creates them, can perform this miracle. Therefore, if things feel, they have no need of angels to move them in their natural processes, although it might be, as St. Jerome says, making clear to me that which I had never before fully understood, that the angels serve as the guardians of each species.

If I am in the right, then, as against the views of my opponents, we must conclude that each thing has just so much sense—be it more, or less—as suffices for its own conservation.

CHAPTER VII

That instinct is a natural impulse of sentient nature, and whoever affirms the one is also committed to asserting the other.

OTHER LEARNED MEN have been aware of these inconsistencies, and were led, as a consequence, to say that things were moved by natural instinct to do whatever it is that they do. In the same way that we, with bit and spurs guide our horses, or as we guide other men by means of words and commands, so God guides all things by means of natural impulses, and men freely, by means of the intellect they possess. Without the necessity of reference to sense, these impulses are supposed to direct all things to their proper ends. St. Thomas seems to have been of this opinion.

But these learned men too became involved with difficulties; for natural instinct is an impulse of nature and, according to them, nature is nothing other than matter or essential form; but as they attribute operations to forms, they should also say that all forms are sentient. Now they do affirm much that is good; for they concede, with Aristotle, that nature operates according to ends; and they hold, against Empedocles, that plants make their fruits in order to immortalize themselves, their thorns in order to defend themselves, and their leaves in order to cover themselves; nature, it then follows, knows its ends, since it would not act, nor would it direct itself to those ends if it did not know them. Hence instinct is the impulse of a cognizant nature. Now if the works of God are perfect, and every nature must know its end in order to operate, it follows that every nature feels; and that fire goes up, motivated by its sentient from which knows its own good to be above, and its evil, below; and the case is entirely similar for hot, cold, and every other thing. In fact, Aristotle, in Book II of his *Physics*, says that plants, as every other entity, operate in virtue of their ends, and there is no need of any special discourse to understand these ends; for just as the practiced player can play without thinking, so every natural thing knows its own proper acts. Nature, as St. Thomas says, is intrinsic art for things, while art is extrinsic nature. Again, in his book *On Dreams*, Aristotle says that nature is daemonic—that is, cognizant; and for this reason, nature is able to inform us of many things in dreams. And to heat, in his book *On the Parts of Animals*, Aristotle gives sense; and says further that in some way all entities are full of soul. But I am surprised that in his *De anima*, in contradicting the great Pythagoras, Aristotle is led to deny sense in plants, and in the elements.

Now if these authors want to consider this instinct of which I have been speaking as coming directly from God, and not as obtaining naturally in natural form, all the arguments cited above oppose them. If they go on to say that this instinct is not violent, and is impressed in the form, for such impression accounts for the faculty of operating, we must say in opposition that it is sense and cognition. But they respond that the arrow sent forth by the archer goes to its goal without feeling it; and that precisely in this way all things are instruments of God who directs them to their ends. To this, I say that the example deceives them—for God is more intrinsic to things than are the forms themselves, as St. Augustine says, and He does not direct them to their goals or ends except through the natures themselves, giving not only the power to reach their goal or end, but knowledge as well of how to accomplish this. Were it otherwise, God would not differ from us who, not being able to give intrinsic motive power to the arrow, move it instead by violence, which lasts for a very short period. Furthermore, if things were moved as the arrow is moved, then when confronted by an impediment they would not return to pursuing their same ends, as in fact they do, but would simply stop as the arrow stops. It is as Solomon says: the first wisdom which extends its power from one end of the world to the other, disposes all things gently. All things, we must note, obey this wisdom and attain their ends by means of that power infused in them which they must obey. It is simply absurd to say that the heat of the fire does not heat, and that the earth does not become cold by reason of its own cold, both of which involve the operation of impulse; it is similarly absurd to maintain that nature proceeds to its ends and operates in terms of these, while lacking in sense. Truly, every sense participates in the first wisdom, as Solomon says; and further, as St. Thomas says, every form participates in God. And because God is powerful, wise and loving, all entities, as I showed in my *Metaphysics;* are made up of power, wisdom, and love; and that each, further, is, because it can be, knows how to be, and loves to be. All entities fight against nonbeing; and when they lack either the power, or the knowledge, or the love of being, they die and are transformed into that which does possess these three.

Now many learned men say that all things have an inner impulse to being, and an appetite for life—and yet they deny sense to all things. But this is simply wrong, since an entity which does not know what hurts or helps it, cannot love what is good for it or hate what is bad; nor could things flee from their enemies if they did not feel themselves to be threatened, or even when they have a presentiment of danger. In this, we must praise the Creator, who impressed in all things His own image, and who held back in no necessary or useful power.

Now a certain author takes pride in asserting that no entity, save man alone, deviates from its end; and this is, as he sees it, because man is composed of reason and of sense which are repugnant to one another, while entities other than man are guided to their proper ends by God. But this is foolish: quite often we do see other entities deviate from their natural ends. I have myself observed one jackass attempting, against nature, to copulate with another; a cat eating its own offspring; a deer giving suck to a young ass—and a thousand other such things which occur contrary to the order of nature. Aside from those cases in which animals are led wantonly to spill their seed, they are not culpable, although man, for the same offense, is subjected to much greater penalties by the Creator. So I say that it is not divine instinct that propels things, but their own sense; and my wise opponents have gone to such an extreme as to deny sense not only to things, but also to beasts—because they think that imputing sensitive discourse to beasts implies that they have as well freedom of choice, as man has; they simply do not see how much difference there is between the human mind and the common sense. But I have already discussed this in my *Metaphysics*. St. Isidore, it should be noted, in addition to appetite, gives knowledge, will, and discourse to all beasts; and he is not in error since he is talking about these things in the way in which they apply to animals, and not humans.

CHAPTER VIII

That all events which happen either through instinct or by instinct, are sensible effects of the whole world and its parts.

MANY HAVE attempted to prove that there is instinct without reason and without sense, by pointing out that the lodestone not only draws the stupid and insensate iron, but that it always, with marvelous instinct, points to the pole; and that the flea, out of natural instinct, leaps into the frog's mouth to be eaten even though this is against its own will; and that when the bull runs into a fig grove, it stops on its own, having come full circle from the place where it was before; and that dolphins love men, and that many animals predict the rains and the winds without being prophets; and that the rooster, which is such a small thing, frightens lions; these, and many more such examples are adduced to make their point.

I say that all these examples point to the sense and consensus of all natures; and that this "instinct" is really impulse of sentient nature. The lodestone, to begin with, does not aim precisely at the pole, but diverges some degrees from it to point toward an island in the north which is itself entirely made of lodestone; for the sense of the lodestone is such that it will always turn to its own source. Just as fire aspires to the sky, and the stone to earth, and water to the sea, so all things look to where their greater part resides; and because of the consensus of that island with the northern stars under which it happens to be located, every other lodestone appears to be drawn to these stars. If you turn the lodestone in any other direction, it returns to its original posture, just as a man, when falling with his face to the ground, immediately will seek to direct it upward to the sky in an effort to return to his own proper position, and the branches of trees, when they are bent downward, seek to return to theirs. I do not know if the lodestone aims at the Antarctic Pole, and I do not wish to enter into a quarrel with navigators, but it is my belief that when a lodestone is brought past the equinox, it aims at the other pole where there are located similar mines of lodestone; for the things at opposite parallels equidistant from the equator are consimilar; although in the west where the sun descends, and in the east where it rises, its actions are different and even the stars are different. Now the lodestone is halfway between marble and iron, and it is thus more animated than iron. Iron is not drawn to iron, as those things which are consimilar in perfection cannot exert greater power upon themselves, but can do so with the lodestone which is a more perfect entity. And just as the animal which cannot ordinarily go up will leap to do so if there is food placed on high, so the ferrous spirit gathers itself together and wins out over its own mass to leap to join the lodestone.

And here the fact of sense being involved is easily demonstrated: when the lodestone is rubbed with garlic it doesn't attract, because the lodestone's odor, which is most pleasing and sweet to iron, cannot be communicated to the iron as it has been overcome by the garlic. Again, if we put the lodestone to the fire it gives off a green flame, and after, it no longer draws the iron because it has lost its unifying spirit; but if we pour its own liquor over it, it will again draw, for this reopens the pores through which the subtle spirit enters. Also, I have seen the lodestone eat and nourish itself with iron-filings—its own similar, although less perfect. Thus too, man eats animals. Now it appears that from the one part which is called a pole, the lodestone draws iron, while from the other it casts it away—but this is not the case; for iron, when it is rubbed with a magnet at one part, takes on the similarity of the lodestone, and then, when it is brought to the other side, it turns back toward the part which it had earlier touched. I believe, further, that the lodestone has poles and positions which are universal and which God has produced in order to show His greatness.

But let us turn to the rest of the instances earlier adduced and show how sense is involved in these. The flea, to begin with, is warm and vivacious, and the odor which issues from the frog's mouth is fresh and perfectly adapted to nourish the flea's fiery spirit. Upon seeing the frog, however, the flea is frightened to go directly to him, and goes instead round and round him, moved with both fear and desire until, at last, the frog, who is vitally attentive, opens his mouth and the flea permits himself to be won over by the pleasurable sensation. In this way too, the crocodile opens mouth. Incidentally, the benefit here is mutual, for this worms in the crocodile's gums, goes willingly into its mouth. Incidentally, the benefit here is mutual, for this works out to the advantage of both bird and crocodile.

The bull, in the example adduced previously, becomes quiet when he is under the fig trees because the odor of the figs is as sweet to it as roses are to us; and just as we stop to sniff the odors emanating from the doors of a spice shop, so the bull stops under the fig tree to smell the fruit which he loves to eat.

Now what marvel is there in the fact that the rooster is feared by the lion? Do we not ourselves fear the serpent and the tarantula which are so much smaller than we? The lion is a heavy-spirited beast because of the heavy food that he eats and the great heat that he contains; the rooster is of subtle and sharp spirits; and when these rooster-spirits pass through the air, they penetrate those of the lion and render them fearful. The same thing happens frequently with sight; as when a man, seeing another, is made submissive by the fierce look in the other's eyes. This sort of thing is even more evident with those who are disposed to respond in this fashion—as when one who suffers nausea at sea vomits in mere anticipation of vomiting when he sees the sea. The voice, as well, is capable of terrifying small animals, as does the sound of cork being cut affect us; for the air is moved with great rapidity in these cases, and this penetrates our spirit causing it to sting. Father Gregory Nicastro cannot hear the bark of dogs, or the crying of little children, or sighs. At Taverna, I observed a dog who whined every time he heard a bell. Animals are particularly susceptible to changes of temperature because they, unlike men, are devoted to their stomachs and do not think of anything else; and it is for this reason that they have presentiment of storms. The warning comes from their stomachs, and they force themselves to fill their stomachs, whining and acting as we do when we anticipate war, or something like that. It happens that the air enters through our pores by respiration, and communicates with the spirit in the head to make it wet, dry, or cold; and whoever is attentive to this can himself sense the change in weather. Those, indeed, who have a hernia, or some other affected part, quite well anticipate the sirocco, which tends to swell them up and make them numb. So also the moon swells the seas, as it changes with various lights; and, in general, humid things respond in this way more than dry things. It is the sun which brings about the ordinary as well as the extraordinary changes, but it is the moon which brings about the minor ones by means of her bland light, swelling them but not attenuating them; and from these antipathies and sympathies, sense and consensus can be proved to obtain throughout the world.

CHAPTER IX

All entities abhor a vacuum, therefore they feel and enjoy mutual contact one with another; and the world is an animal.

EVERYONE should be convinced that natures feel, not only in particular, but as well in their commonality. All bodies abhor the existence of a vacuum, and they rush, with natural impetus, to fill such a void in order to conserve the community entire. This is because all enjoy being together, and cherish their reciprocal contact with one another—which contact comprises their common life. Thus we see that air, in the depths of the sea or in the earth's cavities, will descend with great impetus in order to prohibit the formation of a vacuum; almost, in this rush, seeming to express a particular hatred for the water or the earth into which it rushes for the purpose of promoting the common good. And the water which is sucked upward by funnels of water, rises up and, indeed, often remains suspended, as in the waterclock, a vessel which has but one hole at the top and many holes underneath such that when we seal the one at the top, the water does not descend, but remains in the tube without falling through the lower holes. Indeed, there are an infinite number of demonstrations of this phenomenon; and it is because of this that the marvelous art of *spiritale* has arisen.

We must then affirm that the world is a feeling animal, and that all its parts partake in one and the same kind of life. Just as our own arm does not wish to be separated from the elbow, nor the elbow from the upper arm, nor the head from the neck, nor the leg from the thigh, but all oppose and hate division, so the whole world abhors division—which division occurs when any empty space or vacuum intervenes between any of its parts. Moreover, if the air does not feel pain when it is not being touched by another body it would not rush so swiftly to the aid of the whole, which it does in order to bring itself into contact with other bodies.

CHAPTER X

That a vacuum comes about by violence and not by nature; sensible proof of this, contra Aristotle.

THE PERIPATETICS affirm that not only is a vacuum naturally abhorred in the world, but that it cannot even be created by violence. They argue this be means of certain examples purporting to show that entities can support every evil except a vacuum. Now these men do not hold that there is sense and consensus in things, and they ridicule the Platonists and others who call the world an animal. Then, not willing to admit that all things hate a vacuum, they say that the existence of a vacuum would imply the grave inconsistency that motion through it would be accomplished instantaneously. That, to cite an instance, a stone falling through a void from the roof to the floor of a house would find itself waiting for itself when it arrived at its goal. And this, they argue, is because a mobile moves more slowly through a gross medium than through a subtle one, and faster through water than through honey, and more quickly through air than through water. Therefore, they conclude, if there were a vacuum lacking entirely in resistance to a mobile in motion through it, the motion of the mobile would be instantaneous.

Now this is not an argument worthy of wise men because it does not account for that hatred which sense has for a vacuum, and the love that it has for what is full. Indeed, the explanation given is wholly irrelevant to the question asked: it is as if someone, asked why he was eating, were to reply that he didn't want the food to go to waste! Furthermore, the reasoning is fallacious, as Avempace and St. Thomas have shown, because it is not only the resistance of the medium which accounts for the temporality of motion, but as well the finitude of the mobile; for any mobile of limited power must accomplish its acts in time. Moreover, there is the fact that the termini are incompossibles—the same body cannot be on the roof and the floor at the same time; add to this the fact that space is dimensionate—has length, width, and breadth—and we see that it is requisite that in passing from one extreme to another an object must pass through a midpoint. It follows thus that the common sense of things abhors a vacuum.

Now a vacuum, I insist, can be created by violence. And even if we fill a waterclock with honey, which is heavier than water, and let the honey drip down through the little holes, drawing the little cotton-wrapped stick with it, it still will not pour out of the bottom if you seal off the upper hole; but if you pull it by force it will pour, and when you release it, it leaps back to itself with great impetus. Similarly, when you seal the bellows with pitch, it cannot rise without much force being impressed upon it; and then it returns impetuously to unite itself on all sides because of its hatred for the vacuum within. And the cupping-glass pulls at the flesh because it is empty of air. Other examples, as well, show that a vacuum can be created, as is proved by the path of a cannonball, or the path of a flung stone; for the air immediately behind these objects closes right in upon them. Just as our body, by nature, abhors any division and yet can be made to suffer such division by violence, so it is with the body of the world.

CHAPTER XI

As every nature acts to prohibit
a vacuum, they all must feel or have sense
—contra Aristotle.

OTHER PERIPATETICS, following the reasoning of Aristotle, hold that there can be no vacuum because nature prohibits it—but, in general, they do not say which nature they are referring to, although some maintain that it is universal nature that is meant. This, however, is circular reasoning: what they really mean, that is, is that God, or the angels, or the soul of the world, prohibits the vacuum. Now we have already shown in what sense things take on particular forms, and we have shown that in natural acts, the forms have sufficient power to perform whatever it is that they perform, and that God operates in them only in the special sense which has previously been explained. But all this points to the fact that every form must be understood as feeling that it is evil, or injurious, for it to be divided from the whole, and as attempting, therefore, in every way, to maintain itself in one piece. Now if each particular nature, as we say, abhors a vacuum, then it is clear that every nature has the sense to feel the vaccum when it suffers it—note how they all act to prevent or remedy such a situation. Great rocks, however, with their immense bulk, do not help in this business of filling a vacuum as much as do little things. It is the more tenuous things, generally, which first feel the inconvenience of a vacuum, and being much the quicker and more solicitous, they rush at once to fill it.

CHAPTER XII

Things love space, and do not abhor it.

IT IS TRULY DIFFICULT to understand the status of universal space: whether it too abhors remaining empty, as it seems to since it was created to contain bodies, and when empty draws these bodies to itself. Even in matter we find appetite and sense, so why not in space as well? Now I am certain that space, which was born to give location, draws bodies to itself with appetitive sense; for space has the power of being and the sense of being, just as God gave these to us. Indeed, certain Arabs believed that God was space, since it sustains all, is contrary to nothing, and receives everything benignly; nothing, in addition, dies in it or because of it, but such bodies as are destroyed in space die only with respect to one another. Space is very great—not in terms of material quantity, but rather in incorporeal quantity; and, in addition to being loving and beneficent to all things, it is believed to be infinite in extension beyond the world.

Now I certainly admire the nobility of space, but I do not believe that it is God. Indeed, in my *Metaphysics* I specifically refuted this position. Still I know very well that it is at the base of every being that is created, and that it precedes all beings, if not in time, at least in origin and nature; for, if the world was created, then, as Averroës points out, we must assert that there was first an empty space. He says this because he does not understand where God could possibly be if He were not outside such an arena, and he feels further that immaterial space could not be born of Him. But whoever believes in the created world, as I do, cannot appreciate these arguments very much; for although God is infinite He is not infinite in the sense of possessing incorporeal dimensions that serve as a basis for the material ones of space. God's is a more sovereign magnitude—a magnitude which precedes these. From Him we have being and the possibility of locating bodies, for He is the origin of universal being. And God is not in a place, but the place is in Him; not as if it were physically located in Him, but as participant in His principle. For He is the giver and conservor of space as well as of all other entities. Nor does it dismay anyone that space should be thus, as all other things, created, unless it be those persons who have an extremely low opinion of God.

Now if space is such a divine creature, we can well imagine that things are drawn to it by desire; and that these things, in order to occupy that space which is at the basis of being, rush to fill it, almost as if they desired to acquire a new realm and a new existence. We may conjecture further that since the air hurries in order to prohibit a vacuum, there is joy felt in filling a void; and that the rush is not so much to prohibit the vacuum as it is to spread out in space; for the love of expanding oneself, multiplying oneself, and living full lives in spacious existence obtains in all things that multiply themselves, generate, and expand. Things will behave in this way even to the point of invading the places of their contraries, pushing out or destroying every other thing in their eagerness and need to conserve themselves and, if possible, to make themselves eternal and deify themselves. All things strive in this way to imitate eternal God; they desire to become similar to Him, their own Cause. It is in this way that space draws everything—voluptuously—as I have shown before in my *Metaphysics*.

In the first draft of this book, which I wrote in Latin—that draft which was stolen from me in Bologna by false monks together with other books which I now have to rewrite as I never was able to recover them—I expressed doubt concerning the question of how things come to touch their contraries. This was puzzling, because it would seem, on the face of it, that they would rather face destruction by their contraries than permit a vacuum. And I said then that the vacuum represented a greater threat to the body than even its contrary. Fire, for example, agrees with earth in that, at least, both are corporeal and have agent forms, while the vacuum is neither corporeal nor has it a form. Thus feeling or sensing the vacuum between them, contraries become sad, almost anticipating their annihilation, because a vacuum, as compared to a body, is a nothing. And this, I thought, was the reason why the sky, although encompassed by space, does not expand into that space—because, that is, it enjoys the mutual contact of its parts and it fears the nothingness that it might suffer by spreading. I was amused, too, by Democritus who insisted that the sky was surrounded by a skin which prevented it from expanding its bounds. Now, however, I think that this belief of mine, which does represent a possible view, requires modification; I am now more inclined to say that there is pleasure in the contact between bodies and space because of that desire and love for expanded existence of which I spoke. Further, I see that it is not bodies that give unity to the world, since the world is composed of contraries, but rather space, which interposes itself even between separate bodies and binds the world together. But my original conjecture, that the stars in the heavens and the parts of the world remain together because they are possessed of a similar nature—as dewdrops of water on grass, to employ Solomon's figure—still holds.

CHAPTER XIII

That the world is a mortal animal, and what can be outside it.

ARISTOTLE says that there is nothing outside of the world: neither occupied space, nor vacuum, nor time, nor motion. In fact, Alexander and many of his followers say that God can create nothing outside, and that the primary sphere is not in a place, as it is surrounded by nothing and turns constantly about itself. Democritus and Epicurus, though, say that there are an infinite number of worlds outside of our own. Further, it is the opinion of everyone that the world engages in no rectilinear motion.

Now I certainly do not believe that God's power is exhausted with the creation of this little ball, even if it seems to Copernicus to be incomparably greater than any other. I believe that other worlds can be outside ours, and that God can create an infinite number of worlds of various forms; but that there actually are such, we cannot know unless it is revealed to us by God—God who is both in and outside of them, not as in a place but as the infinite Being who supports everything. And the famous argument centering around the question of what would happen if one were located on the last sphere and fired an arrow proves only that if the arrow does not proceed, there must be a resistant body, while if it does proceed, there must be space and yielding body. And if the sphere itself is limited by nothing, then this nothing would be circular like the sphere. Hence it is being; and cannot be understood as being nothing—as obtaining, that is, neither in the mind nor outside of it, neither in God nor outside of Him—for if there is nothing, both being and God would be finite. It is certain that if fire were infinite in every direction, there would not be the earth, which is its enemy. So also, if God is infinite Being, then nothing else could be found. But they say that God made the world out of nothing, because He did not create it out of any pre-existing matter or form, but gave it being from His Being by simple emanation. I shall say nothing more of this, having dealt with it sufficiently in my *Metaphysics*.

I wish to say that we can never know if the world moves with a rectilinear motion or not: one who is in a covered ship does not know if the ship is moving. But in the four books that I have written on astronomy—against Aristotle, Ptolemy, Telesio, and Copernicus—and to my disciple, Cortese, I have carefully shown that it cannot be known whether it is the stellar sphere or the earth which is revolving, since no one can tell from where he stands whether he is turning or that which appears to be turning is doing the turning. Still by its qualities and motion—prescinding from violent motions—I maintain that it is the sky which is in motion, and that comets move by themselves as do fish in the sea. In my astronomy, I dispense with the concentrics, eccentrics, and epicycles; I render as physical the causes of stellar appearances, and show that the sun descends to illumine the earth; and that to accomplish this, it does not run 23 degrees and 52 minutes toward the tropics from the equator, as it previously did, but rather only 23 degrees and 28 minutes; and that this measure will steadily continue to diminish as its arc toward the earth grows shorter; nor will it ever increase, as Copernicus holds. It is on this basis that we can predict the equinoxes and solstices, which was but occasionally accurate during the 6,565 years of the world. I predict also that the world will be destroyed by fire, as Heraclitus and St. Peter taught before. This animal too, then, will become undone through losing a contrary; God, however, will reproduce it in a better and higher form. However, the mutation of the whole sky, unknown to Aristotle—which sky he thought to be eternal—reveals the coming death of the world. And what Telesio said about the sea holding the sky and earth together by restoring in a sponge-like manner that which the sun takes from it, while the sea gives it back through rains and rivers, is a valid opinion, and one which was held by St. Basil as well; for he referred to the sea as "the blood-water of the earth." But when Telesio adds that the sky is removed from the moisture at the middle of the earth, creating a vacuum, he seems to me to be in error. Because contrariety does not dissolve the world—the combat of contrariety, in fact, incites it to unity and coherence, and thus all things attempt to remedy a vacuum, with each part racing to get their first in order to occupy it before its contrary. Once there, it multiplies, generates, and expands itself in preparation for its enemy. It is clearly seen that these contraries face one another with spontaneous ire. Therefore, this animal will win over itself as does a fever, which is a fervor of armed spirits at war against enemy humors. When these fights occur because of the evil of the enemy, they tend to dissolve the opposition.

Doctors, however, do not understand the secret of fever, and they all think it is something bad, while I think it is something beneficial; for if the spirit were not inflamed against disease, and did not make sudden and violent motions and pulsations attended by an increase in heat, it could not destroy the enemy humors but would soon itself be defeated and bring about death. This, indeed, is what occurs in sudden deaths; for in such instances the spirit did not have time enough to arm itself and to become inflamed. Generally, when the evil humors are not defeated in their fervor, or their fervor is not made to diminish by degrees, one dies; and this—death—is a sign that malignant humors have won out over the spirits, extinguishing them. So far as the world is concerned, however, the very opposite will ultimately occur; for the fervor of the sky will win out over this black and ugly earth, and this construction, as we know it, will perish; and then everything will be made celestial and new and whole in a different way.

It is an error to think that the world does not feel just because it does not have legs, eyes, and hands. Such instruments are proper only to the animal spirit enclosed within gross matter which requires them to move and sense. But for the world, it is enough that its figure be round; its active powers are diffused and operate without being enclosed in heavy arms; its eyes are the stars and luminaries which see, and permit us to see—we who are imprisoned in heavy masses and able to see only through the windows of the senses that which is available to sense in all the air and the sky. It is just as foolish to deny sense to things because they have no eyes, no mouth, and no ears as it is to deny motion to the wind because it has no legs, or eating to fire because it has no teeth, or seeing to one who is in the country because he lacks windows out of which to look, or to the eagle because it has no eyeglasses. It is basically the same foolishness that led others to believe that God has a body, eyes, and hands.

I say that the living God—the living and true God—declares of all things that He has made, that He has given them not only power and the love of being, but also the sense of well-being, so that they might preserve themselves for His glory. Let us turn now to an examination of this, and show it to be the case for all entities.

END OF BOOK I

BOOK V

CHAPTER I

On magic in general, and its divisions.

THE ANCIENT SAGES of the orient were called *magicians*. Particularly adept in magic were the Persians who investigated the occult things of God and of nature which is His art; and they performed marvelous feats in turning magic to human use, as St. Augustine writes. Today, however, the title *magician* is in such bad repute that we apply it only to the superstitious friends of demons: people who, tired of investigating things properly, have tried by short routes to wrest from the demons that which they cannot give. And so astrology, become worthless in the hands of the inexpert, has fallen into disfavor. But only the foolish regard it with disdain. Porta has tried, by careful study, to revive this science, but he is unable to deal with it in terms of causes; and the studies of Imperato can, in part, be considered a basic attempt to reinstate the science.

Now magic consists in three sciences, as Pliny relates: religion, medicine, and astrology. The first serves to purge the soul so that it will be in condition to know—to make us friendly with the First Cause—and to impose trust, honor, and reverence upon the souls of those who pursue it. The second yields understanding of the virtues of herbs, stones, and metals, and the sympathy and antipathy existing between these things and us, as well as the composition and attitude of man, who has need of these insofar as he suffers and acts. The third makes us understand the proper times for action; it studies also the symbolic relations between all things and the fixed stars, comets, and luminaries. This is most significant, since these are the causes of the powers and mutations in all things. So, in the Gospel of St. Matthew, those Magi are lauded who could tell about the birth of the Monarch of the World from the comets; for God—so good and loving is our Maker—displays His works to those who investigate, giving them not only what they seek, but also—when they are purged and well disposed through being virtuous—the grace to arrive at knowledge of supernatural things. This wisdom, then, is not only speculative but practical, as well; for it applies what is known to the use and benefit of man.

Pliny thought that this art is natural to everyone, and that the performance of miracles depends on it, or is made possible by it. He thought that Moses was a great magician, as did the Egyptians Jamnes and Mambre, who fought against him; finally, he says that magic was found on Cyprus, so that when St. Paul was on that island, after first causing Elimas Mago to be blinded, he later cured him by this means in the presence of the proconsul, Sergio Paolo. Nor does Pliny believe that there are demons; for Nero investigated this question and sought to find one in order to prove their existence but was unable to do so; consequently, he believes God to be infused in all things, and he sees God as operating in accordance with that knowledge which is displayed when men use His works. But Trismegistus, who was very wise, says that man is the miracle of the world, and nobler than, or equal to, the gods; and thus man has such power in his mind that he can create marble and bronze gods, and give them soul under certain constellations, so that he can receive oracles from them. And this is believed by Porphyry, and even Plotinus, who adds that there are good and perverse angels, as we know from everyday experience. Indeed, I have seen manifest proof of all this, not when I sought it, but when I was concentrating on other things. Hence it is not surprising that Nero never found the answer. And what they say of Simon Magus' deeds, I would interpret as natural phenomena; indeed, Sventonio Tranquillo relates that even Nero was able to repeat the feat of Icarus.

Now I affirm that there is divine magic: magic that man can neither understand nor employ without the grace of God—and that this was the magic of Moses and other glorious saints: friends of God who, with such little science, performed many miracles, as nature is obedient to the messengers of God. There is natural magic, as that of the stars, and that of medicine and physics, with religion added to give faith to those who hope for favors from these sciences; and there is diabolical magic for those who, by the art of the devil, seem, to those who do not understand, to do marvelous things. Frequently too, although without the devil, this magic is also performed by circus people to the astonishment of the foolish; but these are deeds brought about by cleverness and not by knowledge. Natural magic, then, stands between: and those who exercise it with piety and reverence for the Creator, frequently come to be elevated to the supernatural kind of magic, thus participating in magic of a higher form. But whoever abuses it, and attempts to fool the people, poisoning them and making fools of them, deserves to have the devil intervene and bring them to their perdition.

CHAPTER V

Although all sciences and arts serve natural magic, some are regarded as doing so more than others.

All that scientists do in imitating nature and in working with her to bring about the ends of their arts is known as magic—not only to the peasants, but as well to the entire community of man. Thus not only the sciences already mentioned serve magic, but all the others as well. It was by magic that Archytas made a pigeon that could fly as well as a natural one; and at the time of Emperor Ferdinand's reign in Germany, a German made an artificial eagle and a fly that were able to fly by themselves. Now all arts, so long as they are not understood, are called magic; but after a while they acquire the status of common sciences. The invention of gunpowder and of printing was once regarded as magic; similarly, the use of the lodestone—but now that everyone knows the art, it has become commonly accepted. So also with the art of clock-making; and all other mechanical arts just as easily lose their extraordinary status directly they become familiar to the ordinary man. But physical, astrological, and religious things are very rarely divulged, and it is from these that the ancients drew the art of magic.

CHAPTER VI

On the natural feelings that are employed by the magician to achieve his effects.

Because the animal spirit is both active and passive in nature, it is capable, to some degree, of suffering everything and of acting with everything. The soul in things both suffers and enjoys with the things themselves. The principal passions are pain and pleasure—these are the exquisite sensations of present good and evil. Love and hate are tendencies for goods and against evils which are not sensibly present; for when the objects are sensibly present, the response is either pleasure or pain. Hope and fear are tendencies to flee evils or pursue goods which are not sensibly present.

Trust is sense of something which we are convinced is good: its contrary is diffidence or mistrust. Faith is the mother of trust because it is the sense of good, although the object is not present. True imagination is when the spirit takes in something and thinks of it as it is, not confusing it with another; proof is when the spirit of something is so affected that it cannot be moved in any other way, but every motion reveals the thing to be as it is.

Anyone who knows how to generate these affects in man, by herbs, actions, or other efficacious means, can be called a magician.

CHAPTER IX

In decomposing things there remains old sense and they take on new sense, as well; marvelous proofs in magic.

It is not only the obtuse sense, which we have already discussed in connection with dead bodies, that can be known, but also the particular passions and feelings of a sentient nature; and from this, magic has received great store.

If you make a drum out of the skin of a wolf, and another of lamb skin, and especially if the latter is made of a lamb or sheep that was once frightened by a wolf, you will find that upon beating the wolf drum, the lamb drum will immediately burst asunder. This clearly argues that the passions absorbed in things become revived in such a way that the skin draws unto itself and suffers—even as we draw back when we sight an enemy; or as we are filled with fear when anything that we fear greatly is named, making our hair stand up, as the drawing back of the spirit brings about tightening of the skin on the head; and as, when the devil is mentioned, fearful children become frightened and their hair stands straight up because they feel the fear that the devil himself ordinarily inspires.

The same thing which makes some people happy because they expect good from it can make others unhappy and fearful who anticipate evil from it. The Turks, when in prison, feared the Christians because they might put them to death, while the slaves were happy, for they had a presentiment of freedom; nor is there a man who is about to suffer some great disaster that does not first feel it in an unusual spontaneous sense, or foreboding—because in the air where the disaster is formed the sense of it exists and is communicated to him. So it is that the lamb who once suffered an experience with a wolf retains a latent fear which is spontaneously awakened, just as nausea returns to one who sees the food that he vomited at some other time. In dying, Captain Boemo commanded that a drum be made of his skin to frighten his enemies; and I do believe that drums of wolf skin would frighten horses; and those of dragons, elephants. If you should play on lute strings made of fox intestine, chickens will run; and if made of viper nerves, women will be frightened—those, at least, who are in the habit of fearing that particular snake; and if made of human intestine, vipers will run. As a matter of fact, if the strings on two lutes be made of material originating from contrary animals, when you play one, the other will burst.

The proof of this is manifest when you try to tune two lutes; for when you touch the first string of one lute, if the first string of the other lute is similarly tuned, it will begin to vibrate of itself; and if you put a marker, as a bit of straw or paper, on the string of the other lute, you will observe that when you sound one, the paper on the other will jump up and down and fall off. Now according to some thinkers, this occurs because of the violently moved air. If you place a board between the two lutes, however, the same thing occurs. But the bit of straw does not move on the one string if the other is not stretched as much as the first in such a way that they sound harmoniously; and if it were merely the violent motion of the air that caused the movement of the marker, while the strings were not harmoniously tuned the straw would still move when placed on the other string, but we see that this does not happen. If the motion were caused by simple violence, and not related to sense, then how is it that when they are not in consensus the marker does not move? If these men are right, then even those strings would move which were slack; but instead nothing moves except that string which is the same in diameter and stretched to the same tension as the one which is sounded; and this is a sign that similars enjoy feeling one another—not because air is in violent motion, but because air is the carrier of sensible, felt affection.

It is said that a dead serpent, when thrown under the shadow of an ash tree, which is its enemy by nature, will move in such a way as to get away from the shadow; and a thousand other such phenomena are observed which argue the consensus and enmity of entities which appear, to us, to be deprived of sense. When one suffers from enlargement of the spleen, let him put another spleen in the smoke of a fire and you will find that as the smoked spleen dries, so will the sufferer's. This is not the devil's work, for he can never operate within us; but it comes about because the feeling of the patient generates fear in his own spleen which then shrinks. This is particularly successful with a patient who believes in the efficacy of the treatment, as we shall later see.

Every member has its own proper sense with which it communicates with the whole entity, and so the fear given to the liver by water makes it become soft. And I once saw a spleen opened as if it had been struck with an ax although the patient's belly was never touched. This was accomplished by placing another spleen on a piece of paper and striking at it; the patient's spleen was trembling in consensus, and tried to run away; then the patient was made to eliminate his own spleen's melancholic blood. Some say that by treating the sword with which one is cut, the wound can be made to heal. I have never seen this occur, but I certainly would concede that the wound feels through the air that the sword-enemy which did him harm is being treated in order to do him good; and so the spirit, becoming trustful of help while it is operating in the feverish wound, feels almost the happiness of vendetta, and becomes, thus, well. But of this we shall give many examples later on. It is because superstitious people have told false stories, and the devil intervenes to deceive, that these delicate arts have always been persecuted by priests, with the final result being that we know little about them; but anyone can discover them who understands the sense and consensus in things.

GIORDANO BRUNO

THE ILL-FATED *Giordano Bruno was born in Nola in 1548. At the age of eighteen he entered the Dominican order. The doubts that he entertained concerning some of the teachings of the Church led, in 1576, to the preparation of an indictment for heresy. Bruno fled Italy and undertook an extended adventurous journey throughout Europe. He became a Calvinist in Geneva and went on to Toulouse, where he obtained a degree in theology. In 1586, at the University of Paris, one of his disputations against Aristotle caused such a furor that he thought it best to leave Paris. He journeyed then to Marburg and Wittenberg, where he taught for two years and became a Lutheran. He lectured next at Helmstedt. In 1592 he was induced to come to Venice by one Giovanni Mocenigo, who betrayed him to the Inquisition. After a trial which lasted for many years, Bruno was sentenced to death in 1600, and burned at the stake. Bruno's extant writings are numerous and diverse in con-*

tent. They include dialogues, philosophical poems, and tracts. Of major significance are his dialogues De la causa, principio e uno *and* De l'infinito, universo e mondi.

On the Infinite, the Universe and Worlds

ARGUMENT OF THE FIRST DIALOGUE

Part I

From the First Dialogue we learn:

(1) that the untrustworthiness of sense perception proves that the senses, of themselves, are not a source of certainty. Such certainty as may be attained by their use, which is little or nothing without judgment, depends upon the comparison and checking of one sense report with others. In this way truth may be inferred from diverse sources.

(2) Now we begin to prove the infinity of the universe. The first argument is derived from the actual inability to confine the world, even in fancy, experienced by those who claim it is enclosed within limiting walls.

(3) Our second argument shows that it is improper to refer to the world as finite and self-contained, since this condition is predicated properly only of infinity. Yet another argument which we present is based upon the inconsistency—indeed, the impossibility—of imagining the world to occupy no place. For it would follow necessarily from this that the world does not exist; since all existents, corporeal or incorporeal, have some place, either corporeally or incorporeally.

(4) A further argument is now adduced which, in the Epicurean philosophy, is put in this way:

. . . supposing
A moment the all of space finite to be,
If some one farthest traveller runs forth
Unto the extreme coasts and throws ahead
A flying spear, is't then thy wish to think
It goes, hurled off amain, to where 'twas sent
And shoots afar, or that some object there
Can thwart and stop it? . . .
. . . Since whether there be
Aught that may block and check it so it comes
Not where 'twas sent, nor lodges in its goal,
Or whether borne along, in either view
'T has started not from any end. . . .[1]

(5) The Aristotelian definition of place is inapplicable to primitive, vast, universal space. It is not suitable to take the surface immediately next to a contained body—nor any such foolishness of the type which views space as mathematical and not physical. It is, moreover, unsatisfactory because there is always an intermediate space to be found between the containing surface and the contained body which moves within it, which should rather be called its place. Further, if we insist upon talking about the surface of space, it is requisite that we locate a finite position within the infinite.

(6) If a finite world is posited, then a void must necessarily be accepted as obtaining, since the void is that which contains nothing.

(7) This space in which our world exists would clearly be a void if our world were not in it, since where there is no world, there must be a void. Now beyond our world, one space is like any other. Hence, the potentiality of one is like that of another. Wherefore, this potentiality must accomplish something—for no potentiality obtains eternally without acting. Indeed, potentiality is eternally linked to action or, rather, it is itself action; for in eternity there is no

[1] Lucretius, *De rerum natura,* I, 968–973, 977–979. Bruno quotes the Latin text.

distinction between being and potential being, nor, therefore, between action and potential action.

(8) Sense perception is not opposed to the acceptance of infinity, as infinity cannot be denied merely because it is not sensibly perceived. Sense itself, moreover, is included within infinity; and since reason confirms infinity, we are constrained, therefore, to posit its existence. Further, if we consider the matter well, sense itself presents us with an infinite universe. We perceive, that is, an endless series of objects, each of which is contained by another; nor does experience ever disclose to us—either by internal or external sense—an object which is not contained by another or similar object.

> Lastly, before our very eyes is seen
> Thing to bound thing: air hedges hill from hill,
> And mountain walls hedge air; land ends the sea,
> And sea in turn all lands; but for the All
> Truly is nothing which outside may bound.[2]

From the testimony of our sight, then, we should infer the infinite, as all objects are seen to be limited by other objects, while we cannot experience anything which is self-limited.

(9) It is possible to deny infinite space as some stubborn men do—but only verbally. For that space, called void, where the universe is not, and in which it is pretended that nothing exists, cannot be conceived of as lacking the capacity to contain a lesser magnitude than it actually does contain.

(10) Since it is good that this world exists, the existence of each of the infinity of other worlds is no less good.

(11) The virtue of this world is no more transferable to any other world than my being is transferable to the being of this or that man.

(12) We accept an indivisible, utterly simple infinity, and there is no reason or sense percept which will not permit also a corporeal and extended infinity.

[2] Lucretius, *De rerum natura,* I, 984–988.

(13) Our own enveloping space which appears so immense to us, is neither in part nor in whole relative to the infinite. No more can it be the patient of infinite activity. Compared, indeed, to such activity, that which can be grasped by our weak minds is merely nonbeing. And to a specific objection, we reply that our argument for infinity is not based on the dignity of space but, rather, on the dignity of the worlds of nature—since the same reasons for the existence of our space hold also for every other possible world, and their power of existing is not actuated by our world's existence any more than Elpino's power of existing is actuated by Fracastoro's existence.

(14) If infinite active power does actuate corporeal and dimensionate being, this being must necessarily be infinite. If it were not, there would be implied a detraction from the nature and dignity of both creator and creation.

(15) The universe, as conceived by the uneducated, cannot contain the perfection of all things except in the sense that I contain the perfection of all my members and every globe contains its entire content. But this is tantamount to calling someone wealthy because he does not lack that which he has.

(16) Without the infinite effect, the efficient infinite would be incomplete. We cannot, that is, allow that an infinite effect be itself the efficient infinity. Further, if such were, or could be the effect, this would in no way detract from that which belongs to every true effect; hence, theologians call action *ad extra*, or transitive, in addition to imminent action, so that is quite proper that both effect and efficient be infinite.

(17) To call the universe unbounded, as we have done, satisfies the mind; while holding that it is bounded innumerably multiplies the theoretical inconsistencies and difficulties. Moreover, we reaffirm what was said under (2) and (3) above.

(18) If the world is spherical, then it has figure and bounds. The boundary beyond this figure and its bounds—although you may wish to call this "nothingness"—also has figure; so that the concavity of the latter is joined to the

convexity of the former, since the beginning of your nothingness is a concavity absolutely unrelated to the convex surface of our world.
(19) More is added to that which was said under heading (2), above.
(20) That which was said under (10) above, is here repeated.

Part II

IN THE Second Part of the First Dialogue, that which has already been demonstrated concerning the passive power of the universe is extended to the active power of the efficient cause.
This is accomplished by means of such arguments as:
(1) which argues from the principle that divine power should not be otiose. This argument makes the case with particular reference to any effect outside of the substance under consideration (if, indeed, anything can be outside of it), and points out that it would be no less otiose and invidious for the divine power to produce a finite effect than to produce no effect at all.
(2) the next argument is practical, showing that the contrary view implies a defect in the divine goodness and greatness. From our view, however, there follows no inconsistency whatever with respect to either legality or theology.
(3) This argument is the converse of (12) in Part I, above. Here we mark the distinction between the infinite whole and the completely infinite.
(4) This argument shows that omnipotence is held responsible for the creation and a finite world (on the Aristotelian view) no less from lack of will than from lack of power. They [the Aristotelians] present us with the picture of an infinite agent acting on a finite subject.
(5) The fifth argument demonstrates that if omnipotence does not make the world infinite, then it is incapable of doing so; while if it lacked the power to make it infinite, then it must also lack the vigor to preserve it to eternity.

Further, if finite in one respect, it must be viewed as finite in all respects; for each of its contained modes is an object, and every object and every mode are exactly the same.

(6) The sixth argument is the converse of (10), Part I, above; and gives the reason why theologians espouse a view contrary to ours. It shows also that their arguments are not lacking in expediency; and then goes on to discuss the agreements which obtain between the learned divines and the learned philosophers.

(7) Here we first set forth and discuss the reasons which distinguish active power from diverse actions. Moreover, we here expound on the notion of infinite intensive and extensive power in a more glorious manner than any theologians have ever done.

(8) This argument demonstrates that the motion of the infinite number of worlds is not the result of an external motive force, but results rather from their own nature; and that despite this, there yet does exist an infinite moving force.

(9) The ninth argument shows how infinite motion may be intensively verified in each of the worlds. To this we should add that since each moving body simultaneously is moved and moves itself, it therefore may be seen in every point of the circle which it describes around its own center. This objection is answered later.

ARGUMENT OF THE SECOND DIALOGUE

The Second Dialogue comes to the same conclusion.

(1) Initially, four arguments are set forth:

(i) shows that all of the divinity's individual attributes are united:

(ii) demonstrates that our imagination should not be capable of probing beyond divine action;

(iii) postulates the lack of distinction between divine intellect and divine action, and demonstrates that the divine intellect conceives the infinite as well as the finite;

(iv) makes inquiry concerning what the absolute totality of active and passive power inherent in the totality of things would be if corporeal, sensible qualities were endowed with infinite active power.

(2) We demonstrate that it is impossible for a corporeal object to be terminated by an incorporeal object, but only by a void or a plenum. In either case—void or plenum—beyond the world is space which is ultimately material. Indeed, it is this which is the passive force that rouses the cooperative active force to its activity. Here too, we show the banality of Aristotle's argument concerning the incompatibility of dimensions.

(3) The difference between the world and the universe is made clear. He who holds the universe to be a single infinity must necessarily distinguish between these two terms.

(4) Here opposing arguments, holding the universe to be finite, are leveled against the thesis of an infinite universe. Elpino is the attacker and employs all of the relevant Aristotelian passages to unseat Filotheo, who examines them. Some of these arguments, as it turns out, are derived from the nature of simple, others from that of composite, bodies. The banality is shown of six arguments drawn from the definition of motions which cannot be infinite, and from other propositions which are similarly shown to be meaningless, purposeless, and implausible. Our own arguments demonstrate quite convincingly the reason for the differences and for the termination of motions. So far as is in keeping with the occasion and the place these arguments show the truth about strong and weak motive impulses. We shall later show that an infinite body is in itself neither heavy nor light; and we shall demonstrate how a finite body can or cannot manifest such differences. In this way, we shall show the inanity of Aristotle's arguments aginst those who posit an infinite world when he assumes a center and

circumference, holding that our earth must obtain—whether in the finite or infinite—in the precise center. Finally, every single proposition employed by Aristotle in his attempt to refute the infinity of the world—either in the first book of his *De caelo et mundo* or the third book of his *Physics*—is adequately discussed.

ARGUMENT OF THE THIRD DIALOGUE

(1) In this Third Dialogue there is denied first off that evil delusion concerning the shape of the heavens, their spheres and diversity. Heaven is shown to be a single, general space embracing the infinity of worlds. This is not to say that we deny the being of other infinite heavens if that term ("heavens") is employed in another sense. Just, that is, as this earth has its own heaven (which is its own area), through which it moves and has its course, so the same may be said of each of the innumerable other worlds. We show the origin of the fantasy concerning the great number of moving bodies subordinated to each other, and so formed as to have two external surfaces and one internal cavity. We discuss also nostrums and medicines which nauseate and horrify even those who compound and dispense them, not to speak of the unfortunates who take them.
(2) We explain how both general and eccentric motion, as these pertain to the firmament, are purely illusory: which illusion derives from the motion of the earth's center along the elliptic, as well as from the four varieties of motion which the earth undergoes while traveling around its own center. In this way it is made evident that the proper motion of each star is the resultant of the variation in position which may be verified by viewing the star as a subject body

moving of itself through the spatial field. This makes it clear that all arguments concerning the Primum Mobile and infinite motion are empty and based on ignorance of the motion of this globe of ours.

(3) It is propounded that each and every star has motion just as ours does, and as do those others which are so near to us that we can sensibly detect the deviations in their orbits and motions. But those suns—bodies in which fire is predominant—move differently than the earths—in which water predominates. Hence we can understand the origin of the light which the stars diffuse—some of which glow by themselves and others by reflection.

(4) We show how stars at vast distances from the sun can, just as those which are near to it, participate in the sun's heat. Fresh proof is adduced of Epicurus' view that one sun may suffice for an infinite universe. Further, this explains the true difference between stars that scintillate and stars that do not.

(5) Here we examine Nicholas of Cusa's view concerning the matter and habitability of other worlds and the cause of light.

(6) It is shown that although some bodies are luminous and hot of their own nature, it still does not follow that the sun and earth and water illumine themselves. Light proceeds always from an opposite star. Thus, when we look down from a great height, as from a mountaintop, we perceive the whole sea illumined; but if we were on the sea—on the same plane as the sea—we would perceive no illumination except for a small area where the sunlight and moonlight were opposite us.

(7) Here we discuss the vapid theory of quintessences. It is our position that no sensible bodies are composed of different, primal or proximate principles other than those found on our earth. Nor do they have motions other than those found on our earth. Nor do they have motions other than linear or circular. All of this is proved by means of sensible reasons which Fracastoro makes understood to Burchio. It is further clearly shown that there is no accident here which we may not expect to find on other worlds.

Indeed, if we consider well, we can see that nothing on any other world can be seen from this one, which cannot be seen on this one from any other. Consequently, that beautiful (Aristotelian) order and hierarchy of nature is but a charming fantasy—an old wives' fable.

(8) Although there is a distinction to be drawn between the elements, yet their order, as this is commonly understood, is neither sensibly perceptible nor intelligible. According to Aristotle the four elements are equally parts or members of this globe: *yet it is said that water predominates.* Hence with good reason the stars are called now water, now fire, by the philosophers of nature, prophets, divines, and poets, who in this respect are not fabricating or employing metaphors, but who induce others to spin tales and rave. These worlds must be understood as heterogeneous bodies—animals—great globes in which (the element) earth is no heavier than any other element. In these worlds all particles are in constant motion, constantly changing position and arrangement, just as blood and other humors, spirits, and the smallest parts which ebb and flow are absorbed and again breathed out by us and other lesser animals. In respect of this, a comparison is drawn showing that the earth is no more heavy due to the attraction of its mass to its own center, than any other simple body of homogeneous composition. Moreover, the earth in itself is not heavy, nor does it rise or fall. Further, it is water which is responsible for unifying and bringing about density, consistency, and weight.

(9) Since the famous doctrine concerning the elements is seen to be erroneous, and since the innumerable worlds in the infinite have no less virtue or different nature than our own earth; we now deduce the nature of those sensible compound bodies which exist as so many animals and worlds in that spacious field of air, or heaven, or void, in which there obtain all these worlds which contain animals and inhabitants as does our own.

(10) After we exhibit how the stubborn, the ignorant, and the evilly disposed are accustomed to argue, we show how such disputes are accustomed to end. Some of these dispu-

tants are so wily that they pretend with a sneer, a smile, a certain haughty disdain, and with no loss of composure, to have proved that which they have not succeeded in proving by argument. Indeed, they can't even understand their position themselves; nonetheless, by these tricks they endeavor not only to hide their own painfully obvious ignorance, but to suggest that it is their adversary who is the ignorant one. They do not dispute in order to attain truth, but rather to attain victory; and all the while they attempt to appear as the learned and strenuous champions of contrary opinions. Such persons should be shunned by all who lack the armor of patience.

ARGUMENT OF THE FOURTH DIALOGUE

(1) First off in this Dialogue there is reiterated that which had been said on other occasions concerning the infinity of worlds: how each one of them moves: and in what configuration.

(2) Just as arguments against the infinite mass or size of the universe were refuted in the Second Dialogue after there had been demonstrated by many arguments in the First Dialogue the vast effect of immense vigor and power; so, having in the Third Dialogue demonstrated the infinite number of worlds, we now refute the numerous opposed arguments of Aristotle. The word "world" has one sense when Aristotle employs it, and quite another when employed by Democritus, Epicurus, and others.

Aristotle, arguing from his own formulations of the nature of natural and impressed motion, holds that one earth should move toward another. In order to refute this, we

(i) establish principles important for the clarification of the true foundations of natural philosophy; and

(ii) show that however close the surface of one earth was to that of another, the heterogeneous or dissimilar parts of one—I am not speaking of atoms or simple bodies—would not move to the other earth. Hence we must of necessity more closely examine the nature of heaviness and lightness.

(3) How does it happen that nature has placed these great bodies at so great a distance from one another, rather than placing them nearer so that it would have been possible to pass from one to another? From a more profound perspective we see why worlds could not be placed, as it were, in the circumference of the ether; for they could not be adjacent to a void which has neither power, virtue, nor force, since under these conditions it would be impossible to derive either life or light from one side.

(4) We now consider the respect in which local space may or may not affect the nature of a body. We consider also why it is that a stone midway between two earths will remain in dynamic equilibrium; or, if it did not so remain, why it would move toward one rather than the other.

(5) We consider how wrong Aristotle was in subscribing to the view that there is an attractive force of heaviness and lightness between bodies no matter how far apart they are. From this origin, according to Aristotle, there follows the universal tendency to resist change of state.

(6) We show that rectilinear motion does not appertain to the nature of our earth or of other major bodies, but rather to the parts of these bodies; such that if these parts are not too far apart they move toward one another from even the most diverse positions.

(7) By reference to the behavior of comets we argue that it is false to hold that a heavy body, no matter how far away it is, undergoes attraction or motion toward the body which contains it. This position, indeed, was based on incorrect physical principles resting solely upon Aristotle's purely philosophical suppositions, formulated by him from

a consideration of those parts which are vapors and exhalations of our earth.

(8) Following another line of argumentation we show that simple bodies of identical nature have, in the innumerable diverse worlds, precisely similar motion. Difference of locality is caused by arithmetical diversity: each part having its own center and being also referred to the common center which cannot be found within the universe.

(9) We now demonstrate that bodies and their parts have no determinate upper and lower segments except insofar as the direction of their conservation may be this way or that.

(10) It is now shown that motion is infinite, and that a moving body tends toward infinity and to the formation of innumerable compounds. Heaviness and lightness, however, do not therefore follow, nor infinite speed—indeed, inasmuch as the motion of adjacent parts tend to preserve their own nature, this speed cannot be infinite. Further, the attraction of parts to their containing body can take place only within the local space of the containing body.

THE FIFTH DIALOGUE

Participants in the Dialogue are Elpino, Fracastoro, Filotheo, Burchio and Albertino. Albertino has just entered and speaks first.

Albertino. Just what, I should like to know, is this ghost, this incredible monster, this living prophet, this extraordinary mind? What message does he bring to the world? Or, better, just what are these reborn ancient and obsolete views? What are these truncated roots which are growing fresh shoots in this, our age?

Elpino. They are truncated, but fruitful roots; ancient views which have returned; occult truths which are made manifest. It is a new light which rises over the horizon in the hemisphere of our knowledge and little by little approaches the zenith of our intelligence.

Albertino. If I didn't know you, Elpino, I know what I should say.

Elpino. Say what you will. If you are as wise as I think you are, you will agree with him even as I do. If your perspicuity is greater, you will, as I expect, agree all the more rapidly and completely. Those who find the current philosophy and ordinary knowledge difficult, and those who subscribe to these current and ordinary views even though they are themselves not too bright (as is often the case although they are not aware of it), will not be easily converted to our view. To them, universal consent is the most powerful argument; and they are so awed by the reputation of those authors whom they read that they seek for nothing else than to be reputed expositors and commentators. Some, however, who fully comprehend the transmitted philosophy, have reached the point where they no longer choose to spend the rest of their lives listening to others; they see by their own light and penetrate every cranny with the power of their mind's eye—Arguslike with the eyes of their knowledge, they gaze at this philosophy, unveiled, through a thousand doorways. In this way they are able, upon coming closer, to distinguish matters of belief accepted as truth by habit and universal consent, from that which truly is and must be accepted as certain: as obtaining in the very nature and substance of things. It is true, I hold, that those who have not had the fortune to be blessed by nature with intelligence, or are not at least somewhat familiar with the different branches of knowledge, will not be able to accept our philosophy. Those who are able to do so must have the power of intellectual reflection by means of which they can distinguish between belief based on faith and belief based on the evidence of true principles.

Quite often an opinion is accepted as a principle which, if carefully scrutinized, would be found to lead to an incredible and unnatural conclusion. I say nothing of those mean and mercenary minds that contain no, or little, desire to attain truth, contenting themselves with what passes generally for knowledge: not friends of true wisdom, but greedy for the fame and reputation bestowed upon those who give the appearance of possessing knowledge. I hold him to be poorly equipped to choose between diverse opinions and contradictory statements who lacks soundness and judgment on these matters. He who lacks the ability to compare them will find it difficult to decide, when the differences that distinguish them are beyond his ken. Indeed, it is for him difficult even to understand how such positions differ, since the substance and being of each remains hidden from him. And their differences can never be evident except through a clear grasp of the reasons and principles upon which each is based. After you have looked with the mind's eye, and considered with disciplined sensibilities the foundations, principles and reasons on which diverse and opposed philosophies are based: after you have examined the nature, substance, and peculiarities of each, and weighed one argument against the other on the scales of the intellect: after you have distinguished their differences and compared and judged rightly between them: then, without delay, you will immediately choose to yield your assent to the truth.

Albertino. Aristotle, the prince of philosophers, maintains that it is vain and foolish to waste time in fighting foolish opinions.

Elpino. True: but if you look closely this advice applies against his own opinions too when they are vain and foolish. He who would judge perfectly must, as I said, be able to abstain from the the habit of belief. He must regard two opposed views as equally plausible, and must dismiss all prejudice inculcated from birth: prejudice which is encountered in general conversation as well as that by which we are (as if dying to the mass of men) reborn through philosophy among those scholars who are held by the majority of their contemporaries to be wise. When there arises controversy between different persons held by their contemporaries and countrymen to be wise, I would say that if we would judge rightly we must recall the warning issued by this same Aristotle; who says that we may sometimes too quickly assent to opinions because we focus too narrowly upon an inadequate number of facts. Sometimes, too, an opinion too quickly captures our assent because of custom, so that something appears to us to be necessary which actually is impossible; or we perceive and learn that to be impossible which is actually most true and necessary. And if this can happen with respect to the most obvious things, what must happen in those matters which are somewhat unique, which yet depend upon well-grounded principles and solid foundations?

Albertino. It is the opinion of the commentator, Averroës, and of many others, that that which Aristotle did not know cannot be known.

Elpino. Both he and the mass of his followers had so little genius and were in such profound darkness, that they could see nothing higher and more brilliant than Aristotle. In truth, if he and others when they let fall such opinions were to speak with strict accuracy, they would say that for them Aristotle is a god. In this way they would not so much exalt Aristotle as show their own worthlessness. For to them the matter seems even as it does to the ape, to whom her own children appear the most beautiful creatures in the world, and her own ape husband the most handsome of consorts.

Albertino. "The mountains do bring forth." [3]

Elpino. You will see it is no mouse which they bring forth.

Albertino. Many have crossed swords with Aristotle, but it is their own castles which have fallen, their arrows have been blunted, and their bows broken.

Elpino. What happens when one useless thing makes war against another? One is completely victorious, but remains nonetheless useless; and will it not, in its turn, finally be discovered and overcome by truth?

Albertino. It is impossible, as I see it, to prove that Aristotle is in error.

Elpino. That is much too rash a statement.

Albertino. I say it because I have fully considered and

[3] Cf. Horace, *De arte poetica,* 139.

carefully examined what Aristotle has to say, and have never found him to be in error. Indeed, I can discover nothing concerning divinity which he did not know; and I feel that I must insist that no other man can find that which I have not been able to find in his writings.

Elpino. You gauge the stomach and brain of others, then by your own, and hold that which you cannot do to be impossible for others. In this world there are some not only so unfortunate and unhappy as to be deprived of every good, but who have been selected, in addition, to live forever with that Erinnys and infernal Fury which impels them voluntarily to cover their eyes with the black veil of corrosive jealousy so that they may see neither their own nakedness, poverty, and misery, nor the ornaments, riches, and delights of others. It is their preference to pine away in filth, pride, and penury and to remain buried under the dung of stubborn ignorance rather than be discovered turning to a new discipline or appearing to yield that they had previously been ignorant, and guided by an ignorant man.

Albertino. Are you then suggesting that I become a disciple of this man (Filotheo)? I—a doctor, approved by a thousand Academies of the world—am I now to reject Aristotle and beg to learn philosophy from such as he?

Elpino. As I see it, I would learn not as a doctor, but as a neophyte. I would learn not because I ought to, but because of my lack. I would choose as a master not only this man, but any others whom the gods have selected for that function; for they enable me to understand that which I do not now understand.

Albertino. You would make me a child again?

Elpino. Only so that you may discard childishness.

Albertino. I thank you for your kindness. You do me too much honor in allowing me to listen to this miserable wanderer. Everyone knows how he detests the Academies; all know how he impugns every traditional doctrine. He is praised by few, approved by none, and persecuted by all.

Elpino. True, he is persecuted by all—but what sort of people are they? He is praised by few—but these are the best, the heroes. He opposes traditional doctrine not as doctrine, nor as traditional, but because it is false. He is hated by the Academies, because wherever there is disagreement there is no love. He is in distress because the mass oppose all independents, and he who thus enjoys an exalted position is always a target for the many. To characterize his mind as concerns speculative matters, I should say that he is not so anxious to teach as he is to learn. He will regard it as good news and be quite pleased when he hears that you want to teach him; for his wish is to learn rather than teach, and he regards himself as better equipped to be a student than a master.

Albertino. Welcome most heartily, Filotheo.

Filotheo. And you sir, not less.

Albertino. "If in the forest I chew straw with the ox, the sheep, the goat, the ass and the horse, then, to improve my livelihood, without sin do I come hither to make myself a disciple." [4]

Fracastoro. You are welcome, indeed.

Albertino. I have till now regarded your views unworthy of being heard, let alone worthy of answer.

Filotheo. As a youth, up to a certain age, I too felt as you do, being then entirely captivated by Aristotle. Now, however, that I have seen more and meditated more and have matured, I should be able to judge matters more ably —although, to tell the truth, I may have become foolish and witless. As this is a malady that none can see better than the sick one himself, I am even more inclined to suspect that I have passed from wisdom to ignorance: I am, consequently, most happy to have discovered a physician regarded by all as competent to cure my mania.

Albertino. Neither nature nor I can help if the disease has penetrated to the bone.

Fracastoro. Please, sir, first feel his pulse and examine his urine. Afterwards, if no cure is effected, we'll all be wary of him.

Albertino. The "pulse feeling" which I have in mind is

[4] Gentile notes that this is a quotation from an anonymous sonnet cited also by Luigi Pulci in the *Morgante maggiore,* Canto XXV, 13.

to see whether you can resolve and extricate yourself from certain arguments which I will now set forth. These will prove conclusively that a plurality of worlds is impossible, not to speak of an infinity of such.

Filotheo. When you have taught me this, I shall be greatly in your debt. And if you do not fulfill your intention, I shall still be in your debt for having thus indirectly confirmed my views. Indeed, it seems to me that I shall receive from you the full force of those arguments which are in opposition to my views; and as you are an expert in the traditional sciences, you will be able clearly to exhibit the solidity of the foundation and the whole structure of these sciences as a function of their differences from my own principles. In order that the discussion proceed without interruption, and that each of us may have an equal opportunity to explain his own position, please set forth those arguments which you regard as the most impregnable, significant, and conclusive.

Albertino. Yes. Here they are:

(1) Beyond this world there is believed to be neither time nor space. For there is supposed to be but one primal heaven, a body most distant from us—the Primum Mobile. Thus, we customarily call "heaven" that which is on the farthest horizon of the world. On this are all the still, motionless, fixed, and quiet bodies: the intelligences, which endow the orbs with motion.

The world is divided into a celestial and an elemental body. The latter is bounded and contained, the former the containing limit. This world is ordered hierarchically: from the most dense to the most subtle which obtains above the convex of fire. On this, which constitutes the fifth essence, the sun, moon, and other stars are fixed. The nature of this fifth essence is such that it does not stray into the infinite; because it could not be conjoined with the Primum Mobile. Nor does it meet the other elements; because these would then envelop it causing the incorruptible and divine to be contained and surrounded by the corruptible, which is not appropriate. To the divine there belongs a nature conditioned to form and act, and therefore to the function of containing and endowing others with defining form and limit, being itself without limit, form, or substance.

Having stated this, we now proceed to argue, with Aristotle, that if there is a body beyond this heaven, it must be either simple or compound. No matter which of these you choose, I ask further: will this body occupy a position determined by its inner nature, or by the accident of position and external constraint? We will show that there can be no simple body beyond the heaven, as it is impossible for a perfect sphere to alter its position. Since the center of such a sphere is immutable, its position cannot change, for only by constraint can it change to any but its own proper position—and a sphere can undergo no constraint, active or passive.

Similarly, outside the heavens it is impossible that there be a simple body which moves rectilinearly. Whether this simple body is heavy or light, it cannot be outside the heaven, since the natural place of simple bodies is not beyond the world. Nor can it be held that these bodies are beyond the world by accident or constraint, for in that case other bodies would, of their own nature, already be there.

It is proved then, that there are no simple bodies other than those which make up our own world, and these bodies are endowed with three kinds of local motion. Therefore, no other simple body can exist beyond the world. Therefore also, no compound body can exist beyond the world, since the latter is a compound of the simples and reducible to them. Consequently, it is clear that many worlds do not exist, as there can be but one heaven, since it is unique, perfect, and complete.

From this it follows that there can be neither space, plenum, void, nor time outside of our world. Space could not be there—for if it were a plenum it would contain either a simple or a compound body. If it were void, then, according to the nature of a void which is defined as space capable of containing body, it would be possible for a body to obtain there—but we have already shown that no body can exist beyond the heaven. Time could not obtain there, for time is the number of motion, and motion can only be postulated of a body. Hence where there is no body, there is no motion and, as a consequence, no measurement of motion—*ergo*, no time. Further, since we have already proved that no body exists beyond this world, we have simultaneously demonstrated that there is neither motion, time, nor anything temporal or movable beyond it. Therefore, there exists only one world.

(2) The unicity of the world may be inferred from the unicity of the moving body, the Primum Mobile. Circular motion, it is agreed, is truly one, uniform and without beginning or end. If it be thus one, then it can be the effect of but one cause. If then, there is but one primal heaven below which all the lower heavens are subsumed to make up a single order, then there can be but one guiding or motive power. This cannot be multiplied by the addition of matter, since it is incorporeal. Now if the moving power is one; and if a single moving power can bring only one kind of motion into being; and if motion, whether simple or complex, can occur only within a simple or compound mobile body; it must follow that the mobile world is one. Therefore, there can be no other worlds.

(3) It follows from the positions occupied by bodies in motion that there can be only one world. There are three kinds of mobiles: the heavy, the light, and that which is neither heavy nor light. Earth and water are examples of the heavy; air and fire of the light; and the heavens of the third kind of mobile. Similarly, there are three different regions for moving bodies: the lowest and central, occupied by heavy bodies; the uppermost, at the furthest remove from the lowest; and the middle region, between the central and the uppermost. Thus the first kind of mobile, the heavy, belongs properly to the center; those which are neither heavy nor light belong to the outer circumference; while the light belongs to the space between. There is, consequently, a lowest region to which all heavy objects from any world will tend to move; there is also an upper region toward which all light objects from any world would move; and there is also a region in which the heaven moves, no

matter what world it belongs to. Hence, if there is but one space, there is also one world and not many.

(4) If there were more than one world, I say that there would be various centers toward which the heavy objects of these worlds would move, as well as several horizons toward which light objects would move. In different worlds these positions would not differ in kind but only in number. In this way the center of one world would be more distant from the center of another world than it would from its own horizon. But such centers would be similar in kind, while center and horizon are of opposite natures. Hence the spatial distance between things similar in kind would be greater than the distance between opposed things. But this is contrary to the nature of opposites: for when it is said that contraries are at the greatest remove from one another, this should be understood to refer to distance in the same space. You can see then what follows from postulating more than one world. It is clear that such a hypothesis is not only incorrect but impossible.

(5) If there were more worlds possessed of natures similar to this one, they must be equal, or at least proportional in size to this one—which is to say that they would be equal to one another. If this is the case, then no more than six worlds can adjoin this one. For it is impossible for more than six spheres to touch a single sphere without interpenetrating—just as it is impossible that more than six equal circles can touch one another without their lines intersecting. If this is the case, then six horizons will be grouped around a single center—i.e., at the points where the six worlds touch each other or our world. But as the virtue of two opposed elements should be equal in power, and as a lack of equality follows from the arrangement here being hypothesized, the fact that the upper elements are stronger than the lower will result in making the upper victorious over the lower, thus destroying the totality.

(6) Now if the circular surfaces of different worlds touch only at a point, then there must of necessity remain a space between the convex circumference of one sphere and

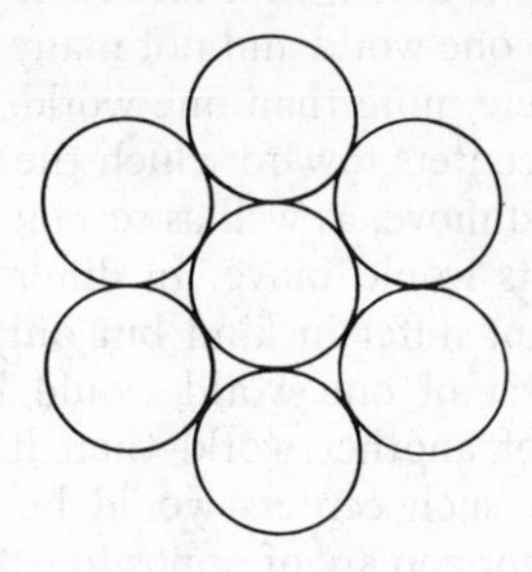

that of another. Either there is something in this space which fills it, or there is nothing. If there is something, then clearly it will not have the nature of an element distant as it will be from the convex surface of a sphere, because, as is quite obvious, this space will be triangular in shape and enclosed within the three arcs that form part of the circumferential surface of three worlds; and in this way the (triangle's) center will be located at some distance from the parts nearest the angles but most distant from the spheres. It then becomes necessary to hypothesize new elements and a new world filling that space—wholly different from our elements and our world. Were this not so, it would be necessary to hypothesize a vacuum in the triangular space, and this, as we see it, is impossible.

(7) If there were other worlds, they would be either finite or infinite. If infinite, then the infinite would have come about as the result of a determined action. For many reasons this is held to be impossible. If finite, they must be a definite number. And then we ask: Why just this many and neither more nor less? Why not one more? What would happen if there were this or that world in addition? Whether even or uneven in number, why should they be of this kind rather than some other? Why is all this matter split into so many worlds rather than unified in a single globe? As unity is better than plurality, *ceteris paribus,* why divide substance among four or six or even ten earths, rather than making a single, great, and perfect globe? Indeed, just as from the possible and impossible there arises a finite

rather than an infinite number, so, in choosing between the consistent and the inconsistent, unity is more rational and natural than multiplicity or plurality.

(8) In all things we observe nature to accomplish her ends with the greatest efficacy: just as she does not lack the necessary, she eschews the superfluous. Since she can, then, produce all of her effects with just that which obtains in this world, it would not be reasonable to assume that there are more worlds.

(9) If an infinity of worlds or, indeed, more than one world existed, this would be so principally because God could make them—or rather because they would depend on God. But as true as this may be, it does not follow that these worlds do exist, for besides God's active power, the passive power of things must also obtain. That which can be created in nature does not depend (solely) upon the absolute divine power, as not every active power transforms itself into passive, but only that which has a subject adequate to itself—i.e., a subject able to receive the efficient act in its completeness. But nothing has such a relationship to the Prime Cause; hence, insofar as the nature of the world is concerned, there cannot be more than one, even though God is capable of making more.

(10) The plurality of worlds is not consonant with reason, for they would contain no civil virtue, which consists in civil intercourse. And had the gods created diverse worlds they would have acted badly in that they had not arranged for the citizens of these worlds to have commerce with one another.

(11) Were there a plurality of worlds they would place barriers in the path of every motive force or divinity. For since the spheres must touch at certain points, one would block the movement of another and the gods could then scarcely control the world through motion.

(12) The only way that a plurality of individuals can arise from a single one is by nature's process of multiplication by substantial division—i.e., generation. Aristotle and the Peripatetics tell us that individuals of a single species multiply only by the act of generation. Those, however,

who hold to the existence of a plurality of worlds made up of the same matter and form do not assert that one is converted into, or generated from, another.

(13) Nothing can be added to perfection. If this world is perfect, then clearly there is no need for another to be added to it. The world is perfect: it is a sort of continuum not bounded by another sort of continuum. An indivisible mathematical point culminates mathematically in a line which is a kind of continuum; the line culminates in a surface which is a second kind of continuum; the surface, in a solid body which is a third kind of continuum. No body migrates or moves to another kind of continuum. But if it is part of the universe, it is bounded by another body; while if it is the universe itself, it is perfect and bounded by itself only. Thus the universe must be one if it is to be perfect. And here are the thirteen arguments which I want, for now, to put before you. If you satisfy me with respect to these, then I shall be completely satisfied.

Filo. But Albertino, anyone who proposes to defend a proposition must first (unless he is a fool) have examined the contrary arguments. The case is the same as with a soldier who would indeed be foolish if he attempted to defend a castle without having investigated the circumstances and places from which it may be attacked. Your arguments—if, indeed, they are arguments at all—are quite well known and oft repeated. The most effective way to respond to them consists in considering, on the one hand, their origin and, on the other, how they stand up to our own assertions. I will make both clear to you in the course of my reply. I shall make my reply brief, and if you require further amplification or clarification I shall refer you to Elpino, who will repeat that which he has previously heard from me.

Alb. Please, first show me that this method will not be fruitless or lacking in satisfaction to one who wants to learn, and that listening first to you and then to him will not weary me.

Filo. To the wise and judicious, among whom I count you, it is sufficient to show the direction of our considerations. They themselves will then be able to proceed deeper into an appraisal of the means by which one or the other of opposing views is to be reached.

Now as regards your Argument (1), we say that your whole system falls because the differences which you mark as obtaining between the various orbs and heavens do not exist; further the stars move through this vast, ethereal space because of their own nature, each revolving about its own and another center. In fact, there is no Primum Mobile that draws the many bodies around ourselves as center. Rather, our globe causes it to appear that this is happening for reasons that Elpino will explain to you.

Alb. I will listen to him willingly.

Filo. And when you have heard him, and noted that such an opinion is contrary to nature while ours is consonant with reason, sense, and verification in nature, you will no longer say that there is a boundary or limit either to the extent or to the motion of the universe. You will then judge the belief in a Primum Mobile—a highest and all-containing heaven—to be an empty fantasy. Rather, you will begin to conceive of a universal field in which all worlds are alike situated, even as this globe, in this our local space, is enveloped by our atmosphere and is in no way fixed or attached to any other body and has no fixed point other than its own center. And should it be discovered that the constitution of our globe differs in no way from that of the surrounding stars, since it contains no accidents different from theirs, then it will become clear that it no more occupies the central place in the universe than any of them, nor is it any more fixed than they, nor will they appear to revolve around it rather than it around them. Since this implies an utter indifference on the part of nature, we must conclude the emptiness of (alleged) inferior orbs; and we must accept the internal impulse toward motion which is implanted in the souls of these globes, the lack of difference throughout the vast space of the universe, and the irrationality of conceiving any boundary or external shape to the universe.

Alb. But these are views which, although not repugnant to nature and perhaps even quite consistent, are still difficult to prove. Great skill would be required to disprove the contrary view and arguments.

Filo. But once the end of the thread is discovered, the tangle is easily unraveled. The difficulty issues from an unsuitable method and presupposition: namely, the weight and immobility of the earth: the position of the Primum Mobile together with the other seven, eight, nine, or more (spheres) on which the stars are implanted, stuck, nailed, knotted, glued, sculptured, or painted: and that these do not reside in the same space as our own star, called by us the earth. But you will hear that her space, figure, and nature are neither more nor less fundamental than those of the other stars, nor is her nature any less adapted to motion than each of these other divine animals.

Alb. True, if this is once fixed in my mind, everything else which you propose will be easily accepted in its turn. You will at once have severed the roots of one philosophy and implanted those of another.

Filo. And you will thereafter refuse, with good reason, to accept common opinions based upon general consensus, such as the existence of a furthest horizon, most lofty and noble, the frontier of the divine, motionless substances which are the movers of these finite orbs. You will then admit that it is at least plausible that this earth, as all the others, is an animal which moves and travels by virtue of her own intrinsic nature. You will regard as mere fable, incapable of any proof, the view that these bodies derive their motion from that of a body which lacks all holding power and resistance—a body more rare and subtle than the air we breathe. You will further see that our view conforms to good sense as well as sound reasoning. You will no longer hold as true the notion of spheres with concave and convex surfaces moving and drawing the stars with them. You will rather see as true, consonant with reason and natural consistency, the view that the stars follow, in conformity with their own intrinsic nature and life—as you shall soon hear—their circular courses around and toward one another without fear of either rising or falling, since in the immensity of space there is no up or down, no right or left, no forward or backward. You will see that beyond the alleged circumference of the heaven there can be a body—either simple or composite—moving in a straight line; for just as the parts of this globe move in a straight line, so also and with similar ease the parts of other bodies can do so. Our own globe is not composed of material different from those beyond our globe; nor does our globe appear to revolve around them any less than they appear to revolve around us.

Alb. I now see more clearly than ever before that the smallest error at the start may cause the greatest difference and danger of errors at the conclusion. A single, simple mistake will multiply little by little and swell into an infinity of others—even as a great plant with numberless branches may grow from a tiny root. On my life, Filotheo, I strongly desire that you prove all of this to me. I do regard your views as both likely and worthy and I wish that you would also show me their truth.

Filo. I will do as much as time and the occasion permit, submitting many things to your judgment which have been previously kept from you not because of your incapacity but because of inadvertence.

Alb. Put the whole matter before me in the form of premise and conclusion. I know that before you came to embrace your present views you carefully examined everything which suggested contrary conclusions, and I am certain that the secrets of the currently accepted philosophy are as well known to you as they are to me. Please then, proceed.

Filo. It is then unnecessary to inquire whether there is space, void, or time beyond the heaven. For there obtains a single, universal space, a single vast immensity which we may freely call *void*. In it are infinite globes like this one on which we live and flourish. This space we declare to be infinite—since neither reason, consistency, possibility, sense, or nature assign any limit to it. In it there are an infinity of worlds, similar to our own and of the same kind. For there is no reason or defect of nature's powers—either active or passive power—that prevents their existence in all the rest of space, which is identical in natural character to our own, just as they exist in the space around us.

Alb. If what you said at the outset is true (and to this point it appears to be quite as likely as the opposite view), then this which you now state follows necessarily.

Filo. Time obtains beyond the alleged convex circumference of the world. For there is found the measure and true nature of motion, since there are similar moving bodies there. Accept this in part as having been proved, and in part as proposed in regard to what you have said in your Argument (1) for a single world. But let me now turn to your Argument (2).

Concerning your Argument (2), I say that there is but one prime and principal motive power. But not that it is prime and principal relative to a second, third, or other motive power in a scale descending to the middle and last, since no such motive powers can or do exist. For where infinite number obtains, there can be neither rank nor numerical order, although rank and order there is according to the nature and value of either different species and kinds, or of diverse grades of the same species and kind. There are, as I see it, an infinity of motive powers, just as there are an infinity of souls inhabiting the infinite spheres. And since these consist of form and intrinsic action, there is relative to them all a governing principle upon which all depends—a first principle which endows spirits, gods, heavenly powers, and motive power with the ability to move. It sets into motion matter, body, animated being, lower orders of nature, and anything which can move. There are, that is to say, an infinity of mobile bodies and motive forces, all of which are reducible to a single passive and active principle, in the same way in which every number reduces to unity, and as an infinite number coincides with unity, and just as the supreme agent and supreme active power coincide in a single principle with all that is possible, as was shown at the end of our book *On Cause, Origin and the One.* In number then, and in magnitude, there is an infinite possibility of motion and movers. In unity and singularity, however, the whole is infinite unmoved mover: an infinite motionless universe. And the infinite number and magnitude coincides with the infinite unity and simplicity in a single, utterly simple and indivisible principle, which is truth and being. Thus there is no Primum Mobile, no order descending from it of second and other mobile bodies, either to a last body or to infinity. But all moving bodies are equally near and far from the prime and universal mover just as (in logical terms) all species are equally related to the same genus, and all individuals to the same species. Thus from a single, infinite, and universal motive force in a single, infinite space, there issues only one infinite universal motion on which an infinite number of mobile bodies and forces depend, each of which is finite in both magnitude and power.

As for your Argument (3), I say that there is no privileged point, no center, in ethereal space toward which heavy objects move and from which all light bodies leave in their search for a circumference. In the universe there is neither center nor circumference; but, rather, the whole is central and every point may be seen as a part of the circumference in relation to some other central point. As concerns us, that object which we regard as being heavy is any object which moves from the circumference to the center of our own globe. We regard as being light that object which moves in the opposite direction—toward the opposite goal. But we shall see that nothing is heavy which is not also light; for every part of the earth changes, in turn, both place, position, and also composition, so that during the long course of centuries no particle in the center fails to reach the circumference, and no particle on the circumference fails to reach the center. We shall see also that weight and lightness are nothing else than the drive of a body's particles to their own containing region, wherever that may be, in which they are best conserved. There are no differences of position, therefore, which attract or repel different parts. But the desire for self-preservation is an inner drive impelling every object—provided that no obstacle intervenes—to fly as far away from contrary matter as possible, and to join with a close neighbor. In this way, then, the particles from the circumference of the moon and of other worlds similar in species and kind to our own, tend to unite in the center of their own globe as though compelled by their own weight, while the more subtle particles, as though compelled by their own lightness, remove themselves to the circumference. This is not a function of the particles taking flight to or from the circumference (because of attraction or repulsion), because if this were the case then the nearer they approached, or the further they went away from the circumference, the more rapid and powerful their motion would become, and observation gives this the lie; for if they are impelled beyond the terrestrial region, they remain balanced in the air and neither ascend nor descend until they either gain more weight by accretion of parts, or increased density because of the cold, in which case they descend, or else they become more rarefied and heat-dissolved, in which case they disperse into atoms.

Alb. I shall be much easier in mind when you have more fully shown me that the stars do not differ in nature from this earthly sphere.

Filo. Elpino will easily make this known to you as he has heard it from me. He will also make you see most clearly that no object is heavy or light in respect to the universe, but only in respect to its own region and the body which contains and maintains it. It is the tendency, you see, to maintain an existing condition which brings about every change of position; as seas, for example, and even drops of water become united, or disperse, as all liquids do when exposed to the sun or other heat. All natural motion, brought about by a body's own internal impulsion, is nothing but an attempt to either escape an inimical or opposed body, or to pursue a friendly and compatible one. Whence nothing changes position unless driven to do so by its contrary. Nothing in its natural position is either heavy or light; but the earthy matter, when it is raised up into the air, strives for its natural position and is felt thus to be heavy, just as water is heavy when suspended in air, though it is not when it is in its own region. In this way, to anyone who is submerged, the whole of the water is not at all heavy, while a little vase full of water will become quite heavy if placed above the air beyond the dry surface. The head on a man's body is not heavy, but if the head of another man is placed on his own it will be heavy—because the latter is not in its natural position. If then, weight and lightness are merely an impulse to a position of safety and escape from a contrary position, it follows that nothing is by nature either heavy or light; and that nothing is endowed with either weight or lightness if it is so far away from its preserving (environment), or so far removed from its contrary as not to be affected by the aid of the one or the harm of the other. If, however, it becomes aware of an inimical environment, and then grows hopeless, perplexed, and irresolute, it will be vanquished by its contrary.

Alb. You promised, and in part you have accomplished great things.

Filo. To avoid repetition, I will now turn you over to Elpino, who will continue with the remainder.[5]

Alb. It seems to me that I understand it all. Just as one doubt fosters another, so one truth demonstrates another. I begin to understand more than I can explain, and I now doubt many things which I had previously held to be certain. In this way, little by little, I feel myself ready to agree with you.

Filo. When you have heard me out, you will yield your full assent. For now, bear this in mind—or at least do not be quite as solidly convinced of the contrary opinion as you were when you first entered the discussion. For little by little, as the opportunity arises, we shall complete the exposition of this subject—a subject which depends, to be sure, on several principles and arguments. For just as one error leads to another, so one uncovered truth is followed by another.

As regards your Argument (4), I say that although there are as many centers as there are individual globes, spheres, or worlds, yet it does not follow that the particles of each are related to any center but their own; nor does it follow that they fly to any circumference but that of their own

[5] Nonetheless, it is Filotheo, not Elpino, who continues.

region. Just as the particles of our earth do not seek any but their own center, nor do they attempt to unite with any but that of their own globe, so it is also that the humors and parts of an animal ebb and flow in their own subject, and do not relate to some other animal.

As regards that which you think unfitting, namely, that a center would become further removed from another center than it would from the circumference of its own globe, although centers are of the same species while centers and circumferences are contraries and should therefore be at the furthest distance from one another, I reply as follows: contraries need not be at the furthest distance from one another, inasmuch as one may either influence or be influenced by the other. We see, for example, that the sun is very close to us among the earths which encircle it, since the order of nature requires an object to subsist, live, and be nurtured by its contrary, while it becomes affected, altered, overcome, and changed by the first.

Further, a short while back we discussed with Elpino the arrangement of the four elements which all contribute particles in the composition of each globe, one particle being placed within another, and one mixed with another. And these are not respectively distinguished as a containing and a contained body. For where there is dry earth, so also there is water, air, and fire, either manifest or latent. The distinction which we made concerning globes—some, like the sun, being fiery, while others, as the moon and earth, being watery—does not depend upon these bodies consisting solely of a single element, but merely on the predominance of one element in the mixed substance.

Furthermore, it is false that contraries are situated at the furthest remove from one another. For the elements have naturally combined and mixed in all objects. The whole universe, indeed, consists solely—both in the principal and secondary parts—of such conjunction and union, as there is no portion of the earth which is not intimately mixed with water. For without water the earth would have neither density, connections between its composite atoms, nor solidity.

Again, what terrestrial body is so dense as to lack insensible openings? Lacking these, such bodies would be indivisible and incapable of penetration by fire or its heat, which latter is, however, sensibly perceived to issue from the substance of these bodies. Where, in this your body, is there any cold, dry segment which is not joined to a moist and warm part of your body? This distinction of elements is a logical, not a natural distinction. If the sun is in a region far removed from that of our earth, yet neither air nor dry land nor water is further removed from it than from our own globe. For the sun, like our earth, is a composite body, though in it a certain one of the four above-mentioned elements predominates, while another is predominant in our earth.

Moreover, if we insist that nature conform to that logic which insists that the greatest distance obtain between contrary bodies, then, between your fire—which is light—and the heavy earth, heaven—which is neither heavy nor light—must be interposed. Or if you would limit your proposition by saying that this order pertains only in respect of the four elements, still you would be forced to arrange them in a different order. Water, I mean, must occupy the central position of the heaviest element if fire, as the lightest element, is on the circumference of the elemental region; for water, which is cold and moist, is opposed to fire in both of these qualities and must, consequently, be at the greatest distance from the hot and dry element; while air, which you hold to be hot and moist, should be at the furthest distance from the cold and dry earth. You see, then, how this Peripatetic proposition falters, whether it is tested according to the truth of nature or according to the Peripatetics' own logical principles and foundations.

Alb. I see it most clearly.

Filo. What is more, you see that our philosophy is not at all contrary to reason. It reduces everything to a single origin and relates everything to a single end; it makes contraries coincide so that there is one primal basis of both origin and end. From this coincidence of contraries we deduce that it is ultimately and divinely right to hold that contraries are within contraries, for which reason it is not difficult to comprehend that each thing is within every other thing—which Aristotle and the other Sophists could not comprehend.

Alb. I listen to you most willingly. I know that so much material and such diverse positions cannot all be demonstrated at once upon a single occasion. But since you have shown me the untenability of those beliefs which I had once regarded as certain, I have been doubtful of all others which for the same, or similar reasons, I would now regard as certain. Therefore, I am prepared to listen to the foundations of your philosophy, your principles and reasons, with rapt attention.

Elp. You will see that Aristotle brought no golden age to philosophy. For now let us dispel your further doubts.

Alb. I am not so curious about those—I am, however, quite eager to understand the doctrine and principles by means of which these and other doubts are resolved in your philosophy.

Filo. We shall turn to those soon. As for your Argument (5), you ought to know that if we conceive of an infinity of worlds possessed of a nature and composition such as you are accustomed to imagine, it would be as if besides a spherical world containing the four elements arranged in the traditional order, and the eight, nine, or ten other heavens of a different nature and substance encircling and rapidly revolving around these, we should then imagine innumerable other worlds also spherical and endowed with motion like ours. But if we conceived of them thus, then we should have to produce arguments and invent ways to explain how one of these worlds could touch or be continuous with the others; we should then proceed with fantastic imaginings to discuss at how many points the circumference of one world may touch those of the surrounding worlds. You would then see that however numerous the horizons around a world, they would not belong to one world, but each one would have the same relation to its own center. For their influence is exerted there where they revolve, and at the center about which they spin in the same way that a number of animals, if bound together and touching one another, would not interchange limbs in such a manner that one or each of them could possess several hands or bodies. We, however—thanks to the gods—are free of the need to employ such explanations. Because instead of these numerous heavens—these many swift, stubborn, and mobile bodies, straight and oblique, to the east and west, on the axis of the world, on the axis of the zodiac, in so far and so much, in greater and lesser declination—we have but one single heaven, a single space through which our own star on which we live, and all other stars, each run their own circuits and courses. These are the infinite worlds, the innumerable stars; this is the infinite space, this heaven embracing all, traversed by all. Gone forever is the fable that the whole revolves around us as the center; for we now know that it is our earth which revolves; and that our earth, spinning about her own center, speeds every twenty-four hours to the successive places of the surrounding luminaries. Gone also is the notion of orbs encircling our own space in which the stars are fixed. To each star we attribute its own motion—named *epicycle*—differing from that of each of the other mobile bodies. These orbs—directed by no motive force other than the spontaneous impulse of the spirit within each—follow, as our own earth, their own course about their own center and around the fiery element, during long centuries if not, indeed, to eternity. Here then is the true nature of the worlds and of heaven. Heaven is just as we see it surrounding our own globe which is, like all the other globes, a luminous and noble star. The worlds are those whose brilliant shining surfaces are clearly visible to us, and they are located at specific distances from one another. But none of them is closer to one another than the moon is to our earth, or our planets to our sun; in this way, those of contrary nature do not destroy but, rather, nourish one another, while those of similar nature do not impede but, rather, give each other space. Thus, from one position to another, little by little, from season to season, our frigid globe is heated by the sun, now from this side, now from that, now on this part, now on that; and by certain changes she first yields, and then takes place from the neighboring earth which we call the moon, so that first one and then the other body is respectively nearer to or further from the sun—for which reason the moon is called the counterearth by Timaeus and other Pythagoreans. These then are the world; each inhabited and cultivated by their own living beings: each the principal and most divine of all living beings in the universe: and each composed, no less than this earth on which we find ourselves, of four elements, although some may be predominantly activated by one active quality, while others are predominantly activated by another, so that some of these are perceptible to us by means of their water and others by their fire.

In addition to the four elements which compose the heavenly bodies there is, as we have said, a vast and ethereal region in which they all move, live, and grow—the ether, which both envelops and penetrates all things. To the degree that this ether enters into and forms part of the mixture of the elements, it is commonly called *air*—the term applying to that misty layer around the waters and within the land, enclosed between the highest mountains, capable of holding thick clouds and strong winds from north and south. To the degree that it remains pure and does not enter into composites, but forms the locale and the enveloping space through which the compound body moves on its course, we call it, properly, *ether*—a term which means *course*. This ether, although identical in substance with the air which is stirred within the earth's bowels, is nonetheless differently named; just as that which surrounds us is called *air*, although when it is in some part of us or has a part in our composition—as when it is in our lungs, arteries, and other cavities and lacunae of the body—it is called spirit. Similarly, the ether, when surrounding a cold body, condenses into vapor; while around a hot body it is attenuated like a flame which becomes sensible only when it is joined to a denser body which then ignites. Thus the ether is of its own nature: it lacks all determinate quality, but takes on all the qualities offered by neighboring bodies and carries them by means of its own motion to the furthest limits of the horizon where such active principles have efficacy.

Now the nature of the worlds and the heavens have been demonstrated to you, so that not only can your present doubt be resolved, but innumerable others. You are now provided with the basis for many true physical conclusions. If some proposition has up to here seemed to you to have been stated but not proved, I shall leave it for the time being to your own discretion and, if you are judicious, then even before you actually discover the supreme truth of such a proposition, you will hold it far more probable than the contrary views.

Alb. Continue, Filotheo, so that I may hear more from you.

Filo. We have already resolved your Argument (6). In that Argument, considering the contact of worlds at a single point, you asked what object could fill those triangular spaces so that it be neither an element nor of a heavenly nature. We, however, posit a single heaven in which each world has its own space, region, and correct area. It diffuses through all, penetrates and envelops all, touches and is closely attached to all, leaving no place vacant—unless, that is, like so many others you prefer to call *void* this site and locale of all motion, this space in which all have their course. Or you may call it the primal subject denoted by the term *space,* in order not to ascribe to it a limited locale, if you wish, by this omission logically to regard it as something existing in the mind not derived, in nature and substance, from being and body; this may satisfy one's insistence that nothing exists which has no position, finite or infinite, corporeal or incorporeal, either as a whole or by means of its parts. Such a subject, in the last analysis, can be nothing else but space; and this space, nothing else but void. If then, we regard this space or void as obtaining, we call it the ethereal field which contains all worlds; if we regard it as an underlying substance, we call it the space within which there obtains the ethereal field with the worlds; and this space cannot be conceived as existing within another space. Observe then, that it is not necessary for us to postulate new elements and worlds—unlike those who begin to designate, upon the slightest pretext, inferior orbs, divine substances, rarer and denser parts of celestial nature, quintessences, and other such fantastic names utterly lacking any meaning or truth.

To your Argument (7), I say that the infinite universe is one: a single continuum: a compound of ethereal regions and worlds. The worlds are innumerable, and they should be understood to reside in diverse regions of the single universe and to exist according to the same law of nature as this world which we inhabit is understood and does reside in its own space and region. I have been telling all this to Elpino during the past days; approving and affirming that which has been expounded by Democritus, Epicurus, and many others who kept their eyes and ears directed always to nature.

> Then, spew not reason from thy mind away,
> Beside thyself because the matter's new,
> But rather with keen judgment nicely weigh;
> And if to thee it then appeareth true,
> Render thy hands, or, if 'tis false at last,
> Gird thee to combat. For my mind-of-man
> Now seeks the nature of the vast Beyond
> There on the other side, that boundless sum
> Which lies without the ramparts of the world,
> Toward which the spirit longs to peer afar,
> Toward which indeed the swift élan of thought
> Flies unencumbered forth.
>
> Firstly, we find,
> Off to all regions round, on either side,
> Above, beneath, throughout the universe
> End there is none—as I have taught, as too
> The very thing of itself declares aloud,
> And as from nature of the unbottomed deep
> Shines clearly forth. . . .[6]

Lucretius rejects your Argument (8), which held that nature should include herself. Although this has been

[6] Lucretius, *De rerum natura,* II, 1040–1051.

tested in great and small worlds, it is yet never observed to be the case in any. Our eye never discovers an end, but is overcome by the immensity of space spread before it. Confused and bewildered by the myriad of ever multiplying stars, our perception falters and reason is then forced to add space to space, region to region, world to world.

> . . . Nor can we once suppose
> In any way 'tis likely, (seeing that space
> To all sides stretches infinite and free,
> And seeds, innumerable in number, in sum
> Bottomless, there in many a manner fly,
> Bestirred in everlasting motion there),
> That only this one earth and sky of ours
> Hath been create . . .
> Thus, I say,
> Again, again, 'tmust be confessed there are
> Such congregations of matter otherwhere,
> Like this our world which vasty ether holds
> In huge embrace. . . .[7]

Lucretius complains too against your Argument (9) which assumes, without proof, that there is no infinite passive power which corresponds with infinite active power; and that infinite matter cannot be patient and infinite space cannot make a field to itself; and that, as a consequence, act and action cannot become comformable to the agent so that it may happen that even though the agent imparts the entire act, yet the whole act cannot be imparted. This latter view clearly and entirely contradicts the former observation. Wisely has it been remarked:

> . . . Besides, when matter abundant
> Is ready there, when space on hand, nor object
> Nor any cause retards, no marvel 'tis
> That things are carried on and made complete,
> Perforce. And now, if store of seeds there is
> So great that not whole life-times of the living
> Can count the tale. . . .

[7] Lucretius, *De rerum natura*, II, 1052–1057; 1064–1066.

And if their force and nature abide the same,
Able to throw the seeds of things together
Into their places, even as here are thrown
The seeds together in this world of ours,
'Tmust be confessed in other realms there are
Still other worlds, still other breeds of men
And other generations of the wild.[8]

To your Argument (10), we say that there is no need of this pleasant exchange between the various worlds any more than it is necessary that all men should be one man, or all animals one animal. I do not here even consider what we learn about this from experience—i.e., that it is best for all living creatures of this world that nature has distributed their different kinds throughout the seas and mountains. If it had been the case that, by human devices, they were to traffic together, good is not thereby added to them but, rather, removed; since such traffic tends rather to redouble vices than to augment virtues. Rightly, then, the Tragic Muse laments:

The lands, well separated before by Nature's laws, the Thessalian ship made one, bade the deep suffer blows and the sequestered sea become a part of our human fear.[9]

To your Argument (11) I reply as to your Argument (5). Each world in the ethereal field occupies its own space so that one neither thrusts against nor touches another. Each pursues its own course and is set at such a distance that the contraries do not destroy, but rather complement one another.

Your Argument (12) asserts that nature, having multiplied by defining and dividing matter, accomplishes this only by way of generation—i.e., when an individual, as parent, produces another individual. But this, we say, is not universally true. For by the act of a single efficient cause there may be produced from one mass many and diverse vessels of various forms and shapes. I mention in passing

[8] *Ibid.*, 1067–1076.
[9] Seneca, *Medea*, vv, 335–339.

the fact that if the destruction of a world, followed by its renewal, should come to pass, the production of animals in it—perfect and imperfect—would come about without an original act of generation: and this by the sole force and innate power of nature herself.

Your final argument, Argument (13), holds that because this or some other world is perfect, no further worlds are requisite. I reply that certainly they are not requisite for the perfection and subsistence of our own world; but in order that the subsistence and perfection of the whole universe obtains, an infinity of worlds is indeed requisite. It follows therefore, not from the perfection of this or of those that they, or this, be less perfect; for this world, as those others, and they even as this, consist in their parts, and each is a single totality in virtue of its members.

Alb. The voice of the mob, Filotheo, shall not deny your noble countenance to me. Nor shall I be deprived of your divine conversation by the indignation of the vulgar, the foolishness of the mentally deficient, the displeasure of sycophants, the emptiness of blockheads, the betrayal of liars, the complaints of the malicious, nor the sniping of the envious. Continue, Filotheo, persevere; do not lose heart or quit the field even though the great and dignified conference of ignorant fools threatens you with many traps and devious devices and tries to destroy your divine task—your exalted task. Rest assured that all will finally see as I now see: that all will agree that it is as easy for everyone to praise you as it is difficult for them all to instruct you. All of them (if they are not wholly perverse) will, when they properly understand you, deliver a favorable verdict of you, just as everyone, at the last, comes to be taught through the kindly mastery of the mind; for only by dint of our own mind can we attain to the treasures of the mind. And since a certain natural holiness is enthroned in the court of the intellect which exercises judgment between good and evil, light and darkness, so it will come about that each individual, by his own private meditation, shall come to your case as just witnesses and defenders. And they who do not make themselves your friend, but stolidly seek the defense of shadowy ignorance, and remain your stubborn and steadfast enemies, will feel the hangman and executioner—your avenger—within themselves; for the more they hide him within the depth of their thought, the more he will torture them. In just this way the Hellish worm dwelling on the bristling hair of the Furies, seeing that his plan against you has failed, will furiously turn on the hand and breast of his unbelieving host and bring him that death which he spreads who disseminates the Stygian poison.

Commence to tell us what is, in truth, in the heavens: what, in truth, the planets and all the stars are: how the infinite space—far from being impossible—is necessary: how such an infinite effect is seemly in the infinite cause. Tell us the true substance, matter, act, and efficient cause of the whole: how every sensible and composite thing is built up from the same origin and elements. Instruct our minds on the infinite universe. Tear to bits the concave and convex surfaces which would limit and separate so many elements and heavens: pour ridicule on inferior orbs and fixed stars: break and fling to earth with the resounding whirlwind of active reasoning those fortresses of the blind and vulgar masses, the adamantine walls of the Primum Mobile and the ultimate sphere: disperse the ideas that our earth is the one and only center of the universe: destroy the ignoble belief in that fifth essence. Make known to us that the composition of our own star and world is the same as that of the many other stars and worlds that are visible to us. Each of the infinity of great and vast worlds, each of the infinity of lesser worlds, is equally sustained and nourished anew through the succession of its ordered phases. Destroy the notion of external motive forces together with that of a limited, bounded, heaven. Open wide to us the gate through which we may mark the lack of difference between our own and all the other stars. Show us that the substance of the other worlds throughout the ether is the same as that of our own world. Make us see clearly that the motion of all of them stems from the impulsion of the inward soul, so that we, illumined by such thoughts, may proceed all the more surely toward a knowledge of nature.

Filo. Elpino, what is the significance of Doctor Burchio's reluctance to consent to what we have said?

Elp. It is typical of an alert mind, that although seeing and hearing little, it yet considers and understands much.

Alb. Although I have not yet seen the whole body of the shining planet, I can yet see by the rays shimmering through the narrow chinks in the closed windows of my mind that this is no meretricious brightness or Sophist's lamp. Nor does it proceed from the moon or any minor star. I anticipate still greater enlightenment in the future.

Filo. Your continuing friendship will be most welcome.

Elp. Let us now go to supper.

END OF THE FIVE DIALOGUES
CONCERNING THE INFINITE,
THE UNIVERSE AND WORLDS

Suggested Readings

BERNARDINO TELESIO

ABBAGNANO, N. *Bernardino Telesio*. Milan, 1941.
CASSIRER, E. *The Individual and the Cosmos in Renaissance Philosophy*. New York, 1964.
COPLESTON, F. C. *History of Philosophy*, vol. 3. London, 1953.
FIORENTINO, F. *Bernardino Telesio*, 2 vols. Florence, 1872-1874.
HÖFFDING, H. *History of Modern Philosophy*, vol. 1. New York, 1950.
KRISTELLER, P. O. *Eight Philosophers of the Italian Renaissance*. Stanford, 1964.
SOLERI, G. *Telesio*. Brescia, 1945.

TOMMASO CAMPANELLA

BLANCHET, L. *Campanella*. Paris, 1920.
CASSIRER, E. *The Individual and the Cosmos in Renaissance Philosophy*. New York, 1964.
COPLESTON, F. C. *History of Philosophy*, vol. 3. London, 1953.
HÖFFDING, H. *History of Modern Philosophy*, vol. 1. New York, 1950.

GIORDANO BRUNO

BRUNO, GIORDANO. *Cause, Principle and Unity*, trans. P. Lindsay. New York, 1964.
———. *Concerning the Cause, Principle and One*, in S. Greenberg, *The Infinite in Giordano Bruno*. New York, 1950.
———. *The Heroic Enthusiasts*, trans. L. Williams, 2 vols. London, 1887-1889.
———. *On the Infinite Universe and Worlds*, in D. W. Singer, *Giordano Bruno: His Life and Thought*. New York, 1950.
CASSIRER, E. *The Individual and the Cosmos in Renaissance Philosophy*. New York, 1964.
COPLESTON, F. C. *History of Philosophy*, vol. 3. London, 1953.
HÖFFDING, H. *History of Modern Philosophy*, vol. 1. New York, 1950.
HOROWITZ, I. L. *The Renaissance Philosophy of Giordano Bruno*. New York, 1952.

KOYRÉ, A. *From the Closed World to the Infinite Universe*. New York, 1958.
KRISTELLER, P. O. *Eight Philosophers of the Italian Renaissance*. Stanford, 1964.
NELSON, J. C. *Renaissance Theory of Love*. New York, 1958.
OLSCHKI, L. *Giordano Bruno*. Bari, 1927.
SPAMPANATO, V. *Vita di Giordano Bruno*, 2 vols. Messina, 1921.
YATES, F. A. *Giordano Bruno and the Hermetic Tradition*. Chicago, 1964.